In this important contribution to development and foreign policy literature, the authors use Africa as a lens to illuminate the ways in which development assistance has served as an instrument of American power, promoting U.S. geopolitical and economic interests from the Cold War to the war on terror.

Elizabeth Schmidt, *Loyola University Maryland, USA*

A thought-provoking excavation of the official discourse of international development. By regarding aid as a tool of power, Divon and Derman construct a critical narrative that contrasts the needs of ordinary Africans with interests embedded in US foreign policy over the years. Worth reading.

Michael Bratton, *University Distinguished Professor of Political Science and African Studies, Michigan State University, USA*

This book studies American policies towards Africa from WWII to the present day. It does so by employing an understanding of power transcending a simplistic interpretation. As policies empowered some groups and changed local dynamics, aid was an extremely important tool in wielding influence. A great book.

Stig Jarle Hansen, *Research Fellow, Belfer Center for Science and International Affairs, Harvard University, USA*

This book is an always readable and provocative deconstruction of American foreign aid, and the interests and ideologies that have long supported it.

Nicolas van de Walle, *Maxwell M. Upson Professor of Government, Cornell University, USA*

Analyzing the exercise of American power in Africa through U.S. development co-operation, this book illuminates the interests and ideologies behind it. Showing how U.S. administrations (1946-2016) have viewed as well as framed the African issues that confronted them, this book is recommended to all those studying great power politics and development theory.

Morten Bøås, *Research Professor, Norwegian Institute of International Affairs (NUPI) Oslo, Norway*

# United States Assistance Policy in Africa

From the end of WWII to the end of the Obama administration, development assistance in Africa has been viewed as an essential instrument of US foreign policy. Although many would characterise it as a form of aid aimed at enhancing the lives of those in the developing world, it can also be viewed as a tool for advancing US national security objectives.

Using a theoretical framework based on 'power', *United States Assistance Policy in Africa* examines the American assistance discourse, its formation and justification in relation to historical contexts, and its operation on the African continent. Beginning with a problematisation of development as a concept that structures hierarchies between groups of people, the book highlights how cultural, political and economic conceptions influence the American assistance discourse. The book further highlights the relationship between American national security and its assistance policy in Africa during the Cold War, the post-Cold War, and the post-9/11 contexts.

This book will be of great interest to students and scholars of Development Studies, Political Science and International Relations with particular interest in US foreign policy, USAID and/or African Studies.

**Shai A. Divon** is a post-doctoral fellow at the Department of International Environment and Development Studies, Faculty of Landscape and Society at the Norwegian University of the Life Sciences, Norway. He has extensive military and security experience and has worked and carried out research in Africa, Asia, the United States and the Middle East.

**Bill Derman** is Professor Emeritus at the Department of International Environment and Development Studies, Faculty of Landscape and Society at the Norwegian University of the Life Sciences, Norway and also at the Department of Anthropology, Michigan State University, USA.

# Routledge Explorations in Development Studies

This Development Studies series features innovative and original research at the regional and global scale.

It promotes interdisciplinary scholarly works drawing on a wide spectrum of subject areas, in particular politics, health, economics, rural and urban studies, sociology, environment, anthropology, and conflict studies.

Topics of particular interest are globalisation; emerging powers; children and youth; cities; education; media and communication; technology development; and climate change.

In terms of theory and method, rather than basing itself on any orthodoxy, the series draws broadly on the tool kit of the social sciences in general, emphasising comparison, the analysis of the structure and processes, and the application of qualitative and quantitative methods.

**Socio-economic insecurity in emerging economies**
Building new spaces
*Edited by Khayaat Fakier and Ellen Ehmke*

**Foreign aid and emerging powers**
Asian perspectives on official development assistance
*Iain Watson*

**The political ecology of climate change adaptation**
Livelihoods, agrarian change and the conflicts of development
*Marcus Taylor*

**China's foreign relations and the survival of autocracies**
*Julia Bader*

**Democratic accountability and human development**
Regimes, institutions and resources
*Kamran Ali Afzal and Mark Considine*

**Rural livelihoods in China**
*Edited by Heather Xiaoquan Zhang*

**Global food security and development aid**
*Ivica Petrikova*

**Southern perspectives on the post-2015 international development agenda**
*Edited by Debapriya Bhattacharya and Andrea Ordóñez Llanos*

**United States assistance policy in Africa**
Exceptional power
*Shai A. Divon and Bill Derman*

# United States Assistance Policy in Africa

Exceptional Power

Shai A. Divon and Bill Derman

LONDON AND NEW YORK

First published 2017
by Routledge
2 Park Square, Milton Park, Abingdon, Oxon OX14 4RN

and by Routledge
711 Third Avenue, New York, NY 10017

*Routledge is an imprint of the Taylor & Francis Group, an informa business*

© 2017 Shai A. Divon and Bill Derman

The right of Shai A. Divon and Bill Derman to be identified as authors of this work has been asserted by them in accordance with sections 77 and 78 of the Copyright, Designs and Patents Act 1988.

All rights reserved. No part of this book may be reprinted or reproduced or utilised in any form or by any electronic, mechanical, or other means, now known or hereafter invented, including photocopying and recording, or in any information storage or retrieval system, without permission in writing from the publishers.

*Trademark notice*: Product or corporate names may be trademarks or registered trademarks, and are used only for identification and explanation without intent to infringe.

*British Library Cataloguing in Publication Data*
A catalogue record for this book is available from the British Library

*Library of Congress Cataloging in Publication Data*
A catalog record for this book has been requested

ISBN: 978-1-138-64719-0 (hbk)
ISBN: 978-1-315-62717-5 (ebk)

Typeset in Baskerville
by Wearset Ltd, Boldon, Tyne and Wear

# Contents

|   |   |   |
|---|---|---|
| *Acknowledgements* | | viii |
| *Acronyms and abbreviations* | | ix |
| 1 | Introduction: power rules | 1 |
| 2 | Words of power: power of words | 29 |
| 3 | Tools of power: the American discourse | 58 |
| 4 | US policy in Africa and the Cold War | 108 |
| 5 | US policy in Africa and the 'new world order' | 178 |
| 6 | The arc of instability: US policy in Africa after 9/11 | 216 |
| 7 | Explaining assistance as power projection | 260 |
| | *Index* | 297 |

# Acknowledgements

This book is the outcome of many years of work, research and experience in Africa and the United States. Through this journey, we received support from family, friends, colleagues and various organisations who recognised value in our work, offered us their time, advice, comments and support.

First and foremost we would like to thank our families, Hege, Daniel and Naomi Divon, as well as Shoshana and Moshe Divon, for their love, patience and sacrifice during the years, and to Anne Hellum for her collaborative work, and to Bill's adult children – Corina, Brandon and Noah for their love and support.

We would like to thank our home institution, the Department of International Environment and Development Studies (Noragric), at the Norwegian University of Life Sciences (NMBU), for its support over the years. This book was finalised in the United States in 2016 thanks to a generous grant offered to Shai A. Divon by the US–Norway Fulbright Foundation. As a Fulbright Visiting Scholar, Shai was hosted at the School of International Service, American University Washington, DC, who granted access to the resources needed to complete this volume.

In addition, Bill would like to thank the African Studies Center at Michigan State University for its longstanding support of Africanist scholarship and engagement as well as his own.

We would like to thank our friends and colleagues who provided various forms of advice, comments, and support during the years we worked on this publication: Nadarajah Shanmugaratnam, Darley J. Kjosavik, Paul Beaumont, Esben Liefsen, Maia Green, Gordon Crawford, Gordon Adams, David Barton, Liv Ellingsen, Josie Teurling, Andrei Marin, Tor Arve Benjaminsen, John-Andrew McNeish, William Warner, Ian Bryceson, Gufu Oba, Pål Vedeld, Poul Wisborg, Stig J. Hansen, Cassandra Bergstrøm, Ingrid Nyborg, Espen Sjaastad, Hans Adam, Frode Sundnes, Lars Kåre Grimsby, Sunetro Ghosal, the late Guy Ben-Ari, Grete Benjaminsen, Nicole Rezende, Ingunn Bohmann, Lena Bakke, Jayne P. Lambrou, Ingvild Jacobsen, Awais Arifeen, Abda Khalid, Simon Nicholson, Paul Wapner, Judith Shapiro, Ken Conca, Malini Ranganathan, Garrett Graddy-Lovelace, Peter Limb, David Wiley, and the two anonymous reviewers who studied the manuscript at Routledge.

# Acronyms and abbreviations

| | |
|---|---|
| ACOTA | African Contingency Operations Training and Assistance Program |
| ACRI | African Crisis Response Initiative |
| AFRICOM | African Command |
| AGOA | Africa Growth and Opportunity Act |
| AMISOM | African Union Mission to Somalia |
| ANC | African National Congress |
| AQIM | Al-Qaida in the Maghreb |
| ATT | Amadou Toumani Touré |
| BNC | Binational Commission |
| CAR | Central African Republic |
| CENTCOM | Central Command |
| CIA | Central Intelligence Agency |
| CJTF-HOA | Combined Joint Task Force – Horn of Africa |
| CPA | Comprehensive Peace Agreement |
| CSIS | Center for Strategic and International Studies |
| DFA | Director of Foreign Assistance |
| DoD | Department of Defense |
| DoS | Department of State |
| DRC | Democratic Republic of Congo |
| EACTI | East Africa Counter-Terrorism Initiative |
| EARSI | East Africa Regional Strategic Initiative |
| ECOMOG | Economic Community of West African States Monitoring Group |
| ECOWAS | Economic Community of West African States |
| EUCOM | European Command |
| FNLA | National Liberation Front of Angola |
| FRELIMO | Mozambique Liberation Front |
| FROLINAT | Muslim National Liberation Front of Chad |
| FTF | Feed the Future |
| FY | Fiscal Year |
| GATT | General Agreement on Tariffs and Trade |
| GCCI | Global Climate Change Initiative |

| | |
|---|---|
| GHI | Global Health Initiative |
| GIA | Armed Islamic Group (translation) |
| GPOI | Global Peace Operations Initiative |
| GSPC | Salafist Group for Preaching and Combat (translation) |
| GUNT | Transitional Government of National Unity |
| GWOT | Global War on Terror |
| ICG | International Crisis Group |
| ICU | Islamic Court Union |
| IDCA | International Development Coordination Administration |
| IMF | International Monetary Fund |
| INPFL | Independent National Front of Liberia |
| LDCs | Least Developed Countries |
| LRA | Lord's Resistance Army |
| MCA | Millennium Challenge Account |
| MCC | Millennium Challenge Corporation |
| MDGs | Millennium Development Goals |
| MNLA | National Movement for the Liberation of Azawad |
| MPLA | People's Movement for the Liberation of Angola |
| MUJAO | Movement for Oneness and Jihad in West Africa |
| NAFTA | North American Free Trade Agreement |
| NATO | North Atlantic Treaty Organization |
| NCP | National Congress Party |
| NEPDG | National Energy Policy Development Group |
| NGOs | non-governmental organizations |
| NIC | National Intelligence Council |
| NIE | National Intelligence Estimate |
| NPFL | National Patriotic Liberation Front of Liberia |
| NSC | National Security Council |
| NSS | National Security Strategy of the United States |
| NSSM | National Security Study Memoranda |
| OAU | Organisation of African Unity |
| OPEC | Organization of Petroleum Exporting Countries |
| PACOM | Pacific Command |
| PDD | Presidential Policy Directives on Development |
| PEPFAR | President's Emergency Plan for AIDS Relief |
| PSI | Pan Sahel Initiative |
| QDDR | Quadrennial Diplomacy and Development Review |
| RENAMO | Mozambican National Resistance |
| RPF | Rwandan People's Front |
| SALT | Strategic Arms Limitation Talks |
| SPLA | Sudan People's Liberation Army |
| SPLM | Sudan People's Liberation Movement |
| SSTRO | Stability, Security, Transition, and Reconstruction Operations |
| SWAPO | South-West African People's Organization |

| | |
|---|---|
| TFG | Transnational Federal Government |
| TSCTI | Trans-Sahara Counter Terrorism Initiative |
| TSCTP | Trans-Sahara Counter Terrorism Partnership |
| UN | United Nations |
| UNAMIR | United Nations Assistance Mission for Rwanda |
| UNITA | National Union for the Total Independence of Angola |
| UNITAF | Unified Task Force (Operation Restore Hope) |
| US | United States (of America) |
| USAID | United States Agency for International Development |
| USIA | United States Information Agency |
| WTO | World Trade Organization |
| ZANU | Zimbabwe African National Union |
| ZAPU | Zimbabwe African Peoples' Union |

# 1 Introduction

## Power rules

### Great expectations

Following the end of World War II (WWII) the United States emerged as the most powerful nation in the World. Although threatened by communism there was a sense of optimism expressed by President Truman as he promised that the US would raise the living standards of the underdeveloped nations and that '[f]or the first time in history, humanity possesses the knowledge and the skill to relieve the suffering of these people' (Truman, 1949). This would be accomplished by sharing technology and by programmes 'based on the concepts of democratic fair dealing' (Truman, 1949). This was Truman's optimistic vision and it was shared by many in Europe after the war.

In general, the US presents itself as the leader of the free world. Since the end of WWII, it has championed democracy, a liberal global economy, modernisation and systems of rules and laws manifesting through institutions such as the World Trade Organisation, the World Bank, the International Monetary Fund and the United Nations. To this end, the US tried to use its power and influence in the world to create what it views as the best political, social and economic system that leads to individual freedoms and prosperity.

Development policies are often delinked or separated from more general foreign policy concerns (Easterly, 2008; Birdsall and Leo, 2015). When the focus is on foreign policy, development is usually backgrounded, a sub-plot, or ignored altogether in favour of high-politics, wars and such. Meanwhile, development theories might use individual case studies to illustrate the rights, wrongs, successes or failures, of a particular policy, but lack a longer perspective, and often leave interests in the background. Development theory aims at a timeless approach, but presents a-historical theories of what works or not, but often omits contextual historical, or even systemic factors.

In this book, we seek to reconnect them in order to explore how American 'interests' are framed. We consider how within a dynamic and changing world certain views in the US, or truths, have remained relatively stable. We do this by examining aid or development assistance in the context of the exercise of US power.

Aid or development assistance has been a key component of US policy since President Truman. In this book, we ask if there have been significant changes in the formulation of US aid policies? How, over the past seven decades, has development assistance been articulated within all the presidential administrations? How have these administrations answered the question: what is the purpose of development assistance? Is it to help transform under-development into developed nations? Is it to help people and states in conditions of 'under-development' to reach an end state labelled 'developed'? Is development assistance about helping those most in need to 'help themselves' or to give them the tools to be placed on a path to development? If not, what are the other embedded agendas, objectives and purposes behind the development assistance policies of powerful states?

Historically, development assistance has a particularly important place in global politics. During the colonial period, colonial administrations sought, through domination and hierarchy, to remake their colonies through processes they framed as assistance to develop. Development became a term through which colonial subjects were seen as inferior an inefficient. Following decolonisation, formal government control seems to have been replaced by informal influence explained as development assistance. This process has been uneven, sometimes peaceful, sometimes violent, but based on the idea that the world was divided into 'rich', 'civilised' and 'modern' nations (often the colonisers), and 'poor', 'barbaric' and 'traditional' nations (often the former colonised). As the colonial world came to an end the world was divided into three – the First (the West), the Second (the East) and the Third World. These terms have fallen out of fashion, and now several terms are used to distinguish powerful (developed) nations from weaker (developing or underdeveloped nations). These terms are usually based on economic criteria with the World Bank's categories based on income the most used.[1] In the remaking of the world, the US has played a particularly influential role. Because the US has seen itself as the leader of the free world and involved in development assistance in many countries,[2] we thought it apt to examine the sources and utilisation of power through assistance policies by the American state post-WWII. The kind of enquiry we propose could be done for any of the major nations providing development assistance. Nevertheless, the influence of the US as a global superpower is of particular interest for this purpose.

This is not intended to be a book examining foreign policy from an international relations perspective. We do not attempt, either, to examine in much detail the influence of domestic power relations in the US on the assistance policy of the US, debates around foreign assistance mechanisms, nor the mechanics of how the US delivers assistance. From an African perspective, this book is not meant to be a comprehensive historical volume on the sub-continent post-WWII. What we do attempt to do is to enter the long-standing debates around the purposes of development assistance explaining how drawing upon various conceptions of power illuminate alternative reading of materials. We do this to help unmask the tensions between the value-based conceptions of granting assistance, and the hierarchy, interests and ideologies that guide assistance policies and practices. Through this book we narrate the position of sub-Saharan Africa in US global priorities. We provide an account of how each president has viewed Africa, the major African issues they faced, how they dealt with them and the place of development assistance in their policies. To do this we look at the hierarchies, interests and ideologies that guide assistance policies over time. We link how political, security, economic and military interests intersect with development assistance from 1945–2016. In order to do this, we explain in this chapter how we view power in the social sciences, and how development assistance can thus be usefully understood as an instrument of power.

While the US is often characterised as the most powerful nation in the world, power in the social sciences is an elusive concept. Different emphases and understandings based on various theoretical perspectives can, in turn, lead to new interpretations. To explore how we might gain new interpretations of development assistance as a tool of power, we begin this book with a discussion on the importance of power in social science thinking, and then in turn, how power can be mobilised and exercised in and among states.

The British philosopher Bertrand Russell once remarked that the most fundamental concept in social science is power (Russell, 1938: 10). Power, he asserted, is like energy: '[it] has many forms, such as wealth, armaments, civil authority, [and] influence on opinion' (Russell, 1938: 10–11). Conceptualising power as energy has important metaphorical values. We can imagine power as located in different places at the same time; we can imagine power flowing from different points of origin to other points, losing influence, gaining influence, modifying parameters or forms depending on a multitude of variables. We can visualise different types of power, resulting in and leading to different effects, in isolation or in relation to a multitude of present and past variables; we can even try to visualise the future effects of power through various forms of analysis. But as Nye remarks (2011: 3), power in the social sciences and subsequently the effects of power on social settings is unlike energy in physics and cannot be captured in a formula where measured components are placed in a relationship that produces an equally measurable result.

As discussed thoroughly by Lukes (2005: 61–62), the meaning of power in a qualitative sense is elusive. The use of the word *power* in spoken and written form leads to various conceptions of its meaning (Clegg and Haugaard, 2009). The issue becomes even more complex when attempting to translate idioms across different languages for different users depending

4  *Introduction: power rules*

on their political agenda, disciplinary background and context of use, leading to various disagreements on conceptualisations and understandings of power.

As outlined below, in this book we propose to draw on the analyses offered in different theoretical traditions to better frame and understand the ways in which national security interests and idealism interact with the development assistance discourses and policies of the US. We will emphasise but not be limited to Michel Foucault, Steven Lukes, James Scott and others to guide how and why US development assistance policy took the shape it did. We will clarify why and how US development policy was never able to escape from the particular concept of American exceptionalism and subsequently how the US views and understands its role which guides the linkage between national security, foreign policy and development assistance.

*Foucault – power and modes of thinking*

Of Foucault's many influential concepts, he is perhaps best known for his reflections and analyses of power. He also altered his own position during his academic career, which added more complexity and depth to his interpretations of social realities, highlighted weaknesses and shortcomings of some of his methodologies, and offered potential solutions and improvements. To understand Foucault's work, one must rely primarily on lectures and interviews conducted with him where he contemplates the meaning of his research, as well as expands and clarifies his thinking and conceptualisations. A rich and large scholarship of Foucault's work has emerged in the years following his death and has led to methods, approaches and theoretical frameworks. We, of course, are most interested in his uses and understandings of the concepts of power and governmentality. We have found his emphasis upon power, discourse and knowledge to render more legible elements of US development assistance.

During the course of two lectures held in January 1976, Foucault (Foucault and Gordon, 1980: 78–109) attempted to identify conceptual coherence in several of his works. He spoke of the 'local character of criticism' and explained that it indicates:

> [A]n autonomous, non-centralised kind of theoretical production, one that is to say whose validity is not dependent on the approval of established regimes of thought.
> (Foucault and Gordon, 1980: 81)

What Foucault underscores is that knowledge is often restricted by a process where 'functionalist coherence or formal systematisation' leads to the production of very specific accounts of reality that become standards of rational thought and are considered as truths (Davidson, 1986: 225).

Foucault suggests that a close critical examination of historical contents can unravel conflict and struggle subjugated by the structural standards under which knowledge was produced. The production of specific truths over prolonged periods of time leads to systematic stratification which results in an elaborate social construction. Stratification in this sense is a slow process where a multitude of individuals, collectives and the unfolding of historical events interact with pre-existing knowledge and truths to produce an accumulation of experiences that lead to societal axioms. In this sense, stratification is a social construction where key narratives are produced, reproduced and reinforced, standardising the shape and validity of knowledge and defining truth as follows:

> 'Truth' is to be understood as a system of ordered procedures for the production, regulation, distribution, circulation and operations of statements.
> 'Truth' is linked in a circular relation with systems of power which produce and sustain it, and to effects of power which it induces and which extend it. A 'régime' of truth.
> (Foucault and Gordon, 1980: 133)

Foucault was studying the history of sciences, exploring it as a mechanism of power that shapes notions of what is defined as acceptable knowledge. Based on these premises, the discourses that appear in a society will grant precedence to certain types of knowledge which are based on, and/or incorporate, the basic truths of a society. This is a description of a circular mechanism through which knowledge is shaped by truth, which then leads to the production of knowledge that incorporates these truths, thus reinforcing them and eventually leading to their reproduction and deeper infusion in society:

> [B]asically in any society, there are manifold relations of power which permeate, characterise and constitute the social body, and these relations of power cannot themselves be established, consolidated nor implemented, without the production, accumulation, circulation and functioning of a discourse. There can be no possible exercise of power without a certain economy of discourses of truth which operates through and on the basis of this association. We are subjected to the production of truth through power and we cannot exercise power except through the production of truth.
> (Foucault and Gordon, 1980: 93)

In a purely theoretical sense, Foucault saw a dynamic mechanism that leads to social constructions. Imagine a mound consisting of several stratified layers where each stratum has some kind of relationship to the previous one. This stratification is generated by three elements that

6  *Introduction: power rules*

enhance each other in a circular relationship: power, knowledge and discourses. Together they produce the ideological foundations of a society: the regime of truth. The longer this mechanism works uninterrupted, the more complex and elaborate the stratification it produces.

History teaches us that paradigms shift as Foucault elaborates in his lectures of 1978.[3] But the main point here is that paradigms which are the ideological foundations of a society can be identified, deconstructed and studied by the analysis of discourses. From discourses we can tease out what can be considered and accepted as knowledge, and to a certain extent we can explain how or what leads to the establishment of societal paradigms or why they shift. In essence, this is the conceptual foundation for a methodological framework that enables us to understand the building blocks of social constructions through the analysis of specific discourses.

Hoy (1986: 124–128) notes that Foucault's approach to the concept of power avoids the discussion between those who assign power to agents (such as Lukes) and those who assign it to structures (such as Marx). Instead, Foucault focuses on the analytics of power by 'mapping the network of power relations that have evolved historically' (Hoy, 1986: 128) as a method of explaining society as follows:

> Power must be analysed as something which circulates, or rather as something which only functions in the form of a chain. It is never localised here or there, never in anybody's hands, never appropriated as a commodity or piece of wealth. Power is employed and exercised through a net-like organisation. And not only do individuals circulate between its threads; they are always in the position of simultaneously undergoing and exercising this power. They are not only its inert or consenting target; they are always also the elements of its articulation. In other words, individuals are the vehicles of power, not its points of application.
> 
> (Foucault and Gordon, 1980: 98)

Using these lenses, Foucault invokes the term 'subjugated knowledge', which is knowledge that has been produced within the frame that defines and legitimises basic truths of a society. Exploring historical content critically with the aim of understanding, uncovering and challenging the functionalist and systematised impositions that frame narratives, will facilitate the exposure of subjugated elements, the 'insurrection of subjugated knowledges' as Foucault terms it (Foucault and Gordon, 1980: 81). In other words, to expose these hidden elements, one must allow for the challenging of the power that dominates and subjugates rationality and truth in a society (Davidson, 1986: 225).

Foucault, as pointed out by Lemke, introduces the notion of a distinction between power and domination. Foucault wrote that people play strategic power games – games that are about determining the conduct of others. These power games are different than states of domination. Indeed, for some, participation in power games is voluntary and associated with various forms of pleasure. Therefore, in specific social settings, subjugation to power and even domination is associated with positive outcomes.

Nichols (2010) in his survey of the influence of Foucault upon postcolonial studies noted that power reorganises peoples' identities and also can re-organise or re-configure peoples' subjectivities. Domination in this light (and which we consider below) becomes a particular type of power relationship. It is in Lemke's words 'stable and hierarchical, fixed and difficult to reverse' (Lemke, 2002: 53).

To superimpose his insights on more contextual examples, Foucault used the term *governmentality* to describe power and privileged systematic ways of thinking about roles, values, ethics, ideas and governance. He also contended that 'governmentality' was born from historical changes in the West (Foucalt *et al.*, 2007: 108–110). Governmentality is, in this perspective: 'the rationalisation of governmental practice in the exercise of political sovereignty' (Foucault *et al.*, 2004: 3, quoted by Lemke, 2007: 44). Foucault tried to embed into one term the conditions in which governance of a sovereign creates the rationality that produces, justifies and enforces the discourses that legitimise the sovereign's governance. It serves to grant precedence to specific goals as well as shape subjects that subscribe to, adhere, justify and help reproduce and empower these discourses (Anders, 2005: 39–40; Dean, 2010: 24–37; Foucault *et al.*, 1991: 102–113).

Foucault employed two styles of study (which he termed archaeology and genealogy) to tease out the subjugated elements he was after. It allowed him to create narratives to uncover the relations of power appearing in discursive practices and explain their effects in societal situations (Davidson, 1986: 227). Archaeology attempts to locate historic statements conducive to the production of truth by isolating discursive practices which are:

> characterized by the delimitation of a field of objects, the definition of legitimate perspective for the agent of knowledge, and the fixing of norms for the elaboration of concepts and theories. Thus, each discursive practice implies a play of prescriptions that designates its exclusions and choices.
> (Foucault quoted in Davidson, 1986: 221–222)

To conduct an archaeology in this sense, one must first problematise the present to identify which threads to follow. Once these threads are identified and isolated, an excavation into historical statements can be conducted to locate where threads begin, end, or assume another form, as well as to locate how, why, by whom and for which purposes modifications occur (Davidson, 1986: 223).

8  *Introduction: power rules*

The second style of study employed by Foucault is genealogy. Davidson (1986: 224) explains that the main focus of genealogy is the relationship between 'systems of truth and the modalities of power'. Unlike archaeology which focuses on identification and isolation of discursive practices, genealogy is concerned with the power connected with these discourses (that is, the governmentality aspects of discursive practices). Genealogy aims to rediscover conflict and struggle tucked away and pushed to the fringes by canonised histories (Foucault and Gordon, 1980: 83). In other words, emancipating subjugated knowledge from the power of canonisation (Foucault and Gordon, 1980: 85).

Foucault distinguishes between archaeology and genealogy by explaining that the archaeological method leads to an analysis of discursive practices, while the genealogical method explains the ways in which discursive practices highlight certain truths and subjugate others (Foucault and Gordon, 1980: 85). Davidson (1986: 225 and 227) notes that Foucault's archaeological and genealogical methods are in fact complementary. The first enables the discovery of discourses relevant to a problematised issue, while the second uncovers the ways in which discursive practices exercise power that lead to specific outcomes.[4]

Nancy Fraser notes that the most problematic aspect of Foucault's work was his assumption that his standpoint was normatively neutral (Fraser, 1989: 18). Foucault believed that his research was based on stoic analyses in the sense that it did not bear on the positivity or negativity of discursive practices, but rather focused on the exposition and explanation of the modalities of power and political regimes located in them (Dean, 2010: 54). Foucault himself termed it as a refusal of 'the "blackmail" of the enlightenment' to be for or against it (Dean, 2010: 54; Foucault and Rabinow, 1984: 42). This position triggered the Foucault–Habermas debate and evoked one of Habermas's central criticisms of postmodernism. Essentially, Habermas pointed out that the archaeological and genealogical methodologies employed by Foucault are in essence the 'analysis of truth' and 'critique of power' respectively. He claimed that no critique of power could be conducted without an analysis of truth, and that Foucault's analysis of truth is not deprived of a 'normative yardstick', despite his claims to the opposite (Habermas, 1986: 108).

Whether it is impossible to conduct a genealogical analysis without being swayed by normativity is an ontological, and subsequently, epistemological question. The answer lies in the stated opening positions of the researcher. Habermas's criticism of Foucault on this matter relates to Foucault's failure to conduct a normative-free analysis, despite his claims to the contrary. Using Foucauldian perspectives (among others) in the analysis of development assistance, and more generally, if and how the US government uses it to promote its own interests, means that we have normative views. By questioning the 'truth' of American exceptionalism and viewing it rather as a form of power and discipline means that we regard normative claims as important to our work. What we would claim, however, is that it is not anti-American. Moreover, we would not claim to be dispassionate. We work in a department of international environment and development studies and our sympathies lie with the world characterised as less developed, underdeveloped, or low income. In our view, the requirements, needs and claims made by peoples of Africa have greater legitimacy than often acknowledged due to their political and economic weaknesses in a capitalist world economy. The African continent has its own specific history where potentials were cut short or diverted by the slave trade, colonialism, and now climate change. Given the special historical relationship between the US and Africa produced by the slave trade (and its aftermaths), an inquiry into the use of power by the US seems highly relevant. Our analysis leads us to pessimism as to the potential for the US government to change how it frames and organises development assistance. It has become an even more fraught arena due to the rise of terrorism and the militarization of US foreign policy more generally. We take this up again in our conclusions.

Using Foucault's archaeological and genealogical methods as markers, we interpret the intentions of development policy as a complex field which is shaped by and serves as a regime of truth through which idealism and national interests are met and to varying degrees satisfied. The terms *developed* and *underdeveloped* carry specific meanings when used to describe encounters between cultures. They indicate a hierarchy rooted in a plurality of conceptions such as race, gender, culture, resources, technology and religion. The justification for investing in and conducting an intervention under the heading of 'development assistance' features the space where ideology and culture merge with the subtext meanings of developed and undeveloped. We attempt to unmask[5] these encounters through a lens of power.

### *The American regime of truth and the formulation of development policy – thinking about Foucauldian power*

We suggest that the regime of truth is the means through which the identity of powerful Americans can be confirmed. The space where 'American' is conditioned. It is the mechanism through which individuals and groups in America make sense of a way of life, the foundations that determine how stories in the society are told and understood, the way *sense* is being made and the way behaviour is being interpreted. The regime of truth is the foundation, to be beyond question if it is to be most effective, upon which the acceptance or rejection of discourses is possible in the context of American society (Guyatt, 2016; Parkinson, 2016). It is the mechanism that grants validation to statements and determines the rejection of others. The regime of truth in a society is what makes it possible to answer the question: 'What is power for?'[6] The regime of truth underscored in this work validates and legitimates (for Americans) the projection of American power. It works to project its own power upon the American people; it is the power to forge 'American'. It is possible, in our view, to locate in narratives and discourses some fundamental building blocks of contemporary American ideology. These blocks are elements that are produced and reproduced by American institutions through which the basic truths of the society are formed (and are often used and presented by political elites). What we sketch here is the American ideology[7] that emerges first in an anti-colonial form to the British colonial rulers and later as a contrast to twentieth-century fascism and communism as America consolidates its hegemonic power. Americans construct and legitimise their actions in the world in reference to the roots of the nation. We find that the regime of truth helps shape the concept of foreign assistance and legitimises its particular operationalisation over time and in different contexts. Our focus is on the conjunction between assistance and national security employed to achieve specific objectives justified by this particular ideology. The American regime of truth which supports the assistance policy is discussed further in Chapter 3. Once a foreign policy course has been established in a context, the analysis of power moves away from a Foucauldian description towards other conceptual frameworks to study the ways in which power is projected.

## Lukes – power as domination

In his seminal work on power, Lukes (2005) produces a lucid conceptual map that facilitates the theoretical and empirical study of power in its application. The underlying debates that led to this publication were linked to the study of American politics. Lukes picked up on certain debates on power in American politics during the 1960s (see below), and identified a number of shortcomings in the way power was conceptualised until then. In his work, he describes the two common conceptualisations of power, and adds another which he calls 'the third dimension of power'.

The debates that triggered the formulation of Lukes' theoretical framework on power took place in the late 1950s, and revolved around questions of domination, especially of elites, in American society. The first dimension of power which Lukes refers to was formulated by Dahl (1961) who disagreed with a hypothesis forwarded by Mills (1956) asserting that American politics were dominated by a group of elites. Dahl studied decision-making in politics, focusing on the behaviour of actors when conflicting preferences were observable. From his analysis, Dahl established that power and influence are not located with one individual or a group of individuals. He demonstrated that no single individual or group could consistently exercise decision power over a plurality of independent issues (Lukes, 2005: 38). Dahl's analysis of power is dubbed by Lukes as the 'one-dimensional view' where power manifests when decisions are made, or through actions that lead to decisions (Lukes, 2005: 19).

The main shortcoming of this view, and subsequently of Dahl's methodology for measuring power, is that his observations were limited to conditions where A exercised power over issues, causing B to do or accept something which is against B's own preference. While this can indicate a great deal about the exercise of power within a system and on particular issues brought for discussion, it does not raise questions such as who decides which issues are or can be raised or omitted from an agenda, or the way in which issues are framed on the agenda. Bachrach and Baratz (1970) point out that Dahl examines power only in situations where an issue is brought up for discussion and decision-making. Dahl does not consider or examine the operation of power manifested by the exclusion of issues from decision-making processes, or by the way in which they are brought to the table. Bachrach and Baratz (1970: 6 quoted in Lukes, 2005: 22) indicate that power is also located beyond observable behaviour and should also be studied in situations where known conflicts of interests exist (as opposed to situations where conflict of interests are observable through direct behaviour). Dahl's study of power is thus confined to contextual behavioural observations and suffers from the reproduction of the biases confined to a system, ignoring power over the system (Lukes, 2005: 38).

The two-dimensional view of power is linked directly to the criticism raised against Dahl's one-dimensional approach. It locates power as being over the system and expands the scope from the exercise of open coercion (where A is observed to cause B to accept or do something B would otherwise not do), to the use of influence where A limits the range of possibilities of B (Lukes, 2005: 22). An important distinction here is that B may or may not realise that A has exercised power over him or her. This issue expands the sphere of a study of power to non-observable behaviours.

As noted by Lukes (2005: 24), conflict, whether overt or covert, is still assumed to be an underlying cause for invoking the use of power when viewed through the two-dimensional lens. While assumed to be present, conflict is not always immediately observable in a case where issues are purposefully not raised or treated as non-issues, making the empirical study of power a complicated endeavour. The three-dimensional view of power suggested by Lukes deals with a more complex exercise of power where conflict is a latent concept. It taps into power exercised to avoid the emergence of conflicts altogether (Lukes, 2005: 28). In this respect, the three-dimensional view of power is linked to a form of power discussed by Foucault where A uses social forces in addition to institutional capacities and individual decisions to shape the basic belief, preferences and perceptions of B, to the capacity that B assumes a course of action that is not in his or her best interests, sometimes without even realising it. But even though the concept connects to linked mechanisms, Foucault and Lukes highlight different components and subsequently study different elements. Lukes' initial conception of power is limited to power as domination, that

12  *Introduction: power rules*

is 'power over' and to a certain extent 'power to' for the purpose of securing compliance (Lukes, 2005: 109). Foucault's views on power change over time. In an essay published after his death (Foucault, 1988; Lemke, 2007) he distinguished between power and domination while also stipulating that when he said power he really meant 'relations of power.' Foucault stated that in order to be relations of power (in contrast to domination) they could not exist unless the subjects are free.[8] These relations of power are then changeable, reversible and unstable. We read this as indicating differing degrees of agency. It follows that in relations of power there must be the possibility of resistance. There are those relationships of power which he called 'strategic games between liberties' where some people try to determine the conduct of others. If there is no possibility of resistance then there are no relations of power. The later Foucault left more space for politics. This is in contrast to his earlier emphasis upon states of domination – economic, social institutional or sexual which are often thought of as the most important face of power. In addition, Lemke (2007) observes that Foucault identified a third type of power relation – government that refers to the 'conduct of conduct' although in general Foucault sought to expand the understanding of power relations beyond government interactions with the population.

Lukes highlights the importance of viewing power agents broadly. He contends that power does not require, when it is at work, the intentions or positive intervention of actors. Viewing power in this way lets us see and understand social arrangements that produce powerlessness or specific outcomes as unconnected to the powerful (Lukes, 2006: 171) To identify a process where power is being exercised requires the identification of the exerciser but does not require direct intentions (Lukes, 2005: 57–58). In this way Lukes does not dismiss the role of structures and their influence on agents. Given his interest in inequality he would favour identifying responsibility. Part of the differences between Lukes and Foucault rests on their disciplinary backgrounds. Foucault as philosopher and historian highlights hidden connections between power and knowledge and how power-knowledge relations change over time. Lukes on the other hand seeks to provide us with the theoretical and analytical tools as to how states regulate and control populations[9] under their control.

In relation to this study, the theoretical framework offered by Lukes is used to inform two different forms of analysis. The first is the relationship between idealism and national interests in the operation of development politics inside the US. It comprises the power game that informs the relationship between different agencies with different areas of responsibilities. This relationship can be studied in historical and contemporary contexts (separately or as a continuum) focusing on how certain societal values[10] manifest in the formulation of coherent foreign policy as viable conscious arguments to influence a course of policy or action. This exercise highlights the inter-agency 'power game' and determines the ever-changing and contextual starting position of the different agents[11] influencing formulation of policy.

The second form of analysis is the power exercised through the operationalisation of a policy in developing countries – in this case, the American development policy in Africa. Lukes' framework serves as a conceptual map to understand the operationalisation of policy that explains the role of development assistance in the strategic relationship between the US as a donor country and African nations as recipients. Using the theoretical framework for this purpose assumes a starting position that possibly regards this relationship as attempted domination: the US attempting to secure the compliance of Africans to achieve its own ends. This may lead to potential criticism that this work is contaminated by a normative bias that colours both the type of investigation and its outcomes. In diplomatic language, the relationship between various countries is described as one of partnership, co-operation and with shared goals rather than attempted domination (excluding cases of open conflict). Our purpose is to analyse how a powerful donor interacts with the concept of assistance to achieve other ends, and examine how this interaction bears on helping the underdeveloped to develop. To clarify why an analysis of US development policy in Africa using a conceptual map inspired by Lukes is not, in this case, anchored in a normative bias against the US, we would like to turn the discussion to the context of power as a tool to achieve American policy objectives.

### *Nye – hard, soft and smart power*

In 2010 the Department of State published its first Quadrennial Diplomacy and Development Review (QDDR) to answer the question: How can America do better? (QDDR, 2010: Forward by Secretary of State Hilary Clinton). The QDDR was a follow-up by Obama's Presidential Policy Directive on Development[12] and was meant to provide a strategic framework to improve the deployment of America's power:

> Secretary Clinton began her tenure by stressing the need to elevate civilian power alongside military power as equal pillars of U.S. foreign policy. She called for an integrated 'smart power' approach to solving global problems – a concept that is embodied in the President's National Security Strategy.
>
> (QDDR, 2010: ii)

Both America's National Security Strategy (NSS) and the QDDR form the basis for the strategic frameworks of the US Agency for International Development (USAID, 2013: 6). Both documents emphasise the concept of *smart power* as a strategy to further US foreign policy objectives.[13]

Smart power is a term arguably coined by Nye in 2003 to refer to contextual combinations of 'hard' and 'soft' power to achieve preferred policy outcomes (Nye, 2004: 32). In 2006, Nye co-chaired, together with Richard Armitage, a Centre for Strategic and International Studies (CSIS) commission on smart power. The efforts of the commission culminated in a report published in 2007 (CSIS, 2007) laying out a set of recommendations to the 'President of the United States, regardless of political party' on how a smart power strategy can be implemented (CSIS, 2007: 1). In 2011, Nye published a book entitled the *Future of Power* (Nye, 2011) where he outlined in a more academic fashion the strategic vision of the smart power concept.

In essence, Nye (2011: 14) describes 'three faces of relational power', correlating his baseline with Lukes' conceptual map for the analysis of power, and then turns the three dimensions of power into conceptual tools for policymakers. The underlying idea is to help policymakers devise informed strategies where the ranges of power options at their disposal, hard and soft, are combined intelligibly to wield influence in foreign affairs. The need to explicitly introduce the notion of smart power came after a decade where the US projection of power was understood to be overly reliant on hard power strategies, damaging the image of America and consequently significantly hampering its strategic influence over a range of foreign policy objectives. He observed that the exercise of power became more complicated due to globalisation and growing interdependency. In turn, these changes require new methods and approaches on new global issues where interests must reflect global and domestic priorities at the same time.[14]

Nye developed a spectrum of power behaviours to indicate the range of options available for policy (Nye, 2011: 21). The spectrum ranges from 'command' which is at the hard power end of the spectrum, to 'co-opt' at the soft power end, introducing 'coerce', 'threat', 'pay', 'sanction', 'frame', 'persuade' and 'attract' as possible behaviours. He defines soft power as the 'ability to affect others through the co-optive means of framing the agenda, persuading, and eliciting positive attraction in order to obtain preferred outcomes' (Nye, 2011: 20–21).

Nye and Armitage explain that to achieve America's interests:

> The United States must become a smarter power by once again investing in the global good – providing things people and governments in all quarters of the world want but cannot attain in the absence of American leadership. By complementing U.S. military and economic might with greater investments in soft power, America can build the framework it needs to tackle tough global challenges.
> (CSIS, 2007: 1)

One of the critical areas listed by Nye and Armitage where a smart power approach will be a useful strategy to achieve policy objectives is global development:

Elevating the role of development in U.S. foreign policy can help the United States align its own interests with the aspirations of people around the world.

(CSIS, 2007: 1)[15]

As illustrated by the QDDR, various documents issued by USAID, and the NSS during the Obama administration (NSS, 2010: 14–16),[16] the concept of smart power was adopted explicitly to better achieve US foreign policy interests. Thus, there exists in the US government a conscious use of a concept of power which firmly rests on Nye's adaptation of Lukes' conceptual framework to achieve policy objectives around the world. The three pillars of American power as explained in various documents (such as USAID, 2012 and references) are defence, diplomacy and development, or 'the 3Ds' as they are often referred to in the Obama administration.

Nye devises a conception of power for the purpose of American policymakers. He adapts Lukes' analysis into a concrete range of options for policymakers so that they can better understand the range of possibilities at their disposal to project America's power and achieve objectives in a smarter way. The smarter way is to project power while reducing the unintended consequences associated with over-reliance and uninformed use of specific power tools. Smart power as a policy tool is also an artefact of the regime of truth, and as such constitutes an object for Foucauldian analysis.

We return now to the question of whether using a conceptual map that studies conscious attempts to exercise power to influence, control, and dominate as a tool for the analysis of development policies, can be considered a bias-free exercise. The formal foreign policy strategy of the US in recent years has been structured around the explicit projection of smart power, which in itself, is a conceptual tool based on the three 'faces of power' described by Nye as the different aspects of relational power. Since the faces of power are based on Lukes' description of the three dimensions of power, the role of this strategy is to plan intelligent ways to exercise 'power over', and to a certain extent 'power to'. This means locating intelligible ways to modify B's behaviour to be consistent with the preferences of A as a form of influence, control, or domination. The word 'domination' often resonates negatively and is associated with open, often violent or coercive imposition. Nevertheless, domination encompasses subtle behaviours which are sometimes not even noticeable. When A devises a set of preferences and then commits to achieve them, it can be argued that A will be engaged in various forms of domination if he or she attempts to induce or modify the behaviours of B. Does this necessarily mean that it is not in the (best) interests of B to engage in that behaviour? If it is in the interests of B to engage in a behaviour suggested by A, does this mean that A's actions with regard to B cannot be called domination? Is the use of the word 'domination' only appropriate when A induces, influences, affects or modifies the behaviour of B when it is not in the interests of B to engage in that behaviour? Lukes (2005: 86) defines 'power as domination' as A's exercise of power over B in order to further (or at least not harm) A's own preferences, when this exertion of power has a negative bearing on B, whether B realises this or not. While this definition of power as domination is useful, it assumes that one can identify whether the exertion of power by A is in fact bearing negatively on the interests of B. That is not always the case; the question is who is to determine that A's power is bearing negatively on B? Is it A? Is it B? Should it be an objective observer? What if B believes that it is in his or her best interests to accept A's exertion of power? Can it be argued that in fact B does not know or understand what is in his or her own best interests? Can it be argued that B is 'primitive' (to utilise the word used by colonial powers and Americans on some occasions when referring to Africans)?

We prefer a more generalised designation of domination, limiting the variables to the actual action and purposes of the entity exercising power. This designation is the following: *power as domination is when A exercises power over B to achieve A's own set of objectives.* Such a definition incorporates all the uses of hard and soft power by A, and underlines that by the exercise of power, A's intentions are first and foremost to achieve A's own set of objectives tied to A's own interests and preferences as A defines them or understands them. This means a conscious attempt by A to project power to achieve first and foremost his or her own objectives (interests and/or ideological-based objectives), whether these have a negative bearing on B or not (see below for a further discussion). But, as argued above, choosing to conduct an analysis based on a framework that studies power as a conscious attempt to modify or induce behaviours (domination), does not necessarily lead to a normative bias against, in this case, the US. It is using the building blocks upon which US foreign policy strategies are built in order to dissect and analyse its effects, consequences and the meanings for development assistance.

There is another type of power that surfaces on the 'dominated' side of the equation which significantly affects the intended outcomes of the 'powerful's' policy and practices. This type of power must also be factored into the analysis.

### Scott – weapons of the weak

To explain the third level of analysis, we will begin with an old Ethiopian proverb quoted in Scott (1990: opening quote): 'When the great lord passes, the wise peasant bows deeply and silently farts'. Albeit colourful, the proverb captures an element of power neglected by Lukes. Though the actions of the peasant in this case have no practical effects on the power of the lord, it indicates that sometimes the relatively powerless can grant the powerful the impression that s/he is more successful than s/he really is. As Scott (1985) demonstrates, subdued people can employ a number of different strategies through which power exercised over them is undermined or nullified, and in many cases, without the knowledge of the dominator.

Using Lukes' own style of formulation to explain the point above: assuming that A is the powerful individual or entity who consciously exercises power over B to achieve A's own ends, often (and especially in development assistance contexts as contended here) B finds ways to use the exercise of power by A: to undermine A; to give A the impression that s/he is more powerful than s/he really is; to allow A to exercise parts of his or her power and to concede other parts; or to gain power, to ends that serve B's purposes and/or interests (sometimes against A's own interests and intentions). This can be achieved: with knowledge of A, without knowledge of A, or with partial knowledge of A. In a reconsideration of resistance in Foucault's work, Flohr argues convincingly that resistance is 'presupposed in the exercise of power' (Flohr, 2016: 48). By this he means that resistance can be an adaptive response or an unpredictable outcome of the exercise of power. In turn, the exercise of power must adapt and respond to the resistance that is produced. In the end, the outcomes of resistance are not known and can end in the reshaping of the original power relations (Flohr, 2016).

This is not really a fourth dimension of power, but rather a parallel dimension of it; it is the locus where an exercise of power over someone enables that person to tap into a source of power he or she did not have before. It is where the application of any of the three faces of power to achieve specific objectives creates opportunities that allow the dominated to employ various sets of strategies to gain more power, which in turn, is exercised in ways that may undermine the objectives of the dominator. It is not necessarily the same as open or latent resistance, which is an aspect of reactionary responses to the use of power, but rather an adaptation to the application of any kind of power, be it hard or soft.

Scott (1985: 315) begins his analysis by questioning Gramsci's concept of hegemony[17] which emerges from an assertion made by Marx and Engels. In *The German Ideology* (1846), Marx and Engels explain that elites who control the modes of material production also control the means of mental production. Gramsci views hegemony as the exercise of ideological domination over culture, religion, education and media (Scott, 1985: 315). Broken down into its elements, the Gramscian notion of hegemony is an application of domination through the third dimension of power as discussed by Lukes. Scott (1985) focused his investigation on everyday peasant resistance to class domination in the context of the Green Revolution. He demonstrated that despite attempts by the ruling class and agricultural experts to exercise ideological domination, peasants continue to resist hegemony. He questioned whether the ideologies of the powerful only *seem* to penetrate the dominated, while in reality, there is a gap between manifested public behaviours and the private ideological beliefs they continue to hold (Scott, 1985: 321–322). In many cases, the subdued hold firmly to their earlier dominant ideologies, do not lose their own sense of justice, and question and demystify the narratives of the powerful (Scott, 1985: 317). Put more simply, the weak may find ways to counter and undermine the power of the strong.

In his critique of development projects in Lesotho, Ferguson (1994) demonstrates a common feature of many development interventions whereby there is an effort to hide or mask the power dimensions required to act. In the case examined by Ferguson he describes how the development objectives of a donor are converted into a project by a recipient state. The recipient state transforms development objectives into 'technical problems' on a project level, which leads to situations where resources provided by a donor (say, to address poverty) end up serving the expansion of state powers over its own population (Ferguson, 1994: 256). Ferguson emphasises that this is not necessarily a result of a conspiracy, but 'just happen[s] to be the way things work out' (Ferguson, 1994: 256). Seen through the lens provided by Scott, we can assign the role of the powerful to the donor and the role of the weak to the recipient state.

Two major issues manifest through Ferguson's example which are relevant for the chapters that follow. The first is that, in this case (and many others), the domination of the powerful are not necessarily a conscious attempt to exercise domination over the recipient to transform his or her behaviour to fulfil the interests of the donor. Ideological biases are socially constructed, and are embedded in identities. As such, a donor may express his or her own ideological biases in discourses without realising that they are that. A donor as such may not be aware of the power (in a Foucauldian sense) that construct in him/her a regime of truth, and unware of the power s/he exercises as a donor to re-create this truth with recipients. A donor who controls the resources and decides how to allocate them will invest in sets of objectives consistent with their view of how development challenges should be tackled. This view might not necessarily reflect the needs or preferences of the recipient, but the recipient might claim that they want to tap into the resources offered by the donor. The recipient might agree with the premise that the donor knows better. It is possible that the intentions of the donor are to accord with the recipient and pays little or no attention to how the recipient has altered their views or actions. In the book, we demonstrate how the US as a donor seeks to alter or support other countries' policies and actions to align with US government broader national security objectives. However, as we also demonstrate, this exercise of power does not necessarily produce the intended outcomes.

The second issue that manifests in Ferguson's example is the introduction of a 'chain' of power relations that can result in significant modifications of initial objectives and intentions of a donor. In this case we have a donor country, a recipient state, and a group of people within the recipient state where the development project or programme is applied. We can formulate it as A, B and $B_1$, where A exercises latent or conscious power over B, and B subsequently exercises power over $B_1$ which may be consistent or inconsistent with the intentions of A. This becomes more complicated when we consider that B might intentionally or unintentionally modify or completely change the intention of A by exercising power over $B_1$. The power that B is able to exercise over $B_1$ is in this case only possible because A initiates and supports the process.

## Interests, power and development assistance – a conceptual map

This work tries to locate and explain development assistance policy both as a result of power in social constructions (the regime of truth) and as a tool of power (through the operationalisation of policy). But the question remains how to incorporate the different types of power and its effects in terms of reactions to it in an analysis that accounts for context, complexity and nuances. In order to justify the type of data gathered and included in this research as well as to clarify the ways in which we interact with the data we sketch a conceptual map anchored in various conceptualisation of power.

Domination is the main category under which we locate power in development assistance; development assistance or aid is based on hierarchy between the givers and receivers of aid. This is discussed in Chapter 2. If we use Lukes' definition of domination, then Nye's concept of power includes elements that are difficult to accept as domination. An example of that is the use of co-operation as an expression of soft power. In a case when B agrees to co-operate because he or she believes it is in his or her best interests to do so, would not be domination as defined by Lukes. But if B's decision to co-operate is related to a current, past or continuous effort by A[18] to (re-)structure B's basic beliefs, we are in fact witnessing domination. If B believes that co-operating with A is in his or her own interests but has been influenced over decades and does not know better, or B has no access to knowledge and information other than that given to him by A,[19] or B is a victim of global Western cultural imperialism, A is in fact dominating B. But asserting that B does not know better, or is a victim of imposed structures, is a qualitative statement closely linked to normative positions. Therefore, domination cannot be linked to how the exertion of power bears on B since the experience of B can be contested ad infinitum. Domination should be defined based on the intentions of A, and not only when A is engaged in a conscious attempt to exercise domination, but rather based on A's fundamental intention to induce or modify a behaviour of B for the objective of achieving A's own preferences. In this case, we can include Nye's range of tools, from hard to soft power, as forms of domination. Domination in this case can be visible, hidden or invisible, but can also range from conscious to unconscious domination. In other words, the dominator does not realise s/he is dominating.

20  *Introduction: power rules*

If one chooses a dictionary definition for *domination* which focuses on supremacy, pre-eminence and mastery, then the term raises controversy as it is saturated with negativity. But domination also involves control and influence, which disarms the negativity described above. As mentioned, domination can be subtle, almost unnoticed. And if we turn back to Foucault, submission to domination can even be voluntary with full understanding of the roles of master and servant. In addition, a dominator might not be conscious of the exertion of domination, acting based on his or her own understanding of 'good' and 'evil' in a fashion that serves the interests of the subject. When a missionary builds a school in Africa, the missionary is not only bringing education to Africans, but is also bringing Christianity and salvation (in his/her mind) to them, as well as his or her own personal redemption.

If we open up a conceptual space where power operates as domination, then which concepts can we use in order to make sense of the range of actions and reactions? First, we consider the operation of power in a simple manner, locating an A which exercises power over a B. Considering the complexity of power that is exercised to achieve objectives, as well as the parallel dimension of power (the power gained by B through the exertion of power by A), we can devise a simplified non-exhaustive framework that allows us to understand some of the complexity to address the content of this book. Table 1.1 examines the operation of power in a space where it is exercised as domination between A, the dominator, and B, the dominated, with feedback of B to the exertion of power by A.

In a chosen context, we can ask ourselves the following questions about A's exertion of power: What type of power is A exercising? What is the level of awareness of A regarding the dominating effect of this power? In which sphere does A's power operate? In Figure 1.1, Divon (2015) uses three indicators on a scale for convenience to describe the form of power in each attribute. In addressing specific cases, the scale would need to be adjusted to taken into specific complexities. Once we define the forms of power exerted by the dominator, we can examine the reaction of the dominated. Consider the example when A is consciously using development assistance (soft power) in country X to invisibly repel Soviet attempts to

*Table 1.1* Conceptual framework for a general analysis of the operation of power as domination

| Attributes | Context | | |
|---|---|---|---|
| | Forms of power | Dominator (action) | Dominated (reaction) |
| Type | Hard-combined-soft | | |
| Awareness | Conscious-latent-unconscious | | |
| Sphere | Visible-hidden-invisible | | |

Source: author

befriend that country. What is the reaction of B to this exertion of power? Does B reject assistance by A because B understands the objectives of A and disagrees with them? Does B reject parts of A's assistance and accept other parts for B's own reasons without understanding A's objectives or without allowing A to know that B understands A's objectives? etc. This framework can be used to analyse specific and generalised contexts. But first one must understand how to define A and how to define B, especially when power moves from A to B in complex ways and through different agents.

Figure 1.1 is a general visualisation of some locations where we expect to identify power that affects the meaning of development assistance in US policy. Naturally, any schematisation such as the one below is a mere generalisation that simplifies a much more complex and infinitely nuanced reality.

For our purposes we can use the Organisation for Economic Cooperation and Development's (OECD) Development Assistance Committee (DAC) definition of Official Development Assistance (ODA) as

> those flows to countries and territories on the DAC List of ODA Recipients and to multilateral institutions which are: (i) *provided by official agencies*, including state and local governments, or by their executive agencies; and (ii) each transaction of which: (a) is administered with the promotion of the **economic development and welfare of developing countries** as its main objective; and (b) is **concessional in character** and conveys a grant element of at least 25 per cent (calculated at a rate of discount of 10 per cent).[20]

We also recognise that the boundaries among military assistance, humanitarian assistance, emergency relief and support to refugees means that the boundaries among the categories are overlapping and slippery. In addition to the complexities within development assistance itself the US government has linked development and the fight against terrorism in the aftermath of 9/11.[21] One way of viewing this linkage is that A (the US) exercising soft power (development assistance) over B (in general terms, recipients of US assistance) to achieve A's interests (fight terrorism) with the assumption that B shares its interests. We contend that this use of power is represented in a long history of US involvement in Africa.

The post-9/11 conceptualisation of development where the explicit links between US national security, the fight against terrorism and the development assistance programme are made, is a starting point for a Foucauldian excavation to locate discursive practices that tie US development assistance policy to national security, interests and American ideology.

The first box in Figure 1.1 represents the places where we expect to locate discourses containing the unique American ideological underpinnings for development assistance, as well as the dominant bearings for the

22  *Introduction: power rules*

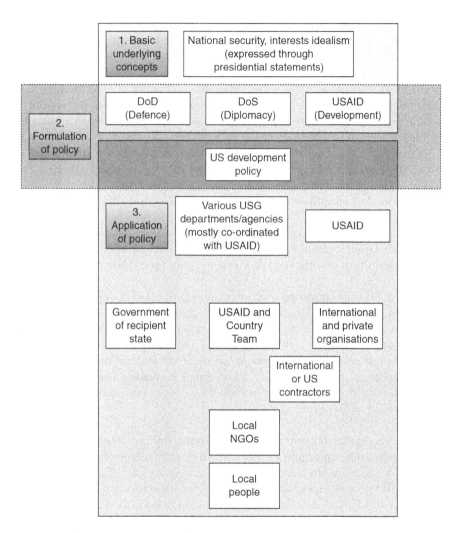

*Figure 1.1* Conceptual map: location of power and levels of analysis.
Source: author.

programme in historical contexts. The box also includes the most important departments involved in inputs influencing the development assistance policy: the Department of Defence (DoD), the Department of State (DoS) and the US Agency for International Development (USAID).[22] These departments formulate discourses adjusted to or reflected through various executive branch statements (once the direction for policy has been decided) that include forms of ideological justifications.

The second box locates the area where strategic goals are transformed into generalised policies, and then carved into more generalised programmes and objectives, reflecting both the ideological underpinning and American interests. Here we can expect to find justifications that link specific agendas to the general discourse in forms that bridge interests and ideology.

The third box represents a further carving of generalised development assistance goals and programmes into country-specific forms, and the application of policy through development projects. Despite USAID being the lead agency on development assistance, a significant number of other agencies are involved in the process. Figure 2–1 in Brainard (2007: 34) illustrates the complexity of US foreign assistance, linking objectives of the programme to the organisation of government in the US. The plurality of the objectives linked to the foreign and development assistance programmes relates to a number of departments and federal agencies, and fall under various bureaucratic jurisdictions and expertise. As Figure 2–1 in Brainard (2007: 34) illustrates, there are many actors involved in the American assistance programme. We will not be focusing on understanding the mechanics of American assistance, but rather on the intersection of objectives with USAID, DoS and DoD as the lead agencies involved in various aspects of international development.[23] The intention is to understand how the concept of development assistance is used to consolidate security, interests and idealism in the process of translation into policies, programmes and projects.

The third box also represents the application of US development assistance programmes by actors external to the US government. These range from recipient states on a bilateral level, international organisations, private contractors (American and foreign) and local and international NGOs. The entire system is geared to create projects and programmes that benefit local people as a part of a grand scheme to help an entire country move towards a developed state – while at the same time addressing national security concerns and ideological preferences of the US. The focus of this book is on the grand scheme under which the system operates and not on specific programming in regional and country level.

Power is the central thread running through the various elements in all three boxes presented in Figure 1.1. There is no meaningful way to represent the various power relationships by incorporating arrows into the scheme. The relationship is much more complex than actor A exercising power over actor B as illustrated by the theoretical discussions above. In such an analysis there is room to locate power as explained and understood by Foucault, Lukes, Nye and Scott, highlighting how development assistance is conceived and how it is being used. This will allow for the formulating of a critical narrative that contrasts the interests and needs of local people in underdeveloped situations with the conceptualisation of development assistance of a donor.

Dissecting the institutional politics of the American foreign assistance programme (of which development assistance is a component) could include a study of the bureaucracy, the lobbying and Congress as well as the executive branch on its agencies and histories. Understanding the plurality of the underlying ideas about development assistance in America means a breakdown to an almost infinite number of interests and positions that represent the world at large as well as domestic ideological and policy prejudices. This is, of course, a task which is beyond the scope of this research.[24]

Nevertheless, it is possible to examine and flesh out the most important underlying concepts that form the dominant American understanding of development assistance at given times and in contexts as influenced by the regime of truth and expressed in discourses. This can be achieved by studying references to development assistance in various executive branch policy statements, assuming that these statements represent the most powerful underlying ideas that make it into policy, and if not, contain criticism of policies rejected or devised by the legislative branch against the opinion of the executive. There are continuous discussions on the importance of the President in the determination of American power, both in general and in contexts. As noted by Nye (2013: 11), this question goes back to the ambiguity of the constitution about the power of the President and Congress in foreign policy. Nevertheless, Nye explains that leadership matters, which underlines the role of agency in structural contexts (Nye, 2013: 137). In other words, presidential statements can represent the formal bearings of the US on different matters in specific times. They symbolise the most powerful ideological and policy interests in a context. So, while presidential statements do not indicate the battles waged with the purpose of winning one perspective or another on a specific issue, they do represent the winning strategies and the rationalisation behind them.

The framework presented here serves as an introduction that guides the way we read and interact with the data presented in this book. Our point of departure is that the concept of development assistance operates in a space where established historical hierarchies between groups of people exist. As such, established power relations on various conceptual levels affect the interactions between developed and underdeveloped nations or states. In Chapter 2 we outline the intellectual and historical foundation for the formation of this hierarchy, and explain how this hierarchy affects the particular interactions and policies between the US and Africa. In Chapter 3 we focus on the American development assistance discourse in the executive branch. It traces the link among the use of development assistance as a power tool to help achieve national security and foreign policy interests and goals in selected African geopolitical contexts. Chapters 4 to 6 describe in some detail the intersections between American interests and changing African realities. They present the American assistance policy towards various African states as a function of national security and foreign policy objectives. These chapters demonstrate how the executive branch viewed and used the assistance policy as a tool to achieve geopolitical objectives during the Cold War (Chapter 4), the post-Cold War years (Chapter 5), and the post-9/11 years (Chapter 6). To form the narrative in Chapters 3 to 6, we gathered a range of data from primary and secondary sources. These include a variety of documents available in archives and online, interviews conducted in Washington DC and Africa with past and present officials working for USAID, the DoS, DoD and other agencies, and a range of scholarly texts examining various aspects of US policies in Africa since the end of WWII. We conclude the book with Chapter 7 where we discuss the relationship between power, US development policy in Africa, and unintended consequences that have undermined the purpose of development assistance, the long-term strategic objective of the US, and the American moral compass that serves as a justification for US power projection.

## Notes

1 The World Bank divides the world into income categories: As of 1 July 2015, low-income economies are defined as those with a GNI per capita, calculated using the World Bank Atlas method, of $1,045 or less in 2014; middle-income economies are those with a GNI per capita of more than $1,045 but less than $12,736; high-income economies are those with a GNI per capita of $12,736 or more. Lower-middle-income and upper-middle-income economies are separated at a GNI per capita of $4,125. http://blogs.worldbank.org/opendata/new-country-classifications
2 USAID, for example, operates in 165 nations.
3 In his lectures at the College de France (see Foucault *et al.*, 2007), Foucault portrays different forms of government and therefore power. For example, what he calls the pastorate where the metaphor of a shepherd caring for his flock of sheep (as a whole and as individuals) characterises the political systems of Pharaonic Egyptian and Hebrew.
4 In 1983 Foucault wrote,

> We must distinguish the relationships of power as strategic games between liberties – strategic games that result in the fact that some people try to determine the conduct of others – and the states of domination, which are what we ordinarily call power. And, between the two, between the games of power and the states of domination, you have governmental technologies.
> (Foucault quoted in Bernauer and Rasmussen, 1988: 19)

5 Unmasking: '[C]hallenging the extra-theoretical effectiveness of a doctrine' (Hacking, 1999: 56).
6 Once determined, we can conduct a separate analysis on how this power is projected. The eclectic framework presented in this chapter explains how to conduct such an analysis.
7 We know that there is an enormous literature beginning notably with de Toqueville attempting to capture the distinctiveness and dynamism of the US. Our purpose however is not to review this literature but to focus on relevant aspects to the construction of development assistance.
8 Foucault's words are as follows:

> Power is exercised only over free subjects, and only insofar as they are free. By this we mean individual or collective subjects who are faced with a field

of possibilities in which several ways of behaving, several reactions and diverse comportments, may be realized. Where the determining factors saturate the whole, there is no relationship of power; slavery is not a power relationship when man is in chains.

(Foucault, 1982: 790)

9 This also became a focus for Foucault in his lectures at the College de France. See the collected lectures in Foucault *et al.* (2007).
10 Here we refer to the institutions that are regarded within a society as attributes of its fundamental character; the regime of truth that can be teased out through a Foucauldian study. The character of a society may not be identical across the society and may assume different forms over time. But most importantly, the character of a society can be identified in discourses, and the fundamental societal values associated with that character can be teased out of discourses.
11 Agents in this sense can be viewed as separate individuals or collectives represented by individuals, for example, the President of the US as representing the direction of American policies, or the administrator of USAID as representing the policy of the agency.
12 A document that was initially confidential, until it was declassified in 2014 following a Freedom of Information Act (FOIA) claim.
13 The NSS (2010) describes various forms of power without referring directly to the term 'smart power', while the QDDR employs the term 'smart power' directly.
14 On the issue of climate change, for example.
15 Note that this statement rests on an assumption that people's aspirations around the world are consistent with US interests, and if not, perhaps they need to be.
16 Unlike the QDDR and various other US government documents, the NSS does not use the term 'smart power', but rather lists the various power tools at the disposal of the US under the title '*A Whole of Government Approach*'.
17 Outlined in Gramsci's *Prison Notebooks*.
18 Or an agent of A, or another entity that shares the same views as A by influence.
19 Where A would often dub B as 'primitive', as we discuss thoroughly in Chapter 2 and *in passim* throughout the book.
20 Available online: www.oecd.org/dac/stats/officialdevelopmentassistance definitionandcoverage.htm
21 Outlined in Chapters 3 and 6 in this book.
22 Choosing once again the most important actors in relation to the assistance policy, fully aware of the fact that a multitude of inputs come from other sources. Dissecting the influence of various agents in American politics is not the aim of this book.
23 During the George W. Bush administration the Millennium Challenge Corporation (MCC) became in important and independent agency for development assistance. In the years after its inception, the MCC turned to USAID for expertise, advice and implementation.
24 In this respect, Figure 1.1 should have included a layer visualising a multitude of actors and agents who play an important role in influencing priorities of development policy. Some of these dynamics are however expressed in the final formulation of policy, although the question of who influenced these policies cannot be answered without a proper analysis. That is not the objective of this book.

# References

Anders, G. (2005) Good Governance as Technology: Towards an Etnography of Bretton Woods Institutions, in Mosse, D. and Lewis, D. J. (eds) *The aid effect: giving and governing in international development.* Pluto, London, Ann Arbor, p. 223.

Bachrach, P. and Baratz, M. S. (1970) *Power and poverty; theory and practice.* Oxford University Press, New York.

Bernauer, J. W. and Rasmussen, D. M. (1988) *The Final Foucault.* MIT Press, Cambridge, Mass.

Birdsall, N., and Leo, B. (2015). *The White House and the World: Practical Proposals on Global Development for the Next US President.* Retrieved from Washington, DC: Cgdev.org/whitehousedev

Brainard, L. (2007) *Security by other means: foreign assistance, global poverty, and American leadership.* Brookings Institution Press, Washington, DC.

Clegg, S. and Haugaard, M. (2009) *The SAGE handbook of power.* SAGE, London; Thousand Oaks, Calif.

CSIS (2007) CSIS Commission on Smart Power: A smarter more secure America. Center for Strategic and International Studies, Washington, DC.

Dahl, R. A. (1961) *Who governs? Democracy and power in an American city.* Yale University Press, New Haven.

Davidson, A. I. (1986) Archaeology, Genealogy, Ethics, in Hoy, D. C. (ed.) *Foucault: a critical reader.* B. Blackwell, Oxford, UK; New York, pp. vi, 246.

Dean, M. (2010) *Governmentality: power and rule in modern society.* SAGE, London; Thousand Oaks, Calif.

Divon, S. A. (2015) Exceptional rules – US assistance policy in Africa Department of International Environment and Development Studies (Noragric), Norwegian University of Life Sciences.

Easterly, W. (2008). *Reinventing foreign aid.* MIT Press, Cambridge, Mass.

Ferguson, J. (1994) *The anti-politics machine: 'development,' depoliticization, and bureaucratic power in Lesotho.* Cambridge University Press, Cambridge, England; New York.

Flohr, M. (2016) Regicide and resistance: Foucault's reconceptualization of power, *Distinktion: Journal of Social Theory* 17 (1): 38–56.

Foucault, M. (1982) The Subject and Power, *Critical Inquiry* 8: 777–795.

Foucault, M. (1988) The ethic of care for the self as a practice of freedom, in Bernauer, J. W. and Rasmussen, D. M. (eds) *The Final Foucault.* MIT Press, Cambridge, Mass., pp. 1–20.

Foucault, M. and Gordon, C. (1980) *Power/knowledge: selected interviews and other writings, 1972–1977.* Pantheon Books, New York.

Foucault, M. and Rabinow, P. (1984) *The Foucault reader.* Pantheon Books, New York.

Foucault, M., Burchell, G., Gordon, C. and Miller, P. (1991) *The Foucault effect: studies in governmentality: with two lectures by and an interview with Michel Foucault.* University of Chicago Press, Chicago.

Foucault, M., Ewald, F. O., Fontana, A. and Senellart, M. (2004) *Naissance de la biopolitique: cours au Collège de France, 1978–1979.* Gallimard: Seuil, Paris.

Foucault, M., Senellart, M., Ewald, F. and Fontana, A. (2007) *Security, territory, population: lectures at the Collège de France, 1977–1978.* Palgrave Macmillan, Republique Française, Basingstoke; New York.

Fraser, N. (1989) Foucault on modern power: empirical insights and normative confusion, in Fraser, N. (ed.) *Unruly practices: power, discourse and gender in contemporary social theory.* Polity Press, Oxford, pp. 17–34.

Guyatt, N. (2016) *Bind us apart: how enlightened Americans invented racial segregation.* Basic Books, a member of the Perseus Books Group, New York.

Habermas, J. (1986) Taking Aim at the Heart of the Present, in Foucault, M. and Hoy, D. C. (eds.) *Foucault: a critical reader.* B. Blackwell, Oxford, UK; New York, pp. 103–108.

Hacking, I. (1999) *The social construction of what?* Harvard University Press, Cambridge, Mass.

Hoy, D. C. (1986) Power, Repression, Progress: Foucault, Lukes, and the Frankfurt School, in Foucault, M. and Hoy, D. C. (eds) *Foucault: a critical reader.* B. Blackwell, Oxford, UK; New York, pp. 123–147.

Lemke, T. (2002) Foucault, governmentality, and critique, *Rethinking Marxism* 14: 49–64.

Lemke, T. (2007) An indigestible meal? Foucault, governmentality and state theory, *Distinktion: Scandinavian Journal of Social Theory* 8: 43–64.

Lukes, S. (2005) *Power: a radical view.* Palgrave Macmillan, New York.

Lukes, S. (2006) Reply to comments, *Political Studies Review* 4: 164–173.

Marx, K., Engels, F., Pascal, R., Lough, W. and Magill, C. P. (1938). *The German ideology.* Lawrence & Wishart, London.

Mills, C. W. (1956) *The power elite.* Oxford University Press, New York.

Nichols, R. (2010) Postcolonial studies and the discourse of Foucault: Survey of a field of problematization, *Foucault Studies* 9: 111–144.

NSS (1987–2012) National Security Strategy of the United States.

Nye, J. S. (2004) *Soft power: the means to success in world politics.* Public Affairs, New York.

Nye, J. S. (2011) *The future of power.* Public Affairs, New York.

Nye, J. S. (2013) *Presidential leadership and the creation of the American era.* Princeton University Press, New Jersey.

Parkinson, R. G. (2016) *The common cause: creating race and nation in the American Revolution.* Published for the Omohundro Institute of Early American History and Culture, Williamsburg, Virginia, by the University of North Carolina Press, Chapel Hill.

QDDR (2010) The First Quadrennial Diplomacy and Development Review. US Department of State, Washington, DC.

Russell, B. (1938) *Power: a new social analysis.* Allen and Unwin, [S.l.].

Scott, J. C. (1985) *Weapons of the weak: everyday forms of peasant resistance.* Yale University Press, New Haven.

Scott, J. C. (1990) *Domination and the arts of resistance: hidden transcripts.* Yale University Press, New Haven.

USAID (2012) 3D Planning Guide: Diplomacy, Development, Defense.

USAID (2013) USAID Forward: Progress Report 2013.

# 2 Words of power
## Power of words

This chapter outlines an intellectual and historical background to the representation of Africa and its inhabitants as underdeveloped. This background serves as a foundation for a critical analysis of the modern concept of development assistance to Africa. As a function of identity within pre-established hierarchies, development assistance operates through asymmetric power relations between those who command resources and the power to decide when and how to allocate them, and those who are in need or wish to access these resources for development.

The story in this book is based on diverse discussions on development assistance, US identity, and US foreign policy in Africa, combined with the historical and intellectual contexts through which hierarchy and power are established and operationalised. The relations between the US and Africa are constituted in a complicated reality where the continent and its dwellers are subjected to hierarchical characterisations.[1] The most dominant expressions of these include racial, cultural, economic and political hierarchies manifested through dichotomies that contrast the Western world with Africa including developed–undeveloped, white–black, civilised–uncivilised, urban–rural, industrial–agrarian, modern–traditional and rich–poor narratives. Through these dichotomies, Africans are described as deficient in multiple ways. The different narratives on Africa and its dwellers are present throughout time, with dichotomies modified to contexts and historical changes.

The specific history of US–Africa relations is attached and influenced by episodes such as slavery, the religious missions to Africa, European colonial rule, the changing interests of the African-American communities, and US economic interests just to name a few. These historical patterns are infused into the post-WWII superpower politics, and the quest of the US to assume and maintain leadership of the 'free world'. The American story expresses a particular regime of truth, identity and ideology which manifests itself through the projection of power around the globe. In this story, development assistance serves as a technology of power deployed to secure various national security and foreign policy objectives. To view and analyse development assistance as a technology of power, we combine the theoretical framework outlined in the previous chapter, with the particular understanding of assistance as a tool deployed by the powerful in settings where clear hierarchies exist.

To understand the particular role of development assistance as a tool of power, we need to unpack the story of the hierarchy between the Western world and Africa. In our case, we will focus not only on the hierarchy established through the labelling of regions and people as underdeveloped, but also how particular identities have shaped and informed this discourse. In the case of Africa, race and ethnicity have played an overarching role despite the availability of alternative frameworks.

Before entering the meaning and role of development assistance, and trace the hierarchical relationship between Western cultures and Africa, we would like to begin our discussion on power and hierarchy by explaining the problem through terminology widely used here and elsewhere in the literature. In this book, we employ the term 'sub-Saharan' Africa for a variety of reasons. First, and most importantly, it is a term of convenience widely used in literature to designate specific regions in Africa and exclude others. Nevertheless, we recognise that the Sahara has not posed a barrier to multiple links between northern and sub-Saharan Africa. But as Lydon (2009: 11) indicates, the notions of the Sahara as a barrier has 'led to a flawed characterisation of Africa as inhabited by two diametrically, racially, and by extension culturally opposed Africans'. The long tradition dividing the continent as such has led to deeply engrained notions that Africa and its people are separated by a natural divide into racially, politically, and economically distinct spaces.

In terms of foreign policy and academic scholarship, Africa is described in much of the literature across disciplines as divided into North Africa and sub-Saharan Africa, with the former region commonly viewed politically and culturally as an integral part of the Middle East, while the latter viewed as Africa proper. This type of division is extremely problematic, and in many cases, ignores a rich history of trans-Saharan ties expressed through culture, religion and commerce.[2]

One important outcome of this division of Africa, as mentioned above, is two strands of literature that are often viewed and studied as separate (Bentahar, 2011: 1). This fact also produces separate academic specialisations across various disciplines dealing with African history, economy, culture and politics. The division of the continent as such also affects the analysis of various geopolitical interests of powerful nations. Subsequently, foreign policies for north- and sub-Saharan Africa are articulated based on different sets of assumptions, interests and outlooks.

Sub-Saharan Africa is a term that effectively replaces the racial term Black Africa that was commonly used since the sixteenth century and through the colonial and early post colonial-periods (Bentahar, 2011: 3; Jordan, 1974: 5). The modern French *Larousse* dictionary explains the term Black Africa as the assemblage of countries south of the Sahara.

We note this point because sub-Saharan Africa is not simply a geographic separation of regions, but can also be understood as a modern euphemism for racial distinctions. The importance of this issue is mostly symbolic, but connects to a long tradition of similar symbolism that perpetuates an order of hierarchy whereas the people of Africa south of the Sahara are assigned to a lower order in various aspects.

Assigning Africans to lower racial, societal, civilisational, political, and economic orders, has been a continuous thread throughout the history of the relationship between the people of the continent and the Western world. In such an analysis, development assistance becomes another expression of the need to elevate Africans from a deficient state of underdevelopment. While today development assistance is associated with various definitions of political, economic and social deficiencies, it is deeply rooted in the view of the African as inadequate in terms of racial, cultural and political inferiority. The history of the relationship between the Western world and Africa is dominated by projections of power fed by a self-perception of superiority and subsequent hierarchy installed over Africa and its inhabitants.

## Unpacking the hierarchy in 'development assistance'

Who are the developed and the undeveloped of the world? Development assistance is intuitively coupled with idealism moulded into plans and actions to help deprived or poor people to access basic needs and other goods and services in a multitude of contextual circumstances. The term *development*, while highly contested, places different peoples and nations in relatively stable hierarchies. How are these hierarchies created and what are they based on?

There are several important elements that we need to explore in order to understand the historical and intellectual trajectories described in this book. First, we need to unpack the historical tensions present in the labelling of people as developed and undeveloped. Subsequently, the concept of development assistance holds within it these tensions, which often manifest through the discourse and application of policy. Second, the concept of development assistance in the American political context, becomes an element of a global projection of power as we outline in detail in subsequent chapters. This is different to how the old colonial powers (England, Portugal, Germany, France, *et al.*) sought to develop (often called civilise) the inhabitants of their colonies. As such, a fundamental tension is created between the political purpose of assistance and the moral- and value-based rhetoric used to justify development assistance. As we will show throughout this book, development assistance is a concept that is deployed as a tool of power to achieve strategic interests. The moral- and value-based justifications for development assistance in such cases functions, consciously or unconsciously, as a mask covering strategic interests of donors.

This section articulates the intellectual and historical construction of developed and undeveloped in Africa as a background for the analysis of US policy towards the continent. The underlying argument is that while various categories linked to development assistance as a policy tool, change over time to fit socio-political ideas and contexts, those who populate these categories remain the same. Consequently, the people in need of development assistance today are defined through modern distinctions between rich and poor. Nevertheless, the rich-poor dichotomy is the latest distinction in a long tradition of separation based on racial, cultural and political categorisations expressed through an order of hierarchy created by the powerful.

At varying times, idealism seemed to blur the fundamental hierarchy preserved between categories of people separated by conceptions of authority and power. To explore the role of hierarchy and power we need to answer a few fundamental questions: who are the people labelled as 'in need of development'? Why are they labelled as such? And, what motivates states to grant development assistance to people inhabiting other states? We do not try to answer these questions in the same way as do the United Nations, the International Monetary Fund (IMF), or the World Bank. We do not seek a taxonomy based on measurements of economic prosperity, level of inequality, level of education, or access to services as these institutions do in order to define development. What we would like to explore is the formation of hierarchy between the categories developed and undeveloped, and the usages of these categories to pursue objectives beyond idealism.

The hierarchy between groups of people implied and enacted through development assistance is established by one group of people based on a self-perception of supremacy. This supremacy is justified in different historical times and contexts by different theoretical conceptions. While differing contexts modify the narrative that explains the inferiority of groups in relation to one another, the hierarchy is preserved. At the centre of these discourses, we find *development assistance* as the term used for a solution devised to modify the inferior groups, for example, in terms of their religion, culture, political system, economic system, governance strategy etc. The justification for modification varies over history, but always seems to be vindicated by a combination of morals, values and interests of the group which views itself as superior and commands the power and resources to decide who should receive aid and how the aid should be granted.

## Framing people as developed-undeveloped

The modern American enterprise of development assistance (foreign aid) is often attributed to President Truman and the ideas he outlined in the fourth point of his inaugural address (Eberstadt, 1988; Escobar, 1995; Esteva, 1992; Rist, 2008; Shenin, 2000):

[W]e must embark on a bold new program for making the benefits of our scientific advances and industrial progress available for the improvement and growth of **underdeveloped** areas. More than half the people of the world are living in conditions approaching **misery**. Their food is **inadequate**. They are **victims** of disease. Their economic life is **primitive** and **stagnant**. Their poverty is a **handicap** and a **threat** both to them and to more prosperous areas. For the first time in history, humanity possesses the knowledge and the skill to **relieve the suffering** of these people.... The old imperialism – exploitation for foreign profit – has no place in our plans. What we envisage is a program of development based on the concepts of democratic fair-dealing. All countries, including our own, will greatly benefit from a constructive program for the better use of the world's human and natural resources. Experience shows that our commerce with other countries expands as they progress industrially and economically. Greater production is the key to prosperity and peace. And the key to greater production is a wider and more vigorous application of modern scientific and technical knowledge. Only by helping the **least fortunate** of its members to help themselves can the human family achieve the decent, satisfying life that is the right of all people. Democracy alone can supply the vitalizing force to stir the peoples of the world into triumphant action, not only against their human oppressors, but also against their ancient enemies – hunger, misery, and despair.

(Truman, 1949; emphasis added)

Truman proposed that the US together with other nations and the private sector, engage in a worldwide effort for 'peace, plenty and freedom' based on 'democratic fair-dealing'. The idea has been criticised by some scholars for emphasising a conception of an ideal state-of-being viewed through 'Western-centric' lenses (Cornwall and Eade, 2010; Doty, 1996; Escobar, 1995; Esteva, 1992; Kothari, 2005; Munck and O'Hearn, 1999; Rist, 2008). Truman explained that the underdeveloped areas of the world are inhabited by people who live in conditions approaching misery. They suffer from hunger, disease and primitive economic life. These conditions, he suggested, were not likely to change without external assistance. He indicated that poverty is an impediment not only for the people who must endure this condition, but also a threat to the prosperous areas of the world. Truman suggested that a concentrated effort be made to provide the underdeveloped areas access and benefit from the scientific advances and progress available to the American people. This would, in his mind, lead to a significant change in their conditions. In effect, Truman combined in his discourse two justifications for development assistance: idealism and self-interests.

The combination of idealism and interests in a discourse justifying sorts of interaction and interference between powerful states and indigenous people was not an innovation offered by President Truman. Christian missions and colonial powers, for example, used the same discourse to justify the instalment of new institutions upon indigenous people, as well as the eradication and dismissal of local knowledge as uncivilised and primitive (Doty, 1996; Said, 1978). As such, the American discourse of development assistance articulated by Truman was reproducing and reinforcing hierarchies which existed between groups of people for decades. This outlook, as proposed by some scholars,[3] may lead to an understanding of development as a concept that emerges from an intention or need to exploit (labour and resources, for example) through domination, either as a direct or indirect extension of elitist and colonial conceptions. Such explanations often reduce or disregard the importance of identity and idealism in development discourses.

The use of *development* as a word that subordinates ideas of religion, culture, intellect, political systems, status, economic practices and technology of one group of people to another is present since the early encounters between European states and indigenous people in the Americas, Middle East, Orient, Asia and Africa. Ideas which place humans on a path of progression from 'primitive and stagnant' to 'advanced and prosperous' can be traced back to early Roman philosophy.[4] During the eighteenth century, thinkers like John Locke, Edward Gibbon, Adam Smith, Marie Jean Antoine Nicolas de Caritat (the Marquis de Condorcet) and many others outlined new ideas to explain that society progresses from primitive to advanced states (Stocking, 1987: 13–18). During the nineteenth century, thinkers such as Auguste Comte, GWF Hegel, Herbert Spencer, Émile Durkheim, Edward Tylor, Lewis Morgan and many others produced new theories of sociocultural evolution concerned with the progress of civilisation (McGee and Warms, 2008: 7). These narratives attempted to explain and typify societies, culture and the organisation of humans. The basic premise of the initial sociocultural evolutionary ideas was based on the notion that progress is a deterministic unilineal movement through stages of maturity (Bowler, 1989: 30–39). It sought to create typologies of human societies and explain the development from 'savage and primitive' to 'civilised and modern'.

Many different concepts emerged to explain the progression of humans. Some of these preceded Darwin's publication, and linked human progress to mental and moral faculties; other explanations linked progress to environmental and material causes. These theories and discussions originated in European and American milieus and often generated typologies that grouped white Western Europeans in the more complex variations of sociocultural organisation while other racial groups were relegated to lower categories (Stocking, 1987: 18). These discussions often used the word *development* at the foundation of narratives that structured hierarchy between groups of people. Such examples are found in narratives that rendered human races as inferior to the white race, and sometimes as a justification for oppressive institutions such as slavery.

As scientists began moving toward concepts of geological and biological evolution, how to understand the worlds' peoples came under new interest. While there were multiple approaches on how to understand human differences, two theories of evolution dominated. The first relied upon social and cultural evolution and the other on biological differences typically formulated in terms of races. A wide range of terms and concepts came to be used to explain British, French, German, American *et al.* superiority. Colonial powers had an array of concepts including *development* to distinguish between their higher morals, values, culture, race, economy and the 'primitive' people they ruled. To varying degrees the colonial powers used these to justify their policies and practices. Therefore, when Truman referred to the underdeveloped people of the world, he was using the well-established notion of hierarchy packed into a word that instantaneously invoked categories of people associated with lesser attributes specified in a variety of typologies created for various reasons.

It is not implied here that categorisation or classification is necessarily hierarchical in nature. Nevertheless, in the contextual cases of encounter between civilisations, Western European rhetoric often indicated a hierarchy between races and cultures.

The American concept of development assistance attributed to Truman was new in the sense that it advocated the operationalisation of progress as perceived by the newly established American hegemony after WWII. This was a process where, in theory, social, political and cultural progress could occur through material advancement led by the American people through the morals, values and purposes of a particular American identity. As such, there is an interest in exploring the expression of hierarchy through development assistance as a reflection of history, society and identity. This nexus is particularly relevant to understanding the evolving relationship between the US and Africa, and the different roles assigned to development assistance as a tool of power.

## Race and development

The classification of humans according to racial hierarchies is as old as historiography. References which group people according to the colour of their skin are found in ancient documents, classical writings, Arab texts, Christian manuscripts, and in modern scientific literature. In many descriptions, there are nuanced distinctions that discern between degrees of blackness and degrees of whiteness, usually coupling people of lighter skins with positive traits and people of darker skins with negative traits.[5]

Before the ideas of biological evolution were forwarded in the second half of the nineteenth century, discourses on racial inequality were not always linked to 'scientific' arguments. It was not uncommon to allocate hierarchy between races based on theology and interpretation of physical characteristics, observed behaviours, with or without explicit linkage to climate, culture and habits (de Benoist, 1999). In many of these discussions, we can find the word *development* as verb, noun and adverb that indicate types of hierarchies between races.

Discussions on race doctrines were given a scientific boost with the theory of evolution. It marked a gradual shift towards finding a 'scientific' basis for racial differences. Intellectuals from several disciplines including the new discipline of anthropology debated the differences among races and whether these accounted for cultural differences. Many of these discussions introduced ideas based on biological evolution and adaptation to environmental conditions to explain the differences between human races. These theories combined observations of the physical, mental and moral characteristics of humans to conclude that one set of features is associated with a more developed (in evolutionary contexts) type of human. In these discussions, moral, intellectual and physical qualities are merged, with the peoples of Africa ranking the lowest during the eighteenth and nineteenth centuries.[6] The 'negro' is described as morally and intellectually inferior, suggesting a hierarchy based on the colour of skin.

Alfred Russel Wallace, the co-originator of the idea of evolution by natural selection presented a paper in 1864 in an attempt to bridge the conflicting theories on human origins. He argued that the main faculty of humans is their intellect, and therefore, from a certain point in history human bodies evolved only marginally because adaptation to natural conditions was achieved using intellectual solutions:

> For it is evident that such qualities would be for the well-being of man; would guard him against external enemies, against internal dissensions, and against the effects of inclement seasons and impending famine, more surely than could any merely physical modification. Tribes in which such mental and moral qualities were predominant, would therefore have an advantage in the struggle for existence over other tribes in which they were less developed, would live and maintain their numbers, while the others would decrease and finally succumb.
> (Wallace, 1864: clxii)

Wallace argued that humans dispersed over the surface of the earth throughout time. The physical features of humans kept changing while their brains were not fully developed. Thus, he asserted, we find varieties of humans whose physical characteristics are adapted to their specialised environments. When the human brain evolved to a point where humans could adapt to their environment through intellect, the physical forms became fixed. Wallace believed that from this point, the intellect continued to evolve in all humans but in a differentiated manner, depending on the environmental conditions. In the temperate areas (inhabited by the light skinned humans), where challenges were harsher, human intellectual capacity evolved further than that of humans in tropical areas (inhabited by dark skinned humans). This, he believed, explained why there are humans with different physical characteristics and different intellectual and moral abilities. Thus, he believed, the intellectual, moral and physical qualities of Europeans are more advanced and therefore they dominate other races. Wallace explains that these superior qualities have a direct significant impact on the wellbeing of humans, and that the developed races of Europe used their intellect to create better weapons, divide labour, anticipate the future and structure complex societies with superior moral and social arrangements compared to the other races. He observes that when races with superior qualities encounter the less-developed races, native production systems and social organisations give way and eventually cease to exist.

Wallace's narrative demonstrates how evolutionary theory could be used toward justifying the supremacy of Europeans. To the extent that it sees all humans are part of a single species, it represents the shift towards a scientific acceptance of the potential equality of humans. The implication became that since the human species is of a homogenous origin, the potential for higher intellectual capacities exists within all. The observed differences in cultural and societal practises were explained through adaptation theory. Nevertheless, these debates structured a hierarchy based on interpretation of moral, intellectual, societal and cultural practices.[7]

The classification of indigenous inhabitants of Africa, Asia, the Americas and Oceania as uncivilised with less developed mental and moral capabilities than the white population of Europe in general, was quite common in European and American history. This constructed hierarchy certainly contributed to the institution of African slavery. While the enslavement of people is a practice traceable to ancient human history, racial classification according to skin colour coupled with hierarchal observations on religion, culture, moral and intellectual faculties of the Negro, was at the foundation for the justification for the modern institution of slavery (Fredrickson, 1988: 11; Jordan, 1974: 53).

But there were also those who rejected racial domination and deplored the subsequent treatment of other races with contempt. These voices intensified during the late eighteenth century. The ideas of the abolishment movement were rooted in the social, political and legal inequalities that led to the American and French revolutions. For centuries, the elites in Europe treated their own populations with contempt and domination. The intellectual ideas that led to the social revolutions in Europe granted that buying and selling humans, tearing them forcibly from their homes, and administrating severe punishments for petty crimes, were inappropriate both morally and religiously (Cohen, 1980: 131; Fage, 1962: 98; Hochschild, 2006: 87; Lovejoy, 2000: 259–260).

Opposing slavery was not necessarily synonymous with equality between races (Cohen, 1980: 150; Hochschild, 2006: 133). Many who did view

Africans as equal humans based on various humanitarian and religious arguments,[8] regarded Africans in a paternalistic manner, viewing them as misguided children who needed proper instruction towards Christianity and civilisation (Lovejoy, 2000: 259–260; Quinn, 2000: 5–6). Some, like the member of the British parliament and a famous abolitionist Sir Thomas Buxton, put forward pro-colonisation arguments as a means to practice humanitarian ideals of assisting the misguided Africans to develop and correct the injustices of the past:

> I now come to the point which I deliberately consider to be beyond all others momentous in the question before us. I lay great stress upon African commerce, *more* upon the cultivation of soil, but *most* of all upon the elevation of the native mind.
>
> This is a wide subject; it embraces the consideration of some difficult questions. They resolve themselves into these: 1st. Are the Africans able and willing to learn? 2d. *What*, and *how shall we teach* them?
>
> It is true that the inhabitants of Africa are in the very depths of ignorance and superstition; but, still, there are amongst them redeeming symptoms, however slight, sufficient to prove that the fault is not in their nature, but in their condition; and to teach us, that when we shall have put down that prodigious evil which forbids all hope of their improvement, it is abundantly possible that the millions of Africa may assume their place among civilized and Christian nations; and that a region, whose rank luxuriance now poisons the atmosphere, may be brought under subjection to the plough, may yield a wealthy harvest to its occupants, and open a new world, as exciting to our skill, capital, and enterprise, as was America on its first discovery.
>
> (Italics in the original; Buxton, 1840: 457–458)

Some abolitionists reasoned that in order to redeem the wrongs done by the slave trade, Europe must help civilise Africa to reveal the positive qualities of culture rather than the destructive ones (Fage, 1962: 105; Rist, 2008: 51). The missionary societies were strong advocates of this rationale, and supported as well as helped finance further explorations of the African continent to expand the reach of civilisation (Fage, 1962: 105).

This short overview points at an intimate connection between race, the dichotomy developed-undeveloped and the ideas and roles of granting assistance to develop both as a tool of power and as a moral duty. Racial distinctions are at the foundation of a hierarchy based on an understanding of the self, and of the other in relation to the self. Through the encounters between Western societies and the other civilisations of the world, this hierarchy served as a justification for Western societies to project power in various ways to modify the culture, religion, governance structures and habits of the 'uncivilised' societies. During colonial rule, racial distinctions were often associated with gaps between mental and moral capabilities of people, and subsequently their ability to effectively exploit their environments. Race was linked to conditions of poverty, pagan faith, uncivilised customs, underdeveloped technologies and poor social organisation. It also justified domination and exploitation of the undeveloped indigenous populations in colonies, partially under the pretext of bridging the development gap. The colonial discourse also incorporated the expression of a moral duty to civilise the natives (Rist, 2008: 51). These types of narratives were also common as part of the movement towards the abolition of slavery as well as part of religious doctrines calling for spreading God's grace to pagans (Rist, 2008: 49–51).

## Race and the American context

Race relations and slavery in the US have been an important subject of study and an integral part of the American identity since 1619 when the first African slaves were brought to Virginia. While it is not possible to summarise the vast literature on this subject to a few paragraphs, we would like to highlight a number of important connections between racial tensions within the US, American identity, the image of Africa in America, and the influence of these on US–Africa relations. What we would like to emphasise in this account is how the view of Africa is influenced by these elements.

In his critical analysis of US foreign policy, Michael Hunt (2009) illustrates the fundamental role of racial conceptions in the formation of American foreign policy during the twentieth century. As in Europe, the idea of racial hierarchy was fundamental in defining the way in which elites and the general public in America understood themselves, and for shaping their attitude towards other groups of people, both domestically and internationally. In America, racial hierarchy linked to higher and lower modes of culture, intelligence and governance, was heavily influenced by the encounters and interactions with the native population of the Americas, and by the importance of slavery as an institution upon which many parts of the economy depended. Bringing progress to the native Americans, for example, was a narrative that employed the same kind of arguments used by the Europeans in their colonies, according to which the lesser races will always yield and fade away when encountering superior races (Hunt, 2009: 57–58).

Africans figured at the bottom of the American map of racial hierarchy. Identifying with the British legacy above all others, the guidelines used by America for setting the standards in foreign policy were anchored in the basic ideas of British social Darwinism after 1850 where indicators of success and superiority were located in the level of 'industrial progress, military prowess, and international influence and control' (Hunt, 2009: 79). This conception informed and reinforced the belief of white Anglo-Saxon Americans in their own superiority in terms of intelligence, culture, morality and the ability to govern (Hunt, 2009: 78). One of the most popular of American thinkers in the nineteenth century Ralph Waldo Emerson (1803–1882) celebrated the notion of the English. In fact, he wrote an essay entitled English Traits in which he finds that this is the finest race.[9] These notions were present in the subtext of American interactions with foreign nations as well during the late nineteenth and early twentieth centuries (Hunt, 2009: 91).[10] Moreover, racial thinking and categories were used to rank the European races (Ripley, 1899) and to prevent immigration of the lower races.

In his important work on the historical origins of racism in the US, Jordan (1974) asks a fundamental question: 'what was it about Indians and Negroes which set them apart from Englishmen, which rendered them *different*; which made them special candidates for degradation?' (Jordan, 1974: 50). This question highlights many important issues: first, that the constructed hierarchy that led to slavery and a subsequent definition of race relations within the US is rooted in long standing European biases that found their way to America with the first settlers. Second, that this constructed hierarchy is rooted in perceived differences that led to the de-humanisation of certain groups of people, rendering them as inferior and inadequate. The question posed by Jordan moves beyond an economic rationale for the justification of chattel slavery in the Americas.[11] It goes towards unmasking fundamental social constructions that structure hierarchy between groups of people. After all, it was the Negros, Indians and other non-white people that were dehumanised and forced into slavery, and not groups of immigrants from Europe. How to justify forcing certain groups of people into servitude and not others? The answer points toward a constructed hierarchy that render certain people as inferior (Davis, 2003: 6; Fredrickson, 1988: 11).

How did the African come to be viewed as inferior by the Englishman? Jordan (1974: 3–25) highlights how skin complexion and other physical distinctions between the Englishman and the African, came to be associated with religious and cultural differences. Skin colour was the most striking external dissimilarity between Europeans and Africans. 'Black', as indicated by Jordan (1974: 6), 'was an emotionally partisan colour', associated through lingual symbolism with evil, impurity, uncleanness, death and foulness. White symbolises the antonyms to all the unwanted qualities. In the eyes of the Englishman, the blackness of Africans was observed together with their heathenism and cultural habits that differed so much from the English ways. Africans were 'naked', 'savages', 'libidinous', 'brutish', 'bestial', 'pagan', 'cannibal', 'violent', etc; Africans were, in brief, – 'uncivilised'. When these attributes were viewed in tandem with Christian religious doctrines, the causes of 'blackness' (within and without), were sometimes explained as disobedience to God and punishment (Jordan, 1974: 23). These descriptions and perceptions of the Africans as inferiors, as the 'other', as 'not one of us' (Davis, 2003: 6) since the early sixteenth-century encounters between the English and the natives of Africa are at the roots of the justification for slavery.

There is no need to repeat that the enslavement of Africans in the US is thoroughly documented. But it is important to highlight that in this history, blacks were forcibly removed from their African environment, torn apart from their family, stripped of their clothing, forced to work as hard labourers, and bought and sold as personal property. Auctions were held to establish the market prices for slaves of different characteristics. Slave owners hired men to track down and recapture slaves who ran away. Heathenism, savagery, or other depictions rendering Africans as uncivilised could only serve as partial justifications concealing a more fundamental view of superiority that justified a doctrine of total domination. After all, slavery persisted in the US even after African-Americans converted to Christianity, wore Western clothing, and appropriated Western graces. In fact, even after slavery was formally abolished in 1865, racial segregation persisted in the US. It has been slowly dismantled through a range of laws. However, racial tensions and discrimination are still significant in present day America as illustrated by recent events in 2016, and protests of movements such as Black Lives Matter against race-related deaths and acts of violence against African-Americans.

While times have changed and the discourse of racial superiority has sometimes been pushed to the fringes of modern American society, there is little doubt that it still persists. The 2016 election campaign in the US demonstrated that racial tensions and white supremacy is still a current issue in modern America. Race relations, both historical and contemporary, are very much present in the consciousness of modern Americans and will always be an integral part of the American identity. The history of racial tensions in the US has influenced both a sense of hierarchy between America and Africa, as well as a sense of duty towards Africans. Over time, the racial overtone of this constructed hierarchy diminished, and was replaced with cultural and political hierarchies as we discuss below.

## A hierarchy of cultures

Culture and the 'lack of culture' often played a part in racial narratives. Protagonists of the classification of culture in an order of evolution often spoke of *development* from the lower 'primitive', 'uncivilised' and 'savage' states, to higher stages represented by European cultures. Nevertheless, there were those who rejected that culture was a reflection of race, and emphasised social Darwinism instead. The influential anthropologist Edward Burnett Tylor, for example, noted that:

> [D]ifferences in the civilization and mental state of the various races of mankind are rather differences of development than of origin, rather of degree than of kind.
>
> (Tylor quoted in Stocking, 1987: 159)

Tylor argued that the cultural differences observed between different races are not linked to racial polygenism but to cultural evolution. The difference is not at all subtle. Tylor rejected an order of hierarchy based on racial theories, and favoured a classification of cultures based on similarities between primitive (historical) European cultures and primitive (contemporary of his time) indigenous cultures of North America, Asia and Africa. He saw in contemporary indigenous cultures a reflection of a primitive stage in which Europeans once dwelt. The word *development* in Tylor's narrative indicates that primitive cultures will evolve to higher states, reaching eventually a level comparable to contemporary European cultures. This was a deterministic approach to the evolution of cultures which implied that all cultures move through similar stages from lower (primitive) to higher (civilised). As indicated by Stocking (1987: 235), Tylor's classification of cultures designated a hierarchy that happened to match the skin colours of people in his groupings; the lowest forms of culture are associated with darker skins. As he moved along the forms of cultures from simple to complex, the saturation of skin colours lightened accordingly. The classification of cultures in an order of hierarchy is an important transition from racial narratives as they partly became obsolete, only to strongly reappear post WWI. Since cultures were seen as a function of social evolution, lower cultures could be elevated, according to this rationale, through purposeful interventions of higher cultures.

The anthropologist Lewis Henry Morgan devised a hierarchical typology of cultures comprising seven stages from a lower status of 'savagery' to a status of 'civilisation' (Morgan, 1877). In his analysis, he identified contemporary societies in the different stages of culture and explained that:

> [T]he principal institutions of mankind have been developed from a few primary germs of thought; and that the course and manner of their development was predetermined, as well as restricted within narrow limits of divergence, by natural logic of the human mind and the necessary limitations of its powers.
>
> (Morgan, 1877: 18)

Morgan believed that the stages of culture were proof of common origins of humankind. He understood that culture develops from a lower stage (comparable to the Australians and Polynesians of his time), to a higher stage (comparable to the United States and European nations of his time). While Morgan's analysis was not necessarily racial, it structured hierarchy between Europeans and other races based on a typology of culture progression. The main difference between racial theory and cultural evolution lies in the notion of potential equality of people and their capacity for change. While racial theories argue that the difference between races is unbridgeable since the hierarchy is biological, cultural evolution opens the door to equality either through evolution or through diffusion.[12]

During the early twentieth century, there was a reaction within the discipline of anthropology to the comparative approach of evolutionary theories. Franz Boas, for example, criticised the notion that societies evolve in a predictable and deterministic fashion (Boas, 1920). He supported the idea of historical particularism emphasising contextual development[13] of civilisations. He stressed that very little can be said about universal laws of development:

> We rather see that each cultural group has its own unique history, dependent partly upon the peculiar inner development of the social group, and partly upon the foreign influences to which it has been subjected.
> 
> (Boas, 1920: 317)

For Boas, cultural development is an intrinsic process with particular characteristics that relate to each case such as environmental and material. His reasoning leads to the idea that all societies develop, but not every society goes necessarily through the same or similar stages of development.

In these debates, development was a key term that helped describe the hierarchy between what was viewed as higher and lower forms between and within cultures. Culture became the essence of narratives that explained gender disparities, institutional formation, scientific knowledge, technology, class and governance (Asad, 1991: 315). This led to hierarchies that were more distinct between cultures being expressed in different times as civilised–uncivilised, modern–primitive, industrial–tribal, complex–simple and Christian–Heathen (Muslim, Hindu, Buddhist and Pagan alike). Reflecting the Eurocentrism of these concepts, the same groups of people were always assigned higher and lower cultural attributes.

## Simple and complex political systems

Early studies of political systems in anthropological contexts derived from the same theoretical perspectives that structured hierarchy between cultures. From the very start of political anthropology, we find typologies of political systems in a hierarchical order (such as in Lowie, 1962 [1927]). Most of the early studies were conducted in colonial contexts, and in many cases, informed the policies and governing practises of colonial authorities.[14] European elitism was a part of the social construction of most anthropologists, and affected the ways in which most viewed, recorded and conceived cultural and political forms in the colonies. This helped to warrant and re-enforce contemporary conceptions of modernity and progress which materialised through hierarchical relationships between colonisers and colonised (Asad, 1991: 315).

Typologies of political systems often designate hierarchy such as the pre-industrial stages of band–tribe–chiefdom–state. We also find typologies that classify the complexity of states in order of hierarchies based on the presence and mode of different institutions such as markets and trade, taxation, ownership of land, judicial systems and mode of successions (for example, Claessen and Skalnik, 1978).

Robert Lowie was the first who attempted to deal with a separate anthropological analysis of political systems. He rejected the idea that political systems pass through deterministic stages of development (Lewellen, 1992: 7):

> What we have tried to do is simply to prove that the germs of all possible political development are latent but demonstrable in the ruder cultures and that a specific turn in communal experience – say, contact with a weaker or stronger neighbor – may produce an efflorescence of novel institutions.
>
> (Lowie, 1962 [1927]: 112–113)

Lowie used the term 'political development' to designate movement from simpler and ruder forms to more complex, as exemplified by his contrast of the Andamanese settlement and the British Empire. He rejected the notion of unilineal evolution, but indicated that when 'advanced' meets 'primitive', the latter may develop, or as he implies, move up in the hierarchy of political systems.

Lowie's narrative exemplifies why the term *development* is not necessarily a synonym of evolution, but a designation of hierarchy based on notions of complexities. The explanations for the cultural and political stages in which many non-European indigenous populations are found in relation to the European and American civilisations, are disconnected through this notion from racial and evolutionary explanations. Fortes and Evans-Pritchard's seminal publication, *African Political Systems*, is an example of an analysis that draws upon functionalism. To establish the novelty of their inquiry, Fortes and Evans-Pritchard (1967 [1940]: 4) explain that earlier attempts to understand political institutions by political philosophers were tainted by evolutionary theory. Based on the deterministic assumption of evolution, it was commonly thought that the origins of modern political institutions could be uncovered by the study of 'primitive' political systems in 'primitive' societies. Fortes and Evans-Pritchard claimed that 'a scientific study of political institutions must be inductive and comparative' (Fortes and Evans-Pritchard, 1967 [1940]: 5). Radcliffe-Brown explains in his preface to Fortes and Evans-Pritchard's book (1967 [1940]) that comparison is possible through classification based on a great number of contextual observations. The comparative method[15] should be used to extract universal laws that explain societies across time and space through induction inference. This, he believed, would help eliminate abstract concepts such as 'primitive', 'feudal' and 'capitalist' societies and replace them with concepts that represented a more accurate description of empirical reality.

While rejecting use of the term 'primitive' in classification as a basis for comparison, Radcliffe-Brown used the terms 'simple societies' and 'complex societies' to distinguish between different forms.[16] He exemplifies how fundamental elements in the organisation of complex societies are also found in 'simple societies' though they assume different procedures and reasoning (Fortes and Evans-Pritchard, 1967 [1940]: xvii). As such, the functionalist approach turned the meaning of *development* from movement through stages in a deterministic unilineal process into a measure of complexity. For the purpose of this chapter, this idea is significant when observing the seam between anthropological research and the practical affairs of colonial administrations.

Colonial administrators needed to establish effective systems to bridge the 'complex' notions of society they brought with them to the colonies, and the 'simple' notions that characterised native societies. The purpose of these systems was first and foremost to serve the needs of colonial powers and their interests. Development became a term that meant applying certain insights revealed through academic knowledge and experiences to create policy that allowed a more effective and efficient rule of the colonies (for example, Asad, 1973; Mamdani, 1996).[17] This was intended to help create complex systems which, on one hand, would allow the natives to interact with the colonial authorities on the required levels, and on the other, would preserve some of the natives' characteristics for a variety of reasons, including racial segregation and romantic notions of preservation (Mamdani, 1996). Development meant modifying the social landscape in colonies to serve the ends of the powerful.

## Colonialism, hierarchy and the purpose of development

The racial, cultural and political hierarchies established between the Western world and Africa manifested through religious, administrative and economic functions created through colonial rule. The extent to which these were due to racial differences or social ones became an important point of contestation.

While racialist theories were gradually fading (though never fully disappearing), Africans were still not regarded as equals. One of the early critical accounts describing the links between development assistance and racial, cultural and political hierarchies through colonial policies can be found in the work of Lucy Mair. A political anthropologist, Mair's early work was conducted before WWII. She studied the effects of European contact upon village life in Africa in colonial settings, and was one of the first scholars to apply anthropological tools to a study dedicated to the transformation of native society by European colonial practices and policies. Mair's aim was not to produce an account that questions the ethical perspectives of the contact between European and 'primitive' civilisations, which she believed to be inevitable, but rather to:

[I]ndicate the main problems of adjustment which it creates for the society which is exposed to it and for the authorities who are responsible for the development of that society.

(Mair, 1934: 7)

Mair (1934: 2–9) identified three main areas of contact between the 'complex' European civilisations and the 'primitive' cultures of the natives in colonies through which development of that society would take place. Through religious contact embodied in missionaries, political contact embodied in administrators, and economic contact embodied in settlers, she observed the asymmetrical relationship of hierarchical power manifested through policies aimed explicitly at the 'development of native life in one direction or another' (Mair, 1934: 2–3).

The religious mission in Africa was set to 'civilise' the primitive cultures by turning them away from their 'pagan and immoral' existence. It was achieved using a set of rules that forbade many of the native cultural practices which were deemed unfit according to Christianity and Western norms and values. An important part of this effort involved the construction of schools, hospitals, and churches as well as the encouragement of new forms of agricultural crops and techniques. The religious mission had an idealistic underpinning for its development activities, but with a heavy taint of self-interest of its practitioners linked to notions of self-fulfilment and the grace of God. The mere practice of these activities necessitated a conviction that natives lacked certain attributes. It placed them in a lower hierarchical position, usually expressed through labels such as 'pagan', 'primitive', 'uncivilised' and 'savage'.

Colonial administrations were the expression of the colonial power and rule. They assumed different forms in different territories depending on the aims, goals and philosophy of the coloniser, as well as contextual native social structures. Colonial administrations were set up to rule the colonies and bridge certain gaps between the natives and European institutions, with the aim of satisfying the interests and needs of the colonisers and for the advancement of the natives along the lines that suited these interests (Kidd, 1894: 65; Lugard, 1926: 57; Mair, 1934: 4; Pakenham, 1992: passim). The relationship between the colonial administrations and the natives was based on power and the subordination of the natives to colonial will and authorisation.

The most evident gap between the notions of the colonisers and those of their native subjects was visible in incompatible economic conceptions (Mair, 1934: 4). This area of contact created the most friction between the settlers and the native cultures and institutions. Here the asymmetric power relationship was most visible. This could be observed on various levels such as the different needs and lifestyle of the settlers in comparison to the natives, the policies and actions taken to secure the needs and wants of the settlers, and the incompatibilities between

European economic philosophies and native production systems (Mair, 1934: 5).

In all three main areas of contact we can locate the duality of the term *development*; it is a strange marriage between idealism and self-interest underlined by a common sense of superiority and power. Consider the 'dual mandate in British colonial Africa' as explained by Lord Lugard, the well-known British colonial administrator and career soldier who served most of his life in the British colonies:

> It was the task of civilisation to put an end to slavery, to establish Courts of Law, to inculcate in the natives a sense of individual responsibility, of liberty, and of justice, and to teach their rulers how to apply these principles; above all, to see to it that the system of education should be such as to produce happiness and progress.... The nineteenth century saw the development of these great colonies into nations enjoying self-government. Its closing decade witnessed the dawning recognition of the vital importance of the tropics to civilisation, and the 'discovery' and acquisition of large non-colonisable areas in tropical Africa – no longer regarded as picturesque appanages of Empire, but essential to the very existence of the races of the temperate climes.
>
> (Lugard, 1922: 5–6)

Lugard's narrative exposes the dichotomy bridgeable through development assistance. Lugard seems to project progressive attitudes towards the native subjects of the colonies, visualising a reality where they can develop without repression or domination (Lugard, 1933: 11). As a soldier, he participated in campaigns for the abolishment of slavery. As an administrator, he was a champion of education as means to prepare indigenous populations for 'indirect rule'. However, his patrician tone reveals hierarchy and power rendering his moral idealism problematic:

> In Africa in those regions where a few thousand Europeans have settled, the conditions are reversed, and the problem is to safeguard the interests of an ignorant majority in the present, and to devise a policy for the future, when the majority has attained a higher level of social development, a policy which shall ensure to each a prospect of harmonious development without domination or repression by the other. If it be the function of education to prepare youth for the responsibilities of maturity, and to realise by a process of trial and error the nature of those responsibilities, then the task of the educator in Africa to-day is one of outstanding importance for the peaceful development of race relations in the world.
>
> (Lugard, 1933: 11)

As observed by Mair (1934: 8), this system of indirect rule has two aspects: political and economic. The political aspects aim at producing a system where the natives achieve a legitimate self-rule for all internal affairs (the international affairs would be managed by the Empire). The economic aspect aims at achieving self-management and exploitation of material resources. This doctrine is also dubbed 'parallel development', 'differentiation' and 'association' (Mair, 1934: 8). Its purpose is 'evolution from lower to higher standards by a process of adaptation and gradual transition' (Lugard, 1933: 1). But Lugard does not suggest that natives should become Europeans through development; what he advocated was a separate development of native institutions through which they will become better subjects of the British Empire (Mair, 1934: 8). The objective of the policy:

> [W]ill be to retain what is best in African tradition, to make the village agriculturalist or craftsman more efficient, to replace superstitious fear by the ethics of a higher religion, to fill in the great hiatus between the illiterate masses and the so-called 'educated' minority. Education, it is hoped, will mean the raising of the standard of the people, not the denationalization of the few, making of the African a better and more efficient African and not an imitation white man.
> (Lugard, 1926: 64)

While he was supporting a policy designed to encourage a process of maturation of the 'subject race', he also echoed Lord Milner's strategy of segregation between the races (Mamdani, 1996: 16), explaining that this notion is not racial, but rather based on sanitary, health and cultural preferences:

> The Indian or African gentleman who adopts the higher standard of civilisation and desires to partake in such immunity from infection as segregation may convey, should be as free and welcome to live in the civilised reservation as the European, provided, of course, the he does not bring with him concourse of followers. The native peasant often shares his hut with his goat, or sheep, or fowls. He loves to drum and dance at night, which deprives the European from sleep.... For these people sanitary rules are necessary but hateful. They have no desire to abolish segregation.
> (Lugard, 1922: 150)

The cultural gap between the Europeans and the natives in colonies was deep, to the point that a segregation of the races was warranted in the eyes of the policymakers. This policy of 'parallel development' bridged interests and idealism, allowing a notion of segregated equality. 'Citizenship will be a privilege of the civilized; the uncivilized would be subject to an all around tutelage' (Mamdani, 1996: 17).

Indirect rule is a policy that proposes equality by the way of segregated adaptation through education (meaning a parallel development leading to a European-like civilisation, but distinct, different and separate). Its most distinct feature is, however, the hierarchical approach toward the culture, institutions, social organisation, manners and livelihood methods of the native subjects in colonies. Development in this case became a process through which natives would participate in a set of activities designed by colonial officials to become more like those who held power over them. There were multiple motivations for these schemes including self-interest of the colonising powers, and desires to genuinely assist the colonial subjects.

This background illustrates how the Africans and their institutions were viewed as less civilised and less developed leaving aside the racist constructions of why they were the way they were. The lower status and position of Africans was expressed in discourses and visible through projections of power. We will describe this in the following chapters where first the US was happy with the colonial control of Africa, then shifted to being supportive of independence movements except in southern Africa where the US continued to support Portuguese colonial rule in Mozambique and Angola and white control of Namibia, South Africa, and Rhodesia.

## The American view of Africa

Like many other New World nations, the US had deep, if often unacknowledged contacts with sub-Saharan Africa through the slave trade. Knowledge about Africa in the early nineteenth century after a century and a half of the slave trade was limited and highly skewed. However, with the return of some slaves to West Africa, the expansion of American missionary activities, especially the American Colonisation Society, and limited if growing trade, interest in Africa expanded (Clendenen *et al.*, 1966; Clendenen and Duignan, 1964; Drake, 1970; Duignan and Gann, 1984; Du Plessis, 1929; Goldschmidt, 1963; Kolchin, 2003; Latourette, 1949; Redkey, 1969). Missionaries worked to lift the pagans of the 'Dark continent' and bring them Christianity (Duignan and Gann, 1984: 90). Slave traders and owners saw the Africans as inferior humans that could be commodified and used for labour (Davis, 2003: 29). And the American Colonisation Society was occupied with repatriating freed slaves, partly as a way of getting rid of unwanted populations in the US. It was only in 1871 in conjunction with Henry Morgan Stanley's explorations of the continent in his efforts to locate Livingstone, that Africa was 'opened to the world at large' and reached a wider and more popular awareness in American society as Stanley went on speaking tours throughout the US to describe the Africa he experienced (Goldschmidt, 1963: 3).[18] Since then, the view of Africa in the American mind was a combination of new insights about a poorly-known continent, and the view of the African-American at home. These combined perceptions produced several discourses about Africa and its inhabitants from the slavery era, the Civil War, the reign of Jim Crow, through the Civil Rights Movement to present day America.

A very important interruption in the American consensus about Africa was provided by Marcus Garvey who founded the United Negro Improvement Association. Garvey, part of the substantial West Indian migration to New York, called for 'pride of race'. Without detailing the contradictions in his messages, he had tens of thousands of followers in the US and in Africa, and was read by Kwame Nkrumah, and the black unionist in South Africa, Clements Kadalie (Duignan and Gann, 1984: 259). W.E.B. Dubois was another African-American intellectual who sought to make African-Americans knowledgeable about their African past. The links between African-Americans and Africans was also deepened through the work of the black historian Carter Woodson who also founded the *Journal of Negro History* (Rudwick, 1959). Indeed, DuBois took part in the Universal Races Congress of 1911 held in London. It was a large international effort to reduce hostility and conflict among races. The object of the Congress was to discuss:

> in the light of science and the modern conscience, the general relations subsisting between the peoples of the West and those of the East, between so-called white and so called coloured peoples, with a view to encouraging between them a fuller understanding, the most friendly feelings, and a heartier co-operation. Political issues of the hour will be subordinated to this comprehensive end, in the firm belief that, when once mutual respect is established, difficulties of every type will be sympathetically approached and readily solved.
> (Weatherly, 1911: 315–316)

DuBois went on to initiate a Pan African Congress held in Paris in 1919. DuBois' rival, Booker T. Washington also became interested in Africa. He initiated a focus on African-Americans who he contended should assist Africans while African students should attend black universities in the US (Duignan and Gann, 1984: 272). In other words, they were using racial narratives themselves to celebrate African achievements (DuBois, 1990; Magubane, 1987). The 'special relationship' between the former slaves and their home continent ebbed and flowed over time. African-Americans were creating complex counter-narratives to challenge and delegitimise racial and developmental narratives although they tended to be in the background.

In her volume on Africa in the American mind, Sears (1997) indicates more generally how American perspectives on Africa were influenced by various milestones in the relationship with the population at home. From fear of the abolishment of slavery, through the civil war and the post-civil war instalment of the Jim Crow rules, to the struggle of the

African-Americans to end lynching and segregation, the African continent is portrayed as a reflection of events at home. In the 1870s, Africa is depicted as a dark continent, wild, dangerous and savage. Sears (1997) interprets this image of Africa in the American mind as a reflection of the turbulent race relations at home. After the end of the civil war, when slavery is abolished but new institutions such as Jim Crow are installed to tame the black population, the African continent appears as a more benign, conquerable frontier where colonial powers are engaged in the development of civilisation. During the 1920s as the continent appears to be less threatening under firm colonial rule, and while race relations in the US appear to be under a status quo, the fear from the untamed African is replaced by an attraction to the natural beauty and wildlife of the continent. The focus became partly conservation and protection of the African wilderness and wildlife toward which President Teddy Roosevelt occupied himself.

With the formation of the United Nations in 1945 followed by the Cold War, racial segregation in South Africa (an original member of the UN) and in the United States became international issues. In Africa, new political parties emerged demanding independence while in the US the civil rights movement emerged demanding an end to segregation, the right to vote and more generally equality. During that time the mainstream press contrasted the violence of the Mau-Mau rebellion in Africa with the refined and peaceful struggle led by Martin Luther King Jr. (Sears, 1997: 352). Sears (1997: 353) indicates that the violent Mau-Mau rebellion was used by conservative Americans to highlight the potential danger of the Civil Rights Movement, while liberals used the Mau-Mau rebellion to mount a defence of the exemplary conduct of the Civil Rights Movement.

The racial situation in the US changed after WWII. The established patterns of racial segregation and discrimination came increasingly under pressure from not just within the US but from around the world. *An American Dilemma* as Gunnar Myrdal *et al.* (1944) framed it, of a nation of individual freedom but excluding blacks became entwined with the Cold War and the growing independence movements in Africa and Asia. The struggle by African-Americans in the US became visible to large parts of the world. When Derman went to Guinea in 1965 he was repeatedly asked, even at the village level, about the racial situation in the US. After the World War, black hopes were cut short by 'white violence' (Emerson and Kilson, 1965: 1057). The NAACP in an anti-lynching campaign advertised how 28 blacks from 1918–1921 were publicly burned by mobs (Emerson and Kilson, 1965: 1058). In addition to competing for the loyalty of new nations (see next chapter) was the attention given by the anti-colonial movements, nations and the Soviet bloc to race relations. Despite the racial history of the US and its support of the colonial powers, Washington now had to begin making changes although as we will describe, not enough. In terms of patterns at home, 'Housing, meals, schools, transportation, recreation – these were all spheres in which rebuffs were likely to be experienced' by diplomats, UN personnel, students and others coming from Africa to the US. Segregation placed the American democracy in an unfavourable light and led to demands that the UN be moved from the US. The Justice Department wrote in support of ending segregation in schools (Brown versus the Board of Education):

> It is in the context of the present world struggle between freedom and tyranny that the problem of racial discrimination must be viewed.... Racial discrimination furnishes grist for the Communist propaganda mills, and it raises doubt even among friendly nations as to the intensity of our devotion to the democratic faith.
> (Quoted in Emerson and Kilson, 1965: 1073)

However, this would not free the US from criticisms of various interventions in African affairs and how it did development assistance. It did mean that the identity of African-Americans (and in the name) was not clearly or irrevocably linked to the continent. How that identity has been realised, changed and contested is beyond the scope of this book. It has meant, however, that US policies did, to varying degrees, have to take into account this constituency. One example discussed in detail later on was the effort by the US government to continuously side with the white settlers of southern Africa.

## Conclusion

*Development* as a term used in the context of encounters between cultures, was widely used in narratives that compared levels of attributes between groups of people in an order of hierarchy. This hierarchy was expressed by linking racial attributes to cultural, political and economic organisation. Racial theories were, for a long while, used to explain differences between what were perceived as simple and complex social organisations. The reference to *development* was often made to contrast the general capacities and skills of different people and relate them to each other, and to describe possible ways to bridge the gaps between groups of people.

Until the end of WWII, race often played a major role in the ways Europeans and Americans viewed the Africans. It was only after the events of WWII, that the classifications of humans and their mental capabilities following racial theories became a taboo. Even then, race continued to play a major role in the interaction between people as exemplified by racial interactions in the US until the 1960s and beyond, and by the apartheid regime in South Africa, abolished during the 1990s.

Colonial encounters expose the impact of hierarchical typologies in conjunction with various ideas of assisting development. The basic common understanding was that a society which was attributed to a lower typological category, could, under certain conditions, achieve progress (partial or whole) through various forms of assistance.

The idea that certain societies retain better attributes than others, and that certain societies possess various types of responsibilities to help the underdeveloped to acquire these attributes, relates to various notions of power. One such notion is the power/knowledge mechanism that forges regimes of truth, and through them the very perception of the self as possessing better attributes, and the other as inferior or unfortunate. These perceptions are then used by the powerful to justify various strategies of interventions to modify the other for a variety of reasons. But, as we shall discuss in subsequent chapters, these strategies often lead to problematic (morally, ethically and practically) policies, that undermine both the regime of truth of the powerful, as well as the objectives of the policies. These are the unintended consequences of power projection.

## Notes

1 Such hierarchical categorisation between Western cultures and other cultures are treated extensively by Edward Said (1978).
2 To begin exploring this issue, see for examples in Lydon (2009) and Bentahar (2011), as well as the references in those.
3 See, for example, Sachs (1992).
4 See, for example, Lucretius *On the Nature of Things*, Book V.
5 For a thorough and nuanced overview on the ideology behind racial and racist narratives, in linkage and disconnection from sociobiological consideration, see de Benoist (1999) and Jordan (1974).
6 An important and influential taxonomy dubbed *Systema Naturae* was introduced by Carl Linnaeus in multiple revised editions since 1735. See also de Benoist (1999) for multiple references to texts that classify the black population of Africa as inferior humans.
7 The well-known and popular American anthropologist Carleton Coon (1965) wrote that hominids did not become fully human until they had a cranial capacity of greater than 550 cubic centimetres and the different grand races (white, black, yellow and red) crossed the cerebral rubicon at different times with Africans having crossed the latest and therefore the furtherest behind intellectually and culturally.
8 See, for example, Armistead (1848); Buxton (1840); Schoelcher (1840).
9   On the English face are combined decision and nerve, with the fair complexion, blue eyes, and open and florid aspect. Hence the love of truth, hence the sensibility, the fine perception, and poetic construction. The fair Saxon man, with open front, and honest meaning, domestic, affectionate, is not the wood out of which cannibal, or inquisitor, or assassin is made. But he is moulded for law, lawful trade, civility, marriage, the nurture of children, for colleges, churches, charities, and colonies.
(Emerson, 1983: 802)
10 For a comprehensive overview see Hunt (2009: 46–91).
11 The economic rationale is explained in detail in several studies on slavery and the political economy in the Americas, for example, see Duignan and Clendenen (1978); Genovese (1989); Kolchin (2003) and more recently by Baptist (2014).

12 A concept that is implied in Morgan's writing, but was developed later by Boas (1937), Lowie (1920, 1924) and Ratzel (1896).
13 Boas uses the term *development* in relation to culture to indicate movement through degrees of complexity. What he rejects is the idea that cultures develop according to universal laws and in addition that diffusion is the explanation for certain similarities between cultures.
14 See, for example, the comment by Fortes and Evans-Pritchard on the matter (1967 [1940]: 1).
15 Radcliffe-Brown asserted that the objective of the comparative method in social anthropology is to 'explore the varieties of forms of social life as a basis for the theoretical study of human social phenomena' (Radcliffe-Brown, 1951: 15).
16 In practice though, Radcliffe-Brown was unable to replace the term 'primitive' in his reference to the societies he explored. See, for example, the collection of essays he published in 1952 entitled: *Structure and Function in Primitive Society*.
17 While there is no agreement in the literature as to the significance of the role of anthropologists in contributing to colonial policy, it is clear that many anthropologists wanted their work to be used by colonial administrations, while colonial administrations did occasionally use or even commission anthropologists to conduct work to inform policy (for example, Lackner, 1973; Lewis, 1973).
18 Stanley became a supporter and admirer of King Leopold of Congo despite the atrocities being committed there (Hochschild, 1998).

## References

Goldschmidt, W. and American Assembly. (1963) *The United States and Africa*. Published for the American Assembly, Columbia University, F.A. Praeger, New York.
Armistead, W. (1848) *A tribute for the negro: being a vindication of the moral, intellectual, and religious capabilities of the colored portion of mankind; with particular reference to the African race*. W. Irwin, Manchester and London.
Asad, T. (1973) *Anthropology and the colonial encounter*. Ithaca Press, London.
Asad, T. (1991) From the history of colonial anthropology to the anthropology of Western hegemony, in Stocking, G. W. J. (ed.) *Colonial situations: essays on the contextualization of ethnographic knowledge*. The University of Wisconsin Press, Madison, pp. 314–324.
Baptist, E. E. (2014) *The half has never been told: slavery and the making of American capitalism*. Basic Books, a member of the Perseus Books Group, New York.
Bentahar, Z. (2011) Continental Drift: The Disjunction of North and Sub-Saharan Africa, *Research in African Literatures* 42: 1–13.
Boas, F. (1920) Methods of Ethnology, *American Anthropologist* 22: 311–322.
Boas, F. (1937) The Diffusion of Cultural Traits, *Social Research* 4: 286–295.
Bowler, P. J. (1989) *The invention of progress: the Victorians and the past*. Basil Blackwell, Cambridge.
Buxton, T. F. Sir st. Bart. (1840) *The African slave trade and its remedy*. John Murray, London.
Claessen, H. J. M. and Skalnik, P. (1978) *The early state*. Mouton, The Hague.
Clendenen, C. C. and Duignan, P. (1964) *Americans in black Africa up to 1865*. Hoover Institution on War, Revolution, and Peace, Stanford University, Stanford, Calif.
Clendenen, C. C., Collins, R. O. and Duignan, P. (1966) *Americans in Africa, 1865–1900*. Hoover Institution on War, Revolution, and Peace, Stanford University, Stanford, Calif.

Cohen, W. B. (1980) *The French encounter with Africans: white response to blacks, 1530–1880.* Indiana University Press, Bloomington; London.

Coon, C. S. and Hunt, E. E. (1965) *The living races of man.* Knopf, New York.

Cornwall, A. and Eade, D. (2010) *Deconstructing development discourse: buzzwords and fuzzwords.* Practical Action Publishing in association with Oxfam GB, Rugby.

Davis, D. B. (2003) *Challenging the boundaries of slavery.* Harvard University Press, Cambridge, Mass.; London.

de Benoist, A. (1999) What is Racism?, *Telos* 1999: 11–48.

Doty, R. L. (1996) *Imperial encounters: the politics of representation in North-South relations.* University of Minnesota Press, Minneapolis.

Drake, S. C. (1970) *The redemption of Africa and black religion.* Third World Press, Chicago.

Du Bois, W. E. B. (1990) *The souls of black folk.* Vintage Books/Library of America, New York.

Du Plessis, J. (1929) *The evangelisation of pagan Africa: a history of Christian missions to the pagan tribes of central Africa.* J. C. Juta, Cape Town and Johannesburg (South Africa).

Duignan, P. and Clendenen, C. C. (1978) *The United States and the African slave trade, 1619–1862.* Greenwood Press, Westport, Conn.

Duignan, P. and Gann, L. H. (1984) *The United States and Africa: a history.* Cambridge University Press; Hoover Institution, Cambridge, Cambridgeshire; New York; Stanford, Calif.

Eberstadt, N. (1988) *Foreign aid and American purpose.* American Enterprise Institute for Public Policy Research; Distributed by arrangement with National Book Network, Washington, DC; Lanham, MD.

Emerson, R. W. (1983) *Essays and lectures.* Literary Classics of the United States, New York.

Emerson, R. and Kilson, M. (1965) The American Dilemma in a Changing World: The Rise of Africa and the Negro American, *Daedalus* 94: 1055–1084.

Escobar, A. (1995) *Encountering development: the making and unmaking of the third world: with a new preface by the author.* Princeton University Press, Princeton, N.J.

Esteva, G. (1992) Development, in Sachs, W. (ed.) *The Development dictionary: a guide to knowledge as power.* Zed Books, London; Atlantic Highlands, N.J., pp. 6–25.

Fage, J. D. (1962) An introduction to the history of West Africa. (Third edition.) [With maps.]. University Press, Cambridge.

Fortes, M. and Evans-Pritchard, E. E. (1967 [1940]) *African political systems.* Oxford University Press, London.

Fredrickson, G. M. (1988) *The arrogance of race: historical perspectives on slavery, racism, and social inequality.* Wesleyan University Press, Middletown, Conn.

Genovese, E. D. (1989) *The political economy of slavery: studies in the economy and society of the slave South.* Wesleyan University Press, Middletown, Conn.

Goldschmidt, W. and American Assembly (1963) *The United States and Africa.* Published for the American Assembly, Columbia University, F.A. Praeger, New York.

Hochschild, A. (1998) *King Leopold's ghost: a story of greed, terror, and heroism in Colonial Africa.* Houghton Mifflin, Boston.

Hochschild, A. (2006) *Bury the chains: the British struggle to abolish slavery.* Pan, London.

Hunt, M. H. (2009) *Ideology and U.S. foreign policy.* Yale University Press, New Haven, CT.

Jordan, W. D. (1974) *The white man's burden; historical origins of racism in the United States.* Oxford University Press, New York.
Kidd, B. (1894) *Social evolution.* Macmillan, London; New York.
Kolchin, P. (2003) *American slavery, 1619–1877.* Hill and Wang, New York.
Kothari, U. (2005) *A radical history of development studies: individuals, institutions and ideologies.* David Philip; Zed Books, Cape Town, London.
Lackner, H. (1973) Colonial adminstration and social anthroplology: Eastern Nigeria 1920–1940, in Asad, T. (ed.) *Anthroplogy and the colonial encounter.* Ithaca Press, London.
Latourette, K. S. and National Foundation for Education in American Citizenship. (1949) *Missions and the American mind.* National Foundation Press, Indianapolis.
Lewellen, T. C. (1992) *Political anthropology: an introduction.* Bergin and Garvey, Westport (Conn.); London.
Lewis, D. (1973) Anthropology and Colonialism, *Current Anthropology* 14: 581–602.
Lovejoy, P. E. (2000) *Transformations in slavery: a history of slavery in Africa.* Cambridge University Press, Cambridge.
Lowie, R. H. (1920) *Primitive society.* Boni and Liveright, New York.
Lowie, R. H. (1924) *Primitive religion.* Boni and Liveright, New York.
Lowie, R. H. (1962) *The origin of the state.* Russell, New York.
Lugard, F. J. D. B. (1922) *The dual mandate in British Tropical Africa.* London: William Blackwood and Sons.
Lugard, F. J. D. B. (1926) The White Man's Task in Tropical Africa, *Foreign Affairs* 5: 57–68.
Lugard, F. J. D. B. (1933) Education and Race Relations, *Journal of the African Society* XXXII: 1–11.
Lydon, G. (2009) On trans-Saharan trails Islamic law, trade networks, and cross-cultural exchange in nineteenth-century Western Africa. Cambridge University Press, Cambridge; New York, pp. xxviii, 468 p.
Magubane, B. (1987) *The ties that bind: African-American consciousness of Africa.* Africa World Press, Trenton, N.J.
Mair, L. P. (1934) *An African people in the twentieth century. [A study of the Baganda people. With plates.].* G. Routledge & Sons, London.
Mamdani, M. (1996) *Citizen and subject: contemporary Africa and the legacy of late colonialism.* Princeton University Press, Princeton, N.J.; Chichester.
McGee, R. J. and Warms, R. L. (2008) *Anthropological theory: an introduction history.* McGraw-Hill Education, New York; London.
Morgan, L. H. (1877) *Ancient society; or, Researches in the lines of human progress from savagery, through barbarism to civilization.* H. Holt and Company, New York.
Munck, R. and O'Hearn, D. (1999) *Critical development theory: contributions to a new paradigm.* Zed Books, London.
Myrdal, G., Sterner, R. and Rose, A. M. (1944) *An American dilemma; the Negro problem and modern democracy.* Harper & Brothers, New York; London.
Pakenham, T. (1992) *The scramble for Africa: 1876–1912.* Abacas, London.
Quinn, F. (2000) *The French overseas empire.* Praeger, Westport, Conn.
Radcliffe-Brown, A. R. (1951) The Comparative Method in Social Anthropology, *The Journal of the Royal Anthropological Institute of Great Britain and Ireland* 81: 15–22.
Ratzel, F. (1896) *The history of mankind.* Macmillan, New York.
Redkey, E. S. (1969) *Black exodus: black nationalist and back-to-Africa movements, 1890–1910.* Yale University, New Haven, CT.

Ripley, W. Z. (1899) *The races of Europe; a sociological study (Lowell Institute lectures)*. D. Appleton and Company, New York.

Rist, G. (2008) *The history of development: from Western origins to global faith*. Zed, London.

Rudwick, E. M. (1959) W. E. B. Du Bois and the Universal Races Congress of 1911, *The Phylon Quarterly* 20: 372–378.

Sachs, W. (1992) *The Development dictionary: a guide to knowledge as power*. Zed Books, London; Atlantic Highlands, N.J.

Said, Edward W. (1978) *Orientalism*. 1st edn. New York, Pantheon Books.

Schoelcher, V. (1840) *Des colonies Francaises: abolition immediate de l'esclavage*. Pagnerre Editeur, Paris.

Sears, C. (1997) *Africa in the American mind, 1870–1955: a study in mythology, ideology and the reconstruction of race*. PhD Dissertation, University of California, Berkeley. https://siarchives.si.edu/collections/siris_sic_3754 (accessed 12 March 2017).

Shenin, S. Y. (2000) *The United States and the Third World: the origins of postwar relations and the Point Four program*. Nova Science Publishers, Huntington, N.Y.

Stocking, G. W. (1987) *Victorian anthropology*. Collier Macmillan, London.

Truman, H. S. (1949) Truman's Inaugural Address, *Harry S. Truman Library and Museum*.

Wallace, A. R. (1864) The Origin of Human Races and the Antiquity of Man Deduced from the Theory of 'Natural Selection', *Journal of the Anthropological Society of London* 2: clviii–clxxxvii.

Weatherly, U. G. (1911) The First Universal Races Congress, *American Journal of Sociology* 17: 315–328.

# 3 Tools of power
## The American discourse

### The American discourse of assistance

The evolution of development assistance policy in the US is tightly linked with power and to ideas of exceptionalism in American culture. Power and exceptionalism nurture concepts that guide national security strategies, foreign policy and conceptions of development assistance (Hodgson, 2009: 10; Hunt, 2009; Jordan *et al.*, 2009: 29; Mead, 2001: 96–97; Ruttan 1996: 2). But there are many nuances within the fundamental schools of thought around US foreign policy, and subsequently the justification for development assistance and its links to national security and foreign policy objectives. In this chapter we explore the assistance discourse of the executive branch. We focus on the justifications for US foreign assistance in three distinct periods: the Cold War; the post-Cold War years; and the post-9/11 years. The objective of this chapter is to demonstrate the discursive links made between American idealism, exceptionalism and national security. This serves as the foundations upon which US foreign and assistance policy towards Africa was formed.

There is a significant body of literature discussing the uniqueness of American culture. Many of these discussions locate the roots of Americanism with the emerging ideologies of the pioneers and the founding fathers. Throughout history and in contemporary settings, these ideologies are interpreted, appropriated and used by political elites to justify policy. The link between these foundational ideologies and their use in contemporary contexts can help bridge the sometimes paradoxical use of idealism with pragmatism and nationalism in the justification of development assistance.

A set of subjects often appears in the literary landscape dealing with the topic of Americanism. Among the plurality of headings used to describe the uniqueness of American ideology and culture, we find the words 'individualism', 'race', 'puritanism', 'democracy', 'the rule of law', 'elitism', 'capitalism', 'frontier', 'exceptionalism', 'manifest destiny', 'city on the hill'[1] and 'special providence'. Frequently used to describe and explain the uniqueness of American thought, these terms are fundamental in understanding the link between idealism (secular and religious) and pragmatism as it manifests in the formulations and justification of the foreign and development assistance policies of the US.

One way to enter the subject of Americanism is by reference to the famous nineteenth century American author, Horatio Alger. Alger's accounts repeat a specific narrative, sometimes called 'rags-to-riches', which embody the historical and contemporary pursuit of the American dream. The reference to Alger's narratives can tease out the putative American values widely represented in contemporary political discourses as the essence of Americanism (Nackenhoff, 1994: 3–5). We refer to Alger's narratives to highlight the elements used in the construction and reproduction of the regime of truth.[2] The elemental characteristics of the American dream are anchored in popularised views and interpretations of the history and foundation of the US as a nation. Alger's protagonists are often the ragged, poor, uneducated, orphaned and abused. His narrative describes how, despite impossible odds and unfortunate circumstances, optimism and dignity are never lost. With hard work, determination,[3] religious conviction and self-control, Alger's young protagonists accomplish the American dream, which usually means achieving fame and/or fortune.[4] We locate the importance of the 'rags-to-riches' narrative in the context of foreign assistance mainly in the underlying values it conveys[5] rather than the dream it propagates. Individualism, hard work, religion, dignity and heading towards a frontier, are important building blocks of Americanism and the way Americans understand and interact with their social, political and physical environment. Safeguarding the possibility to achieve the dream is a democratic system embodied in a declaration of independence that protects economic success and the God-given rights for 'Life, Liberty and the pursuit of Happiness'.[6] Democracy and the rule of law are the sacred mechanism through which the possibility of economic equality is granted. The American regime of truth is canonised ink-on-parchment, memorised, studied and repeated by all Americans and anchored in the words 'We hold these truths to be self-evident.'

A central pillar of Americanism is the concept of exceptionalism. Simply put, exceptionalism is the belief that America, by the grace of God, is exceptional among nations and destined to fulfil the role of the 'city upon the hill', 'the new Jerusalem', the beacon of light and hope chosen to lead and inspire other nations towards the righteous path.[7] In a contemporary context, the notion of exceptionalism, which implies superiority of ideas and ideals (Restad, 2015: 17), is coupled with post-WWII American power. This leads to the operationalisation of the regime of truth through foreign policy and subsequently, the creation and justification for development assistance, bridging the gap between American idealism and interest-driven pragmatism. Exceptionalism provides an ideological justification to propagate American ideas and show others how to improve. It also justifies to Americans why the country has to continuously enhance its own power. Our basic premise is that the self-notion of exceptionalism is a fundamental idea that influences the formulation of American foreign policy.[8] We use this point of departure to understand the ways development assistance serves as a tool shaped by power and as a tool for the projection of power.

The fundamental regime of truth that shapes the assistance policy of the US as it emerges from the narratives and discourses presented below, is centred on the notion expressed repeatedly by political elites, Democrats and Republicans, liberals and conservatives, that America is an exceptional nation. Many scholars[9] isolate in their analysis of the influence of exceptionalism on foreign policy two main approaches which are often labelled the *missionary* and *exemplary* strands. The missionary strand extracts from exceptionalism an interventionist foreign policy, arguing that America has a responsibility to promote and disseminate its ideals and values. The exemplary strand, so it is maintained, assumes a more isolationist approach, arguing that America's role lies in being the paragon for other nations, remaining distant from conflicts and behaviours that contradict American ideals and values, safeguard the values at home, allowing other nations to aspire to become like America. But as indicated by Restad (2015), the exemplary strand is not at all isolationist. What is usually identified in the literature as an exemplary approach is clearly interventionist as Restad (2015: 80) argues throughout her book. According to her, American foreign policy has been consistently unilateral and internationalist since the beginning of the Republic. Based on ideas of exceptionalism and in attempts to enhance its own power, American policymakers pursue a path of unilateral internationalism with the objective of achieving its own interests above all other considerations. Nevertheless, when it comes to the assistance policy, we can locate strategies that link exceptionalism to missionary and exemplary stances. Both are used as strategies to achieve the American mission of protecting its own interests and ideology through an internationalist foreign policy, but employing different strategies to safeguard and enhance American power through its assistance policy. We come back to these notions and their interactions with development assistance in Chapter 7.

While the labelling of American foreign policy as missionary and exemplary captures a link between exceptionalism and archetypes of foreign policy approaches, other building blocks of Americanism together with historical contexts produce even more nuanced approaches to foreign policy. These combine notions of exceptionalism with pragmatic concerns, and produce foreign policies that are set primarily to safeguard American interests, leaving ideals and values present, but functioning as stage-sets of varying importance to achieve American goals. In reference to the critique of Reinhold Niebuhr of American exceptionalism, Bacevich (2008) contends that the US has sought global dominance in order to sustain the American way of life which has meant an ethic of self-gratification and excess. Recalling George W. Bush's words following September 11: 'Get on board. Do your business around the country. Fly and enjoy America's great destination spots. Get down to Disney World in Florida' (quoted in Bacevich, 2008: 60), and 'I encourage you to all to go shopping more' (quoted in Bacevich, 2008: 61), it is not a surprise that Bacevich asks: 'can freedom be understood as meaning many more things to buy?' (Bacevich, 2008: 63).

Interacting with the idea that America is an exceptional nation, are the values embodied in the 'rags-to-riches' narrative, which form the basis for the pursuit of economic success. The economy and means of accumulation are safeguarded by democracy and the rule of law,[10] together forming the means to preserve the system and protect it from external threats. A vibrant market-based economy forms the basis of power that preserves the possibility of accomplishing the American dream (and by extension, preserving the fundamental American ideals and values underlying the dream), as well as safeguarding it from the world at large. The economy becomes the source from which America draws its ability to project hard and soft power, to both protect America from the outside, and to preserve a position which allows it to disseminate its ideas and values.[11] The desires to remain economically and militarily powerful will compete and undermine some core ideals and values and their manifestation in practices of foreign policy. This has sometimes led to an unbridgeable double standard and, as a result, to the weakening of American power which we discuss in subsequent chapters.

In general, one can identify a fundamental duality of motives in the justification for the American development assistance programmes. Ruttan (1996: 2–3) speaks of *idealism* and *realism* stemming from American exceptionalism. Idealists argue that it is the manifest destiny of the US to lead the world towards democracy and prosperity. Realists claim that the ideas and values of the US are in perpetual threat from anti-democratic and corrupt forces, and therefore, constant vigilance and proactive engagement to secure interests and the American way of life should guide strategy (Bacevich, 2010: 28). These conceptions are not necessarily mutually exclusive, though a focus on one or the other can relate in different ways to national security strategies, national interests and foreign policy, and will influence how priorities and goals of development assistance are defined and operationalised.

The following chapter focuses on presidential narratives containing underlying reasons for foreign assistance as expressed publicly throughout various administrations since the end of WWII. These narratives are analysed in conjunction with various documents from different governmental agencies, the legislative branch and foreign policy analysis. The chapter will be divided into historical periods. In each period, we highlight two main issues: the formation and evolution of the concept of development assistance in the US; and the links among the concepts of development, foreign policy and national security.

The basic premise here is that America's foreign policy is designed to enhance American power and safeguard the American way of life at home. Based on this, we will examine the assistance discourse as a tool to project power, justified by the ideas of exceptionalism, thus reproducing and enhancing a regime of truth.

## The foreign assistance discourse during the Cold War

### From Truman to Eisenhower

As WWII drew to an end, it became apparent that a new world order needed to be structured to prevent future physical and psychological devastations caused by the onset of extreme ideologies such as Nazism, fascism and increasingly communism. The US, which gained substantial authority and recognition for its leading role in shifting the tides of war towards a decisive victory, found itself in a new position of leadership and global status.

Constructing a new world order 'under law, dedicated to peace, security, freedom and general well-being of all mankind' was one of the main objectives of the Yalta Conference.[12] But the deep ideological gap separating capitalism and communism emerged in force after the war and the battle to consolidate the victory was about to begin.

The newly established US hegemony meant the ability to influence the creation of a global system that could promote the values, needs, interests and ideologies that guided America (Johnson, 2004; Peck, 2010: 13). The Soviet doctrine of communist expansion was seen as a threat to this vision. Kennan wrote, '[The US] must formulate and put forward for other nations a much more positive and constructive picture of sort of world we would like to see' (Kennan quoted in Viotti, 2005: 192).

President Truman did not hide his concerns about the rise of Soviet power. He identified both military and ideological threats that might devastate the world and endanger American values. As a response to an urgent request by Greece and Turkey for financial assistance to rebut communist pressure, Truman outlined his doctrine to Congress. He explained the foreign policy and national security concerns emanating from Soviet pressure, and viewed the situation as an existential danger to a Greece threatened by 'terrorist activities' led by communists, and to 'the future of Turkey as an independent and economically sound state' (Truman quoted in Viotti, 2005: 197–199). Truman believed that the US had a responsibility to block communist expansion, and that the world expected and welcomed American support in maintaining freedom. A hesitant response to the Soviet threat, in his view, would not only undermine world peace, but also endanger the welfare of the US. Truman concluded that America must support the political institutions and sovereignty of countries threatened by the totalitarian communist regime.

For the US, the apparent appeal of the Soviet ideology was a major concern. Communist doctrine threatened to sweep across the post-war, poor, devastated world, by underlining the injustice of class disparities and the dangers of capitalism and imperialism; it promised redistribution of resources, and encouraged people to stand for their rights against oppression through revolution (Peck, 2010: 21–22). This undermined the foundation of US ideology based on individual liberties, economic prosperity, democracy and non-interference as a government policy. To counter the Soviet narrative, the US had to engage in a campaign to convince the poor, deprived and marginalised people of the benefits associated with American ideology.

The Truman doctrine became the foundation of the post-war American approach to the Soviet Union and marked the onset of the Cold War. This was the beginning of major shifts in US foreign policy focusing on a more direct involvement in international affairs (Jordan *et al.*, 2009: 45–46). On March 12, 1947, President Truman appeared before a joint session of Congress and stated:

> I believe it must be the policy of the United States to support free peoples who are resisting attempted subjugation by armed minorities or by outside pressures. I believe that we must assist free peoples to work out their own destinies in their own way. I believe that our help should be primarily through economic and financial aid which is essential to economic stability and orderly political processes.
>
> (Truman quoted in Viotti, 2005: 198)

Against this backdrop, the American concept of foreign assistance was conceived to disseminate and win over support to American values as a part of the anti-Soviet campaign. The rationale for the Marshall Plan (the first official development assistance programme) included a containment strategy to secure US national security interests, and to ensure the future welfare of the American people:

> Any government which maneuvers to block the recovery of other countries cannot expect help from us. Furthermore, governments, political parties, or groups which seek to perpetuate human misery in order to profit therefrom politically or otherwise will encounter the opposition of the United States.
>
> (Marshall, 1947)

Thus, American assistance would not be granted to those who attempt to 'block the recovery of other countries', and those who 'seek to perpetuate human misery'. Essentially, assistance was tied to a return to the normal economic health of the world, as a fundamental precondition to political stability and peace. It required the acceptance of a doctrine which is not aligned with communist ideas.

In his inauguration speech[13] Truman (1949) highlighted his concern for the underdeveloped areas of the world. Handicaps such as poverty, hunger, disease and lack of economic growth were not only consequential to the people who endured them, but were described as a direct threat to the more prosperous areas of the world. The pre-eminence of the US among nations in the development of industrial and scientific innovations was key, in Truman's view, to emancipate the underdeveloped from their burdens (Truman, 1949). The solution he advocated for underdevelopment was modernisation (Peck, 2010: 35), a counter narrative to the revolutionary options offered by communism, as well as emancipation from the old colonial constraints (Peck, 2010: 37). Whether the Cold War was principally about 'finding ever more effective ways to break down barriers for American influence' as suggested by some (Peck, 2010: 41), or whether it was 'to reduce the power and influence of the USSR to limits which no longer constitute a threat to the peace, national independence and stability of the world family of nations', as formulated by the US National Security Council (NSC, 1948), foreign assistance would become a strategic tool to pursue such objectives. This is not to say that a moral rationale for assistance was absent from the American discourse. American foreign policy traditions emphasising democracy and human rights have been present since the early days of the republic (see, for example, Kane, 2008; Mead, 2001: 132–173). Senator J. William Fulbright[14] (1967: 248–255) identified two main strands of moralism in American history: democratic humanism and intolerant puritanism. The first is based on reason and moderation, while the second is a crusading spirit that manifests itself in periods of difficulty and misfortune, or when 'some event or leader of opinion has aroused the people to a state of high emotion' leading to 'a harsh and angry moralism' (Fulbright, 1967: 250). Those who belong to the puritan tradition are 'men with doctrines, men with faith and idealism, men who confuse power with virtue, men who believe in some cause without doubt and practice their beliefs without scruple' (Fulbright, 1967: 248). These were later described by James Forrestal as 'semi-warriors' (Bacevich, 2010: 27), a term coined to designate those who believe that the US is in a perpetual condition of danger and threat. This idea of unending struggle grants an everlasting justification for the national security discourse and maintains its importance in American foreign policy.

The link between the national security paradigm and the moral duty of the US, is embodied in one of the most important policy documents composed in the early years of the Cold War: NSC-68.[15] Written by a joint committee of the DoS and DoD, NSC-68 identifies Soviet ideologies as 'animated by fanatic faith' antithetical to American principles, and aiming to 'impose absolute authority over the rest of the world'. The US has a 'fundamental purpose' laid down in the constitution to 'assure the integrity and vitality' of a free American society. NSC-68 refers to the Declaration of Independence, the Constitution, Bill of Rights and Divine

Providence, to highlight the need to defend the American way of life (NSC, 1950). According to the authors of this document, the US was destined to play a fundamental role to defeat the Soviet threat, but to succeed, America must expand its circle of allies and harness their efforts to the cause. If instead, nations were allowed to adopt a course of neutrality, the Soviet Union would achieve domination. Soviet political and economic engagement in the world was viewed as psychological warfare which, if left unchecked, would endanger the leadership of the US and the values of its institutions (NSC, 1950).

To reduce the power and influence of the Soviet Union without resorting to total war, the authors of NSC-68 recommended that the US assume a foreign policy strategy that will strengthen the orientation of the world towards American ideology. Such a strategy would be achieved through a 'rapid and sustained build-up of the political, economic, and military strength of the free world, and by means of affirmative program intended to wrest the initiative from the Soviet Union' (NSC, 1950).

This strategy informed the linkage between national security and foreign assistance for the following years. In June 1950, Congress approved the Act for International Development[16] which authorised funding for 'Point Four' of Truman's inaugural address, promising to fulfil the American commitment for technical assistance programmes (Butterfield, 2004: 18; Truman, 1950). With this Act, Congress emphasised that any American programme for international development must be consistent with US foreign policy objectives (Ruttan, 1996: 51). This tied US foreign assistance to economic, political, social and humanitarian interests and values as defined by the DoS. In the post-war reality of the 1950s and the growing power of communism, this meant that foreign assistance priorities would be guided by security concerns with a heavy emphasis on military assistance programmes (Ruttan, 1996: 63).

The election of Eisenhower in 1953 reflected the strengthening of conservatism in the US. Eisenhower's first inaugural address highlighted the growing concern with national security issues in the shadow of the Korean War, fear from nuclear weapons, and the battle whereby 'Freedom is pitted against slavery; lightness against the dark.' (Eisenhower, 1953). Eisenhower believed that his most important task was to strengthen the power of America to withstand the threats that could jeopardise its security and leadership in the free world. To this end an effort must be made to support 'proven friends of freedom' and enhance their security and well-being (Eisenhower, 1953).

In May 1953, Eisenhower delivered a special message to Congress concerning the Mutual Security Program. Developed by his administration for Fiscal Year (FY) 1954, the programme highlighted linking foreign assistance and national security through economic, technical and military aid to enable the US to preserve its leadership position in the world (Eisenhower, 1953a).

Eisenhower had to repeatedly justify to a conservative congress the links between foreign assistance to the national security strategy and the welfare of the American people (Eisenhower, 1953b). He explained that in order to effectively combat Soviet ideology, it is important that 'people see evidence of improved conditions of living flowing from freedom and independent sovereignty as contrasted to totalitarian methods' (Eisenhower, 1953b). Technical assistance programmes, bi-lateral, and through the UN, where substantial mechanisms to convey this message to underdeveloped areas. Eisenhower emphasised that such programmes are in essence an 'integral part of our program for America's security' (Eisenhower, 1953b).

In the following years, Eisenhower consistently linked foreign assistance to US national security interests and to the struggle against communist aspirations for world domination.[17] Military, technical and economic assistance to developing countries, were viewed as vital components of US security and the well-being of the American people. The distinct emphasis was, however, on military components, both in rhetoric and in requests for funding. Even though Eisenhower often framed the assistance programme as a part of the American moral ideology and heritage (Eisenhower, 1955), it was clear from his speeches and addresses that the *raison d'être* for the programme was support for US national security and economic interest in opposition to Soviet actions around the world.

This was emphasised by key figures throughout the Eisenhower administration including Secretary of State John Foster Dulles who stated that foreign aid was an essential part of US foreign policy, and a long-term strategic tool to fend off communism (Ruttan, 1996: 73). Nevertheless, Eisenhower maintained that the motivations for the American programme were distinctively different from those of the Soviets. For America, peace and justice were the driving forces, not the intention to dominate and subjugate people to foreign political, economic and cultural interests (Eisenhower, 1956). As such, foreign assistance programmes from their origins were linked to a realist view of the international system with an objective to contain competing socio-political and economic ideologies.

By 1958, Eisenhower's administration was working hard to gain congressional support to secure long-term commitment for foreign assistance to address security threats and economic self-interest in a strategic manner (Ruttan, 1996: 75–76). The recommendations for a long-term strategy for the programme included the creation of an independent agency for the administration of the programme and a multi-year financing plan to replace the year-to-year system (Ruttan, 1996: 75–76). Eventually, Congress accepted the need for a comprehensive long-term strategy for foreign assistance which materialised in the form of the Foreign Assistance Act of 1961.

## The Kennedy administration

The link between national security and development assistance continued during the Kennedy administration, but with an important distinction. President Kennedy expanded and formalised development assistance as a foreign policy tool. He viewed aid as a fundamental mechanism in the battle against communism, as well as a moral imperative of the American people (Kennedy, 1961). Kennedy saw the rise of nationalism in the Third World as a powerful and unstoppable current. He recognised the need of the US to assume a clear position consistent with America's general support of freedom and self-determination (Mahoney, 1983: 244). He pushed forward the Foreign Assistance Act, passed by Congress in 1961, and believed in the need to separate development assistance into distinct military and non-military components for greater efficiency and effectiveness. In his inauguration address, Kennedy underlined a value-based rationale for aid:

> To those people in the huts and villages of half the globe struggling to break the bonds of mass misery, we pledge our best efforts to help them help themselves, for whatever period is required – not because the Communist may be doing it, not because we seek their votes, but because it is right. If a free society cannot help the many who are poor, it cannot save the few who are rich.
>
> (Kennedy, 1961d)

As the founder of the Peace Corps, he often emphasised that their mission was carried on behalf of the American people, and stressed that aid was a partnership between the national government and the American people (Kennedy, 1962). The Peace Corps was set up as an arm of the US government that contributed to development assistance abroad through private institutions and organisations (Kennedy, 1961a). Kennedy stated that the 'Peace Corps is not designed as an instrument of diplomacy and propaganda or ideological conflict. It is designed to permit our people to exercise more fully their responsibilities in the great common cause of world development' (Kennedy, 1961a). He also expressed his hope that the Peace Corps concept would inspire other nations to follow suit and contribute to international development (Kennedy, 1961a). The Peace Corps allowed the US government to do a few things: popularise a moral justification for development assistance and reduce government costs in delivering assistance by inspiring the American public to volunteer; and harness the international community for development aid through encouraging other nations to establish similar voluntary organisations.

But when Kennedy addressed the concept of assistance strategically, he stressed the national security aspect through an anti-communist discourse. He fended off voices opposed to the aid programmes by emphasising that investment in assistance programmes offer returns in terms of welfare, security and freedom (Kennedy, 1961b, 1961c). Kennedy stated that while aid is a way to fulfil humanitarian responsibilities, it is first and foremost a programme that enhances the security of the US in the battle against communism through a new kind of war that is being waged (Kennedy, 1961b, 1961c). Aid allows the US to confront the Soviet Union in the battle for the hearts and minds of poor people in Africa, Asia and Latin America (Kennedy, 1961b).

The Foreign Assistance Act emphasised the duty of the American people to help those who suffer from conditions of hunger and poverty. But the Act also underlined the importance of assistance for the welfare of the American citizens.[18] The passing of the Foreign Assistance Act led to the creation of the United States Agency for International Development (USAID) designed to implement long-term economic and social development programmes.

USAID was described by Kennedy as the alternative to sending troops for the defence of freedom (Kennedy, 1962a). Working for economic development with people in underdeveloped countries was a tool designed to demonstrate how problems of poverty, misery and inequality could be solved without adopting Soviet ideology and falling behind the Iron Curtain (Kennedy, 1962a). Foreign assistance was claimed to be a distinct American contribution and 'a tremendous source of influence for a President of the United States' (Kennedy, 1962a).

When the House Appropriation Committee threatened to cut foreign aid funds, Kennedy framed it as a threat to the security of the free world:

> You cannot separate guns from roads and schools when it comes to resisting Communist subversion in under-developed countries.... To mutilate the aid program in this massive fashion would be to damage the national security of the United States.
>
> (Kennedy, 1962b)

Kennedy also highlighted the importance of aid for the creation of jobs in America for American trade interests (Kennedy, 1962b). For Kennedy, aid programmes were 'just as important as any military spending abroad' (Kennedy, 1962b). The Foreign Assistance Act of 1961, the re-organisation of foreign aid assistance, and the creation of USAID and the Peace Corps, were vital components of US national security strategy to stop Soviet and communist expansion. For Kennedy, development assistance was one of the most important tools to advance the cause of freedom. In his Special Message to Congress on Foreign Aid, Kennedy announced that the upcoming years would be the 'Decade of Development' where 'less-developed nations' would transit to self-sustained growth (Kennedy, 1961). He contended that development assistance could be used to frustrate communism without the need to explicitly require that recipients align with

America. Foreign aid was not a tool designed to 'negatively' fight communism (Kennedy, 1961). Rather, it was a tool that focused on practising and disseminating American ideals, which, he believed, were based on good and righteous intentions. This kind of focus could help promote a free and secure world that applauds America for its values and efforts, and in this way could contribute to the rejection of communism. America should, according to this rationale, focus on granting help and support to less-developed countries because America strives to do good. Less developed countries would not only feel the benefits of development assistance, but would also appreciate the pureness of motives, and thus be encouraged to strengthen their ties with the US and reject communist attempts to link friendship with ideology.

American values, moral conviction and the fight against communism were for Kennedy, inseparable concepts that formed a comprehensive justification to create a dedicated, well-designed and thoughtfully executed development assistance programme administered by newly-created agencies devoted to this purpose (Kennedy, 1961, 1962c).

## *President Johnson*

When Johnson took over the presidency after the assassination of Kennedy, he brought a distinct change of rhetorical emphasis into the foreign assistance discourse that should be viewed and understood in relation to the war in Vietnam. While the linkage between assistance and the containment of communism was a regular feature in Kennedy statements and addresses, Johnson underlined moral duties and economic benefits. Though the anti-communist rhetoric in the assistance discourse was present in many of Johnson's statements, it was gradually toned down, and became increasingly absent in later addresses.

In his first Special Message to Congress on Foreign Aid, Johnson emphasised a moral commitment to development alongside an anti-communist justification (Johnson, 1964). He made a similar reference to communism in his Special Message to Congress on the Foreign Aid Program on 14 January 1965. But the explicit connection between foreign assistance and communism is almost absent from the two following Special Messages on 1 February 1966 and 7 February 1967 (Johnson, 1966, 1967). It remains only as a hint in an allusion to the security and peace of the world. Instead of emphasising communist threats, Johnson underlined the moral imperatives of assistance. He highlighted the dividends from supporting such a programme to the current and future economic interests of the US, and the importance of assistance for security and peace.

Ruttan (1996: 267) notes that Johnson's emphasis on the moral imperatives of economic and development assistance was part of his attempts to deflect the growing domestic criticism over the military involvement in Vietnam, and the substantial costs (both human and monetary) related to the war effort. To continue justifying economic assistance, of which USAID programmes in Vietnam were substantial (Dacy, 1986: 26–29), Johnson kept highlighting America's values, and especially flagging peace, plenty, and freedom as pursued by the founding fathers in contrast to the 'misery' in developing nations (Johnson, 1966).

Much like Kennedy and Truman, Johnson believed that the role of the US was to help people help themselves. He underlined that it was the responsibility of leaders in developing countries to invest in improved farming techniques, build schools, hospitals and industry, reform land and tax systems, address demographic concerns and 'create the climate which will attract foreign investment, and keep local money at home' (Johnson, 1966). But development assistance should prioritise those countries ready to adopt these changes. He recommended that Congress support the US food aid programme by increasing funding to USAID, and that these funds would be used by the agency to promote import of fertiliser, farm equipment, pesticides and farming techniques from the US, as well as help finance road building, irrigation systems and promote research on soil and seeds improvements. The aid programme's expenditures, he declared to Congress, will only be used where it serves the interests of the United States (Johnson, 1966).

Johnson (1967) outlined six guiding principles for strategic foreign assistance:

1   Self-help: the United States will help nations who are ready to help themselves.
2   Multilateralism: developed countries must share the cost of development assistance.
3   Regionalism: cooperation between countries to develop resources shared with neighbours.
4   Agriculture, health and education as the key sectors to help the underdeveloped nations to advance.
5   Balance of payments: keeping the dollar strong as a basic condition to assist other nations.
6   Efficient administration: so the American people will know that their tax dollars are spent wisely.

To achieve this, Johnson recommended that USAID go through a reorganisation 'to better carry on the War on Hunger and to promote private investment and the growth of private enterprise in the less-developed world' (Johnson, 1967).

This change of emphasis should be viewed along with the contextual events that defined the US in the mid to late sixties. The growing importance of the civil rights and anti-war movements within the US had a strong influence both on Kennedy and Johnson. As President, one of Johnson's first actions was to pass the Civil Rights Act (1964). He then convinced the

89th Congress to adopt legislation to combat social disparities in American society (Fulbright, 1967: 132). But in the shadow of the Vietnam conflict, Congress began to scrutinise every attempt by the executive branch to administer military and economic aid (Butterfield, 2004: 113). To justify foreign assistance in these circumstances, Johnson used narratives which incorporated elements regarded as social handicaps in many urban and rural societies in the US: poverty, collapsing infrastructure, lack of education and poor health care (Butterfield, 2004: 113). To harness support for a foreign assistance programme, he explained how investing in developing countries would produce growth in America, linking his arguments to the contemporary crisis in the US induced by the war in Vietnam. While muted in his rhetoric, the assistance programme did play a major role in the effort to contain communism during his administration. 'Cold warriors' such as Walt Rostow[19] considered the programme of economic and technical assistance to South Vietnam as one of the most important tools of containment, directly countering Soviet attempts to spread its ideology (Rostow, 1960: 294–298). As noted by USAID Assistant Administrator Poats in a testimony before Congress in 1962, USAID was:

> engaged in Vietnam in two crucial aspects of the war – the fight against communist subversion and insurgency ... and the fight against inflation and critical commodity shortages in the market place.
> (Quoted in Dacy, 1986: 29)

In the shadow of the Tet offensive in 1968, Congress and the American people lost much of their confidence in the administration. Among the various steps that reflected that scrutiny, Congress called upon the executive branch to review the development assistance programmes (Butterfield, 2004: 115) which was mostly invested in Vietnam and assisted the war effort (Eberstadt, 1988: 34–35). This task was left to the Nixon administration.

### *The Nixon and Ford administrations*

In his first Special Message to Congress on Foreign Aid in 1969, Nixon explained that for many years Americans had viewed foreign assistance in the light of national interests: Americans believed that military assistance helped secure the world and by extension the US; that economic assistance improves the development of US markets; and that technical assistance gains respect and friendship for the US (Nixon, 1969). Nixon clarified that while all these were 'sound and practical reasons' for foreign aid programmes, they did little justice to the main character and purpose of the American people. He stated that the 'moral qualities' of the US compelled it to do 'what is right to do' (Nixon, 1969), and that this was why foreign aid existed. But when he began to outline his 'fresh approach' to aid, stating that 'US assistance is essential to express and achieve our national goals in the international community – a world order of peace and justice', he linked foreign assistance back to US national interests.

The changes that Nixon offered to the American development discourse relate to his efforts to reduce the government share in costs while still maintaining the dividends offered by the programme to national interests. His plan was to expand US technical assistance, and to internationalise the costs through multinational organisations. In this way, private enterprises inside America would be encouraged to provide technical assistance to develop farms, commerce and industry in developing countries. In addition, increasing joint contributions to multilateral organisations would help reduce the costs endured by the US government, while internationalising actions that were vital for US interests. In fact, this was an effort to strengthen the US economy and help achieve domestic interests through assistance.

To anchor support for his agenda, Nixon established a Presidential Task Force on International Development in September 1969 chaired by Rudolph Peterson, the President of the Bank of America. Aligning with Nixon's wishes, the 'New Approach' to foreign aid suggested by the Task Force, echoed Nixon's view. It suggested an emphasis on military aid under the authority of the executive branch while economic assistance would be channelled through an International Development Corporation (instead of USAID). The development programme would be funded by a three-year programme for foreign assistance, which would give the executive branch considerable flexibility and render aid funds more fungible. This suggestion would have given the President substantial room to manoeuver on matters of military aid and reduce the costs and involvement of the government in economic aid programmes (Ruttan, 1996: 96–98).

The Senate rejected Nixon's foreign assistance bill. The realities of the American conflict in Vietnam, together with a bill authorising considerable authority to the President to dispense funds for military assistance, as well as a suggestion that economic aid to developing countries should be managed in a business-like fashion – did not sit well with the legislators (Butterfield, 2004: 114). Congressional committees were working in parallel on new legislation in order to introduce comprehensive changes to the Foreign Assistance Act and reduce the influence of the executive branch on the programme (Nowels, 2007: 257). In 1973, Congress introduced amendments to the Foreign Assistance Act initiating 'New Directions' in development assistance. These reflected a further emphasis on humanitarianism and recognition of the global interdependence of the economic system. It also reflected the growing influence of interest groups, especially those who pushed for a human rights agenda alongside arguments to strengthen the US economy through exports to underdeveloped countries, and the creation jobs in the US (Ruttan, 1996: 113–114).

The relationship between US foreign assistance and world peace was sketched in the context of increased globalisation and interdependence of states. In a document outlining to Congress recommendations for new direction in development assistance, USAID explained the main objectives of the programme as: to strengthen the US capability to serve as a negotiator of peaceful solutions in conflicts; to deliver post-conflict economic and humanitarian help to alleviate suffering; to deliver assistance to combat poverty and its implications; and to build the ability to intervene with assistance when natural or manmade disasters occurred (USAID, 1975). Appendix 1 of the document USAID links the assistance programme and US foreign policy through contributions to world peace. USAID argued that the objectives of foreign assistance, are not only consistent with American values, generosity and humanitarianism, but are also important for American business and industry. Developing countries were essential sources for raw materials needed for production. In turn, developing countries depended on American exports, technology and skills for economic, institutional and industrial development to exploit resources. According to this document, a policy of isolationism in a globalised world could lead to negative outcomes for the US and the global economy including increases in oil and gas prices. (USAID, 1975: Appendix I).

To address the 'food and energy crisis' and maintain access to raw materials, USAID proposed an approach that concentrated development assistance in three main sectors: food and nutrition; population and health; and education and development of human resources. Programmes would focus on reaching the poor, reforming government institutions, and gender empowerment to further develop these sectors (USAID, 1975: Article IIA and Appendix I).

The rise of the civil rights and anti-war movements led to a growing awareness of human rights issues. This is reflected in presidential narratives from the Kennedy administration onwards, where the emphasis is expanded from the anti-communist discourse with a heavy weight placed on a security rationale, towards a value-based rationale with economic interests and human rights justifications for the policy. During the Nixon administration, Congress moved to reduce presidential powers over the assistance programme, subjecting it to stricter oversight and control. This trend culminated in 1971 when Congress rejected the Foreign Assistance Bill for the first time since WWII (Callaway and Matthews, 2008: 41). The disagreements between Congress and the executive branch on the nature and purpose of the foreign assistance continued during the Ford administration.

Gerald Ford assumed his role as President in the shadow of the Watergate scandal and the final stages of the Indochina wars. The situation led to congressional pressure on the executive branch, and severe domestic opposition to the war in Vietnam. An unelected President Ford had to deal with a democratic Congress elected during the Watergate scandal that sought to limit the power of the executive branch to provide assistance without consulting Congress first (Kissinger, 2003: 425). The disagreements between the executive branch and Congress on foreign assistance were partly an expression of tensions between the administration's national security strategy and human rights issues as viewed by Congress. Many in Congress opposed the Nixon–Kissinger realpolitik which tended to place national security above all other considerations, even at the cost of pursuing problematic or even illegal policies (Callaway and Matthews, 2008: 41).

Aware of these tensions, Ford sought to build an atmosphere of collaboration and compromise with Congress. Nevertheless, Congress introduced several restrictions to the Foreign Assistance Act of 1974, as well as a number of restrictions on development appropriations throughout the Ford administration to which the President objected.

In 1976, Ford vetoed the Congress Foreign Assistance Bill Authorisation S. 2662 for FY1977. He believed Congress violated the constitutional separation of executive and legislative branches (Ford, 1976). The bill imposed a ceiling on arms sales; required the US to restrict foreign assistance to countries that violated human rights standards set by Congress; removed trade restrictions with North and South Vietnam; and subjected the authorisation of military assistance and advisory groups to Congress. Ford saw this as direct interference with the President's constitutional responsibilities, handicapping the ability of the executive branch to 'implement coherent and consistent foreign policy' (Ford, 1976).

Incorporating human rights as criteria for foreign aid was considered by some in Congress as a vital component of national security. Assistance to other governments was often interpreted as formal approval from the US to regimes it supported, and by extension acceptance, if not support, of their practices. Disregarding human rights criteria was believed to hamper US power by seemingly granting legitimisation to problematic regimes through assistance (Apodaca, 2006; Cohen, 1982: 247).

## *The Carter administration*

Coming out of the Vietnam conflict and the amoral Nixon–Ford–Kissinger administrations which openly disregarded Congressional legislation on human rights since its enactment in 1973 (Cohen, 1982: 249), Carter who had initially framed his calls for the US to be moral and good, shifted to the language of human rights. According to Nancy Mitchell (2016: 88) Carter campaigned more on the restoration of core values and US redemption and not on human rights despite those who argue the contrary (for example, Carleton and Stohl, 1985: 214; Apodaca, 2006: 55; Peck, 2010: 45).

The election of Jimmy Carter reflected the domestic criticism of the late 1960s and 1970s including the anti-Vietnam protests, the Watergate affair, and growing public awareness of human rights abuses by oppressive regimes (Peck, 2010: 53–58). This was also expressed through congressional criticism of a foreign policy that offered support to oppressive regimes to achieve national security, economic and anti-communist agendas (Peck, 2010: 45). Carter promised to bring back the basic idealism upon which the nation was founded, pledging to pursue the course that emphasised the moral righteousness of the American way (Ambrose and Brinkley, 1997: 219; Apodaca, 2006: 55; Peck, 2010: 45). The Vietnam War led to open contestations of containment and questioned the very basic premises of American ideology to the point that many Americans viewed their country as destructive, which led to substantial shifts in public opinion. Ambrose and Brinkley (1997: 216) note that the war in Vietnam linked the containment of communism to the death of thousands of Americans and Vietnamese.

In his inaugural address, Carter detailed his commitment to human rights and pledged America's support to fight poverty, ignorance and injustice based on its founding ideals. Absent from his speech was the narrative that related foreign assistance directly to US national security and communism. His emphasis was on approaching foreign policy based on moral considerations because it was the essence of America, and consequently best served America's interests. He wanted to eliminate US interventions abroad that contradicted the ideals upon which the American society functioned domestically (Carter, 1977).

Carter's efforts to improve the foreign assistance programme began immediately. In March 1977, he sent a message to Congress to present his plan. He tried to address the criticism accumulated against the programme over the years, and to underline the moral principles that would guide it henceforth (Carter, 1977a).

In order to consolidate the foreign assistance activities of the government and improve their effectiveness, Carter proposed to create an International Development Coordination Administration (IDCA).[20] In his first message to Congress on the plan to create the IDCA, Carter's focus was on improving the efficiency and effectiveness of spending and efforts to encourage growth of developing economies (Carter, 1979). However, Congress raised some concerns on the proposed legislation reflecting various interests and resistance from different agencies involved, such as USAID and the Peace Corps who would lose control of significant parts of their programmes and activities under the new plan (Ruttan, 1996: 448).

As noted by Apodaca (2006: 58), the realities of domestic and international politics overshadowed Carter's intentions. His human rights emphasis was often criticised as naïve, disconnected from reality, and even as a threat to America's interests and influence overseas. His attempts to manoeuver between his moral convictions and the criticism against him led to policies, messages and decisions that seemed to be inconsistent and erratic.

The emphasis on the political, economic and security interests of the US was more pronounced towards the end of Carter's term. It reflected both the need to address the criticisms against his policy, the unfolding of global events (such as the Soviet invasion of Afghanistan in 1979 and the Iran hostage crisis), and the growing threat of global terrorism. Carter emphasised that foreign assistance is a tool that allows the president to meet 'promptly and effectively ... unforeseen foreign policy and security emergencies' (Carter, 1980). Carter explained to Congress that foreign assistance is used to stabilise and enhance economic prosperity of 'developing countries, already important markets for US exports, and whose participation in the world economy is steadily increasing' (Carter, 1980).

Carter's rhetoric over the years indicated that he meant to inject his idealism into both the economic and security aspects of the foreign assistance programme. Nevertheless, America's politics, national security and foreign policy interests overshadowed his intentions to base assistance on idealism, and remained as significant considerations for aid allocations throughout his administration (Apodaca, 2006: 59). In certain cases, oppressive regimes and human rights abusers received assistance despite the formal rhetoric (Carleton and Stohl, 1985: 216). Concerns such as influence, national security, political opposition and bureaucratic complications within the administration led to decisions that contradicted the official policy, and resulted in aid allocations that continued to support oppressive regimes (Callaway and Matthews, 2008: 44–45). In fact, some scholars claim that Carter's foreign policy was remarkably similar to the Nixon–Ford–Kissinger policy, and that the main difference was in the rhetoric (Carleton and Stohl, 1985: 214). In practice, Carter had to give precedence to national security concerns, while he was able and willing to concede some diplomatic and economic interests to pursue his human rights agenda (Carleton and Stohl, 1985: 224). His efforts to do this were also limited by the notion that the Cold War was a zero-sum game. The sense of weakness stemming from Vietnam and the hostage crisis led Americans to exaggerate Soviet strength and to underestimate the difficulties faced by the Soviet Union (Mitchell, 2016: 689).

The energy crisis of 1979[21] that began with the disruption of production in Iran, and the Iraq–Iran war from 1980 to 1988 led to a global rise in oil prices and Carter's unpopular efforts to reduce US dependence upon Middle Eastern oil. The international debt of developing countries had risen, and resulted in severe inflation and an economic crisis that shifted the focus of assistance from an emphasis on human needs and the rural poor, towards macro-economic policies targeting assistance to governments in developing countries to address their debt management (Butterfield, 2004: 199). This led to a new shift in US foreign assistance which suited the views held by Ronald Reagan.

## The Reagan administration

The main criticisms offered by Reagan and his advisors to Carter's foreign policy revolved around the human rights approach, the scale of the Soviet threats, and foreign assistance to the Third World. The principal division between Reagan and Carter goes back to the fundamental distinction between idealism and realism in the American approach to policy.

Carter believed that American leadership was legitimised by the ideals upon which the nation was established. While sharing the fundamental beliefs in American foundational mythologies, Reagan measured Carter's foreign policy by the impact of the human rights approach on the ability of America to influence global political dynamics and secure its interests and way of life. Kirkpatrick[22] (1979) attributed Carter's approach to Brzezinski's analysis of a world beyond the Cold War where global perspectives driven by scientific and technological advances will lead to common understandings that will transcend culture and politics, and diminish individual nation state perspectives (Brzezinski, 1970: 274). In such a world, projecting power through economic leverage will gain importance and will be seen as a more legitimate tool than overt political coercion. Brzezinski argued that to maintain leadership role in such a world, the US should assume an increasingly depoliticised approach to foreign assistance (Brzezinski, 1970: 288).[23] Kirkpatrick labelled Brzezinski's outlook as an overly optimistic, deterministic and moralistic approach. She believed it would lead US foreign policy towards support of economic change in the Third World out of commitment to promote a perception of constructive global change, rather than protecting American interests and national security (Kirkpatrick, 1979).

Reagan argued that Carter's human rights approach led to withholding support to friendly autocratic regimes (such as Iran and Nicaragua) resulting in the loss of valuable allies and customers for American products. He believed that the collapse of such regimes weakened the overall position of America in the world. Instead of moderate pro-American right-winged autocrats, the US now faced radical pro-Soviet left-winged totalitarians with an even worse human rights record of accomplishment. In addition, he criticised Carter's hesitant reaction to the collapse of allied regimes (such as the Shah in Iran), which, he thought, signalled to other friendly regimes and potential allies that the US was unreliable (Carleton and Stohl, 1985: 205).

Despite his criticism, Reagan also believed that the issue of human rights was a foundational component of American ideology (Apodaca, 2006: 82). But he also found Carter's approach to be misguided, and therefore redefined the concept of human rights to support his anti-Soviet ideology and strengthen the regimes that helped serve that purpose (Callaway and Matthews, 2008: 55–56). For Reagan, the struggle between the US and the Soviet Union was a battle between good and evil, freedom and tyranny, prosperity and oppression (Apodaca, 2006: 83). He labelled international terrorism (anti-state attacks) as a human rights violation, and identified the Soviet Union as the instigator of terrorism, thus linking human rights abuses to communism (Apodaca and Stohl, 1999: 186). In practice, Reagan focused on fighting the expansion of communism, and gave support to people and groups that actively fought against communist regimes in the Third World (Apodaca, 2006: 86).

Shortly after he took office, Reagan began shifting the focus of foreign assistance to serve his concept of foreign policy. He believed that bilateral programmes would better serve the security and economic interests of the US. He sought to limit US involvement in multilateral efforts, where it was harder to advance military and security concerns (Ruttan, 1996: 121). While keeping an undertone of idealism in his approach, Reagan believed that the main purpose of foreign assistance was to serve the national security interests of the US (Reagan, 1981).

To address the growing dissatisfaction of Congress with aid, Reagan formed a Commission on Security and Economic Assistance chaired by Deputy Secretary of Defence, Frank Carlucci. The mandate of the commission was to examine the relationship between security and development assistance and issue recommendations to improve the coherency of foreign assistance. Secretary of State Shultz stated that the report would help improve the assistance programme and ground it in US national interests (Shultz and Reagan, 1984). Reagan noted that beyond moral duties, economic and security assistance lead to strong alliances and partnership that help bolster a safer world and the national security of the US (Shultz and Reagan, 1984).[24]

Ruttan (1996: 122) explains that US foreign assistance under the first Reagan administration was based on two guiding principles. The first rested on the four pillars of development assistance[25] based on the tenet that people in developing countries should be helped to help themselves. The second principle outlined by Secretary of State, George Schultz, linked development assistance to economic and security interests by stressing that America's economic well-being is dependent on economic growth in the Third World, and that security and peace for the American people were linked to stability and peace in developing countries. These two principles reflect the struggle to connect idealism and realism in foreign policy, and to underline the importance of development assistance as the selected tool for the task. The main challenge for the Reagan administration was to 'fit the rhetoric of the four pillars into a foreign policy design that secured US national interests' (Ruttan, 1996: 122), or in other words, to devise a development assistance programme that spoke the language of idealism, while designed to serve US national interests.

During the second Reagan administration, the premises of the Cold War strategies began to change. The cracks in the Iron Curtain led to improved relations between the US and the Soviet Union. The US began to strengthen its economic ties with the Soviet satellite states, and long-term economic stabilisation gained increased importance in foreign assistance rhetoric (Ruttan, 1996: 131–132). The collapse of the Soviet Union led to a redefinition of US interests in Third World countries. There was a growing understanding that without the Soviet threat, American interests no longer lay primarily in military and security concerns; a new focus on economic, political and humanitarian issues in the Third World would best serve America (Sewell and Contee, 1987: 1016). Faced with budget deficits, Congress together with Secretary of Treasury Baker, sought to modify the emphasis of foreign assistance from security to development with the objective of creating growth in the Third World and resolving debt problems (Ruttan, 1996: 132).

The shifting global tides led to an increased international collaboration. Towards the end of the Reagan administration, the US had decreased its overall assistance levels, focusing investments on growth and channelling more funds through multilateral assistance. Reagan remained committed until the end to the support of democracy against communism, including open support and funding to the Nicaraguan Democratic Resistance fighting against the leftist Sandinista National Liberation Front that had overthrown the US-supported dictator Anastasio Somoza, and supported the military ruler of Guatemala, General Efrain Montt. Until the end of his tenure, Reagan remained true to his outlook that linked American idealism, exceptionalism and realism that judged the world as a struggle between forces of good and evil (Reagan, 1988) thereby supporting anti-communist rulers in Africa and Central America.

In the battle between the USSR and the United States, America won. The US became the sole hegemonic power after the collapse and fragmentation of the Soviet Union and its ideology. With these dramatic events, foreign assistance required change and rethinking to adapt to the new dynamics of international and domestic economics (Ruttan, 1996: 454).

## Foreign assistance after the collapse of the Soviet Union

### *The George H. W. Bush administration*

When Bush entered the White House, he brought with him the knowledge of a seasoned public servant who had the widest foreign policy experience since Eisenhower (Barilleaux and Rozell, 2004: 115). Bush was a conservative pragmatist who believed in prudence. He viewed the Reagan presidency as generally successful, and aimed at continuing with similar policies while gradually introducing improvements. He did not believe in ideological crusades and preferred a cautious approach to the various challenges he faced. One of his major strategies was to constantly work to achieve consensus before committing to action. Bush worked hard to reconcile Congress after years of strenuous relationship between the executive and legislative branches which characterised the late Reagan administration. This management style underlined the way Bush addressed the unique challenges of his short presidency.

Bush faced some of the most complicated and unique challenges an American president has had to address in decades. Most notably, Bush was the first president since WWII to formulate a national security doctrine that did not include a containment strategy. He called it a change of 'almost Biblical proportions' (Bush, 1992); a new world order. With President Gorbachev's resignation and Yeltsin replacing him, the Soviet Union was dissolved in December 1991. The US became the dominant world power and emerged as the victor of the Cold War. It meant that a president and his staff members who built their entire careers in the reality of a bi-polar world (Kegley, 1989: 727) needed to free themselves from the Cold War blinders and devise a fresh foreign policy for a new reality.

'The single most unifying rationale for foreign AID' was, according to Zimmerman[26] (1993: 191) the Cold War. The other major rationale – expansion of world trade and global economy – became the most important endeavour now that the Cold War was over (Butterfield, 2004: 217). Bush believed that the US needed to assume its responsibility and moral obligations as the sole superpower, and engage globally as the leader of the free world (Kegley, 1989: 719). Against this backdrop, America had to deal with domestic struggles, including a weakening economy, soaring crime, collapsing infrastructure and poor education and health systems (Bush, 1989; Kegley, 1989: 729; Lundestad, 1993: 246–247f). On the global level, a number of major international challenges emerged, including the events that led to the US invasion of Panama, the Iraqi invasion of Kuwait and subsequent Gulf war, the Madrid Peace Conference of 1991, the Earth Summit, the Somali civil war and the North American Free Trade Agreement (NAFTA), to name a few.

One way to observe the adjustments made by the US to a new world order through examining the changes in the National Security Strategy (NSS) during the transition period away from the Cold War. As a result of the Goldwater-Nichols Department of Defence Reorganisation Act (1986), the President was required to report to Congress his strategic national security vision on an annual basis. The conceptual transition is clearly illustrated through the NSS published in 1987, 1988, 1990, 1991 and 1993. Snider (1995: 6–10) notes that as of 1988, the NSS reflected the realisation that national interests were increasingly detached from a military contest against the Soviet Union, towards an emphasis on domestic prosperity as a foundation for US leadership in a post-Cold War era. The incorporation of US economic policy as an element of national power received increasing attention. The most fundamental changes to the NSS occurred in 1991 (Jordan et al., 2009: 59). Devised under the Bush administration, the strategy shifted the prism of national security towards regional challenges affecting military, political and economic interests. Snider (1995) also notes that the choice of the instruments of power shifted from military power instruments popular during the Reagan administration towards soft power elements such as diplomacy and economic tools during the Bush administration.

Bush believed in an American leadership for peaceful change. He saw the increasing importance of global interdependencies in a post-Cold War world. The role of the US was to assume the responsibility of leadership and seize the opportunity to secure its interests through globalising its ideals. Bush stated in his preamble to the last NSS document authored by his administration, published shortly before the onset of the Clinton administration, that 'the impoverished, the oppressed, and the weak have always looked to the United States to be strong, to be capable, and to care. Perhaps more than anything else, they have depended on us to lead' (NSS, 1993). He re-iterated his position that global peace can be achieved by adhering to democratic values as a basis for the freedom of people and free economies. He called it the 'Age of Democratic Peace' (NSS, 1993). To achieve and maintain a position of global leadership in an interdependent world, the US had to renew its 'domestic vitality – in economic productivity, investment, technology, education and energy' (NSS, 1993). This was to be the 'peace dividend' of a post-Cold War era where military spending would decrease, freeing funds for economic spending and new investments on domestic levels (Jordan *et al.*, 2009: 59).

The Bush administration identified five major interconnected policy objectives for a new world order that could be addressed through the foreign assistance programme (Baker, 1991):

1 To promote global cooperation for a transition to democracy based on the American ideals of respect for human rights, free and fair elections and political and economic freedom.
2 To promote free market principles and encourage deregulation, privatisation, free trade and investment in order to 'graduate' countries towards developing a friendly environment to US exports, which in turn will help creating jobs domestically and strengthen US competitiveness.
3 To assume a leadership role in the mediation of regional conflicts to promote peace. Recipients of security assistance are viewed as vital allies through their acknowledgment and support of American leadership on issues of peace, security and non-proliferation.
4 To acknowledge and deal with transnational threats, both domestically and globally. This necessitates the identification and acceptance of potential hazards to global security and welfare posed by environmental degradation, crime and terrorism.
5 To assume global leadership in addressing humanitarian needs through responding to natural and man-made disasters.

The strategy devised by Secretary of State Baker to achieve these objectives relied on Congress allowing further flexibility in the structure of foreign assistance accounts to match the quick pace of geopolitical changes. To promote American interests Baker suggested strengthening multilateral institution; promoting understanding together with partners on common agendas and goals; using trade and investment policies more creatively to promote interests; enhancing US economic strength; and pursuing a more vigorous US diplomacy. Baker believed that bilateral assistance (military and economic) would be the most essential tool to advance interests in the 1990s.

In many ways, the state of disarray in which USAID found itself during the late Reagan and the Bush administrations (Butterfield, 2004: 217; Ruttan, 1996: 459–460) is a testimony both to the declining position of development assistance and to the lack of clarity about its role in the new world order. These elements converged with weak leadership in USAID and a Congress that was demanding reduced foreign assistance expenditure (Ruttan, 1996: 439). Together, these reflect the struggle to redefine and justify the concept and purpose of development assistance in a post-Cold War reality despite the foundational idealism underlying the justifications for the programme. Aid was used mainly to promote the interests and objectives of the US. A USAID report from 1989 concluded that aid helped to increase the dependency of recipients on assistance rather than bolstering their own development. Zimmerman (1993: 3–4) explains this as a reflection of the importance of political agendas over development objectives.

Despite the many voices calling for reforming foreign assistance, Bush failed to pass a new agenda for the programme (Ruttan, 1996: 455). This is attributed to both the weakness of USAID administrators,[27] and the lack of priority given to the agency by Secretary of State Baker. The new policy challenges outlined by Baker were translated into a re-draft of the Foreign Assistance Act submitted to Congress in 1991. But the lack of commitment on the part of the administration expressed itself in exerting only minimal efforts to secure its passage (Ruttan, 1996: 460). Congress rejected the administration's reform on the grounds that it would allow too much discretionary authority to the executive branch.

Apodaca (2006: 119–121) notes that while Bush's rhetoric implied a new world order, his actions reflected his inclination to pragmatism and his tendency to introduce changes through slow bureaucratic procedures aimed at maintaining the status quo. In practice, Bush pursued human rights policies only when there were no costs. His foreign policy strategy advanced US interests before idealism.

The Bush years are thus characterised by the need to redefine and adapt foreign policy to a new reality. USAID administrator Ronald Roskins who was appointed in 1990, began a process of reformulating a coherent new post-Cold War strategy for USAID in support of advancing economic liberalisation and democracy (Butterfield, 2004: 219). But Congress continued to cut foreign assistance appropriation regularly in the following years; this was a trend that continued during the Clinton administration.

## The William J. Clinton administration

'It's the economy, stupid' – was one of the main messages conveyed by Bill Clinton during his successful presidential bid in 1992. Indeed, the economy was at the heart of Clinton's two-term tenure in the White House and guided his priorities in both foreign and domestic policies (Apodaca, 2006: 162; Brinkley, 1997: 113; Clinton, 1993).

Clinton entered the White House as the first president who did not have the Soviet Union as a direct threat to US national security. For the first time since WWII, a presidential candidate could run for office using domestic challenges as his prime ticket without the need to invoke containment of the Soviet Union (Apodaca, 2006: 138; Hyland, 1999: 18; Mandelbaum, 1996: 19). While Clinton did focus mostly on domestic issues rather than international affairs in his White House bid, he inherited Bush's 'new world order' multinational doctrine in practice: US marines were engaged in Somalia, the navy was in Haiti, and the air force in Iraq (Albright and Woodward, 2003: 141; Brinkley, 1997: 112; Mandelbaum 1996: 16). The United Nations (UN), responding to an American initiative, imposed economic sanctions on Bosnia, and sanctioned a European-led 'blue helmet' mission for that country. America was in the process of leading major economic and trade initiatives, including NAFTA and the transformation of the General Agreement on Tariffs and Trade (GATT) into the World Trade Organisation (WTO). The reality during the first months of the Clinton administration was of a US heavily engaged in world affairs as the sole superpower, committed to several military missions and multinational economic and trade policies.

From the beginning of his tenure, Clinton tried to relate domestic challenges to foreign issues. Similarly to Bush, he understood that the new post-Soviet reality meant greater international interdependence. He appropriated jargon such as 'world economy', 'world environment', 'world AIDS crisis', 'world arms race' and agreed that assuming a leadership role would help shape a world of opportunities for the US economy (Ambrose and Brinkley, 1997: 402; Clinton, 1993). He promised that his engagement with the world would be based on protecting peace and prosperity at home by promoting international security through a global market economy, international co-operation, the pursuit of human rights and the enlargement of democracy (Albright and Woodward, 2003: 429; Apodaca, 2006: 137; Peck, 2010: 177–178) .

Clinton was heavily criticised in the beginning of his presidency for not articulating a coherent 'grand strategy', and for reducing foreign policy to 'band-aid diplomacy' (Albright and Woodward, 2003: 141; Brinkley, 1997:

113; Snider and Nagl, 2001: 134). This criticism intensified after 18 US army rangers were killed in Mogadishu, a failed intervention in Haiti, a lack of firm response against the Serbian ethnic cleansing in Bosnia (Mandelbaum, 1996: 16), and the failure to intervene with the UN during the Rwandan Genocide (Des Forges, 2004; Power, 2002: 329–389).

Clinton's National Security Advisor, Anthony Lake, attempted to devise a clear foreign policy strategy that would link international affairs to domestic challenges in a way that was consistent with the statements Clinton made in his inaugural address concerning domestic issues (Brinkley, 1997: 114). The new doctrine had to include tangible benefits to the American people to justify US involvement in world affairs and to be consistent with the domestic ticket that won Clinton his presidency. Lake's challenge was to link between engagement in the world and the welfare of the American people, using idealism in conjunction with American interests in the absence of a major and clear national security threat.

On 27 September 1993, Clinton outlined before the UN General Assembly his democratic enlargement strategy which explained how America related to a post-Cold War world as the sole superpower committed to global leadership. He identified two forces threatening to undermine the sovereignty of nation states: an external force – globalisation, and an internal force – nationalism. From the global perspective, economic opportunities drove the world towards integration and political liberalisation, which reduced the independence of national economies. From a nation state perspective, the reduced economic security of individuals as a result of decreased insularity and increased dependence of national economies, was woven together with the absence of the Soviet Union. Former Soviet satellite and dependent states were now free to repossess their national, religious and ethnic identities. These inner forces gave birth to domestic, religious and ethnic awakenings that threatened the traditional nation state (Clinton, 1993). Clinton promised that America would assume leadership and remain engaged to address these challenges through supporting the expansion of market-based democracies. He explained that democracies lead to prosperity and increased co-operation, thus encouraging the formation of a global community of nations co-existing peacefully.

Clinton understood that to sustain leadership, military force and economic power, America must revitalise its own economy (Brinkley, 1997: 120). The key to this end lay in a foreign policy that promoted the adoption of free market principles, especially in the former Soviet satellite states and Latin America (Clinton, 1993). Free market and trade works best in democratic settings and where human rights are upheld (Clinton, 1993). Such conditions create the necessary security and peaceful conditions for the promotion of trade agreements (Clinton, 1993). With this, Clinton sought to promote national security, American ideology and moral obligations (Clinton, 1993).

These aspirations are reflected in the NSS documents published between 1994 and 2000. Clinton's policy is echoed in the different titles of the NSS documents, modified from 'National Security Strategy of the United States' to 'A National Security Strategy of Engagement and Enlargement' (1994–1996), 'A National Security Strategy for a New Century' (1997–1999), and 'A National Security Strategy for a Global Age' (2000).[28] All titles reflect Clinton's strategy to enhance America's engagements in international affairs from a leadership position, aiming at globalising the core American values of democracy, free market and respect for freedom. Snider and Nagl (2001: 135) note that Clinton's NSS contained a different vision for America's security in the absence of a military threat. This transition was based on the recognition of opportunities that help create a safer and more prosperous America alongside security challenges. Theoretically, this meant that the US can, and mostly likely should, engage with the world using a different type of power, a transition from coercion through military might and economic incentives to a strategy of co-option to protect the American people, the American territory and the American way of life.[29]

Criticism against Clinton's foreign policy highlighted that his engagement and enlargement strategy lacked concrete focus and long-term planning. The criticism indicated that often his decisions were based on popularity criteria rather than a grand strategic design (Hyland, 1999: 203). In practice, there was a gap between the idealistic intentions voiced by Clinton, and his foreign policy practice, which was often hesitant (Apodaca, 2006: 138; Callaway and Matthews, 2008: 58–59; Hyland, 1999: 25). Some critics believe that this eventually led to the domestic and global weakening of US hegemonic power and of the presidency as an establishment (Hyland, 1999: 203–204).

Since the end of the Cold War foreign assistance needed to be reformulated in order to convince Congress and the American people that it merited budgetary support. Many voices criticised the assistance programme claiming that USAID, for example, had become inefficient, overemployed, surrounded by complicated bureaucracies and needed to be streamlined and reinvented (Ruttan, 1996: 466–467).

Shortly after he assumed office, Clinton appointed Brian J. Atwood as the new USAID administrator. Atwood identified a number of areas through which USAID could remain relevant to foreign policy in a post-Cold War reality. These areas included global economy, population growth, environmental degradation and political repression (Ruttan, 1996: 467).

The review process of USAID culminated during February 1994 into an AID reform legislation submitted as H.R.3765 to the House for examination (Ruttan, 1996: 468). The proposed bill clarified the relevancy of USAID in the new era, and underlined sustainable development as the post-Cold War assistance policy. It contained a policy statement that explained the links between globalisation and US interests through the promotion of human rights and democracy. Peaceful resolution of conflicts, free and open trade and sustainable use of resources were outlined as the main characteristics of a world that contributes to US interests and ideology. Sustainable development was underscored as the primary goal for US policy. A lack of focus on sustainable development was described as a potential long-term economic burden which could lead to resource scarcity, but also threatens peace and prosperity through political, economic and security turmoil. The importance of democracy was explained through the relationship between the form of government and the free market. Democratic regimes were described in H.R.3765 as peaceful, co-operative and reliable partners who respect human rights and freedom, and promote the resolution of differences in peaceful ways. Addressing the effects of globalisation was described as a platform to domestic economic prosperity that would benefit American workers through the expansion of global markets alongside a prosperous and more secure world. In addition to the clear outline of benefits to American interests through AID programmes based on such objectives, H.R.3765 incorporated the link between AID and the American ideals as an additional justification to maintaining the programme. Diplomacy and foreign assistance were as such crucial tools in a post-Cold War era to strengthen co-operative arrangements with allies and build new relationships based on: the promotion of sustainable development, democracy, growth, trade and investment, building democracy and providing humanitarian assistance.

Despite the rhetoric and intentions, the foreign assistance programme, and especially AID, were continuously downsized during the Clinton administration. Congress continued to cut foreign aid budgets (Callaway and Matthews, 2008: 60), while Vice President Gore's 'rethinking government' initiatives led to substantial staff reductions in USAID (Butterfield, 2004: 222).

While Clinton's rhetoric recalled Carter's idealism, the foreign assistance policy during his tenure was a continuation of past policies where decisions were based on alliances, needs and economic interests (Callaway and Matthews, 2008: 60). Clinton emphasised global peace and prosperity, and talked of the importance of democracy as a condition that leads to international security, free market economy and international co-operation, but he granted foreign assistance support that contradicted this rhetoric (see for example Apodaca, 2006: 144–148; Callaway and Matthews, 2008: 59–60).

As with some of his predecessors, Clinton's idealism was overshadowed by US national interests. Preserving the leadership role of the US in the world, and decisions based on economic gains were the main drivers behind policy in practice (Callaway and Matthews 2008: 61). These trends continued with his successor, George W. Bush, until the US faced another major event that would lead to a major reformulation of national security and foreign policy.

## US foreign assistance after the events of 9/11

*The George W. Bush administration*

As noted by Condoleezza Rice in her memoir, George W. Bush was not the seasoned diplomat his father was; he had virtually no competence in foreign affairs and international politics when he entered the White House (Rice, 2011: 6–7). He seemed almost disinterested in international affairs and diplomacy and preferred involving the US only when interests were imperative, and then mostly in a unilateral fashion (Kane, 2008: 311). Before the events of 9/11, his lack of experience and engagement produced a foreign policy that lacked focus and direction (Callaway and Matthews, 2008: 61).

Very much like his father, destiny brought to his doorstep a formative event. In their magnitude and implications on American domestic and foreign policy, the events of 9/11 proved to be as important as the Japanese attack on Pearl Harbor, the onset of the Cold War and the dissolution of the Soviet Union. The fall of the Iron Curtain led to the loss of an enemy that occupied the entire American security and diplomatic apparatus since the end of WWII. The entire system was structured and geared to contain a Soviet threat. The collapse of the Soviet Union led to a complete reformulation of foreign and domestic policies under George H. W. Bush followed by Bill Clinton to fit a 'new world order' paradigm (Adams and Williams, 2010: 223–224). The events of 9/11 introduced a 'new enemy' (Callaway and Matthews, 2008: 61). It gave back policymakers what they lost when the Cold War ended: a clear and tangible foreign policy objective – to fight and defeat global terrorism.

While Al-Qaida had a face, name and flag, it did not have an address as such. As a non-state actor it used guerrilla strategies and hit-and-run tactics. It embedded itself in local populations and exploited weak states and weak governance structures to gain strongholds. It took advantage of poverty and marginalised people to spread doctrines and recruit followers. Most importantly, it had the potential to hit anywhere using terror tactics. The 9/11 attacks forced America not only to retaliate against Al-Qaida, but also to reformulate its entire approach towards global and domestic security risks, and establish a new engagement policy for international and domestic affairs to protect its interests and citizens.

Bush's initial reaction to the 9/11 attacks was to invoke the old 'good versus evil' narrative. He sent a clear message to the world: 'You are either with us, or you are with the terrorists' (Bush, 2001). In practice, this statement represented the onset of a new national security paradigm that shifted the American diplomatic and security apparatus towards a new kind of projection of power. This new doctrine became the main feature of US global engagement throughout the Bush administration.

The immediate American response to the 9/11 attacks was centred on the use of hard power against Al-Qaida in Afghanistan and other places in the world. A war in Iraq was justified by invoking alleged links between Saddam Hussein and terrorism, fearing weapons of mass destruction would reach terrorists. Eventually, the war on terror became global and involved action by countries from every continent.

While hard power was the tool of choice for the Global War on Terror (GWOT), it became clear to the administration that the efforts to combat terrorism must incorporate a more comprehensive effort, including soft power tools such as foreign assistance instruments (Callaway and Matthews, 2008: 62). In his preamble to the NSS (2002), Bush linked American exceptionalism and responsibility to lead, to global freedom and the GWOT. Once again, the justification for the assistance programme was tied to a national security objective and anchored in American exceptionalism.

The war on terror provided a solid foundation for justifying an investment to fight poverty and disease, viewed as the 'recruiting sergeants' for terrorism and extremism. For Bush, however, there was a direct link between 9/11, the role of America in the world, the righteousness of American ideals, and his own religious convictions: 'We fight against poverty because hope is an answer to terror ... because faith requires it and conscience demands it' (Bush, 2002). In his memoir, Bush named the chapter devoted to his development and humanitarian assistance agendas the 'Lazarus Effect' (Bush, 2010: 333–354). For Bush, the resurrection of Lazarus by Jesus was a parable for America's efforts to assist the poor and the sick in Africa and elsewhere in the world. Condoleezza Rice named the chapter in her memoir devoted to the President's development and humanitarian efforts in Africa: 'Bush the African' (Rice, 2011: 225–233). These titles illustrate some of the ideas, convictions and roles behind the development and humanitarian assistance programmes. Bush linked his understanding of essential American values to the idea that America is destined to play the role of a saviour, to the actions that America must take after the 9/11 attacks. The GWOT was a solid justification to pour taxpayers' dollars into assisting poor and suffering people across the globe. Bush emphasised that 9/11 led him to understand that fighting disease and poverty has a bigger purpose than satisfying conscious: '[b]y confronting suffering in places like Africa, America would strengthen its security and collective soul' (Bush, 2010: 336).

Bush decided to devote some foreign policy attention and resources to fight underdevelopment in Africa before America's engagement in GWOT (Bush, 2010: 333–354). Since he regarded the American foreign assistance programmes and the UN multilateral mechanisms as inefficient and ineffective, he preferred committing resources to the Global Fund rather than engaging USAID or contributing through the UN (Bush, 2010: 335–336). He viewed the American assistance programmes as a design fitted to support the anti-communist strategy during the Cold War, implying that necessary adjustments to properly function outside this context were not sufficient (Bush, 2010: 335–336). He also believed that the programmes were 'paternalistic' in their design, attitude and requirements from recipient nations, and decided to introduce reforms, especially after the assistance programme became a part of the GWOT (Bush, 2010: 335–336).

By 2006, development assistance became a major soft power tool that helped strengthen the two pillars of US national security strategy reflecting America's most solemn obligation to protect the security of the American people: fighting against tyranny through the promotion of 'freedom, justice and human dignity', and supporting the expansion of democracy (NSS 2006, preamble by Bush). Underdevelopment was described as a condition that leads to transnational challenges, including spread of diseases, crime and terrorism (NSS 2006, preamble by Bush).

Four major changes were introduced to the aid programme during the Bush administrations:

- The creation of a new development agency – The Millennium Challenge Corporation (MCC).
- The creation of the President's Emergency Plan for AIDS Relief (PEPFAR).
- The creation of the office of the Director of Foreign Assistance (DFA) at the DoS.[30]
- The expansion of the role of the DoD in delivering development, humanitarian and economic aid.

Lancaster (2008: 15) indicates that these reforms constituted the most substantial changes introduced to the programme by any American president since Kennedy. They reflect the combination of idealism and national interest in the strategy behind the development assistance policy.

The MCC was established in 2003 as a new result-oriented programme brought by Bush to the UN Financing for Development Conference held in Mexico in 2002 (Lancaster, 2008: 16). As a new and independent US foreign aid agency for the fight against global poverty, the MCC works through a bilateral development fund called the Millennium Challenge Account (MCA). By establishing the MCC, Bush tried to address a number of issues at once: it was a step in reforming what he viewed as the inefficient and ineffective assistance programme; it was a market-based programme deliverable that addressed his religious convictions; it allowed him to act upon his commitments to several people, especially to an altruist rock star[31] (Bush, 2010: 348–350; Rice, 2011: 225); and it was one of the tools in the fight against global terrorism.

The link between poverty, the GWOT and the MCC was expressed in the speech Bush delivered during the conference in Mexico announcing the creation of the MCC (Bush, 2002; see quote in this chapter, p. 88). It was based on the assertion that there is a link between poverty, weak institutions, corruption and vulnerability to terrorism (NSS, 2002, preamble by Bush).

This was a similar argument to the Cold War assumptions that linked poverty to vulnerability to communist ideology (Lancaster, 2003: 20). Establishing the MCC helped addressing the linkage between poverty and terror by assisting eligible[32] developing countries to address governance, human rights and economic growth issues (ICG, 2005: 29).

Eligibility does not guarantee MCC assistance. Once a country qualifies for assistance, it must submit a plan for review to the MCC board. The plan must be designed with civil society and work towards supporting economic growth and poverty reduction. Even though the MCC is defined as an independent government entity that operates separately from the DoS, the Department of Treasury and USAID, the board of directors of the MCC includes the administrator of USAID, the Secretary or Treasury (Vice Chair of the Board), the US Trade Representative and the Secretary of State (Chairman of the Board).

The PEPFAR agenda is not generally viewed as designed to protect the security of the American people. Indeed, it is difficult to link security to a vast humanitarian endeavour that addresses the suffering and deaths of millions. Nevertheless, the relationship between HIV/AIDS and US national security was made explicit in a number of reports authored by the National Intelligence Council (NIC).[33]

The HIV/AIDS relief plan was announced by the President in the State of the Union address delivered before Congress in January 2003. While arguing the importance of investing money in HIV/AIDS relief abroad, Bush invoked American exceptionalism to justify its role in the battle against evil as the defender of peace and protector of human dignity (Bush, 2003).

PEPFAR took the American commitment to fight HIV/AIDS above and beyond the pre-9/11 promise to support the Global Fund with a contribution of 200 million dollars (Bush, 2010: 336) to 30 billion dollars for five years following FY2008 (Adams and Williams, 2010: 48).

Aside from the moral responsibility to help fight HIV/AIDS and the religious and personal values expressed by Bush based on his understanding of American ideals and values, there were several security-related reasons for investing in HIV/AIDS.

In September 2002, the NIC issued a report discussing the potential impacts of HIV/AIDS on long term strategic interests. The report flagged five countries of strategic importance with a growing HIV/AIDS problem. It emphasised that HIV/AIDS was 'likely to have significant economic, social, political and military implications' (NIC, 2002: 3). HIV/AIDS incapacitated and eventually killed millions. It was feared that the illness would have serious implications for viable work forces in infected countries and would harm economies in various ways. In addition, AIDS was common among soldiers and some in the DoD raised concerns that it may weaken the military power of some countries, and undermine America's efforts to train African units. The authors of the NIC reports viewed HIV/AIDS as a security threat through its impact on populations and economic growth, contributing to the destabilisation of governments (see also Rothchild and Emmanuel, 2005: 89). HIV/AIDS has been mentioned in the National Security Strategies of the US as a transnational threat since 1991. A firmer linkage between security and HIV/AIDS was introduced during the late Clinton administration (Dietrich, 2007) where the potential global economic implications of HIV/AIDS were underlined. Both NSS documents published during the Bush administration (2002 and 2006) highlight the links between poverty and terrorism, and mention HIV/AIDS as one of the main obstacles for development, stability and security (NSS, 2002: 10).

The NSS, published in 2006, lists PEPFAR as the main programme which addresses both the moral imperatives of the US and the security-related challenges of HIV/AIDS (NSS, 2006: 31). Nevertheless, Bush remained consistent in his statements that the fight against HIV/AIDS was mainly a question of conscience tied directly to his religious convictions and his view of America's role in the world (Dietrich, 2007). Today, PEPFAR is lauded as a remarkable achievement of US foreign assistance that advances interests while fulfilling humanitarian values, increasing health security and helping promote stability and long-term development (Morrison, 2013: 1).

Reflecting the impact of 9/11 and the subsequent shifts in US foreign policy, USAID published a White Paper in 2004 addressing the growing role of development assistance in a post-9/11 foreign policy. The paper emphasised links between globalisation and markets, tying poverty to the surge of infectious diseases and corruption, crime and terrorism (USAID, 2004: 3).

The office of the DFA was established first and foremost to create coherency between the two main instruments of soft power available to the President (diplomacy and development), and to ensure that these instruments worked in-sync with programmes led by the DoD (Nowels and Veillette, 2006: 2; Rice, 2008). The creation of the DFA was a part of the transformational diplomacy agenda that recognised the important role of soft power in encouraging the formation of responsible and well-governed states in the world (Lancaster, 2008: 29; Nowels and Veillette, 2006: 2). Randall Tobias, the first DFA, built on USAID's White Paper to establish a strategic framework which categorised countries according to their level and trajectory of progress (Lancaster, 2008: 31). The experiences in Afghanistan and Iraq illustrated the complexity of the post-9/11 security challenges, especially those arising from the inability of certain states to enforce their sovereignty on areas under their control.[34] Failed states and complex emergencies were viewed as principal foreign policy priorities to ensure America's national security, and USAID emphasised its essential role in complementing defence and diplomacy tools (USAID 2004: 3).

The growing role of development assistance in contributing to an overall coherent national security policy was stated numerous times during the Bush administration.[35] The justification arguments linked core American ideals such as liberty, democracy and human dignity to the fight against terrorism and US national security. Linking development and humanitarian assistance to national security also led to an increasing involvement of the DoD beyond traditional mission support and humanitarian roles.

In 2005, the DoD issued Directive 3000.05 to define the purpose and scope of military support for Stability, Security, Transition and Reconstruction Operations (SSTRO). Military operations involving provision of humanitarian assistance, especially in relation to complex emergencies such as natural disasters was not new, nor was the military involvement in various forms of security assistance including training of soldiers and police. The innovation of Directive 3000.05 lies in the roles of the military and other US security agencies in activities which were the professional domain of the DoS and USAID. The Directive emphasises that SSTRO missions will be prioritised in a comparable way to combat operations, and that they will be 'conducted to help establish order that advances U.S. interests and values' (DoD, 2005: 2). Section 4.3 of Directive 3005.05 specifies that stability operations include activities to establish a private sector in target countries, which involves 'encouraging citizen-driven, bottom-up economic activity and constructing necessary infrastructure, and [d]evelop representative governmental institutions' (DoD, 2005: 3). The Directive also specifies that in order to conduct these operations, the DoD will develop its working relationships with civilians and with representatives of various other government agencies, international organisations, NGOs and the private sector (DoD, 2005: 4).

The four major changes to US foreign aid programmes introduced after 9/11 reflect a shift in foreign policy toward securitisation. The President's rhetoric now strongly emphasised American ideals alongside national security and US interests. The focus on the GWOT and the growing importance of security agencies in this context allowed the DoD to appropriate soft power tools into its arsenal. In practice, these changes contributed to the fragmentation of the assistance programme and led to inconsistencies, inefficiencies and ineffectiveness in the deliverance of development and foreign assistance (Adams and Williams, 2010: 45–46, 92; Lancaster, 2008: 46). It also created an increased inconsistency between the rhetoric of idealism, values and human rights associated with aid and the national security, GWOT, and other interests targeted by it (Bacevich, 2010: 22–23; Lancaster 2008: 95; Peck, 2010: 280).

*The Barack Obama administration*

Barack Obama's bid for presidency focused on improving the image of the US damaged by the post-9/11 unilateralism of the Bush administration. This meant redefining America's global role, and within that, balancing the power between defence, diplomacy and development, with a greater emphasis on the last two instruments.

When President Obama entered the White House, America was in crisis. Since the events of 9/11, America has exercised its global leadership mainly through the projection of hard power. By the time Bush moved out of the White House, the American economy was in severe recession. The military was engaged on several fronts, and deployed *en masse* in Afghanistan and Iraq. The popularity of the US as the 'leader of the free world' sank, even with its close allies.[36] And at home, constitutional liberties were threatened by the paradoxical need to preserve them.

The links between the inception of the crisis and the ways in which America was projecting its power since the events of 9/11 have been discussed by several authors (for example, Bacevich, 2008; CSIS, 2007; Johnson, 2010; Nossel 2004). Ending the crisis and restoring America's economic stability and prestige as a leader was of the utmost importance for Obama (Obama, 2009).

There was a certain irony to the situation in which America found itself at the dusk of the Bush administration. Since 9/11, the ability of the US to project hard power has greatly increased with respect to the capacity to deploy and the technological sophistication of its armed forces. It would appear that US power was unmatched and at its peak. There was no doubt that American forces could win every battle they engaged in with very little effective resistance. But despite that, America was losing the war. Not losing the war in the traditional sense when an army is defeated by another, or controlled spaces fall into the hands of the enemy, or regimes are toppled by dissenting forces. Indeed, America had succeeded in defeating militarily, almost without resistance, the armies it was engaging, assuming control over vast geographical spaces, as well as replacing 'enemy' regimes with 'friendly' ones. However, relying on the governments of Iraq and Afghanistan to hold these territories proved fruitless. America's victories were slowly turning into defeats. The economic costs of the wars were underestimated while the housing bubble in the US produced a financial and economic crisis. America's hegemony was weakening while its projection of power created opportunities for emerging economies to advance their own interests.

The paradox of losing the ability to capitalise on winnings while still being the most powerful nation on earth could be epitomised by a phrase articulated by Senator Fulbright four decades earlier, as 'the arrogance of power'. Fulbright was speaking of American power during the Vietnam war. He was not only referring to the weakening of the US due to the tremendous military, human, economic and ethical costs inflicted through the engagement in Indochina. Fulbright was also referring to the economic and cultural impacts the war inflicted on other nations, especially on countries subjected directly to American power. Such impacts led to societal earthquakes that removed the legitimacy of US projections of power, even in the eyes of its allies. These 'fatal impacts', as Fulbright describes them, could slowly transform a legitimate, welcomed application of power into something viewed as an imperial endeavour (Fulbright, 1967: 20–21).

While written about Vietnam, Fulbright words resonate through the post-9/11 GWOT. His description depicts the essence of the crisis faced by President Obama when he assumed office – the gradual but steady decay of American power expressed through the loss of leadership, deterioration of the economy and the ability to compete with other emerging powers, severe antagonism against the arrogant way the war was conducted, and the moral bankruptcy American officials and troops demonstrated during the war.[37] These all occurred while American military power was increasing exponentially. Joseph Nye and Richard Armitage expressed this issue to the Senate Foreign Relations Committee by indicating that the question was not whether or not America was powerful, but whether America was 'perceived as a bully or a friend' (Armitage and Nye, 2008: 2).

As advocated by Armitage and Nye, the Obama administration turned to the concept of 'smart power' in an attempt to regain a balance and halt the decay of American global leadership. The idea was to deploy a full spectrum of tools to effectively cap the drainage of American power and regain legitimacy for leadership by creating a balance between the use of hard and soft power in pursuance of national interests. On her confirmation hearing, Secretary of State Clinton stated that smart power would be the essence of America's foreign policy under the Obama administration, deploying 'the full range of tools at our disposal – diplomatic, economic, military, political, legal, and cultural – picking the right tool or combination of tools for each situation' (Clinton, 2009).

In an address before the Council on Foreign Relations on 15 July 2009, Clinton provided further details of the administration's approach to smart power and the intention to combine 'principles and pragmatism' in an intelligent way through foreign policy in five core areas:

> First, we intend to update and create vehicles for cooperation with our partners; second, we will pursue principled engagement with those who disagree with us; third, we will elevate development as a core pillar of American power; fourth, we will integrate civilian and military action in conflict areas; and fifth, we will leverage key sources of American power, including our economic strength and the power of our example.
> (Clinton, 2009a)

One of the most important strategies was the elevation of development assistance to a core pillar of American power alongside diplomacy and defence. Secretary Clinton explained that to re-establish American leadership and achieve the national interests of the US one must recognise that 'defense, diplomacy and development were not separate entities either in substance or process ... and that the whole of government ... had to be enlisted in their pursuit' (Clinton, 2010). Secretary of Defence Gates, agreed with Secretary Clinton that the role of diplomacy and development are indispensable to secure American interests (Gates, 2010).

To devise a sound strategy for the elevation of diplomacy and development to an equal status of defence as a 'whole-of-government' approach, the DoS launched a review process in July 2009 (Clinton, 2010a). The process, termed QDDR, was the equivalent of the legislatively mandated review of the DoD's strategy and priorities (the QDR). The first QDDR released in December 2010 was subtitled 'Leading Through Civilian Power'. It drew justification from two main documents: the NSS, released in May 2010, and the Presidential Policy Directives on Development (PDD) issued in September 2010.

In the NSS, Obama underlined that America had over-extended its power, leading to a loss of global leadership and national decay. To regain power, he emphasised the need to acknowledge the integrated challenges presented by globalisation. Obama noted that to advance interests, the capabilities of the American military must be integrated with the experience, knowledge and knowhow of diplomats and development experts (NSS, 2010, preamble by the President). The importance of development assistance in the whole-of-government approach to national security was emphasised in the NSS as both a moral imperative, and as a tool of power. Development assistance had the potential to help manage security threats, but also to help create economic opportunities as well as encourage the expansion of 'democratic institutions that serve basic human needs' (NSS, 2010: 15). Development assistance could help America regain its reputation and legitimacy where it has been lost or eroded.

The core elements of the NSS document mentioned above are also featured in the PDD (PDD, 2010: 2). The PDD was issued by President Obama as the formal global development policy of the US. Initially, the administration released information about the document in the form of a fact sheet. The full document was deemed distributable strictly on a 'need-to-know basis' as it communicated 'sensitive foreign policy and national security topics' (PDD, 2010, attached memorandum for recipients).[38] Development assistance was described in the PDD as an essential tool to advance US national security objectives listed as 'security, prosperity, respect for universal values, and a just and sustainable international order' (PDD, 2010: 2). Development assistance would become an essential tool to re-establish the reputation and leadership of the US in a world shaped by new emerging powers competing for resources. It would help mitigate threats from fragile states whose weaknesses inflicted misery on their own population through poverty, hunger and disease and by extension, allow terrorism and transnational crime to prosper (PDD, 2010: 2).

In other words, Obama saw the role of development assistance as a tool which could contribute to the enhancement of American power. But, as he indicated in the PDD, pragmatism was not the only reason to use development assistance; American exceptionalism and the obligation to disseminate the 'just' American values was another. According to the document, the US has a moral obligation to all humankind. Fulfilling this obligation is a service America owes to the world because of its exceptional nature and the position of power it occupies (PDD, 2010: 2). This argument has a circularity to it, since to fulfil this destiny, America needs to be in a position of power to lead and to persuade the world of its just purpose: America can lead through the use of power. Projecting that power in a smart way can grant America legitimacy, and can also help to create a global system which enhances its power base. In this way, the American regime of truth is preserved at home and disseminated globally, which further enhances American power (PDD, 2010: 2–3).

The PDD sought to create a broad-based consensus for the elevation of development assistance to the status of a core pillar of national security alongside diplomacy and defence. Obama stated that the new approach to global development would centre on three elements (PDD, 2010: 4):

1. A focus on development policy outcomes that bring about broad-based economic growth, democratic governance, 'game changing innovations' and systems that help people meet their basic needs.
2. A focus on placing the United States as an effective partner to leverage its leadership through a new operational model.
3. A focus on creating a new architecture where development capabilities are used across government as a pillar of foreign policy.

In this model for development policy, the status of USAID would be elevated, and the administrator of USAID would be granted a seat at the NSC when appropriate. This would require re-building USAID's capabilities which had been slowly deteriorating since the end of the Cold War. The new architecture calls for the establishment of an inter-agency process where development is co-ordinated with defence and diplomacy to create coherency, streamline processes, and avoid duplicity and uniformed interventions. The PDD also recognises the important role played by Congress in terms of development policy and commits to establishing a bipartisan consensus regarding the importance of development in the overall national security architecture.

The opening paragraph of the QDDR sheds light on the way the purpose of development assistance is viewed by the Obama administration as a tool of power to promote American interests and values:

> Somewhere in the world today, a jeep winds its way through a remote region of a developing country. Inside are a State Department diplomat with deep knowledge of the area's different ethnic groups and a USAID development expert with long experience helping

communities lift themselves out of poverty. They are on their way to talk with local councils about a range of projects – a new water filtration system, new ways to elevate the role of women in the community, and so on – that could make life better for thousands of people while improving local attitudes toward the United States.

(QDDR, 2010: 1)

As specified, the QDDR builds on previous initiatives such as transformational diplomacy, introduced during the Bush administration, to find ways to promote coherency between the various arms of government to protect America's interests and project its leadership (QDDR, 2010: 2):

We help prevent fragile states from descending into chaos, spur economic growth abroad, secure investments for American business, open new markets for American goods, promote trade overseas, and create jobs here at home. We help other countries build integrated, sustainable public health systems that serve their people and prevent the spread of disease. We help prevent the spread of nuclear weapons. We support civil society groups in countries around the world in their work to choose their governments and hold those governments accountable. We support women's efforts to become financially independent, educate their children, improve their communities, and help make peace in their countries. This is an affirmative American agenda – a global agenda – that is uncompromising in its defense of our security but equally committed to advancing our prosperity and standing up for our values.

(QDDR, 2010: 2–3)

The QDDR focuses in essence on building and promoting civilian power to better serve the American people and the strategic objectives of the US. It observes the important contribution of civilian power for confronting a wide range of challenges, recognising that soft and hard power mechanisms combined in an intelligible way could help America advance its interests and values through partnership. In this way, America could regain its legitimacy and roll back the damages of the unilateral foreign policy of the Bush administration.

One of the main objectives listed by the QDDR is to elevate the status of USAID to become the pre-eminent global development institution. The document underlines six specific areas where US development efforts would be concentrated: sustainable economic growth, food security, global health, climate change, democracy and governance and humanitarian assistance, emphasising gender and empowerment of women as a main objective in each area (QDDR, 2010: 10).

Both the QDDR and the PDD flag three presidential initiatives where USAID would play a significant role in support of the smart power approach. These are: Feed the Future (FTF), the Global Health Initiative (GHI) and the Global Climate Change Initiative (GCCI). Together these three initiatives represent the core elements of Obama's new development strategy (PDD, 2010: 8).

The FTF initiative is a US contribution to a multilateral commitment undertaken by the G8 in July 2009, and to the global effort to achieve the Millennium Development Goals (MDGs) (FTF, 2010: 1). FTF is a multi-pronged effort aimed at 'addressing the root causes of hunger' (FTF, 2010: vi) by accelerating economic growth through agricultural productivity, enabling the poor to access markets and generate income and combat malnutrition (PDD, 2010: 8). This initiative is led by USAID which promotes food security by supporting country-led initiatives focused on the reduction of hunger. The justification for the FTF links poverty, disease and resource scarcity, to America's national security interests, as well as to moral values and obligations (FTF, 2010: vi).

The GHI builds on the success of PEPFAR to expand the global health effort of the US to improve healthcare systems, address other tropical diseases and contribute to the achievement of the health-related MDGs (PDD, 2010: 8). Similarly to the FTF, the GHI focuses on country-led initiatives to improve health and health systems, and includes a series of objectives such as significant reduction of maternal and young infant mortality, reduction of under-nutrition, prevention of unintended pregnancies, and combat of HIV/AIDS, malaria, tuberculosis and other tropical diseases. In the GHI strategy document, the initiative is described both as a significant contribution to US security and economic interests, as well as a moral obligation (GHI, 2011: 3).

USAID emphasises in its webpages a dual purpose of GHI, invoking both morality and security: the GHI saves lives by fighting diseases and creating a better world; and the GHI protects the security of the US by preventing the spread of diseases that might cross borders and affect the American people (USAID, 2015).

In the PDD, the Obama administration recognises that the future effects of climate change are unavoidable, and as such, the US must engage in bilateral, multilateral and private efforts to build resilience into climate change. Through the GCCI, the Obama administration promotes programmes for the reduction of emissions and the encouragement of the growth of low-carbon societies in developing countries. The role of USAID is to implement GCCI with bilateral assistance, while the DoS (together with the Department of Treasury) assumes the role of promoting GCCI through multilateral mechanisms (Lattanzio, 2013). The initiative has three main components: investing in clean energy, promoting sustainable landscapes and supporting climate change resilience and adaptation. The importance of climate change to US national security and wellbeing, beyond addressing the moral imperatives of its impacts and the serious environmental implications, is described in USAID's Climate Change and

Development Strategy (2012) as a 'threat multiplier', enhancing poverty, social and economic wellbeing and political instability, thus directly threatening national security and economic interests (USAID, 2012: 3–4).

President Obama entered office determined to alter the way in which America interacts with the world. His administration recognised that unilateralism and hard power undermined America's leadership. On the dawn of 9/11, the entire world stood with the US in sorrow, ready to back the country in a war to eliminate terrorism. By the time Bush stepped out of office, the US was seen as a bully state that ignores international opinions and norms, and pursues its own interests unilaterally, driven by GWOT. While Obama was determined to fight terrorism and secure the interests of the US as much as George W. Bush had done, he understood the limits of power. His policy, like policies of many past presidents, was driven by a deep conviction in the exceptional nature of the US (Obama, 2013). So, while the objectives remain the same, the way in which America pursues them, has changed.

## Conclusions

Having traced how 12 US presidents have viewed and pursued development assistance, we find a long and consistent narrative of the specialness of the US place in the world. While US dominance resulted from WWII, it could only be retained by using American power to prevent the spread of communism. An anti-communist ideology and policy focus continued until the end of Reagan's presidency. Adjusting to a world without the Soviet Union proved difficult for both the Bush and Clinton administrations. Clinton's emphasis upon the benefits of globalisation and economic competition provided a clear rationale for development assistance but lacked congressional support in part due to the events in Somalia and Rwanda (see Chapters 4 and 5). The initial bombing of the World Trade Centre in 1993, and the bombings of the American embassies in Nairobi and Dar Es Salam, indicated the US would face grave new difficulties in its global leadership. With the destruction of the World Trade Centre in 2001, and the resultant GWOT, the US turned to its military to try to contain what it regarded as new threats to its security and well-being. As part of the US response to terrorism, it formed a new military entity, AFRICOM (see Chapter 6), increasing the US military's activities in sub-Saharan Africa. Obama attempted to rebalance the relationship between security and development activities. He has, like past presidents, relied upon the idea that the US is a special nation with a special role to play in the world. And it is development assistance which can change lives in poor African nations while protecting American security, thus continuing the regime of truth. How the dynamics of development assistance and how the US has acted in changing African historical contexts forms the basis of the next three chapters.

## Notes

1 'Ye are the light of the world. A city that is set on an hill cannot be hid'. King James bible version of Matthew 5:14.
2 For a thorough and critical analysis on the role of Alger's narratives and the production of the American 'regime of truth' see Nackenhoff (1994).
3 In the American myth, this is often associated and accomplished by 'going West' towards the new frontiers. A substantial body of literature discusses the seminal idea forwarded by Frederick Jackson Turner (1894) on the importance of 'frontiers' in American history.
4 Through politics or by becoming a successful industrialist.
5 By 'conveying', we mean here three things: first as revealing the fundamental American values to the reader; second, the reproduction of these values in discursive practices, which we later highlight in relation to the development assistance discourse; and third, as the American conception of development, that is the possibility to develop by accepting these values.
6 A common analysis of this sentence quoted from the American Declaration of Independence refers to John Locke's *Two Treatise on Government* where he asserts the God-given rights for 'life, health, liberty and property', thus linking Jefferson's *Pursuit of Happiness* with accumulation of property.
7 Referring to the sermon given by John Winthrop on board the flagship *Arbella* before it set sail at the head of a fleet holding a group of the Massachusetts Bay Company colonists on their way to the New World.
8 For a thorough account establishing the influence of the view that America is exceptional in the formulation of foreign policy, see McCrisken (2003).
9 McCrisken (2003: 8–11); Restad (2015: 7); Bell (1989: 41); Brands (1998).
10 We recognise how the US military, private interests and individuals acted outside the law to achieve narrow economic or national interests.
11 We will not consider the US as an imperial power although there is a persuasive literature which does so including Burbank and Cooper (2010); Johnson (2004, 2010).
12 See the Yalta Agreement, Article II.
13 See quote in Chapter 2, p. 33.
14 Senator James William Fulbright was chairman of the Senate Committee on Foreign Relations between 1959 and 1974.
15 Entitled: United States Objectives and Programs for National Security signed by Truman on 30 September, 1950; declassified in 1975.
16 Also known as the Foreign Assistance Act of 1950 (Butterfield, 2004: 18).
17 See Eisenhower (1953b, 1954, 1955, 1956, 1957, 1958, 1959, 1960).
18 See the Foreign Assistance Act, 1961: Chapter 1.
19 Who served as a National Security Advisor to Johnson, succeeding McGeorge Bundy.
20 The creation of the IDCA was based on a bill introduced by former Vice President and Senator Hubert H. Humphrey. It reflected Congress's concern with the growing disorganisation of aid efforts stemming from the plurality of agencies, departments and interests involved (see Ruttan, 1996: 445–450; Butterfield, 2004: 197–198). The IDCA never co-ordinated US policy. It was eventually eliminated from statutes with the introduction of the 1998 Foreign Affairs Reorganisation Act.
21 The first being in 1973 in relation to events in the Middle East.
22 Jeane J. Kirkpatrick, was Reagan's foreign policy advisor. She wrote an article in November 1979 that was brought to Reagan's attention and was later described as an accurate outline of the ideology that guided his criticism of Carter's administration (Carleton and Stohl, 1985: 205, footnote 1).

23 It is important to note that Brzezinski's analysis was still emphasising US national interests and ways to address those in a future where political relationships between nations will not be based on the bi-polar world.
24 Brainard (2007: 258) notes that by the time the commission issued its list of recommendations late in 1983, its relevance was overshadowed by the growing importance of Central America. Consequently, more policy attention was given to the findings of the Kissinger Commission on Population and Development in Central America issued in January 1984.
25 The four pillars were: policy dialogue and reform; institutional development; technology transfer; and private sector development.
26 Robert F. Zimmerman was a development professional with more than 25 years' experience in the Peace Corps, USAID and the DoS.
27 USAID administrator Allan Woods died of cancer in 1989 and was temporarily replaced by his deputy Mark Edelman until 1990 (Butterfield, 2004: 218–219).
28 The NSS, published in 2000, is mostly aimed at documenting the accomplishments of the Clinton administration focusing on the past rather than an outline of a strategy for the future.
29 These three elements appear as the pillars of American security in all the NSSs which were published during the Clinton administration.
30 The name of the office was later modified to The Office of US Foreign Assistance Resources.
31 In reference to Bono, the lead singer of U2.
32 Countries' performances are measured by 17 indicators that determine eligibility for funds.
33 In the US intelligence community, the NIC, is the body that conducts mid- and long-term strategic analysis, and answers to the Director on National Intelligence and the National Security Council.
34 See also the Foreign Assistance Framework in USAID Strategic Plan for FY2007–2012 (DoS, 2007: Appendix A).
35 The rhetoric is present in numerous documents, statements and speeches given by the President and other senior members of the executive branch (for example, Bush, 2005; Natsios, 2006; NSS, 2006; Rice, 2008).
36 See, for example, the document summarising a series of hearings by the Subcommittee on International Organizations, Human Rights and Oversight of the House Committee on Foreign Relations entitled 'The Decline in America's Reputation: Why?', published in 2008.
37 To name a few: the unjustified war in Iraq, the torture of prisoners, the humiliation of prisoners in Guantanamo and the disregard of the sovereignty of nations.
38 The document was the first of its kind and the fact that it was kept away from the public eye was questioned by development scholars and concerned citizens. The Centre for Effective Government, formerly known as OMB Watch, filed for the release of the document under the Freedom of Information Act. The Document was made available to the public in March 2014.

## References

Adams, G. and Williams, C. (2010) *Buying national security: how America plans and pays for its global role and safety at home*. Routledge, New York.

Albright, M. K. and Woodward, W. (2003) *Madam secretary*. Miramax Books, New York.

Ambrose, S. E. and Brinkley, D. (1997) *Rise to globalism: American foreign policy since 1938*. Penguin Books, New York.

Apodaca, C. (2006) *Understanding U.S. human rights policy: a paradoxical legacy.* Routledge, New York; London.

Apodaca, C. and Stohl, M. (1999) United States Human Rights Policy and Foreign Assistance, *International Studies Quarterly* 43: 185–198.

Armitage, R. L. and Nye, J. S. (2008) Implementing Smart Power: setting an agenda for National Security Reform – Statement before the Senate Foreign Relations Committee, 24 April 2008. CSIS.

Bacevich, A. J. (2008) *The limits of power: the end of American exceptionalism.* Metropolitan Books, New York.

Bacevich, A. J. (2010) *Washington rules: America's path to permanent war.* Metropolitan Books, New York.

Baker, J. A. I. (1991) Foreign Assistance funding proposal for FY 1992: statement by Secretary of State James Baker (transcript). US Department of State. 2 (10).

Barilleaux, R. J. and Rozell, M. J. (2004) *Power and prudence: the presidency of George H. W. Bush.* Texas A&M University Press, College Station.

Bell, D. (1989) American Exceptionalism Revisited – The Role of Civil Society, *Public Interest* 95: 38–56.

Brainard, L. (2007) *Security by other means: foreign assistance, global poverty, and American leadership.* Brookings Institution Press, Washington, DC.

Brands, H. W. (1998) *What America owes the world: the struggle for the soul of foreign policy.* Cambridge University Press, Cambridge.

Brinkley, D. (1997) Democratic Enlargement: The Clinton Doctrine, *Foreign Policy* 106: 111–127.

Brzezinski, Z. (1970) *Between two ages: America's role in the technetronic era.* Viking Press, New York.

Burbank, J. and Cooper, F. (2010) *Empires in world history: power and the politics of difference.* Princeton University Press, Princeton, NJ.

Bush, G. H. W. (1989) Inaugural Address, 20 January 1989.

Bush, G. H. W. (1992) Address Before a Joint Session of the Congress on the State of the Union, 28 January 1992.

Bush, G. W. (2001) Address to a Joint Session of Congress and the American People, 20 September 2001.

Bush, G. W. (2002) Remarks by Mr. George W. Bush, President, at the International Conference on Financing for Development, Monterrey, Mexico, 22 March 2002.

Bush, G. W. (2003) Address Before a Joint Session of Congress on the State of the Union, 28 January 2003.

Bush, G. W. (2005) Inaugural Address. 20 January 2005.

Bush, G. W. (2010) *Decision points.* Crown Publishers, New York.

Butterfield, S. H. (2004) *U.S. development aid – an historic first: achievements and failures in the twentieth century.* Praeger Publishers, Westport, Conn.

Callaway, R. L. and Matthews, E. G. (2008) *Strategic US foreign assistance: the battle between human rights and national security.* Ashgate, Aldershot.

Carleton, D. and Stohl, M. (1985) The Foreign-Policy of Human-Rights: Rhetoric and Reality from Jimmy Carter to Ronald Reagan, *Human Rights Quarterly* 7: 205–229.

Carter, J. E. (1977) *Jimmy Carter – Inaugural Address.* 20 January 1977. www.bartleby.com/124/pres60.html (accessed 15 July 2012).

Carter, J. E. (1977a) Foreign Assistance Programs Message to the Congress, 17 March 1977.

Carter, J. E. (1979) International Development Cooperation Administration Message to Congress on the Proposed Agency, 7 March 1979.

Carter, J. E. (1980) International Development and Security Assistance Letter to the Speaker of the House and the President of the Senate Transmitting Proposed Legislation, 27 February 1980.

Clinton, H. R. (2009) Transcript – Senate Confirmation Hearing: Hillary Clinton, *New York Times*, 19 January 2009.

Clinton, H. R. (2009a) Council on Foreign Relations Address by Secretary of State Hillary Clinton, 15 July 2009. Council on Foreign Relations.

Clinton, H. R. (2010) Remarks on the Obama Administration's National Security Strategy – The Brookings Institute, Department of State, 27 May 2010.

Clinton, H. R. (2010a) Leading Through Civilian Power – Redefining American Diplomacy and Development, *Foreign Affairs* 89 (6): 13–24.

Clinton, W. J. (1993) Confronting the Challenges of a Broader World – President Clinton. Address to the UN General Assembly, New York City, 27 September 1993, *US Department of State Dispatch Magazine*, 4 (39). Retrieved from http://dosfan.lib.uic.edu/ERC/briefing/dispatch/1993/html/Dispatchv4no39.html.

Cohen, S. B. (1982) Conditioning United States Security Assistance on Human-Rights Practices, *American Journal of International Law* 76: 246–279.

CSIS (2007) CSIS Commission on Smart Power: A smarter more secure America. Center for Strategic and International Studies, Washington, DC.

Dacy, D. C. (1986) *Foreign aid, war, and economic development: South Vietnam, 1955–1975*. Cambridge University Press, Cambridge; New York.

Des Forges, A. (2004). Learning from disaster – U.S. human rights policy in Rwanda, in D. Liang-Fenton (ed.), *Implementing U.S. human rights policy: agendas, policies, and practices* (pp. 29–50). United States Institute of Peace Press, Washington, DC.

Dietrich, J. W. (2007) The Politics of PEPFAR: The President's Emergency Plan for AIDS Relief, *Ethics & International Affairs* 21: 277–292.

DoD (2005) Directive 3000.05, 28 November 2005.

DoS (2007) Strategic Plan – Fiscal Years 2007–2012: Transformational Diplomacy. Department of State; US Agency for International Development, Washington, DC.

Eberstadt, N. (1988) *Foreign aid and American purpose*. American Enterprise Institute for Public Policy Research; Distributed by arrangement with National Book Network, Washington, DC; Lanham, MD.

Eisenhower, D. D. (1953) Dwight D. Eisenhower: First Inaugural Address. 20 January 1953.

Eisenhower, D. D. (1953a) Special Message to the Congress on the Mutual Security Program. 5 May 1953.

Eisenhower, D. D. (1953b) Letter to the Chairman, Senate Appropriations Committee, on the Mutual Security Program. 23 July 1953.

Eisenhower, D. D. (1954) Special Message to the Congress on the Mutual Security Program. 23 June 1954.

Eisenhower, D. D. (1955) Statement by the President on the Mutual Security Program. 11 April 1955.

Eisenhower, D. D. (1956) Special Message to the Congress on the Mutual Security Program. 19 March 1956.

Eisenhower, D. D. (1957) Special Message to the Congress on the Mutual Security Program. 21 May 1957.

Eisenhower, D. D. (1958) Special Message to the Congress on the Mutual Security Program. 19 February 1958.

Eisenhower, D. D. (1959) Special Message to the Congress on the Mutual Security Program. 13 March 1959.

Eisenhower, D. D. (1960) Special Message to the Congress on the Mutual Security Program. 16 February 1960.

Ford, G. R. (1976) Veto of the Foreign Assistance Bill. 7 May 1976.

FTF (2010) Feed the Future. https://feedthefuture.gov/sites/default/files/resource/files/FTF_Guide.pdf (accessed 15 March 2017).

Fulbright, J. W. (1967) *The arrogance of power*. Random House, New York.

Gates, R. M. (2010) Remarks by Secretary Gates to the Marine Memorial Association, San Francisco, California. Department of Defense, Press Operations.

GHI (2011) The United States Global Health Initiative: Strategy Document.

Hodgson, G. (2009) *The myth of American exceptionalism*. Yale University Press, New Haven, CT; London.

Hunt, M. H. (2009) *Ideology and U.S. foreign policy*. Yale University Press, New Haven, CT.

Hyland, W. G. (1999) *Clinton's world: remaking American foreign policy*. Praeger, Westport, Conn.

ICG (2005) Islamist Terrorism in the Sahel: Fact or Fiction? *Africa Report*. International Crisis Group, 31 March 2005. 92: 42.

Johnson, C. (2004) *The sorrows of empire: militarism, secrecy, and the end of the Republic*. Metropolitan Books, New York.

Johnson, C. (2010) *Dismantling the empire: America's last best hope*. Metropolitan Books, New York.

Johnson, L. B. (1964) Special Message to Congress on the Foreign Aid Program. 19 March 1964.

Johnson, L. B. (1966) Special Message to Congress on the Foreign Aid Program. 1 February 1966.

Johnson, L. B. (1967) Special Message to Congress on the Foreign Aid Program. 9 February 1967.

Jordan, A. A., Taylor, W. J. Jr., Meese, M. J. and Nielsen S. C. (2009) *American national security*. Johns Hopkins University Press, Baltimore, Md.

Kane, J. (2008) *Between virtue and power: the persistent moral dilemma of U.S. foreign policy*. Yale University Press, New Haven, CT.

Kegley Jr, C. W. (1989) The Bush Administration and the Future of American Foreign Policy: Pragmatism, or Procrastination? *Presidential Studies Quarterly* 19: 717–731.

Kennedy, J. F. (1961) Special Message to the Congress on Foreign Aid. 22 March 1961.

Kennedy, J. F. (1961a) Statement Upon Signing Order Establishing the Peace Corps, 1 March 1961.

Kennedy, J. F. (1961b) Address by President John F. Kennedy to the UN General Assembly: 25 September 1961. Department of State.

Kennedy, J. F. (1961c) Remarks to the Citizens Committee for International Development. 10 July 1961.

Kennedy, J. F. (1961d) Inaugural Address. 20 January 1961.

Kennedy, J. F. (1962) Remarks Upon Proclaiming Voluntary Overseas Aid Week. 9 April 1962.

Kennedy, J. F. (1962a) Remarks to a Group of Overseas Mission Directors of the Agency for International Development. 8 June 1962.

Kennedy, J. F. (1962b) Statement by the President on Foreign Aid. 19 September 1962.

Kennedy, J. F. (1962c) Special Message to the Congress on Foreign Aid. 13 March 1962.

Kirkpatrick, J. J. (1979) Dictatorships and Double Standards, *Commentary* 68: 34–45.

Kissinger, H. (2003) *Crisis: the anatomy of two major foreign policy crises.* Simon & Schuster, New York.

Lancaster, C. (2003) Poverty, Terrorism and National Security, in Farraro, V., Lancaster, C., Pinstrup-Andersen, P., Sachs, J. D. and Sewell, J. (eds) *ECSP Report 9: Should Global Poverty be a U.S. National Security Issue?* Wilson Center, Washington, DC.

Lancaster, C. (2008) *George Bush's foreign aid: transformation or chaos?* Brookings Institution Press, Washington, DC.

Lattanzio, R. K. (2013) The Global Climate Change Initiative (GCCI): Budget Authority and Request, FY2010-FY2014. Congressional Research Service.

Lundestad, G. (1993) Beyond the Cold War: new and old dimensions in international relations, in Lundestad, G. and Westad, O. A. (eds.) *Beyond the Cold War: new dimensions in international relations.* Scandinavian University Press, Oslo, pp. 245–257.

Mahoney, R. D. (1983) *JFK: ordeal in Africa.* Oxford University Press, New York.

Mandelbaum, M. (1996) Foreign Policy as Social Work, *Foreign Affairs* 75: 16–32.

Marshall, G. (1947) *The 'Marshall Plan' speech at Harvard University, 5 June 1947.* OECD, www.oecd.org/document/10/0,3746,en_2649_201185_1876938_1_1_1_1,00.html (accessed 23 April 2012).

McCrisken, T. B. (2003) *American exceptionalism and the legacy of Vietnam: US foreign policy since 1974.* Palgrave Macmillan, Basingstoke, Hampshire; New York.

Mead, W. R. (2001) *Special providence: American foreign policy and how it changed the world.* Knopf, New York.

Mitchell, N. (2016) *Jimmy Carter in Africa: race and the Cold War.* Woodrow Wilson Center Press, Washington, DC; Stanford University Press, Stanford, California.

Morrison, J. S. (2013) U.S. Health Engagement in Africa: A Decade of Remarkable Achievement – Now What? Center of Strategic and International Studies, Washington, DC.

Nackenoff, C. (1994) *The fictional republic: Horatio Alger and American political discourse.* Oxford University Press, New York.

Natsios, A. (2006) USAID in the Post-9/11 World, *Foreign Service Journal*, June: 19–24.

NIC (2002). The Next Wave of HIV/AIDS: Nigeria, Ethiopia, Russia, India and China. www.fas.org/irp/nic/hiv-aids.html (accessed 15 March 2017).

Nixon, R. (1969) Special Message to the Congress on Foreign Aid. 28 May 1969.

Nossel, S. (2004) Smart Power, *Foreign Affairs*. March/April issue. www.foreignaffairs.com/articles/united-states/2004-03-01/smart-power (accessed 15 March 2017).

Nowels, L. (2007) Foreign Aid Reform Commissions, Task Forces, and Initiatives: From Kennedy to the Present, in Brainard, L. (ed.) *Security by other means: foreign assistance, global poverty, and American leadership.* Brookings Institution Press, Washington, DC, pp. 255–275.

Nowels, L. and Veillette, C. (2006) Reconstructing U.S. Foreign Aid: The role of the Director of Foreign Assistance, *CRS Report for Congress*. Congressional Reserach Service, Library of Congress, Washington, DC.

NSC (1948) U.S. Objectives with Respect to the USSR to Counter Soviet Threats to U.S. Security (NSC 20/4, 23 November 1948), *Foreign Relations of the United States Vol. 1*. Department of State Washington, DC: Government Printing Office, pp. 663–669

NSC (1950) United States Objectives and Programs for National Security. 31 January 1950.

NSS (1987–2012) National Security Strategy of the United States. http://nssarchive.us/ (accessed 15 March 2017).

Obama, B. (2009) Inaugural Address. 20 January 2009.

Obama, B. (2013) Inaugural Address. 21 January 2013.

PDD (2010) U.S. Global Development Policy http://fas.org/irp/offdocs/ppd/ppd-6.pdf (accessed 15 March 2017).

Peck, J. (2010) *Ideal illusions: how the U.S. government co-opted human rights*. Metropolitan Books, New York.

Power, S. (2002) *'A problem from hell': America and the age of genocide*. HarperCollins, London.

QDDR (2010) The First Quadrennial Diplomacy and Development Review. US Department of State, Washington, DC.

Reagan, R. (1981) Statement on Signing International Security and Foreign Assistance Legislation. 29 December 1981.

Reagan, R. (1988) *Address Before a Joint Session of Congress on the State of the Union. 25 January 1988*, www.presidency.ucsb.edu/ws/index.php?pid=36035 (accessed November 6, 2012.

Restad, H. (2015) *American exceptionalism: an idea that made a nation and remade the world*. Routledge, Milton Park, Abingdon, Oxon; New York.

Rice, C. (2008) Remarks on Transformational Diplomacy. Georgetown University, 12 February 2008.

Rice, C. (2011) *No higher honor: A Memoir of My Years in Washington*. Crown Publishers, New York.

Rostow, W. W. (1960) *The United States in the world arena; an essay in recent history*. Harper, New York.

Rothchild, D. S. and Emmanuel, N. (2005) United States: The process of decision-making on Africa, in Engel, U. and Olsen, G. R. (eds) *Africa and the north: between globalization and marginalization*. Routledge, London; New York, pp. 74–91.

Ruttan, V. W. (1996) *United States development assistance policy: the domestic politics of foreign economic aid*. Johns Hopkins University Press, Baltimore.

Sewell, J. W. and Contee, C. E. (1987) Foreign-Aid and Gramm-Rudman, *Foreign Affairs* 65: 1015–1036.

Shultz, G. and Reagan, R. (1984) Remarks on Receiving the Report of the Commission on Security and Economic Assistance: 21 February 1984, Ronald Reagan Presidential Library and Museum.

Snider, D. M. (1995) *The national security strategy: documenting strategic vision*. Strategic Studies Institute, US Army War College, Carlisle Barracks, PA.

Snider, D. M. and Nagl, J. A. (2001) The National Security Strategy: Documenting Strategic Vision, in Cerami, J. R. and Holcomb, J. F. Jr. (eds) *U.S. Army War College Guide to Strategy*. U.S. Army War College.

Truman, H. S. (1949) Truman's Inaugural Address, 20 January 1949. *Harry S. Truman Library and Museum.*

Truman, H. S. (1950) Statement by the President Upon Signing the Foreign Economic Assistance Act. 5 June 1950.

Turner, F. J. and State Historical Society of Wisconsin (1894) *The significance of the frontier in American history.* State Historical Society of Wisconsin, Madison.

USAID (1975) Implementation of 'new directions' in development assistance, report to the committee on international relations, 22 July 1975. US Goverment Printing Office, Washington, DC.

USAID (2004) White Paper: U.S. Foreign Aid – Meeting the Challenges of the Twenty-first Century. Bureau for Policy and Program Coordination. U.S. Agency for International Development.

USAID (2012) Climate Change and Development Strategy. USAID.

USAID (2015) *The Global Health Initiative,* www.usaid.gov/what-we-do/global-health/cross-cutting-areas/global-health-initiative (accessed 26 January 2015).

Viotti, P. R. (2005) *American foreign policy and national security: a documentary record.* Pearson/Prentice Hall, Upper Saddle River, NJ; London.

Zimmerman, R. F. (1993) *Dollars, diplomacy, and dependency: dilemmas of U.S. economic aid.* Lynne Rienner Publishers, Boulder, Col.

# 4 US policy in Africa and the Cold War

## The formation of an independent American policy towards Africa

Until 1937, foreign policy towards Africa was planned through the Division of European Affairs at the Department of State (DoS) to ensure consistency with the main priorities, needs and interests of the colonial powers (Hubbard, 2011: 22; Williams, 1969: 164). Africa gained strategic importance during WWII as a port of transition for military supplies and trade. After 1937, the responsibility for Africa was divided between the Near East Division and the European Division at the DoS, with most substantive responsibilities remaining with the European Division reflecting the importance of co-ordinating the African policy and the interests of European powers. It was only in 1949 that the DoS created a new Bureau for Near Eastern, South Asian and African Affairs headed by an Assistant Secretary of State. The responsibility for Africa was given to the Office of African Affairs within the new bureau. This represented the beginning of a separate US policy towards the continent (Williams, 1969: 164).

During WWII, the US opened liaison posts in several locations in West Africa to co-ordinate consular affairs and trade issues. During the war and as a part of the effort to assist it, these posts turned their attention to the vast natural resources available in Africa (Williams, 1969: 163). When the war ended, European powers, and especially Portugal, France and Belgium, viewed American attempts to provide assistance to their African colonies with suspicion. They were reluctant to openly credit the US in instances where assistance was accepted, fearing it would undermine their authority in the colonies (DoS, 1952). But since nationalism was on the rise in Africa, the US became increasingly interested in the inclinations and preferences of natives in colonies. There was a growing understanding at the DoS that information coming from European powers about indigenous populations under their rule did not truly reflect native ideologies. Officers in charge of African affairs were advocating that the US should increase its efforts to understand needs and reach natives in Africa 'who are over-ripe with communism' (DoS, 1952a). The rationale linked colonial injustice to racial and political tensions, and by extension economic instability which created fertile grounds for communist ideologies (DoS, 1953). This was viewed as a direct risk to the 'free world', undermining its ability to access key natural resources, and potentially undermining American power (DoS, 1953).

A National Intelligence Estimate (NIE) published at the end of 1953 identified the rise of nationalism in Africa as a most significant force of change that could have serious strategic implications for the US (NIE, 1953). The NIE identified three major priorities for US interests in Africa:

1 Securing access to current and potential US military bases in the region and the ability to send US forces to Africa in times of war without inhibition.
2 Access to strategic raw materials in Africa as needed.
3 Supporting the efforts of European powers to maintain their 'responsibilities for security, political and material progress of the African people and the latters' adherence to the free world' (NIE, 1953).

Security, resources, and keeping communism at bay became the main objectives of this policy. But while Africa remained under colonial rule, pursuing these objectives meant a close alignment with European interests. Nevertheless, the US prepared for the 'day after colonialism' in Africa, devising plans to keep future African governments and local people friendly and orientated towards America and the free world. Allowing African nations to fall behind the Iron Curtain would have the potential to jeopardise access to essential raw materials, and subsequently, to undermine the power of the free world (NIE, 1953).

The document record indicates[1] that colonial powers often complained that US officials were openly supporting and sympathising with African nationalism. Undermining colonial powers in Africa, they argued, was strengthening the Soviet Union.

The US had often assumed an anti-colonial position based on both ideological and strategic considerations (Clough, 1992: 5–6). On the ideological side, two main issues influenced the rhetoric: The first was related to racial discrimination and the exploitation of natives in Africa by colonial powers, an issue closely linked to domestic politics and the racial history of the US. The American criticism against racial policies in colonies was often met with counter-rhetoric from European powers, highlighting the ongoing racial discrimination within the US (DoS, 1953a). The second issue was related to the many private foundations and religious missions working in Africa and lobbied the US government (DoS, 1952, 1955b). On the strategic side, the racial and political tensions in Africa were causing political and economic instability that had the potential to jeopardise the three major US interests in Africa (DoS, 1953). Since the strategic concerns in Africa converged with turmoil caused by colonial discriminatory policies, the anti-colonial feelings of Africans had to be addressed. It was therefore important for the US to signal to the native population in Africa that America was sympathetic and did not side blindly with its colonial allies and their policies in Africa (DoS, 1955, 1955b). But America also feared that the African quest for self-determination was a communist plot. Secretary Dulles believed that African nationalism was instigated by the Soviet Union to undermine colonial rule and win over African allegiances (Muehlenbeck, 2012: 3–4).

The official policy response revolved around cautiously manoeuvring between the aspirations of Africans for self-determination and the strategic preferences of the colonial powers. The DoS feared that Africans were not yet ready for self-determination. In a letter from the American Consul General in Nairobi to Mason Sears, the American representative to the United Nations Trusteeship Council (DoS, 1955a), the Consul wrote:

> Is self-determination a right that is axiomatic, automatic and divinely bestowed? Or is it a right that one must earn? Most of our American public statements seem to leave this clouded in doubt. People here have the impression we believe in the former. But I think upon reflection nearly all of us would agree that the latter is closer to the truth. Does a child have an 'inalienable right' to self-determination? Does even an adult have that right unless he is able to live up to his community responsibilities?
>
> (DoS, 1955a)

By 1955 it was becoming evident that tensions between colonialism and the struggle for independence in Africa warranted a new approach to the continent. The US could no longer continue to adjust policies according to the interests of European colonial powers and at the same time acknowledge African aspirations for independence without being caught up in the conflict of interests. America needed an independent policy for Africa. The guiding principles of an independent policy outlined by the DoS were attached to economic, military, political and cultural issues – in a descending order of importance (DoS, 1955b). The economic stakes in Africa were considered the most tangible by far at that time (Clough, 1992: 14). America relied on a wide variety of African resources, and the general trend indicated increasing future markets. Africa was also significant for the economic well-being of European allies. But US military and strategic stakes were not substantial, and included an air force base in Liberia and a military mission in Ethiopia. The political stakes in Africa were related to the balance of power and keeping future independent African countries in the Western orbit. The policy document recognises that America's interests in Africa are bound to increase over the coming years and that an independent policy will best serve US interests while preserving the crucial relationships with colonial powers. The document outlined six general goals for an independent policy in Africa (DoS, 1955b):

1   That the continent remain free from inimical foreign influence, whether communist, Indian or Arab.
2   That the political, economic and social evolution of this continent be in a friendly manner to the United States.
3   That the United States obtain, on the most favorable possible terms, access to the economic resources of the area.
4   That the United States increase its commercial, industrial and agricultural activities in the continent.
5   That the United States consolidate its cultural and moral position with respect to Africans.
6   That American strategic needs with respect to the continent be fully safeguarded.

Six courses of action were suggested to achieve the policy goals, underscoring the importance of assistance strategies and diplomacy. The first course of action calls for a 'change of tone of American policy', namely adopting a neutral approach that does not antagonise colonial powers, and does not undermine African national aspirations. The second emphasises the importance of increasing the productivity of Africa. The document recommends supporting private investment of capital in Africa and providing investors with information together with political and diplomatic support to ensure favourable conditions. It also emphasises the importance of supporting development loans and increasing direct US technical assistance to Africa. The third course of action was to assume a multiracial approach for potential solutions to the problems in Africa. It was to mitigate future white settler and black conflicts. The fourth course of action highlighted the significant need for information and education in Africa: 'the demand is so great that whoever brings the African education has the power to influence him in basic fashion' (DoS, 1955b). A fifth course of action recommended encouraging the involvement of private organisations and to have them align themselves with the long-term interests of the US in Africa (DoS, 1955b). And the final course of action called for strengthening the diplomatic resources of the US in Africa, including representation, support personnel and infrastructure.

However, because Africa lacked concrete military significance for the US, it was difficult to argue its importance to the public. A memorandum published in 1955 states that since Africa is not important for current military objectives, there is a need to set up distinct 'American, realistic, and realizable' goals for Africa which do not depend on military action (DoS, 1955c). The document links together the harsh realities of life in the 'primitive' society in Africa living under the oppression of colonialism, to American exceptionalism and subsequent responsibility to champion self-governance, democracy and freedom, to the fight against Soviet attempts to propagate communism while using colonial oppression to instigate anti-Western feeling among Africans. To achieve these aims and befriend Africans, the authors of the document called for institutionalising a co-operation scheme between Europe and the US and the conception of a Marshall-type-plan for the continent. This meant helping Africans raise their standards of living, education and economic development in ways that would lead to co-operation with the US and its European allies.

An NIE report from 1956 on the conditions and trends in Africa (NIE, 1956) acknowledged the diminishing influence of colonial powers and the possibility that emerging states in Africa would focus on seeking recognition and much-needed economic assistance. In this context, the NIE specified that the Soviet Union had attempted to offer aid to African countries and would continue to intensify these efforts in the future. The report emphasised that Africans may decide to turn towards the Soviet Union and Arab states, not because of ideological reasons, but rather as an opportunistic strategy to access resources. Consequently, not meeting African requests for economic assistance by the US or Europe would increase the risk that Africa would align with the USSR. The document also indicated the potential strategic importance of Africa in a future war scenario in relation to maritime routes, lines of communication and access to forward bases of operations.

The increasing importance of Africa for American interests was reflected in the presidential campaigns for elections in 1956 (Walton, 2007: 24–25). In 1956 the democratic candidate, Adlai Stevenson, suggested a reformulation of US policy towards Africa. This suggestion was made principally to address domestic race issues, to gain support from the African-American community, and to address American interest in African affairs. The Republican candidate, Dwight D. Eisenhower, matched Stevenson's statements by vowing to reform the African foreign policy at the DoS. Indeed, after the elections, Eisenhower led a series of actions, including the appointment of an African-American ambassador to the newly independent state of Ghana, a tour of the continent by Vice President Nixon and the creation of a new Bureau of African Affairs at the DoS headed by an Assistant Secretary.[2] Nevertheless, the continent remained on the margins of US foreign policy priorities. American resources were mainly channelled towards securing US economic and national security interests in Asia, the Middle East and Latin America (Ruttan, 1996: 75–76).

Vice President Nixon's tour of Africa was summarised in his report where he suggested that the US devise plans of action to assist European powers to secure their future influence in former colonies, and help induce a pro-Western orientation of future independent governments. Nixon also recommended increasing the DoS presence in Africa by sending additional staff, opening new missions, and raising the level of representation. He also suggested that the US would make an effort to support African transition to independence with technical and economic assistance to help construct pro-Western viable states. Such a policy would achieve several goals, including resisting communism and the Arab influence in Africa (DoS, 1957a). The Vice President believed that the communist threat in Africa tended to be underestimated and pressed for a policy to address what he viewed as the growing communist influence on post-colonial Africa (DoS, 1957b).[3]

By 1957 the various fact-finding missions, discussions, opinions and analyses of trends and future directions of Africa culminated in a statement of policy towards sub-Saharan Africa known as NSC 5719/1 (NSC, 1957). The statement reflected major concerns, and identified the most relevant issues for US policy as:

- Nationalism vs. colonialism
- Racialism
- The communist threat
- Military and strategic value of Africa
- Economic potential of the independent states
- Education and training
- Detribalisation
- Islam.

The two main power tools to address these issues were diplomacy and assistance (technical and economic). Regarding assistance, the policy asserted the importance of both direct US assistance as well as contributions through multilateral mechanisms alongside European investments in development assistance to maintain a pro-Western orientation and influence in Africa. Since Africans were considered 'immature and unsophisticated' when it came to world politics, the concern was that Soviet and Islamic propaganda would capitalise on 'xenophobic nationalism' and influence Africans to orient themselves against Western interests (NSC, 1957). The document suggested that the future orientation of African states would be decided by leaders who would make choices based upon the independence and equality with the 'white man' (NSC, 1957):

> Our policies therefore must be designed to convince the African that by association with the West he can best achieve his goals in a manner which in the long run will be most to his advantage. These policies cannot be effective if the African feels he is merely a pawn in a power struggle.
>
> (NSC, 1957)

In other words, the policy indicates that based on the level of political 'maturity' and 'sophistication' of Africans, and building upon aspirations for independence and equality, a 'soft power' approach could help gravitate Africa towards adopting policies that serve US security and economic interests. In 1958, Secretary Dulles sent his Special Assistant, Julius C. Holmes, on a 10-week study of the continent to introduce recommendations for a future African policy.

In his report, Holmes (DoS, 1958: 2–3) described the conditions of under-development in Africa, characterised as 'primitive population ... largely illiterate, more than half Pagan, and ... practically leaping from the Iron Age into the 20th Century', as an opportunity to prepare Africa for modernisation. The new Africa would need to transit abruptly from a simple form towards 'a more complicated existence for which they are, in the mass, almost totally unprepared'. The transition into

> modernity involves the abrupt abandonment of ancient folk-ways which provided a sense of social, economic and even religious security and an attempt to take on a new set of rules of life, little understood, and for which the African is not yet fitted by education or experience.

To help mould a pro-Western Africa, Holmes recommended support to African leaders to 'produce tangible results in the form of economic and social improvement'. This would be achieved by through 'aid programmes and by the encouragement of investment and development by private enterprise'. (DoS, 1958: 2–3). Holmes recommended increasing substantially the involvement of the US in Africa, including the anticipation of new missions and training of new personnel to qualify for positions in Africa.

The Policy statement towards Africa, NSC 5719/1, was revised once again in 1958. The revision focused mainly on the role of assistance considering more in-depth and differentiated analysis of the economic potential of Africa and more specific policy guidance resulting from the analysis (NSC, 1958: paragraphs 21–27). An emphasis was placed on US economic and technical assistance, as well as providing education and training while the goals remained the same. The aid component of the document highlighted seven priorities for the assistance programming:

- Agricultural productivity and crop diversification
- Improve education
- Combat disease and malnutrition
- Business development
- Industrialisation
- Road infrastructure
- Development of communications systems.

This type of reasoning and formulation about the role of the US in Africa repeated itself in the next few years. It was referred to as 'ride along with the nationalist bandwagon without actually climbing on board' for the purpose of befriending Africans, not antagonising allies, and blocking the influence of the Soviet Union in Africa (DoS, 1959).

European powers also began recognising the need to form a new strategy towards Africa and co-ordinate efforts with the US. In 1958, de

Gaulle proposed a tripartite consultation on African strategy including France, the United Kingdom and the US. In a meeting with de Gaulle on 15 December, Secretary Dulles remarked that:

> Africa is vital to the West. If studied from a North-South viewpoint, Africa was the hinterland of Western Europe. Today Africa is being penetrated by Communist agents, and is caught up in the worldwide movement for premature independence.
>
> (DoS, 1958a)

The content of the tripartite talks was held confidential at the time, mostly because the Western powers did not want Africans to realise the role they may play in a potential East–West confrontation (DoS, 1959a). The most important topic of immediate strategic importance was North Africa, namely the war in Algeria and Soviet influence in Egypt. Africa south of the Sahara was not considered crucial for immediate strategy, but was deemed important considering its vast resources and increasing power emanating from joining multilateral institutions as independent and free nations. One concern regarding Africa's influence in the UN was the Afro-Asiatic bloc that 'often acted most irresponsibly' (DoS, 1959a). America estimated that by 1970 there would be 100 member nations in the UN, 49 of which would be in the Afro-Asiatic bloc. If African nations would not be supportive of the US vote in the UN, America's power in relation to the USSR would be considerably degraded (DoS, 1960a). The members of the tripartite talks identified a Soviet strategy to gain a foothold in Africa by befriending all independent nations and establishing programmes for technical and economic assistance (DoS, 1960a).

Recognising their mutual interests, the three states agreed to collaborate to help Africans move to independence in a manner that would preserve the 'complementary' interests of Europe and Africa. The 'immaturity and lack of sophistication' (DoS, 1959a) of Africans was viewed by the US and Europe as vulnerability in face of communist, pan-African and Islamic pressure (DoS, 1959a). Africans would determine their best interests based on the 'prospect of achieving equality with the white race' (DoS, 1959a). It was therefore important to befriend Africans through offering economic, technical and military assistance that is not explicitly attached to 'political or military strings' (DoS, 1959a).

The US emphasised that while it supported orderly evolution towards independence in Africa, it would offer direct support to African nations when interests were involved. The process of co-ordination between interests of European powers and the US was not without tensions, especially when it came to co-ordination with France. When Guinea, for example, opted out of the French community, the French pulled out all their resources, leaving Guinea, from an American viewpoint, vulnerable to communism. Indeed, the French Communist Party and the then Soviet

Union sent assistance (Attwood, 1967). Despite this, the US welcomed the president of Guinea as a head of state on his visit to the US in October 1959 (as did Germany and the United Kingdom). De Gaulle protested that America was being too friendly to Guinea because accepting Guinea and its president, Sekou Touré, (whom de Gaulle despised) might encourage other African countries to opt out of the French community. The US emphasised that it wished to remain mainly uninvolved in French interests in Africa.

In the following year, the US outlook on Africa became more nuanced. Various documents include more attention to regional contexts and/or in relation to colonial affiliations. The primary and secondary policy objectives in Africa remained to preserve the orientation towards the free world and deny Soviet domination of Africa, with the first objective being a pre-condition to the second (DoS, 1960). Eisenhower believed that America should use economic and development assistance programming to encourage Africa to adhere to Western values, and that this policy should also be implemented even where communism was not emerging as a threat. In cases where African countries were orientating themselves towards communism, the President believed that America should refrain from investing in economic and political development (DoS, 1960).

The discussions on how to execute the policy in Africa included the idea that Africans should be given the impression that they are important (DoS, 1960). This was to be achieved by continuously issuing statements by high-level American officials on the importance of African independence and equality, through granting economic and technical assistance, and by de-emphasising the links between Africa's importance and the Cold War. There was a real concern that if Africans realised that the main interest of the West in the region was linked to the Cold War and control of resources, it might drive Africans to 'cynical neutralism or worse' (DoS, 1960b).

As the policy evolved, many issues were raised as concerns for further study. One such concern was the growing economic burden inflicted on the US as a result of granting assistance to Africa. The recommendations to mitigate this burden included: encouraging private organisations to take part in Africa's development in co-ordination with the US government; studying the challenges and benefits of involving multilateral institutions in the process; and encouraging independent African nations to acquire membership in Western economic institutions such as the International Monetary Fund (IMF) and the World Bank (DoS, 1960b).

It was also recognised that the US government should make an effort to identify the unique development challenges of Africa and prepare adequately for the different contexts by dispatching experts to various countries and preparing adequate plans. There was a concern that inadequate investment and planning could lead to programme failures and would then contribute to African disappointment with the West, jeopardising US presence and future interests on the continent (DoS, 1960b).

## Africa for the Africans

Coined by Kennedy's Assistant Secretary of State for African Affairs, G. Mennen Williams,[4] 'Africa for the Africans' was a statement that not only mirrored the various objectives of US policy under Kennedy, but also the realisation that America needed a more independent and direct policy on Africa (Williams, 1969: 163).

Africa for the Africans meant that the US supported African aspirations for self-determination. Kennedy explained that Africans were all those who deemed themselves as such regardless of colour or race, thus joining blacks and whites under one label (Kennedy quoted in Williams, 1969: 159). The phrase also indicated to Africans that America was an ally concerned with their wellbeing, recognising their aspirations and struggles. It implied that Africa should remain neutral in the Cold War without alluding to or stating this directly. Williams sought to represent the best and purest national ethos of America. It combined the primary objective of foreign policy (to secure US interests), together with America's goal to build 'a world of peace and freedom' (Williams, 1969: 169).

From a US perspective, it was in the best interests of Africans to maintain a Western orientation and reject Sino-Soviet ideology. The American strategy of granting economic and technical support to Africa would help move the continent towards these objectives, and at the same time assist in building new independent nations. Williams specified the win–win strategy of the policy by emphasising its five main tenets:

1   Support of self-determination and nonalignment of African nations.
2   African solutions to African problems.
3   Raise African standards of living with aid and trade.
4   Prevent arms races and arms build-ups in Africa.
5   Encourage Europeans to fulfil their responsibilities as former colonial masters.

Contextualising the five tenets, Williams stated that 'supporting freedom over Communism is basic to and a product of the tenets guiding U.S. policy' (Williams, 1969: 170). Interestingly, the American policy under the Kennedy administration did not explicitly advocate the emulation of a specific system of governance as the model system for African countries. Instead, it emphasised that governance systems should be self-determined as long as they are anchored in the consent of the governed (Kennedy quoted in Williams, 1969: 171). The assessment stipulated that Africans were seeking equality and recognition rather than an ideology. This was a major difference from the containment strategy suggested in NSC-68, and Eisenhower's African policy which called for limiting assistance to countries that orient themselves with the Soviet Union or China (DoS, 1960; Noer, 2005: 227). NSC-68 stated that nations should not be allowed to assume a course of neutrality in relation to the Cold War; neutrality appeared as an advantage to the Soviet Union and would eventually lead to Soviet domination. But since the Soviet Union stepped up its economic and technical assistance to countries in Asia, the Middle East and Africa, 'cold warriors' such as Walt Rostow began emphasising the importance of economic development alongside military components of assistance in a containment strategy (Millikan and Rostow, 1957: 1–8; Rostow, 1960: 294–298). The US wanted to focus on supporting and befriending Africans without introducing conditionality. This could be achieved by encouraging Africans to assume a course of neutrality. The rejection of the West by some countries in Africa was explained as an outcome of colonial policies rather than ideological subscription to communism. Subsequently the focus of the policy was on helping African nations to achieve self-determination, assuming that Western orientation would be accomplished by legitimising and helping countries to achieve their aspirations rather than conditioning assistance with alignment (Noer, 2005: 227–228).

Williams explained that the third tenet of the policy towards Africa, aid and trade, had several important justifications. First, it helped African countries to raise their standard of living and join the world community by using a discourse that tapped into the moral ethos of America. Second, it promoted what the US viewed as the path to global peace and security. Aid appeared as an essential tool for the promotion of trade and investment, as well as exercising influence and leverage on developing countries (Attwood, 1967: 313).

Williams noted that African countries also considered technical assistance and trade investment to be fundamental components of their relationship with the US. Africa needed help, but the US also needed Africa's vote, especially when it came to supporting America's leadership and global policies in multilateral frameworks (Williams, 1969: 173). Africa was also a major provider of raw resources including asbestos, iron ore, industrial diamonds, bauxite and others that supplied the American industry and were essential for the continuity of a healthy American economy (Williams, 1969: 175).

Kennedy's approach to Africa was indeed different and distinct from previous administrations. As the former chair of the Senate Sub-Committee on Africa during the Eisenhower administration, Kennedy supported Africa's quest for freedom from colonial domination and self-determination. His voice was in opposition to formal US policy at that time, which focused on avoiding antagonising European allies. Kennedy did not support the idea that premature independence in Africa might weaken their orientation towards the West and allow the Soviets to spread their ideology (Noer, 2005: 225) and with Eisenhower's attempts to delay self-determination in Africa to please colonial powers (Mahoney, 1983: 18; Muehlenbeck, 2012: 34). His approach stressed the need for an independent and separate US policy on Africa which focused on helping

Africans help themselves to achieve freedom because it was 'right', and because that kind of support would win the friendship of Africans and encourage their Western orientation (Muehlenbeck, 2012: 35). He also questioned the idea that the rise of nationalism in Africa was a Soviet design to frustrate the West[5] (Muehlenbeck, 2012: 34), but acknowledged that disregarding African aspirations for freedom and failing to grant them assistance to fight poverty, sickness, injustice and inequality will eventually push Africa towards the Sino-Soviet bloc (Muehlenbeck, 2012: 35).

Once America decided to commit resources to deliver development assistance to African nations, a number of additional issues began to surface. In a memorandum sent to Under Secretary of State, Chester Bowles (DoS, 1961), Williams expressed his concerns regarding two 'disturbing' developments. The first related to postponing the implementation of many projects in Africa; the second related to devoting assistance resources to a number of countries while ignoring others. The Kennedy administration formed task groups to review the assistance programmes. This process led to postponing the implementation of planned projects until the review process was completed and recommendations for improvement submitted. Williams believed that delaying assistance programmes would have 'catastrophic' consequences on the relationship between the US and Africa. In his opinion, America needed to continuously provide assistance in order to demonstrate its goodwill and convince Africans of America's genuine intentions. Since Kennedy proclaimed the 1960s as the 'Decade of Development' (Kennedy, 1961) America could not afford to concentrate assistance in a few selected countries. Williams argued that America must demonstrate to all underdeveloped countries its will to provide assistance. Hesitation in implementation, or failure to follow up on statements with action, could very quickly lead to disappointment among African nations, with counter-effective consequences (DoS, 1961).

By granting political and economic development assistance, the US expected that African nations would develop peacefully and would acquire firm economic foundations that would help them reject communist attempts to harness them to the Soviet bloc.

Kennedy devised a four-pronged approach towards improving relationships with African nations (Muehlenbeck, 2012: 44–57). First, he opposed colonialism publically, and engaged in active efforts to end colonial rule on the continent.[6] Second, he was openly supportive of a neutral Africa, not conditioning US aid with alignment, and thereby rejecting the rationale of the former containment strategy which called for non-neutrality. Third, he committed resources for the development of Africa and engaged USAID and the Peace Corps[7] in an effort to modernise Africa and develop trade and economy. Fourth, he engaged in personal diplomacy inviting African leaders to the White House, ensuring their participation in various formal ceremonies, treating them as friends and equals. An important part of this strategy included devoting time and attention to the African-American community, including appointment of African-Americans to official positions, and fighting racial discrimination and segregation inside America (Muehlenbeck, 2012: 50–52; Tillery, 2007: 46).

Since Kennedy played a personal role in African diplomacy, his assassination raised immediate concerns about the future of the policy. On 23 November 1963, a day after Kennedy's tragic death, Williams sent a memorandum to Secretary of State, Dean Rusk, outlining the need to continue Kennedy's approach to Africa under President Johnson.

## A policy of residual interest in Africa[8]

Without Kennedy at the helm, the African policy fell behind more pressing issues during, namely, the growing crisis in Indochina and the increasing involvement of America in Vietnam.

With other pressing matters on his plate, President Johnson preferred to leave African matters to the bureaucracy at the DoS, and to involve himself only when presidential decisions had to be made (Lyons, 1994: 245). Initially, Johnson avoided making major changes in personnel to the bureaucracy, and kept the main African policymakers at the DoS from the Kennedy administration at their posts, including Assistant Secretary Williams (Walton, 2007: 33).

The main change to the African policy during the first few years of the Johnson administration was the diminishing involvement of the President (Muehlenbeck, 2012: xv). Johnson's first speech on Africa as President was held over two years after he assumed office (DoS, 1966) during a reception marking the third anniversary of the Organisation of African Unity (OAU). This carefully planned speech was the product of a process initiated to form a distinct 'Johnson Doctrine for Africa' (DoS, 1966), and was linked to a review process of the African policy initiated by Williams in May 1965 (DoS, 1965). US policy towards Africa did not change significantly as a result of this review process. As a matter of fact, a number of officials involved in the process suggested that the African policy should be labelled 'Strengthen policy for Africa' instead of 'New Policy for Africa' (DoS, 1965a). However, Johnson viewed aid as politics, and subsequently aid policy had to be linked to 'clear cut returns, either in terms of demonstrable economic improvement, or in political favours, or both' (quoted in Packenham, 1973: 89). The most significant elements that surfaced during the review process were reported in a memorandum to McGeorge Bundy, the President's Special Assistant for National Security, in June 1965; they included the following observations:

a  [AID] should be used as a political weapon with more aid going to our friends than to our critics and a minimal presence in all African political units.

b   While aid for long-term economic development is sound, an increase in 'impact' aid pays higher political dividends.
c   [Development assistance p]rocedures should be simplified and speeded up and criteria tailored to African capacity to develop projects (DoS 1965a).

When it came to communism, America estimated that in general, Africans were keen to keep the Cold War off the continent 'at all costs' (DoS, 1965a), and that America was mostly successful during this time period in its strategy of countering communism through aid and friendship.[9] The central policy recommendations were to continue strengthening the US–Africa relationships; work towards projecting a positive image of President Johnson in Africa, and locate efficient ways to increase the impact of aid without committing more resources (DoS, 1965a, 1965b). Williams suggested four concrete steps to strengthen to these ends (DoS, 1965c):

1   That the President will publicly associate himself with Africa.
2   That the President will publicly associate himself with the principal of self-determination.
3   That economic aid will be used for political as well as development objectives.
4   That America intensifies its efforts to promote itself and combat communism through dissemination of information, cultural and educational exchanges.

William's recommendations were supported by Secretary Rusk. He agreed that in general, US policy towards Africa was sound. He underlined the necessity of fostering a 'climate of trust and respect' between the President and African leaders. Rusk indicated that

> the greater the effectiveness of our non-military programs in contributing to African economic and social development and to developing African attitudes favorable to the West, the less need there will be for large military outlays to resist Communist encroachments (perhaps 'Wars of liberation') in Africa.
> 
> (DoS, 1965d)

There were critics of this approach. Deputy Special Assistant for National Security Affairs Komer, believed that visible aid programmes and high-level messages were necessary, but would not win Africans over. He held that US interests would be better served through the adoption of supporting African opposition to the continued colonial presence in southern Africa. He observed that the US presence in Vietnam, South Asia and Berlin was interpreted by Africans as imperialism, and linked to their own struggles for independence. Komer pointed to the increasing importance of the African vote in the UN, and that the US was in competition with China and the Soviet Union to win these votes (DoS, 1965e). Rusk concurred with Komer on the main underlying importance of the African policy (DoS, 1965f).

Between June 1965 and March 1966, there were seven military coups in Africa.[10] The Bureau of African Affairs viewed these events as a reaction of young generation idealists and pragmatic Africans to a corrupt and ineffective political leadership. The Bureau believed this was an opportunity for the US to serve its immediate and long-term interests by capitalising on this new wave of 'nationalism, idealism, and efficiency' in Africa (DoS, 1966a[11]). To benefit from these new opportunities the DoS recommended the following: befriend the next generation of leaders, expand the programmes of USAID and the Peace Corps in selected African countries, increase US influence through the Food for Peace programs and use it as an instrument for economic development, and urge the World Bank and European allies to expand advice, loans and investment in assistance programmes (DoS, 1966a).

As the third anniversary of the OAU approached, the DoS and the national security advisors worked together on an approach to Africa which the President would convey in his speech for the occasion. Johnson's remarks would focus on indicating a personal interest in the welfare of Africa, and to present a new policy initiative (DoS, 1966b). Rostow proposed to highlight through the President's speech a set of common principles shared by the OAU (based on the charter of the organisation) and the US, as well as emphasise US support for development in Africa, and assure that US assistance would expand support for economic, education, health and communication issues. In addition, Johnson would announce that the US was prepared to lead an international effort to aid Africa (Johnson, 1966).

In his speech, Johnson highlighted parts of the OAU charter that emphasised freedom, equality and justice and related those to American values, underscoring that the legitimacy of governments should derive from the consent of the governed. He also referred to freedom from colonialism and racial domination, and stated that the US opposed any form of racial and political injustice in Africa. He then explained that these principles were at the core of US policy around the world, mentioning Rhodesia, Vietnam, and other countries, in an attempt to curb African suspicions of US policies in these countries as being neo-colonial. He delivered a number of promises to increase US investment in assistance programmes to strengthen the collaboration with the continent, strengthen regional economic activities, invest in educational programmes, help develop effective communication systems in Africa, and develop infrastructure such as roads, rail, power grids and air links (Johnson, 1966).

During the speech, the President announced that he had mandated US Ambassador to Ethiopia, Ed Korry, as the leader of the Task Force charged with reviewing the development policies of the US for the continent. On 22 July 1966, the Task Force delivered its recommendations for a development policy in Africa (DoS, 1966c). The new policy confirmed that Africa was not the most important strategic area for US foreign policy, and that the main concern for the region was to prevent the escalation of events taking place on the continent from disturbing peace and interfering with American interests in other regions. The Task Force indicated that successful attempts to moderate communism in Europe led to an increase of Cold War confrontations in Africa in the form of encouraging the formation of specific economic and ideological systems.

When it came to assistance, the Task Force indicated that the US approach to Latin America and Asia which was based on the attempt to eliminate obstacles to growth as the main strategy, had not worked in Africa and had led to serious problems. Africa suffered from a larger variety of obstacles, resulting in hundreds of different projects that scattered the limited resources the US dedicated to the continent. In addition, in an attempt to satisfy African leaders, the US channelled resources to address specific political problems that 'damage the credibility of aid as an objective instrument of development' (DoS, 1966c).

Since Africa's development issues could not be resolved quickly, a long-term approach to development could help foster the necessary progress that would spur stability and independence. Such an approach would require investing more resources in Africa for long-term returns. The suggested policy argued that the current operationalisation of development assistance was largely based on non-development criteria, inefficient and ineffective (in terms of implementation and bureaucracy), scattered (across space and across donors), unfocused, and eventually caused more frustration against the US and the free world. The document list of 16 recommendations emphasised the need to formulate priority sectors for development assistance, and concentrate on large development efforts in fewer countries based on a combination of economic and political considerations. It also underscored the importance of multilateral organisations such as the World Bank and the IMF in terms of concentrating development efforts and combining the different objectives and purposes of assistance programmes delivered by different countries involved in Africa's development.

The DoS was generally positive towards Korry's report, but suggested that its content should remain unpublished so as not to cause antagonism among Africans and allies alike in response to some frank comments about the role of development and the approach and implementation of assistance programmes by allies and other organisations (DoS, 1966d). There was a concern that publishing the report would weaken the position of the US in future negotiations relating to aid (DoS, 1966d). Rostow concurred with the DoS on the quality of the report and its main findings and recommendations (DoS, 1966e). On 5 October 1966, the National

Security Council approved the Korry report and assigned the primary responsibility for preparing its application to the DoS assisted by USAID. Rostow was appointed to serve as a liaison to the White House on this effort (DoS, 1966f).

By April 1967, the DoS was well underway implementing many of the Korry report's recommendations. The World Bank, the African Development Bank and the UN Economic Commission for Africa were working together on a plan to co-ordinate major infrastructure development programmes, including telecommunications, power and roads. USAID was initiating major conferences on agriculture and improved food production in Africa, and devising plans to promote educational collaboration and exchange with African students. There was also greater involvement of the private sector in development initiatives, and USAID was reducing the number of African countries benefiting from bilateral assistance and streamlining their objectives and bureaucracy (DoS, 1967).

During this time, there were increased objections in Congress to allocate funding for Aid due mainly to dissatisfaction with the war in Vietnam and the immense costs inflicted on America. The other reason was related to increased dissatisfaction with the effects of aid in Africa, largely due to the initial exaggeration of the prospects of Africa and the potential effects of external aid on the continent (DoS, 1967a). In 1968, the DoS prepared a summary of the foreign policy issues in Africa for the coming year. The document stated that the US objectives on the continent should be guided by:

> (a) safeguarding of U.S. strategic interests; adoption by African governments of favorable attitudes; fostering U.S. trade and investments; (b) realization of the principle of self determination in southern Africa; (c) achievement of an environment which will permit the African nations to develop their national interests without external interference.
>
> (DoS, 1968)

The document estimated that the main concern in Africa would continue to be the instability linked to lack of economic development. The challenge for the executive branch would be to address these issues in a period when Congress was limiting aid resources (DoS, 1968). The Korry report favoured shifting the American aid strategy towards large, multilateral, joint ventures, regional projects for African development over smaller-scale localised projects.

Nevertheless, the African policy during the Johnson administration remained in the shadow of the Vietnam War. The heavy American involvement with troops and economic assistance kept African matters (and others) in the background of foreign policy during those years.

## Africa – a low priority on the President's agenda

The Nixon–Kissinger realpolitik approach to foreign policy had important effects on the African policy of the US. Focusing on pragmatism and realism, the main priority of Nixon's foreign policy was to increase the security and prosperity of the US by maintaining and regulating the balance of power with the Soviet Union. The approach rested upon President Nixon's 1969 speech in Guam where he enunciated what came to be known as the Nixon doctrine. The core of the Nixon doctrine stipulated a new approach to containment: the US would be willing to provide military and economic assistance to friends against aggression, but would not be prepared to bear the primary responsibility for the defence of sovereign nations. Countries assisted by the US would have to provide their own manpower for their own defence. The relaxation of tensions with the Soviet Union would be accomplished through closer political contact and negotiations on agreements to limit the nuclear arms race.[12] The realpolitik approach focused on attaining US strategic objectives to the exclusion of moral considerations or commitments that did not increase or contribute to their achievement (Apodaca, 2006: 31; Stohl et al., 1984: 216).

As a low priority region, US foreign policy towards Africa focused on maintaining the status quo and avoiding Cold War confrontations on the continent (Cohen, 2003;[13] Schraeder, 1994: 33). In public, idealism and development dominated presidential statements on Africa (see Nixon, 1970, 1971, 1972). In practice, Nixon granted very little priority to the African policy. In a memorandum sent in early March 1970 to Kissinger, Ehrlichman[14] and Haldeman,[15] Nixon explained that he had always believed in concentrating on fighting and winning big battles. He did not believe in devoting a significant amount of his time to lower priority issues, and therefore he instructed his senior aides to only bring to his attention foreign policy issues relating to East–West relations, Soviet Union, Communist China, Eastern Europe on matters relating to East–West relations, and Western Europe on matters relating to NATO and the major partner countries Britain, Germany and France (Nixon, 1970a). When it came to Africa and several other low priority regions, Nixon instructed that he did not want matters submitted to his attention unless they require presidential handling and decision-making (Nixon, 1970a). He explained that he did not want to give the impression he did not care: 'I do care, but what happens in those parts of the world is not, in the final analysis, going to have any significant effect on the success of our foreign policy' (Nixon, 1970a).

The consequences of Nixon's approach, at least until 1972, were that the involvement of the President and his senior staff in African matters was 'rare' and 'episodic' and usually occurred in relation to a crisis situation or when the President had to make a public statement on Africa (Schraeder, 1994: 36). Within this, the most important factor affecting presidential involvement in the African policy during a crisis was usually linked to the degree of involvement of the Soviet Union (Bienen, 1978: 449; Schraeder, 1994: 28). Otherwise, the main priority was to maintain the status quo as indicated by Kissinger in a memorandum sent to the President:

> The essential point of the speech[16] ... will simply be to let the Africans know we have them in mind – despite the low priority of our interests in the continent, and despite the low levels of aid. But for countries whose pride and sensitivity run in inverse proportions to their power, this will be a worthwhile and important gesture.
>
> (Kissinger, 1969)

Thirteen years before his successful presidential bid, Nixon was sent on a fact-finding mission to Africa as Vice President of the US. His significant input in the many NSC meetings chaired by Eisenhower became the pillar of US policy guidelines on Africa during that time. Now as President, Nixon faced a different Africa and a different domestic attitude towards foreign aid. Since aid was the main tool of choice for the African policy since the 1950s, there was an important relationship between the status of Africa in the overall US global interests, the evolving events on the continent, and the domestic attitudes in the US towards aid spending.

Towards 1970, there was a profound disillusionment in the US government with the process of African independence. The pursuit of self-determination in Africa was on the whole characterised by authoritarian rule, conflict and corruption. African leaders installed governance systems based on one-party democracy that banned or co-opted opposition, and nationalised major institutions. Political elites took control of major businesses and production systems and failed to manage them for the benefit of the people (Cohen, 2010: 212). In terms of colonialism and independence in the early 1970s, Portugal was still clinging to its colonies in Africa despite armed opposition. In Namibia, South Africa and Zimbabwe white minorities continued to hold power exercised through racialised policies against the black majority.

Domestically in the US, there was a growing dissatisfaction with the government. The Vietnam conflict and the rise of the civil rights movement contributed with rising awareness of human rights abuses around the world, including in Africa. Congress was weary of presidential powers and sought to increase oversight over various engagements of the government. There was growing discontent with aid spending, and Congress was closely scrutinising government expenditures, demanding frequent justifications, explanations and asking to clarify and redefine aid and its purpose (Eberstadt, 1988: 37; Ruttan, 1996: 23–24). As the conflict in Vietnam escalated in the mid-sixties, almost half of all US aid allocations and resources went to that country (Eberstadt, 1988: 34). Development work in Vietnam became an integral part of the war effort, shifting the declared purpose of aid from providing technical and economic assistance, and encouraging private investment – to assisting relocated civilians (humanitarian and economic assistance) and winning the hearts and minds of the Vietnamese population (Eberstadt, 1988: 34–35). One of the consequences of this was congressional barriers over aid spending and the rejection of Nixon's foreign aid proposals in 1971 and 1972 (Eberstadt, 1988: 36–37). Both Congress and the President were attempting to redefine and reform US foreign assistance, culminating in the 'New Direction' legislation of 1973 (Cohen, 2010: 210; Eberstadt, 1988: 37; Ruttan, 1996: 98). The general trend was a significant decline in bilateral assistance to Africa between 1971 and 1973 (DoS, 1973a).

The aim of Nixon's Africa policy was to ensure that Africa would continue to develop and remain outside Cold War rivalries. Policy statements throughout the administration involved three main themes (Haig, 1970;[17] Newsom, 1970; Nixon, 1970, 1971, 1972): the importance of Africa to the US, the US position on the problems in southern Africa (including Rhodesia); and on the Portuguese colonies in Africa. Towards 1973, the additional issue of the drought in the Sahel and subsequent relief efforts received ample attention from the executive and legislative branches. Nevertheless, the dominant issue in the African policy during the Nixon years was the racial and colonial issues in southern Africa and the possibilities for Soviet intervention.

In addition to communist activities in Africa, there were three other main considerations that affected the Africa policy (Nixon, 1972): the concerns of the African-American community and their domestic activities to influence policy; the increasing importance of the African vote in world affairs; and the growing importance of African natural resources for the US economy. Other important, albeit not crucial, strategic concerns were: rights to use African air space for civilian and military flights and refuelling options, access to shipyards that could accommodate the needs of American aircraft carriers,[18] control of shipping routes around the Cape, electronic listening posts and air monitoring stations, NASA communication stations important for the space programme and the strategic interests of allies in Africa (Bienen, 1978: 454–458).

The southern African problems consisted of three main issues: the UN declared illegal government headed by Ian Smith in Rhodesia subject to an international boycott beginning in 1965; white minority rule in South Africa together with its mandate over the former German colony in Southwest Africa (Namibia); and the persistent colonial presence of Portugal in Guinea-Bissau, Angola and Mozambique. These three issues, together with the severe 1973 drought in the Sahel, were the main African foreign policy items that made it to Nixon's desk.

Portugal declared that its 'colonies' were not colonies but overseas provinces and part of the nation of Portugal. This claim was rejected by most nations and all African countries. Portugal was therefore regarded as a colonial power on a continent that rejected colonialism and foreign rule.[19] While the US openly rejected colonial rule it hedged with respect to Portugal. First, Portugal was a NATO ally, and granted the US access to refuelling and space mission monitoring stations in her African territories (NSC, 1969[20]). In parallel, the Soviet Union, China and later Cuba, provided various types of support to the Mozambique Liberation Front (FRELIMO), the People's Movement for the Liberation of Angola (MPLA) and the African Party for the Independence of Guinea and Cape Verde. In addition to undermining Portugal's power both in Africa and Europe, this situation created a concern that communism might encroach in the region (Bienen, 1978: 445).

Minority rule and racial domination in southern Africa were a major concern for American policymakers. There were international calls for economic boycotts and sanctions while some countries suggested the use of force against South Africa and Rhodesia.[21] The US policy stance towards Rhodesia during the Nixon administration was greatly affected by the policy interests in South Africa (Lake, 1976: 127). In 1965, the white minority in Rhodesia led by Ian Smith, declared its independence from Britain. This led the Security Council to condemn the unilateral declaration of independence made by a racist minority in southern Rhodesia and called upon Britain to end the rebellion.[22] Britain imposed selective economic sanctions (1966) and comprehensive sanctions (1968). The US supported the United Nations and Britain.

In 1969, Kissinger commissioned a foreign policy review on southern Africa.[23] The study suggested five policy options towards southern Africa (including South Africa, Rhodesia and the Portuguese colonies) ranging from full normalisation of the relationship to severing all contacts. True to his realpolitik approach, Kissinger preferred the second option offered by the study, which called for a partial relaxation of tensions based on the premise that the white minority in southern Africa 'is here to stay' and that change in the region may be achieved through constructive rather than punitive measures (Schraeder, 1994: 206–211). Option Two, the 'tar baby' option,[24] argued that through relaxation of tensions and continuous diplomatic and economic aid to Africa, the US would preserve its economic, scientific and strategic interests, expand opportunities for trade and investment, ease tensions with Portugal, and continue to encourage 'black states' to reject communist influence in Africa (NSC, 1969).

There was a basic disagreement between the DoS and the national security staff at the White House about the approach to southern Africa and the white minority regimes.[25] While the DoS argued to maintain a policy of sanctions towards Rhodesia, and open condemnation of both the South African and Rhodesian regimes to maintain credibility with the 'black states' (Option Three of NSSM, 39), the national security staff preferred better communication and toned down rhetoric (Lake, 1976: 126). The main argument was that sanctions would not force the white regimes to relinquish their claims nor affect the racial segregation policies and colonial rule in southern Africa. The national security staff argued that US policy towards southern Africa between 1965 and 1968 led to economic losses to American-owned businesses. They believed that the relaxation of tensions would lead to economic development and would facilitate negotiations for a peaceful change of attitudes (Lake, 1976: 126). Kissinger recommended that the President adopt Option Two (Lake, 1976: 130). It incorporated rhetoric that condemned the minority rule and racial segregation regimes in southern Africa, while redefining sanctions, embargos and political pressures to allow increased economic and military transactions with South Africa, Portugal and Rhodesia (Lake, 1976: 133; see also Kissinger, 1970). Economic assistance was to play an important role in curbing the anticipated criticism from 'black Africa':

> We can, by selective relaxation of our stance toward the white regimes, encourage some modification of their current racial and colonial policies and through more substantial economic assistance to the black states (a total of about $5 million annually in technical assistance to the black states) help to draw the two groups together and exert some influence on both for peaceful change. Our tangible interests for a basis for our contacts in the region, and these can be maintained at an acceptable political cost.
>
> (NSC, 1969)

Officially, this policy was kept secret from the public to avoid controversy and condemnation both domestically and internationally (Lake, 1976: 123).

Illustrating the tensions between the DoS and the national security staff is a memorandum sent from Haig[26] to Kissinger in March 1970 about the DoS draft policy statement on Africa (Haig, 1970). The statement Haig attached to the memorandum contains suggested changes incorporated by Kissinger's national security staff. These changes represent the two approaches to southern Africa. The DoS statements on South Africa, Rhodesia and Portuguese Africa reflected their preference to lean towards the pan-African position stated in the Lusaka Manifesto which condemned the injustices in the southern part of the continent. The National Security staff suggested removing some of these statements while toning down others to be more consistent with Option Two of NSSM 39. In the conclusion section of the draft policy statement, the DoS included a quote from the Lusaka Manifesto and an additional concluding paragraph:

> Last fall the Organization of African Unity adopted its eloquent manifesto on southern Africa. Among other things it said:
>
>> [W]e do not accept that any individual or group has any right to govern any other individuals or groups of citizens, without their

> consent; and we affirm that only the people of a society acting together as equals, can determine what is, for them, a good social, economic and political organization.
>
> We Americans warmly welcome that statement. It charts the future. We had another document which did the same for us almost 200 years ago.
>
> That document, our own Declaration of Independence from colonial status, contained concepts as valid for human liberty today as they were to our forefathers – and as the Lusaka Manifesto suggests for the 300,000,000 people of Africa (deleted paragraph in Haig, 1970: 28).

The national security staff suggested replacing this section with the following text:

> As the President said in his Report to Congress on Foreign Policy:
>
>> We Want Africans to build a better life for themselves and their children. We want to see an Africa free of poverty and disease and free too of economic and political dependence on any outside power. And we want Africans to build this future as they think best, because in that way both our help and their efforts will be most relevant to their needs.
>> (Suggested replacement paragraph in Haig, 1970: 28)

On a continent that was not a priority for the White House (Nixon, 1970a; Schraeder, 1994: 206) and of very little concern for Congress (Schraeder, 1994: 211), the problems in southern Africa were considered the most significant foreign policy issues. The realpolitik that guided the approach to policy led America to cast its first veto in the Security Council to prevent severing all contacts with Rhodesia.[27] In 1971, Congress passed the Byrd Amendment[28] that allowed the US to import strategic materials from Rhodesia, most importantly chrome,[29] and in contradiction with international sanctions imposed on that country.[30] The African policy was in essence a balancing act between the need to address domestic concerns raised by the African-American community and civil rights movement, trade and commercial interests in Africa, pan-African politics, and the realpolitik of the Nixon–Kissinger administration that attempted to preserve the balance between the great superpowers.

While 'black Africa' was displeased with US policy towards the southern part of the continent, it was only in 1972 that America became concerned with this criticism (DoS, 1973). On 9 December 1971, the US renewed its agreement with Portugal regarding US rights to use the air and naval bases in the Azores.[31] In return, the US would grant Portugal a substantial aid package which included economic, educational, development, scientific and military assistance (USIS, 1972). This was understood by Africans as evidence of a close alliance between Portugal and the US. Subsequently, the US was charged with indirectly supporting Portuguese colonialism since US assistance to Portugal was being channelled to support control of their colonies in Africa (Gleijeses, 2002: 230; Litwak, 1984: 177–178). The Azores renewal agreement came a month after Congress passed the Byrd Amendment. These two issues led to criticism by many African countries, predominantly Nigeria, which accused the US of not only 'being unsympathetic to Black Africa' but of 'favoring minority-ruled southern Africa' (DoS, 1973). In an attempt to curb the new wave of criticism, Fernando Rondon of the National Security Council staff recommended a number of steps (DoS, 1973):

1 To promote US–African economic ties and try to encourage greater American private investment in African development. For this purpose, the NSC suggested that the President appoint an Assistant Secretary of State for Africa.
2 That Kissinger will initiate a new series of NSSM on sub-Saharan Africa.
3 That the President will increase his contact with Africa and will plan a presidential visit to the continent.
4 To consider an attempt to convince Congress to repel the Byrd Amendment.

Rondon reiterated the relatively low importance of sub-Saharan Africa to US global interests, but listed 10 American priorities in the region:

1 Natural resources
2 Investment
3 Trade
4 Strategic military facilities
5 Monitoring Soviet and Chinese facilities and intentions
6 Forestalling conflict
7 Science–technology
8 African voting power
9 Growing domestic interests in Africa
10. Humanitarian interests.

Humanitarian interests occupy the last position in this list and the justification paragraph reads: 'With sixteen of the world's twenty-five least-developed nations in sub-Saharan Africa, there will be a continuing humanitarian desire on the part of governmental and private institutions to assist Africa' (DoS, 1973).

Africa's poverty and aspirations to develop were consistently used by the President and other members of the executive branch in public statements, to explain how American ideals guide US engagement in development assistance. The public statements emphasise the morality behind development assistance, while in the non-public documentation the justification for assistance represented a realpolitik approach to foreign policy.[32]

In response to the drought in the Sahel there was a mobilisation of American resources to lead a relief effort to the affected regions in Africa. USAID Deputy Administrator Maurice J. Williams was appointed as the special co-ordinator for US emergency efforts in Africa. The US relief operation had two parts: immediate relief (namely delivering grain) and long-term efforts to help the recovery of affected African countries. One of the main objectives was to transform pastoralists into ranchers through development-oriented interventions, taking no account of systems in place with the aim of transforming herders into capitalists (Derman, 1978, 1984; Franke and Chasin, 1980). Secretary of State Kissinger often filtered correspondence addressed to Nixon, summarised it, and added his recommendations before sending it forward to his desk. In relation to Secretary Rogers' memorandum to the President on the Sahel drought crisis, Kissinger concurred with Rogers' proposal on the American response to the drought, and explained to Nixon that it was 'both a useful way to highlight our ongoing efforts, thereby evidencing our concern, and to enhance the effectiveness of our response' (Kissinger, 1973). While Rogers' letter highlighted the humanitarian aspects of US relief efforts, Kissinger's remarks focused on how such efforts would contribute to elevating the image of the US.

Africa was one of the main locations where Kissinger's realpolitik approach began to crack. Litwak (1984: 92–93) noted that the 'Nixon–Kissinger strategy grossly underestimated the importance of local actors in the determination of political outcomes along the periphery' and that it was 'overly optimistic … of the American ability to wield incentives and sanctions at its disposal so as to moderate Soviet behaviour'. The idea of détente was focused on easing the tensions between the superpowers. While the Soviet Union and the US worked to neutralise the dangers emanating from the Cold War, namely the risks of a direct nuclear conflict and the arms race, the sources of international instability moved to the periphery – to the Third World regions (Litwak, 1984: 167).

Although removed from sub-Saharan Africa, the October War in the Middle East during 1973 had important consequences contributing to a re-evaluation of the African policy. First, the evolution of the October War was an example of Cold War politics played in the periphery (see Kissinger, 2003). Most African nations stood in opposition to Israel, coupling the occupation of people and territories as a type of colonialism, and expressing their discontent to American officials of the support granted to Israel by the US[33] (see DoS, 1974, 1975). The October War also led to an energy crisis which underscored the importance of Africa as the second largest supplier of oil to the US (DoS, 1974: 22, 1974a).

Several events occurring in 1974 undermined US policy objectives in Africa. In January 1974, a civil war broke out in Ethiopia. Emperor Selassie was an important American ally and a major beneficiary of American aid (Bienen, 1978: 449). The Derg, (abbr. Coordinating Committee of the Armed Forces, Police and Territorial Army) ruled Ethiopia from 1974 to 1987. It took power following a period of military uprisings which led to the ousting of Emperor Haile Selassie I. Because of the importance of Ethiopia and the treaty of friendship signed between the USSR and Somalia, the US continued its substantial military assistance to the Derg. According to Mitchell (2016: 178), US military assistance to Ethiopia dramatically increased despite concerns about human rights abuses carried out by the Derg. However, it was not enough. As Ford left office, the Derg signed an arms agreement with the Soviet Union.

In southern Africa, one of the main tenants of Option Two forwarded in NSSM-39, namely that 'the whites are here to stay', proved to be inaccurate. On 25 April 1974, the Estado Novo regime in Portugal was ousted by a military coup. An important cause of the coup was the unpopular colonial wars waged by the regime in Mozambique, Angola and Guinea-Bissau. The coup led to a social revolution in Portugal that, among other things, led to the termination of the Portuguese colonial adventure. As a result of the coup and the instalment of democracy in Portugal, the outlawed Portuguese Communist Party re-joined politics and became a major force in that country. In a hearing before Congress, Kissinger noted that:

> The overthrow of the Portuguese government in April 1974 and the growing strength of the Portuguese Communist party apparently convinced Moscow that a 'revolutionary situation' was developing in Africa.
>
> (Kissinger quoted in Litwak, 1984: 178)

The communist involvement in the events that took place in Ethiopia and Portuguese Africa signalled the deterioration of détente (Cohen, 2010: 212). During the Ford administration, this reality led to a re-evaluation of the African policy and to a greater US involvement on the continent, including intensified military aid and covert CIA operations.

## The Cold War intensifies in Africa

As a reflection of the low priority assigned by Kissinger to Africa south of the Sahara, the US still did not have a detailed separate country by country policy. The tendency to be reactive to internal disruptions in individual countries and communist activities on the continent indicated that US Africa policy still lacked long-term planning (Bienen, 1978: 449; Easum, 2010). This was recognised in a major review of US African Policy conducted by DoS together with AID in 1975 (DoS, 1975a) and by the Black Caucus in Congress (DoS, 1975d).

In the early seventies, it appeared that global power was shifting in favour of communism. It certainly seemed as though American power had weakened. Ford assumed the Presidency as Nixon stepped down in the wake of the Watergate scandal. The US retreated from Vietnam after years of fighting a bloody and expensive war and without achieving its objective of preventing South Vietnam from becoming communist. The NATO alliance had been weakened from tensions between Greece and Turkey and the coup in Portugal which strengthened the communist party in that country. The oil embargo imposed by the OPEC cartel during the Middle East crisis of 1973 led to soaring prices and a recession that affected the West as well as the Third World. In southern Africa, liberation movements were supported by the Soviet Union and China and adopted Marxist ideologies as Portugal retreated from its colonies. A civil war in Ethiopia (1974) instigated by a *coup d'état* led by Marxists resulted in a further alienation of the US (Cohen, 2010: 212; Schraeder, 1994: 136). The CIA was increasingly involved in covert operations to help repel communism and protect US economic and strategic interests in many African countries (Lemarchand, 1976; Paterson *et al.*, 1991: 589; Schmidt, 2013). US–Africa relations were on a downturn (DoS, 1975a). Despite the effort of past policies to prevent it, the continent was slowly becoming an arena for the Cold War. This situation was slowly leading to a recognition that the African continent south of the Sahara merited more policy attention (DoS, 1974a, 1975a). At the same time, Congress was set on limiting presidential powers and increasing its oversight over the executive branch in an effort to avoid another Vietnam, thus closely scrutinising attempts to spend money abroad and engage in covert action (Callaway and Matthews, 2008: 41–42; Paterson *et al.*, 1991: 591; Schraeder, 1994: 47). Kissinger believed that the 'national hysteria on Vietnam' was driving congressional reluctance to allow action against ongoing Soviet attacks on the détente strategy (Cohen, 2010: 212; Kissinger, 1979: 1257).

A month before the 1974 *coup d'état* in Portugal, Kissinger appointed Donald Easum to the position of Assistant Secretary for African Affairs. Easum, a former US ambassador to Upper Volta, was set to adjust the African policy to the shifting geopolitical reality. He proceeded with a five-week visit to several African countries where he met US ambassadors and African leaders. In meetings conducted during the visit, Easum indicated that the US was leaning towards shifting its policy on southern Africa, seeking to recognise and establish relations with new nations regardless of the political orientation of ruling parties, as well as to adopt a stricter line against the white minority regimes (Bender, 1978: 71–72; Easum, 2010). Kissinger was unhappy with the 'missionary zeal that Easum brought to southern African affairs' (Cable, 1974), and especially his statements indicating that America would work to change the status quo in southern

Africa (Cable, 1974, 1975; Easum, 2010). Upon his return from his African trip, Kissinger removed Easum from his position and appointed former US ambassador to Chile, Nathaniel Davis as Assistant Secretary for African Affairs. The Africans voiced concerns that Davis's appointment indicates an American intention to address the geopolitical changes in Africa through CIA covert action. These concerns were linked to Davis's former position as the US ambassador to Chile during the *coup d'état* supported by the US and the CIA against Salvador Allende. African leaders feared that the US had made a decision to destabilise Africa (Bender, 1978: 72; DoS, 1975b, 1975c).

Previously the US adopted a policy towards southern Africa that balanced its criticism of the white regimes with its various strategic and economic interests. This came at the cost of antagonising much of Africa, a price that Kissinger was willing to pay to pursue his grand strategy. With the dissolution of Portuguese power, there was a need to embrace new independent states and counter elements that had the potential to install pro-Soviet governments. Two regions were at the centre of US strategic interests in Africa during the Ford years: southern Africa and the Horn of Africa[34] (DoS, 1975a). Kissinger viewed the Soviet interference in former Portuguese Africa as an aggressive act of expansionism and adventurism (Kissinger, 1979: 1257). For him, Africa was in a 'revolutionary situation' (DoS, 1974b). In the former Portuguese colonies, the three liberation movements in Angola: the MPLA, FNLA (National Liberation Front of Angola), and UNITA (National Union for the Total Independence of Angola) signed in January 1975 the Alvor Accords to end the liberation war and start a peaceful transition towards an independent state. However, ideological differences between the parties soon led to an outbreak of civil war where the Soviet-backed (and later Cuban-backed) MPLA fought against the American- and South African-backed FNLA[35] and UNITA. In Mozambique, the Marxist–Leninist party FRELIMO took control of the country in June 1975, and a year later a civil war began pitting FRELIMO against the anti-communist party RENAMO (Mozambican National Resistance), supported by Rhodesia and South Africa.[36] Both South Africa (which controlled Namibia by mandate) and Rhodesia had an interest in the instalment of governments in Angola and Mozambique that would continue the economic collaboration that had existed under Portuguese rule, and minimise criticism against the white minority regimes. They therefore backed, assisted by the US (Stockwell, 1978: 68) certain political parties in those countries which promised the preservation of mutually beneficial relationships.

Against this background, new US policy guidelines for sub-Saharan Africa were drafted (DoS, 1975a). The document included an outline of American interests in sub-Saharan Africa, an estimate of how future prospects in Africa were going to affect these interests, and recommendations for policy. The emphasis was that the interests of individual African countries differed from each other. To overcome the plurality of interests they recommended that the US identify a broader context through which a useful and coherent policy could be formulated to address the continent. The suggestions included addressing Africa through the OAU; categorising African countries in ways that policy could address a group of countries and similar broad issues, for example, adopting sub-regional categories such as the Horn of Africa, the Sahel, or southern Africa; or categorisation according to identifiable interests such as affiliation with a former colonial power, or according to an economic category such as Least Developed Countries (LDCs). Kissinger once explained at a meeting with the Black Caucus in Congress that he had not made a policy statement on Africa since he was unable to formulate a statement that would 'serve all the various African countries' (DoS, 1975d). The main problem, he explained, was that he could not find a common denominator, and promised the Black Caucus that he would devote more attention to the African policy (DoS, 1975d).

Interests in Africa were divided into four categories: strategic, economic, political and US domestic. The strategic interests in Africa were considered modest in relation to other regions. During the time this document was drafted (June 1975), communist activity on the continent was considered limited (DoS, 1975a). It was specified that a strategic objective of the US was to obstruct communist and 'unfriendly' Arab governments from gaining political influence on the continent. The strategic assets in Africa included listening and tracking stations in Ethiopia and other locations, overflight and landing rights for US civilian and military aircraft, access to ports for US navy ships and oil tankers, and secure shipping lanes in proximity to the Horn of Africa and around the southern Cape. The most significant concerns were related to losing overflight and landing rights, and losing access to port facilities in Mozambique, Angola and Ethiopia.

The most important economic objectives for the US were to keep access to resources at acceptable prices and terms. In addition to chrome and tin, most importantly, 20 per cent of all US crude oil imports originated in Nigeria, and the estimates indicated that this would likely rise in the future. The document indicated that African countries in general and especially the LDCs held economic and political grievances against developed countries, and as a result, they would often 'organize economic pressures against the rich' (DoS, 1975a). This led African countries to seek more control over their own resources to extract concessions from developed countries, including revisions of trade and monetary agreements as well as aid. One suggested way to curb the attempt to organise economic pressure against the US was to strengthen, where appropriate, the direct bilateral relations between the US and selected important countries.

US political interests in Africa fell into two categories: protection and promotion of important bilateral interests (which usually meant US access to natural resources), and ensuring African support of US positions on international issues. Winning support from African countries was viewed as a poor prospect. The assessment was that African opposition to the West in international institutions was tainted by an 'emotional element' against ex-colonial powers and as a demonstration of independence from 'white' nations (DoS, 1975a).

The estimate was that African obstructionism to US international initiatives was likely to continue, especially as long as the US avoided a firm stance against the white minority regimes in the southern Africa. Nevertheless, the estimates predicted that even if US policy towards the white minority regimes was to change, there would still be significant divergent interests, mostly economic, which were likely to influence the voting strategy of African countries in international forums (DoS, 1975a). Domestically, there was a growing outcry by black minorities and human rights movements against morally questionable policies, especially in relation to the white minority regimes in Namibia, South Africa and Rhodesia. These domestic trends were important enough to be factored into the formulation of the African policy.

To address these issues, protect and promote US interests in sub-Saharan Africa, eight recommendations were formulated (DoS, 1975a):

1   Promote bilateral relations with 'key black African countries' where major resources, significant investments, and key strategic objectives are located. These countries were grouped into three categories based on the volume of trade and investment as well as strategic importance: in the first category, South Africa and Nigeria were listed as the main countries. In the second category were countries of 'major importance', which included Angola, Zaire and Ethiopia. In the third and largest category, the coastal states of East Africa[37] and West Africa.[38] They offer natural resources and future prospects for investment. The document notes that the remaining very poor states were mainly of humanitarian interest and possible future natural resources.

2   'Tailor' foreign assistance (development and military) 'to Africa in such a way as to derive optimum bilateral benefit for this assistance.' It advises to minimise assistance to countries able to develop on their own (Nigeria and South Africa) as well as to countries who received assistance from other sources (for example, Europe). To lessen congressional and public criticisms, aid could be increased to the 'poorest of the poor' despite the lack of economic and political objectives in those countries. Doing so 'will lend credibility to the contention that our development aid is disinterested and not given solely to advance our own fortunes in major recipient countries' (DoS, 1975a).

3   Promote a separation between political disagreements and mutually beneficial economic relationships.

4   Accommodate specific African wishes on investment and trade to create a better investment climate, 'reduce governmental harassment', and reconsider elements in trade agreements. This could help remove some bureaucratic barriers for investment as well as curb African criticism against US trade policies.
5   Limit the expansion of US strategic facilities in Africa. This recommendation sought to reduce criticism against American ties with South Africa and promote keeping Africa away from Cold War rivalries.
6   Recognise that Africa (as a bloc) would continue to oppose US positions on international issues and tailor a suitable strategy. For example, consider being less negative to Afro-Asian initiatives where the impact on US principles are minimal.
7   Pay more attention to the way in which the US treats African countries and leaders. This was viewed as matter that would affect the ego of African leaders, which leads to a significant impact on the relationship between the US and specific countries. It was recognised in the document that attitudes towards African countries plays a significant role and that Africans 'very much resent being treated by [the US] as the runt of the international litter' (DoS, 1975a).
8   The document recommends pursuing the current policy towards South Africa where the costs of changing policy would outweigh the current benefits. US interests in Rhodesia and Namibia were 'far less important'. The recommendations were to adopt a firmer stance, such as repealing the Byrd Amendment, enforcing the embargo on Rhodesia, and discouraging US investment in Namibia. Toward newly independent Angola and Mozambique the recommendation was to respond positively to 'requests of development assistance or emergency food and financial aid would help demonstrate to the many skeptical leaders in Africa that the US truly welcomes self-determination in South Africa' (DoS, 1975a).

Despite the estimates, during 1975, Moscow stepped up its involvement in sub-Saharan Africa. The new Soviet activity[39] was centred on the former Portuguese territories and included positioning of naval and air force assets in Guinea-Bissau as well as granting renewed support to the MPLA in Angola,[40] arms shipments and technical assistance. An intelligence report indicated that the Soviets were now providing military aid to 17 African countries (DoS, 1976). In return for their support, the Soviets were gaining strategic access for military assets, as well as enhancing their political and economic influence on the continent.

Beginning in mid-1975, the foreign involvement in internal Angolan power struggles escalated (Schmidt, 2013: 122–123). Committed to preventing Moscow from gaining advantage over America, Kissinger viewed the situation in Angola as a US–Soviet-relations problem rather than as an

African situation (Bender, 1978: 65; Davis, 1978). In June 1975, President Ford authorised new CIA operations in Angola[41] in an attempt to counter the Soviet support to the MPLA (Stockwell, 1978; Weiner, 2007: 348–349). By January 1976, troops from Zaire and South Africa were fighting alongside UNITA and the FNLA against the MPLA. The Soviet Union was backing the MPLA with relatively advanced weapons and providing military advice and expertise, while Cuba expedited thousands of soldiers by air and sea to assist combat operations on behalf of the MPLA to repel an attack by South Africa. While the situation was deteriorating, Assistant Secretary for African Affairs Davis resigned his post in disagreement with the course chosen by Kissinger and the President to intervene in Angola through military aid and covert operations rather than following the DoS advice to use diplomacy (Davis, 1978). The resignation brought public attention to the involvement of the US in the Angolan civil war, raising concerns that the situation could give rise to another Vietnam-like debacle[42] (Paterson et al., 1991: 591). Consequently, Congress decided to cut all aid to Angola[43] leading eventually to another perceived American policy failure although the US continued to support UNITA in its military campaigns against the government. In Mozambique, tensions ran high between the US and the newly independent FRELIMO government. Since the dissolution of Portuguese power, America made several efforts to improve its relationship with FRELIMO. But the party distrusted the US due to the support granted to Portugal during the late colonial period, as well as the support for the other white minority regimes. In addition, America's position against the MPLA in Angola, as well as Kissinger's removal of Easum as Assistant Secretary shortly after his return from the African trip,[44] increased Mozambican suspicions of US motives (Isaacman and Davis, 1978: 38–40). The media in the US and conservative congressional representatives publicly accused FRELIMO of being racist and imperial and of turning Mozambique into a Soviet satellite country also contributed to tensions between Washington and Maputo (Isaacman and Davis, 1978: 41–43).

Since Mozambique was granting support to the Zimbabwean African National Liberation Army (ZANLA)[45] against the Smith regime, Mozambique found itself in a direct military conflict with Rhodesia (Isaacman and Davis, 1978: 44–46), and eventually in a bitter civil war between FRELIMO and the anti-communist party RENAMO supported by South Africa and Rhodesia.

The worsening situation in southern Africa was seen by Kissinger and his staff as a warning that Africa was heading towards radicalisation. On 29 January 1976, two days after the Senate decided to cut covert aid to Angola (The Clark Amendment), Kissinger appeared before the Senate Foreign Relations Committee to present an analysis of the events. He began by emphasising that the Soviet Union had begun an 'unprecedented intervention in the internal affairs of Africa' (Kissinger, 1976). He presented the situation in Angola as a unilateral Soviet breach of détente understandings. He explained that an American response was required to preserve the global balance of power. He also expressed his dissatisfaction with the congressional decision to intervene with the authority of the executive branch by withholding covert aid to Angola (Kissinger, 1976). Kissinger indicated that US covert actions in Angola were intended to respond to the 'unprecedented' application of Soviet power in sub-Saharan Africa by way of their client state, Cuba, and to grant support to US 'friends in black Africa' against the Soviet Union and Cuba. He explained that when Congress impedes the actions of the executive branch in such cases when vital interests of the US are affected, the repercussions may undermine the security of the world.

With congressional limits, Kissinger decided to visit Africa where he would meet with leaders and make several announcements in an attempt to prevent further deterioration and radicalisation of the continent (DoS, 1976a). President Ford later commented in his autobiography that Kissinger:

> [W]as going to tell the nations of black Africa that they could not achieve what they wanted through war, and that only with U.S. help could they hope to gain majority rule in Rhodesia, independence for Namibia and the rejection of apartheid in South Africa.
> (Ford, 1979: 380)

Ford explained that sending Kissinger to Africa with this message was not an easy decision during an election year in the US. He believed that it would be difficult to win over the southern states in America while his staff released statements supporting black majority rule in African countries currently governed by white minorities (Ford, 1979: 380; Rodman, 2009: 112). Despite the invocation of moral imperatives, international law and world peace by President Ford (1979: 380) and Kissinger (1976a: 672),[46] the main reason for the African trip was to protect the vital interests of the US against Soviet expansionism.[47] As discussed below, development assistance was to be a main tool in this strategy.

As a part of Kissinger's preparations for the African trip, USAID administrator Daniel Parker sent an action memorandum to the Secretary of State to support an international development investment programme for the Sahel. Kissinger's approval of the initiative was crucial for the inclusion of relevant budgetary requests from Congress (DoS, 1976b). Parker outlined a number of foreign policy considerations that justified supporting the programme. The first was related to the new 'tensions' in Africa (referring to white minority regimes), thus tying development assistance in the Sahel[48] to the current situation in southern Africa. Parker explained that '[a] significant demonstration of interest in African development would be perceived positively, and would be highly visible, well beyond the directly-benefitted nations' (DoS, 1976b). He supported the idea that a substantial Western investment in African development would help keep a focus on 'positive achievement rather than rhetorical radicalism'[49] (DoS, 1976b). An investment in development assistance in Africa would therefore contribute to a significant improvement of US relations with the continent and help reduce tensions created by political differences. Finally, Parker reminded Kissinger that Africa was rich in raw materials of significant importance to the US. A focus on African development would contribute to US economic interests through improvement of investment, trade, access to natural resources and development of untapped resources on the continent.

A few days before he left for Africa, Kissinger met with African ambassadors to outline and explain the purpose of the tour. He highlighted the American commitment to African development and explained that peace in Africa, progress and development are important to the 'developed world' because Africa is 'a major continent and because of conflicts in Africa have a tendency of spilling over as conflicts in other parts of the world' (DoS 1976g).

On 24 April 1976, Kissinger began his visit to six African countries to introduce 'a new era in American policy' (Kissinger, 1976a: 673)[50] indicating a new importance for Africa. The main policy statement was announced in Lusaka, Zambia, in a symbolic attempt to relate the statement to the Lusaka Declaration of 1971 (Kissinger, 1976a: 674). As Kissinger explained to the President and the NSC upon his return from Africa, the strategy behind the 'new policy' was focused on preventing 'the further radicalization of Africa and prevent it all from becoming a black–white issue where even the moderates would have to be against the US (DoS, 1976d). By a 'new policy' Kissinger was referring to an approach to two linked challenges: the strengthening of Soviet and Cuban presence in Africa,[51] and assuming a firmer position against the white minority regimes in rhetoric and action,[52] and on introducing new commitments for economic and development assistance.[53] In Lusaka, Kissinger emphasised common interests, namely 'to build a secure and just future for Africa' (Kissinger 1976a: 673). To the President (DoS, 1976d) and to the NSC (1976), Kissinger reported the main gains of his trip. In return for a firmer position on southern Africa and larger packages of development and economic assistance, he secured commitments from Tanzania, Zambia, Mozambique and Botswana on the following:

1   There will be no call for Cuban troops.
2   There will be no direct dealings by outsiders with the liberation movements, a decision designed to prevent the communists from influencing the Rhodesian struggle.
3   All arms shipments are to go through neighboring governments.
4   While they could not prevent armed struggle … [the] struggle had to be ended by negotiations.

> 5   It was agreed that [the United States] ... would deal more actively with South Africa and ... would not continue to treat them as pariahs. Thus [the United States] ... gained more freedom of movement with respect to South Africa.
>
> (NSC, 1976)

To address the current presence of Cuban troops in Angola, Kissinger hoped to secure the help of various African nations through assistance programmes:

> If we succeed in giving African states a positive program to rally around, then the moderates would be able to show the benefit of working with us and the radicals may begin to feel differently. This was the reason for my suggestions for a reconstruction of the Sahel.
>
> (NSC, 1976)

The new African policy was part of a way to address the failure to curb the Soviet threat in Africa. Kissinger's strategy was to harness support from African nations antagonised by previous US policy. While Kissinger reported that he secured support from several nations, he hoped to win over others with development programmes such as the Sahel programme and other major programmes focusing on Kenya, Zaire, Senegal and Zambia[54] (NSC, 1976).

Kissinger also worked to establish a Special Fund for African Development to address the radicalisation of Africa and establish a 'politically effective organisation to give immediate economic assistance to Western oriented African countries' (DoS, 1976e). This was a French–American initiative that would include 'European nations with historic ties to Africa' (DoS, 1976e). In practice, the operationalised objectives of the Fund would consist of granting support to improve infrastructure, combating drought, develop mineral resources and modernise agriculture. Kissinger welcomed the idea of the Special Fund as an effective means to co-ordinate the efforts of industrialised countries to bring about peace and stability in Africa (DoS, 1976f).

This new focus on economic and development assistance was, in effect, a turn towards fighting the Cold War with soft power. This was not Kissinger's preferred way, but since Congress limited his hard power options, he had to consider other possibilities. In addition, the administration was also exploring military assistance avenues. In 1976, shortly after Kissinger's African trip, President Ford sent a Secretary of Defence (Donald Rumsfeld) for the first time to Africa. This was a signal that the military dimension of US assistance was still relevant alongside the economic and political dimensions (DoS, 1976c).

As a part of the new policy approach to Africa, President Ford ratified towards the end of his administration the membership of the US in the African Development Fund, pledging America's participation in multilateral efforts for development. In January 1977, Jimmy Carter was sworn in as President, promising a new American focus on human rights and a fresh approach toward developing countries.

## SALT lies buried in the sands of the Ogaden[55]

The elections that took place in November 1976 were the first opportunity for the American people to express their frustration over the defeat in Vietnam and the Watergate scandal through a ballot. During his presidential bid, Carter repeatedly flagged the loss of idealism and morality in the executive branch. He criticised Ford for his lack of leadership in foreign policy and for allowing Kissinger to dominate decisions. For Carter the Nixon–Ford–Kissinger years were a time when the executive moved away from the fundamental principles that define America. He vowed to change the image of America by conducting policy based on moral principles and American values where human rights would be championed. He wanted the government to be open and honest, and eliminate the secrecy that characterised the Nixon and Ford administrations. He believed that Ford and Kissinger were attending to matters in developing countries with paternalism and with excessive interference with their internal affairs. He promised a 'greater foreign policy focus on developing nations in general and Africa in particular', and vowed to help install black majority rule in southern Africa (Debate-Briefing, 1976).[56]

However, it is important to emphasise that like his predecessors, Carter was a cold warrior.[57] His distinct foreign policy was based on his personal convictions and a world view which yielded an innovative approach to communism. He was a born-again Christian deeply devoted to his faith. He served his country on a nuclear submarine, and was deeply influenced by his formation as a naval officer (Paterson *et al.*, 1991: 624).

Carter based his approach to foreign policy on the essential character of the US: a democratic nation established upon fundamental values, which uses its power and influence to promote human purpose (Carter, 1977). He promised in his inaugural address a commitment to human rights and to deal with the world based on the same principles applied at home. This was a striking contrast to the Nixon doctrine and Kissinger's realpolitik which assumed a globalist approach[58] to counter the accumulation of Soviet power. He contended that America would handle any situation based on context with an emphasis on human rights to reflect American principles. The Soviet Union would be defeated by conducting a moral and ethical foreign policy where assistance is granted based on human rights criteria rather than responding to Soviet policy (Apodaca, 2006: 54). This would eliminate support to oppressive and problematic regimes given under the pretext of fending off communism; it would avoid dragging America into proxy wars; and it would restore America's position as a positive world power. This approach would also be consistent with the wishes of the American people and Congress who linked human rights to US foreign assistance in 1974.[59] Those wishes were often ignored by previous administrations (Cohen, 1982).

Nancy Mitchell argues that Carter's deep Cold War instincts have not been fully understood or appreciated. Because of his referrals to morality, values or human rights his emphasis upon restoring America's image was based simultaneously on restoring Washington's values and power (2016: 8–9). He believed that if the US behaved toward the world as it did toward its own citizens this would lead by its nature to a more positive image of America and would eventually result in more support and friendship from the world community to US positions. However, the application of human rights criteria as a condition for American assistance led Carter to insist on human rights for some countries but not for ones that were close allies.[60]

Using human rights as the focal point for foreign policy helped raise the overall importance of Africa in the general agenda (Smith, 1986: 133). There were many issues on the continent that needed a clear policy statement by the US, and adherence to human rights principles served as a ladder to climb down from problematic past policies, especially towards southern Africa. In general, Carter endorsed Kissinger's policy approach towards Africa introduced in 1976, assuming a firmer stance in support of majority rule and enhanced development and economic assistance, but he believed it was long overdue, perhaps even too late to win back African support for the US (Debate-Briefing, 1976).[61]

The strategic interests of the US in Africa remained relatively unchanged. The Cuban and Soviet presence established in Angola was a source of serious concern, as was the tightening relationship between Moscow and Addis Ababa in the Horn. National resources and especially Nigerian oil were of consequential economic and strategic importance, and as a result, the political positions and preferences of the Nigerian government were taken into consideration when relevant. The racial tensions in southern Africa loomed large, and were affecting almost every other policy issue on the continent. Carter's moralistic approach to foreign policy and his commitment to human rights demanded a clear-cut American position on the white minority rule in Africa, which meant sustained efforts to resolve the issues in Rhodesia, Namibia and South Africa. Nevertheless, communist presence on the continent created tensions between idealism and realism. This manifested most forcibly through the disagreements between National Security Advisor Brzezinski and Secretary of State Vance, especially on policy issues in Africa. The rapid collapse of Angola into a pro-communist regime created two major concerns for American geopolitics in the region. First, the mere presence of the Soviet Union and Cuban troops undermined American influence and power. Second, there was a concern that after the inevitable future collapse of the white minority regimes in Rhodesia, Namibia and South Africa, the entire southern part of the African continent could fall behind the Iron curtain. The approach to Africa was therefore constituted by the intention to conduct a human rights-based policy, but with full awareness of Cold War realities.

Carter came into office with a strong commitment to racial equality and he saw in southern Africa many of the same issues he confronted when he was governor of Georgia. Carter believed that as long as the Smith regime in Rhodesia rejected majority rule, and as long as South Africa governed Namibia, there was little chance of achieving an agreement with Angola and removing the presence of Cuban troops. As long as the prospect of instability existed in southern Africa, there was a concern that the Soviet Union would interfere to exercise its influence on the outcomes.

On the Rhodesian issue, Carter followed up Kissinger's policy by assuring the repeal of the Byrd amendment by Congress as an important step of reconciliation with black Africa (1977). He made several public statements clarifying that America did not recognise the legality of the Smith regime, nor did it accept the racial policies imposed by its rule. There was little disagreement between Brzezinski and Vance on this approach, which can be taken as an indication that on Rhodesia there was no conflict between idealism and realism (Mitchell, 2007: 268). The US and the British were pressing Rhodesia in concert; Ian Smith proposed an internal solution that involved the free election of a new government in Rhodesia to include representatives of the black majority (Vance, 1983: 260). He conducted elections in 1979, and Bishop Abel Muzorewa was voted into office. Carter met with him in July of 1979 and found that his was not an acceptable government (Mitchell, 2016: 600–604). In agreement with Vance's and Andy Young's[62] views and in opposition to many in Congress who advocated lifting sanctions against Rhodesia due to the steps taken by Smith, Carter did not recognise the new government. First, there was a concern that the 'internal solution' was a compromise devised by Smith to appease the world while preserving the status of whites in Rhodesia; second, the internal solution excluded from the settlement the two important opposition groups fighting against Smith, the Zimbabwe African National Union (ZANU) and the Zimbabwe African Peoples' Union (ZAPU)[63] (Brzezinski, 1983: 142; Mitchell, 2007: 263). Without the participation of the popular opposition groups in the elections, the war for independence could not be ended. If the war did not end there was the increasing likelihood that Cuban troops could enter (Andrew Young quoted in Mitchell, 2007: 274). American and British persistence in this case led eventually to a peaceful solution in 1980, beginning with the temporary restoration of the British rule in Rhodesia, followed by free elections that brought about an independent Zimbabwe and Robert Mugabe as Prime Minister, the lifting of sanctions against Zimbabwe and granting economic aid to the newly independent nation (Smith, 1986: 142).

Carter's genuine concern for racial justice and his commitment to human rights also led him to adopt a firm rhetorical stance against the apartheid regime in South Africa (Brzezinski, 1983: 139; Schraeder, 1994:

216), especially in the shadow of the Afrikaner use of force during the Soweto uprising in June 1976 (Schraeder, 1994: 215). Carter clarified to the South African President, BJ Vorster[64] that America would not condone apartheid, would support the independence of Namibia, would pursue a just solution for Rhodesia and would adopt punitive economic measures against South Africa, including restricting American private economic activities in Namibia (Schraeder, 1994: 215–216; Vance, 1983: 265). Dismayed by the administration's stance against his regime, Vorster accused America of meddling with the internal affairs of South Africa. Consequently, the relationship between South Africa and the US began to deteriorate. Vorster intensified the repression of the black population[65] despite international protests, and made alarming announcements that South Africa was not obligated to avoid the production and testing of nuclear weapons (Smith, 1986: 144–145). The US continued to publicly oppose the apartheid regime, denouncing it as racist, and taking symbolic diplomatic measures,[66] but stalling its support for the imposition of sanctions against South Africa due to the complicated issue of Namibian independence (Gleijeses, 2010: 885; Schraeder, 1994: 216–218). The independence of Namibia connected the South African policy to the presence of the Soviet Union and Cuba in Angola. The South-West African People's Organization (SWAPO) fighting for the liberation of Namibia from South Africa, was carrying out military campaigns in Namibia against South African troops. SWAPO bases were located across the border in Angola where 20,000 Cuban troops were situated (Vance, 1983: 272). This was a major source of tension between South Africa and the newly independent state of Angola. The presence of Cuban troops meant that if South Africa would venture deeper into Angola in pursuit of SWAPO, the situation had the potential to deteriorate into a South African–Cuban conflict that could inflame the region (Vance, 1983: 274). Vance believed that as long as Namibia was under South African rule, it would be impossible to negotiate the removal of Cuban troops from Angola and diminish Soviet influence in Africa.

In an attempt to achieve a solution on Namibian independence, the Americans with Western members of the Security Council formed a negotiation framework (the 'Contact Group') to create a bridge between South Africa and SWAPO to enable free elections in Namibia and to end the South African mandate. Economic sanctions by the UN against South Africa due to the apartheid regime were delayed by the Contact Group because of a concern that it might lead to a deadlock in the Namibian negotiations (Vance, 1983: 275). But, as Vance noted in his memoirs:

> The existence of the process, the determined efforts of the contact group to move it forward, and the real, if incomplete, progress that it produced were essential to rectify the damage done to Western relations with sub-Saharan Africa over prior years. Without the Namibia

negotiating process – together with the Zimbabwe settlement – the United States would have no workable strategy for improving its relations with black Africa and blocking the spread of Soviet and Cuban influence in southern Africa.

(Vance, 1983: 313)

Brzezinski held a different view than Vance. He contended that sanctions against South Africa would target the wrong side whereas what should guide foreign policy, was the Cuban and Soviet threat (Gleijeses, 2010: 887). This meant that the apartheid regime, the racial injustice and the illegal rule in Namibia were important, but secondary to the concern of Soviet expansionism and influence in Africa.

Tensions between the American regionalist and globalist approaches to the interpretation of challenges in Africa occurred in two other major border conflicts during the Carter administration: the conflict between Angola and Zaire during the Katangan invasions of the Shaba region in 1977 and 1978, and the conflict between Ethiopia and Somalia in the Ogaden region occurring at the same time. On both accounts, the involvement of the Soviet Union and the presence of Cuban troops were at the heart of the disagreements between Secretary Vance and National Security Advisor Brzezinski. Vance wrote in his memoirs that the administration's response to the events in Africa in 1977:

[W]ould have a major effect on Third World perception of [U.S.] policy toward the developing nations, and would set the tone for the remainder of the administration.

(Vance, 1983: 70)

Brzezinski preferred a policy approach that would actively use the idea of détente to demand that the Soviets halt their support of military build-up around the world (especially in the Third World). Vance preferred focusing on foreign policy responses that regarded the context of challenges as the main issue rather than creating linkages to a grand-design of global Soviet expansionism (Brzezinski, 1983: 146–150, 178–179; Smith, 1986: 153–154; Vance, 1983: 84–85, 91). Vance argued that linking foreign policy towards Africa to Soviet activities on that continent would prevent America from achieving its separate African policy objectives, as well as lead to a failure to conduct principle-based foreign policy (Vance, 1983: 85). Brzezinski believed that the US should respond to Soviet activities by organising international pressure against them, threatening to withdraw from détente understandings, and with a more proactive demonstration of US resolve and power.

President Mobutu of Zaire was a close ally of the US as well as a military dictator and a human rights abuser (Schraeder, 1994: 90). During the conflict for power in Angola, Mobutu supported covert CIA operations assisting UNITA and the FNLA against the MPLA. Mobuto also granted the FNLA permission to conduct raids into Angola from Zaire. Perhaps in retaliation, the government of Angola supported exiles from the Shaba (Katanga) province in Zaire. In March 1977, the Katangans invaded the mineral-rich Shaba province[67] with the intention to overthrow Mobutu (Mitchell, 166–174; Schraeder, 1994: 87). Mobutu turned to his American allies for support, claiming that the Katangan invasion was a Soviet design and assisted by Cuban military advisors. True to the regionalist approach, America refused to intervene with military support, but agreed to continue supporting Zaire with non-lethal aid. Schraeder (1994: 89) notes that Mobutu's inability to address a relatively limited invasion after years of receiving substantial American economic and military aid exposed the ineptitude of his regime, and led to criticism by some in Congress, demanding to cease American support for his corrupt regime (see also Vance, 1983: 70). The US was not prepared to allow the collapse of Mobutu's regime and the uncertain prospects associated with the loss of another ally in the region (Schraeder, 1994: 89; Vance, 1983: 70). In response to the Shaba I conflict, America decided to focus on support that consisted of 'non-lethal military equipment and further economic assistance to Zaire' (Vance, 1983: 70) and assisted the French to rescue Mobutu (Mitchell, 2016: 170) despite the corruption, ineptitude and his human rights record. The invasions were finally repelled with the help of Moroccan and French troops, and the US managed to address the Shaba I conflict without turning it into a Cold War issue. But less than a year later, the Katangans staged another invasion of the Shaba province.[68] In response to this conflict, America assumed a globalist approach, linking it to the Soviet Union and Cuba. To understand this shift we need to connect the Shaba II conflict to the events that took place in the Horn of Africa and the disagreements between Brzezinski and Vance on the linkages between the African policy and East–West tensions.

The disagreements between Brzezinski and Vance were on display during the crisis in the Horn of Africa during 1977 and 1978 between Somalia and Ethiopia. The US always considered the Horn of Africa as a strategic area. General William Odom[69] once remarked that the Horn of Africa ties the Arab peninsula through Egypt to Africa and should be regarded in strategic terms as a part of the Middle East–South-west Asian States grouping (Odom, 1992: 158). Until Emperor Selassie was ousted by the Derg in 1974, the US enjoyed close military and economic relations with Ethiopia. This friendship translated into American access to military and civilian facilities in Ethiopia as well as support in the international arena. In return, Ethiopia enjoyed American foreign assistance and support against Soviet-backed hostilities in Eritrea[70] and from Somalia (Henze, 1986: 27). After the Derg assumed power, Ethiopia moved steadily closer to the Soviet Union at the expense of American interests.[71]

On the eastern border of Ethiopia lay Somalia, an ally of the Soviet Union since 1963. Somalia, which was formed through the unification of British and Italian Somaliland in 1960, had claimed that its national territory should include Djibouti, parts of northern Kenya and the Ogaden region in Ethiopia, all inhabited by a majority of ethnic Somalis (Lefebvre, 1998: 613). This claim was categorically unacceptable according to the OAU Cairo Resolution of 1964, which stated that African nations agree to respect the territorial borders as conceived on the day of their independence, and agreed to respect the territorial integrity of other African countries. Following the assassination of the Somali President Shermarke in 1969, the commander of the army, General Siad Barre, assumed power through a *coup d'état* and became the ruler of the country as the head of the socialist-oriented Supreme Revolutionary Council. While the West condemned his putsch which overthrew a legitimately elected government, Barre formally aligned his new regime with Moscow (Jackson, 2007: 38).

Between 1976 and 1977, Moscow became an important supplier of military assistance to both Ethiopia and Somalia. After the Derg assumed power over Ethiopia in 1974, the initial Soviet reaction was to enhance its military assistance to Somalia (Jackson, 2007: 40). When Mengistu became the ruler of Ethiopia in 1976, he moved closer to the communist bloc. He signed a military aid agreement with Moscow, and in May 1977, a formal alliance with the Soviet Union which included military, economic and technical assistance co-operation (Jackson, 2007: 49). In March 1977, Fidel Castro visited Ethiopia and shortly after, Cuban military advisors and troops arrived in Addis Ababa (Jackson, 2007: 49). In parallel, the relationship between the US and Ethiopia continued to deteriorate. In protest against violation of human rights in Eritrea, the Carter administration suspended military aid to Ethiopia at the beginning of 1977 (Smith, 1986: 154). Mengistu officially abrogated the defence treaty with the US and ordered the closure of most American facilities as well as a substantial reduction of US personnel in the country (Jackson, 2007: 49–52; Mitchell, 2016).

While Barre was supporting an insurgency against Ethiopia in the Ogaden and preparing an invasion (Henze, 1986: 54), Ethiopia signed a substantial arms deal with the Soviet Union, and Castro began sending advisors and troops to support Mengistu. Despite their historical ties with Somalia, the Soviets considered Ethiopia a more significant prize while Castro considered Mengistu a true socialist, not Barre (Mitchell, 2016). At the beginning of 1977, Barre began to approach the US in an attempt to replace Soviet military and political support with American backing (Vance, 1983: 73). Carter hesitated; the strategic importance of Somalia did not escape the Americans. Somalia was garnering support from Egypt and Saudi Arabia and Carter had made friendship with the Barre government a priority. However, despite US concerns, Somalia invaded the Ogaden in July 1977 hoping for greater American backing and support.

The alliance between the Soviet Union and Somalia was abrogated by Barre in November 1977 in an attempt to signal to America that Somalia had shifted allegiance. Carter indicated once again that the US would be willing to supply defensive weapons to Somalia on the condition that Somalia withdrew from the Ogaden (Vance, 1983: 73). At the same time the Soviet Union and Cuba were actively supporting Ethiopia in the Ogaden war against the Somali aggressor (Mitchell, 2016: 253–283).

The US response to the events in the Ogaden and to the communist bloc involvement in the conflict was a major source of disagreement in the administration (Brzezinski, 1983: 178; Vance, 1983: 84). Brzezinski advocated a globalist approach to the situation in the Horn. He believed that the issue went beyond a border conflict in Africa, and that the Soviet Union should be directly challenged as an aggressor, supplier of weapons and a patron of Cuba. He thought that the Ogaden war should be linked to détente, and to clarify to the Soviet Union that America would not tolerate unchecked Soviet expansionism (Brzezinski, 1983: 178). Failure to react in a decisive manner, would weaken the confidence of the world in America and would damage its political power. Vance disagreed; he did not subscribe to the idea that Soviet actions related to a grand strategy of expansionism, and thought that their involvement in the Horn was opportunistic rather than part of a larger design (Vance, 1983: 84). He argued that for the US to achieve its policy objectives, it must adopt a strategy that combines 'diplomacy, negotiations, concerted Western action, and the powerful forces of African nationalism' to achieve the resolution of disputes, and 'remove ostensible justification for Soviet involvement' (Vance, 1983: 85). Brzezinski wanted to send a carrier group to the Horn (Brzezinski, 1983: 182–183) and signal to the Soviet Union that their involvement would potentially affect the ratification of the SALT II agreement (Brzezinski, 1983: 180). Vance objected to both suggestions. He believed that the US should not send the navy as a threat unless it was prepared to use it (which was not the case), and that SALT should not be linked to situation in the Horn since it was a separate issue and an important American interest that should not be undermined (Vance, 1983: 85, 88).

Carter and the NSC agreed with Vance's approach to this matter; they informed Siad Barre that in principal America agreed to support Somalia with military and economic assistance, but conditioned the support with the end of hostilities in the Ogaden. In parallel, America turned to the Soviet Union and asked for guarantees that Ethiopian and Cuban troops would not attempt to cross the border into Somalia once Barre retracted his troops (Smith, 1986: 156–157). Somalia eventually retreated from Ethiopia and received American foreign assistance, while Ethiopia did not cross the border into Somalia, but was seen to be under greater Soviet and Cuban influence.

It was apparent that Carter's regionalist approach was successful in terms of preventing America's entanglement in an African conflict to address a Cold War rivalry. Brzezinski did not concur. He believed that America's failure to meet Soviet and Cuban involvement in the Ogaden War with American power led the Soviets to be more 'emboldened' (Brzezinski, 1983: 189) and eventually to their invasion of Afghanistan and the collapse of SALT. In this respect, he stated that SALT was buried in the sands of the Ogaden, meaning that the soft power approach to the events in the Horn was the first nail in the coffin that would eventually bury détente (Brzezinski, 1983: 189).

Linking the Vance–Brzezinski disagreements back to the conflict between Zaire and Angola: less than a year after the first Shaba conflict, the Katangan separatists staged another invasion of the province (Shaba II). The second invasion took place in May 1978, two months after the end of the Ogaden conflict. This time the Katangans managed to capture, in a matter of days, key locations in the mineral-rich Shaba province (Schraeder, 1994: 92). Brzezinski believed that the Katangans could not stage such an invasion without Soviet and Cuban backing (Vance, 1983: 84). He linked the events in Shaba to a grand Soviet design, relating it to their meddling in other global affairs, including in the 'arc of crisis' covering the Arab peninsula, Yemen and Ethiopia (Brzezinski, 1983: 316). Now Mobutu was being attacked once again by guerrillas backed by Angola and, he believed, by Cuba and their Soviet patron. After almost two years of weighing the disagreements between Vance and Brzezinski and usually leaning towards the regionalist approach, Carter began to shift his stance (Ambrose and Brinkley, 1997: 285; Carter, 1982: 222; Smith, 1986: 149). The public statements made by Brzezinski and Carter during the month of May 1978 on the role of the Soviet Union and Cuba in the Shaba II conflict were unequivocal and parallel to the old Cold War rhetoric used by previous administrations (Schraeder, 1994: 92). In a meeting between Carter and the Soviet Foreign Minister, Andrei Gromyko, on 27 May 1978 in Washington, DC, Carter expressed his dismay at Soviet adventurism in Africa (DoS, 1978: 367). Referring to the Soviet support of Angola and the Cubans in the Shaba II conflict, he indicated that this sort of behaviour would have consequences for Soviet–American relations (DoS, 1978: 367). Unlike Shaba I, Carter authorised direct American assistance to repel the Katangan invasion. It consisted of combat support operations to the Belgian and French troops who were aiding Mobutu's army to force back the invaders (Schraeder, 1994: 92). This was an indication of a shift in the Carter administration towards a classic Cold War interpretation of geopolitics, leading to increased willingness to adopt military and covert solutions to foreign policy challenges.

Carter and Thatcher did succeed in bringing Mugabe, Nkomo (representing the patriotic front) and Muzorewa to negotiate at Lancaster House in London. Lord Carrington, the British foreign secretary, succeeded in getting all parties to agree to a cease-fire and then move to a new constitution and vote. While no Americans negotiated in London, the Americans played an important role and were included in all stages of the talks (Mitchell, 2016: 624). Carter maintained the sanctions against Rhodesia despite congressional resistance until after Zimbabwe's first multiracial election that installed Robert Mugabe as the leader.

With the onset of the Iranian revolution, the hostage crisis, and the Soviet invasion of Afghanistan in 1979, Carter reverted fully to a globalist foreign policy approach to regain American deterrence against Soviet actions and curb criticism at home. This came to be known as the Carter doctrine, which was heavily influenced by Brzezinski, and presented to Congress during the State of the Union Address in 1980:

> An attempt by any outside force to gain control of the Persian Gulf region will be regarded as an assault on the vital interests of the United States of America, and such an assault will be repelled by any means necessary, including military force.
>
> (Carter, 1980)

Despite his intention to place human rights at the core of American foreign policy, and his initial effort to approach global challenges armed with American principles, Carter did not manage to elevate human rights as the primary guiding principle in foreign policy. A study conducted by Lebovic (1988) indicated that the primary considerations for foreign assistance allocation during the Carter administration were political and military, followed by economic interests as a significant determinant in the relationship between the US and least-developed countries. Human needs were a secondary consideration (Lebovic, 1988: 129). The main recipients of development aid during the Carter administration were countries that aligned themselves with the US, including countries with a problematic human rights record (Lebovic, 1988: 129).

Nevertheless, Carter was the first President to institutionalise human rights as a significant element of foreign policy, a principal to which subsequent Presidents attached importance (Apodaca, 2006: 80).[72] Even Reagan, who was a staunch critic of Carter's foreign policy, recognised the importance of referring to human rights as a guiding principal of foreign policy (Apodaca, 2006: 82). But while Carter succeeded in anchoring the importance of human rights, he failed to follow through in the application of policy. As indicated by Lebovic (1988: 129), the foreign assistance allocations during the Ronald Reagan administration were remarkably similar to Carter's.

## Constructive engagement

Arthur Schlesinger (1983: 5) once noted that Reagan brought back the messianic approach to foreign policy. This approach, firmly anchored in religious conservatism, underscored and contrasted two convictions: that the US is exceptional among nations and guided by divine providence; and that the Soviet Union is an evil empire that stands against the good that America represents (Apodaca, 2006: 82–83; Mead, 2001: 75–76; Schlesinger, 1983: 5). This approach was at the heart of Reagan's interpretation of contemporary challenges, and informed the actions taken by the administration to restore America's leadership and deterrence. The administration believed that a number of linked issues undermined America's position in the world: the perceived weakening of American power (due to Vietnam and Carter's regionalist policies), the global economic crisis and its effects on the American economy, and Soviet-backed subversive actions – especially in Third World countries. Reagan believed that economic growth and the strengthening of the US military were the foundations upon which America would be able to regain its power. The Soviet Union was seen as a subversive force which undermined the security of the world by intentionally targeting the vital economic and security interests of the US and its allies (Haig, 1981b: 6; Reagan, 1984: 3). Secretary of State Haig explained that economic well-being was crucial for American power (Haig, 1982: 40). America had to address three trends that impaired its leadership. The first was the military power gained by the Soviet Union during the economic crisis that weakened the US and its allies. The second was the emergence of Third World countries as vital suppliers of resources while being plagued by conflict, weak governance, weak economies, and conditions of poverty. The third trend was the conscious and designed attempts by the Soviet Union to weaken the US by seizing every opportunity to exploit fragile geopolitical situations to damage Western interests.

To address the fragility of states in the Third World, Reagan (1981: 14–17) advocated a co-operative strategy for global growth where assistance would play a pivotal role. Haig (1981: 5–7) explained that US foreign policy faced a number of interlinked challenges. The economic crisis inhibited growth, and in some countries it led to political disturbances, conflict and subsequently to resource scarcity – which exacerbated hunger, poverty, disease and the ability of governments to address these impediments. Africa was considered one of the critical regions[73] where the US needed to reinvigorate alliances and encourage peace (Haig, 1981: 6). Unlike the Soviet Union, which was seen as a provocateur supplying arms and encouraging conflict in Africa, Haig emphasised that America worked for political freedom, development, political stability and economic progress in Africa and elsewhere. It was crucial for the US that friendly developing countries would enjoy visible benefits to encourage other countries to align themselves with American interests (Haig, 1981: 7).

This outlook yielded criticism of the development assistance strategy of past administrations. The Secretary of State saw three distortions that influenced past policy in developing countries: first, that assistance offered mainly material benefits; second, that America opposed change when its interests were jeopardised; and third, that Soviet involvement in developing countries was not of material importance (Haig, 1981a: 8). The promotion of economic reforms and humanitarian assistance would not be successful without a strategy that countered Soviet attempts to target vital American interests affecting its economic well-being (Haig, 1981).

The Reagan foreign policy approach was based on the following four pillars (Haig, 1982: 18):

1  Restoring the economic health and military strength of the US.
2  Restoring, preserving and fostering new alliances.
3  Promoting peaceful progress in developing nations.
4  Establishing a relationship with the Soviet Union based on friendship and reciprocity.

However, the background was the Soviet military build-up and the need for the US to re-engage with Soviet subversive actions around the globe.

Haig explained to the Subcommittee on Foreign Affairs of the House Appropriation Committee that aid should not be 'dismissed as naïve idealism or ineffective philanthropy' (Haig, 1982a: 36). The budgetary requests to fund the assistance programmes were put forth before the committee because they served the 'national security, foreign policy and economic needs' of the US (Haig, 1982a: 36). Haig emphasised that without foreign assistance, there would be critical setbacks in the southern Africa peace negotiations; America would possibly lose its access to critical military facilities including in Kenya and Somalia, and risked losing an important naval presence along the critical oil shipping routes from the Middle East across the shores of Eastern Africa (Haig, 1982a: 36). Without foreign assistance to Sudan, Somalia and other countries, Soviet subversive action would be encouraged (Haig, 1982a: 36). Haig stressed that a quarter of US agricultural and manufactured exports went to developing countries and that the assistance programmes helped maintain American access to these important markets (Haig, 1982a: 36). And finally, without US assistance to multilateral financial institutions, their influence would be weakened and would damage the attempts to induce the much-needed global economic growth (Haig, 1982a: 36).

Haig's replacement as Secretary of State, George Shultz (1983: 25) explained that without stability and economic growth in the Third World, there could be no peace and security for the American people. The overarching approach to the Third World[74] was carved into the new African policy. Assistant Secretary for African Affairs, Chester Crocker, argued that both the globalist approach that explained events in Africa in relation to the bipolar struggle for power, and the regionalist approach which explained events in Africa as contextual and local issues, were flawed (Crocker, 1982: 22). He asserted that every African situation was anchored in local issues, and simultaneously influenced by, and exercised influence on global politics. He explained that the most fundamental US interests were not served by a perpetual East–West conflict in Africa, but by a peaceful, prosperous and co-operative continent.

There were two sets of shared objectives between the US and Africa according to Crocker: economic interests, and the search for peace. To address the economy, America could offer development and economic assistance, both bilaterally and multilaterally, as well as encouraging private investment to help Africa develop a healthy free market system, solve the debt problems, achieve self-sustained growth and participate in the international economic system (Crocker, 1981: 24). The search for peace was a crucial element of economic recovery and subsequently important for the interests of the US. America believed that Africa's interests were best served by keeping the continent clear of the East–West conflict which were a result of Soviet, Cuban and Libyan actions (not the US or other Western powers) (Shultz, 1984: 9). America's goal in that respect was to establish an understanding among powerful nations to avoid exploiting local conflicts to enhance the influence of superpowers (Crocker, 1981: 25).

There were a number of evolving situations across Africa that occupied Reagan's White House. The situation in southern Africa (with the exception of Rhodesia/Zimbabwe) remained unchanged when Reagan assumed office. US policy was focused on ensuring continued access to key strategic minerals, promoting regional stability, and reducing Soviet-backed involvement in the region, most importantly by eliminating the presence of Cuban troops in Angola. The question of Namibia's independence from South Africa continued to be a source of regional tension. US interests limited the position against imposing harsher sanctions on South Africa. This was indirectly helping to perpetuate the apartheid regime and South Africa's hold on Namibia.[75] It created a gulf between America's statements supporting the independence of Namibia and condemnation of the apartheid regime, and American actions in the UN vetoing sanctions against South Africa and linking Namibian independence to the withdrawal of Cuban troops from Angola.[76]

An important source of concern for the US was Libya. Led by Gaddafi since 1969, Libya was using its oil resources to subsidise insurgency in Africa (Liebenow, 1983: 98). Armed with oil-induced wealth and backed by the Soviet Union, Gaddafi was vocal about his anti-Western position and his support for 'anti-imperial' causes (Hollick, 1982: 300; Pollack, 2002: 413). America's concern with Libya's involvement in sub-Saharan Africa and the Mediterranean demonstrates the geopolitical complexity affecting America's national interests. Gaddafi's involvement in African geopolitics in the Sahel and the Horn, was viewed as a potential threat to America's interests in the Middle East, thus relating the Middle Eastern policy in sub-Saharan Africa, to the East–West power struggle.

The Soviet–Cuban presence in southern Africa and the Libyan involvement in sub-Saharan Africa were the two main African policy issues that occupied the administration (Crocker, 1992: 74). These issues extended over the entire continent. Chad, for example, was a country ravaged by civil war induced by geographic, ethnic and religious tensions. The West and Africa devoted very little interest to Chad and its 15-year-old civil war before Libya stepped up its involvement in the conflict in December 1980 (Hollick, 1982: 297). Gaddafi viewed the Aouzou Strip in northern Chad as a natural part of Libya (Pollack, 2002: 375). He supported insurgency against the government of Chad by providing arms and training to the Muslim National Liberation Front of Chad (FROLINAT). In 1973, Libyan forces invaded northern Chad and occupied the Aouzou Strip. Since the government in Chad was backed by France and the US, Gaddafi's involvement in support of FROLINAT and the backing provided to him by the Soviet bloc, linked the civil war in Chad to the East–West power struggle (Wright, 1989: 124–146). In 1979, after rebels conquered the capital leading to the collapse of the government in Chad, the OAU sponsored negotiations in Lagos which eventually led to the establishment of a Transitional Government of National Unity (GUNT), and a resolution that called for the withdrawal of foreign troops from Chad to be replaced by peacekeeping forces. GUNT was in effect a fragile alliance between the fighting factions in Chad. After the members of the GUNT turned on each other leading to a resumption of the civil war, the leader of the GUNT, President Goukouni, a former militant of the FROLINAT, turned once again to Gaddafi for support. In January 1981, Goukouni and Gaddafi announced their intention to merge Chad and Libya. This was a serious concern for the US (DoS, 1981). The US viewed Gaddafi's involvement in Chad as part of a grand design to transcend the boundaries of sovereign nations in Africa to create a Muslim bloc penetrating sub-Saharan Africa under Libyan leadership (Lyman, 1982: 27). Libya was considered a negative force of destabilisation in the region, working to topple sovereign governments, including the Sudan, Mali, Niger, Senegal and The Gambia (Lyman, 1982: 27). While Chad later withdrew from its intention to merge with Libya, Gaddafi continued to intervene in support of Goukouni against his opposition which was regrouping in Sudan with Western support (Lyman, 1982: 29; Pollack, 2002: 381). In August 1981, Gaddafi signed a treaty of friendship and co-operation with Ethiopia and southern Yemen to join forces against Western 'conspiracy and aggression' and to counter Western policy in the Indian Ocean and the Gulf. The treaty included provisions allowing the deployment of military units from each country in the other's territory under certain circumstances (Cowell, 1981). The US was also concerned by Gaddafi's statements that threatened Niger's sovereignty and would potentially threaten the entire Sahel from Liberia in the west to Sudan in the east (Liebenow, 1983: 135; Lyman, 1982: 29).

During the Reagan administration, Sudan enjoyed friendly relations with America, and had a record of supporting American initiatives in international arenas (Crocker, 1986: 35). Sudan broke diplomatic relations with the US after the Israeli–Arab war in 1967, and consequently US aid to Sudan was cancelled (Johnson, 2011: 57). Sudan adopted a Marxist orientation after President Nimeiry assumed power in 1969, but after a failed Soviet-backed *coup d'état* against Nimeiry in 1971, he began to approach the West and diplomatic relations with the US were reinstated in 1972. When Soviet weapons began to shift the regional balance of power towards Ethiopia, Sudan like Somalia, turned to the US for military and economic assistance. Located near the vital oil shipping routes to and from the Middle East (Crocker, 1982a: 62, 1986a: 29). America wanted Sudan to be a regional ally against Soviet-backed Ethiopia (Johnson, 2011: 57). An effort was made to help bolster Sudan's stability through economic revitalisation to protect American interests in the region (Lyman, 1982: 28). Libya threated Sudan's stability in 1981 by bombing[77] Sudanese villages along the Sudan–Chad border where Goukouni's rivals were regrouping. America feared further Libyan subversion against the Nimeiry government and the potential Libyan infiltration of sub-Saharan Africa (Lyman, 1982: 29). The administration requests for assistance for FY1983 included support for Sudan against Libyan subversion. In addition to military assistance were US$25 million for development assistance (focused on integrated rural development), US$30 million as food assistance, and US$70 million through the Economic Support Fund (Crocker, 1982a: 62). In the 1980s, Sudan was the largest recipient of US foreign aid in sub-Saharan Africa from USAID (Bush, 1986: 13–14), which made that country dependent on American (and IMF) conditions for economic reforms (Johnson, 2011: 43–44).

Looking to the western part of the African continent, requests for foreign assistance were linked to protection from Libyan adventurism. The Reagan administration feared that Libya's attempts to penetrate sub-Saharan Africa were taking advantage of poverty in the Sahel and the regional economic weakness to encourage destabilisation to damage Western interests. Some countries in West Africa, like Niger and Chad, had borders with both Libya and Nigeria. Many other unstable countries in the region vulnerable to Libyan interventions[78] were very close to Nigeria and other regional Western interests (Crocker, 1982a: 62–63).

The policy of the Reagan administration towards southern Africa labelled 'constructive engagement' was primarily formulated to counter 'Soviet–Cuban adventurism', this being the primary concern of the US on the continent (Crocker, 1992: 94). As Crocker remarked, the issue of Namibia's independence from South Africa was on the table – not because it was of particular interest to the US as such – but rather because it was consistently the dominating topic raised by African nations at various discussion forums with the rest of the world (Crocker, 1992: 74–75). The southern part of the continent held nearly 60 per cent of direct US investment in sub-Saharan Africa (Crocker, 1981a: 25). Concentrated in strategic minerals, this investment was linked to the health of America's economy and military strength. Crocker explained that for these reasons, the US should support the economic development of southern Africa and encourage trade and investment through 'the provision of timely and carefully tailored foreign assistance' as well as using development and diplomatic tools to discourage conflict, violent solution and foreign interventions (Crocker, 1981a: 25).

Constructive engagement was a regional policy through which America hoped to balance its interests with the wishes and interests of African nations (Crocker, 1985: 5; Shultz, 1985: 22–23). The US did not wish to weaken South Africa with sanctions because of its economic and security interests (see Dam,[79] 1985: 37). By not taking a firm stance against South Africa's racial regime and its colonial hold of Namibia, US leadership and credibility, domestically and internationally was weakened. Constructive engagement created a separation between the issue of harsh punitive measures against South Africa, and the abhorrence of the apartheid regime.[80] The policy focused on engaging the entire region in this endeavour, harnessing the support of the 'frontline states': Botswana, Lesotho, Malawi, Swaziland, Zaire, Zimbabwe, Zambia, Mozambique and Tanzania, to work towards Namibian independence and the elimination of apartheid, while ensuring continued access to key strategic minerals, promoting regional stability and reducing the opportunities for Soviet subversive action and regional influence. The administration sought to avoid debating the nature of South Africa's apartheid regime and its illegitimate hold on Namibia (Crocker, 1985: 6).

Controversies concerning the constructive engagement policy became more accentuated after Reagan's re-election, and domestic criticism on the southern African policy from both right and left was mounting (Crocker, 1992: 253–260). While opposing comprehensive UN sanctions against South Africa, Reagan issued an executive order[81] in September 1985 imposing 'symbolic' sanctions.[82] The executive order was issued not because Reagan had had a change of heart regarding his South Africa policy, but rather because Congress was about to force the administration to impose its own version of sanctions (Crocker, 1992: 276–277; Schraeder, 1994: 229; Ungar and Vale, 1985: 234). The sanctions focused on sales and import restrictions targeting specific South African government agencies, particularly those involved with enforcing apartheid. There were also restrictions on bank loan approvals to the government of South Africa, restrictions on nuclear-related exports, restrictions on the imports of South African manufactured arms, and the granting of support to US firms operating in South Africa employing a certain number of people in opposition to apartheid-related labour regulations (Reagan, 1985: 2–3). By issuing this executive order, two main purposes were served: first, it allowed the US to demonstrate that moral principles and opposition to the apartheid regime were important and had been acted upon beyond rhetoric. Second, it allowed the US to demonstrate to its domestic and international critics that, despite the opposition to UN sanctions, the policy of constructive engagement was not a carte blanche for South Africa to continue to defy the international community. America was taking tangible action (albeit limited) against the apartheid regime (Crocker, 1992: 276–278). In terms of domestic politics, this executive order allowed Reagan to pre-empt an attempt by Congress to force his administration to accept a harsher version of sanctions, and temporarily stalled Congress from taking further action to force the administration to accept modifications to the South African foreign policy.

Other than sanctions, the US embassy in Pretoria and USAID constituted dedicated programmes in South Africa to advance human rights and help victims of apartheid. The South African Human Rights Programme was established in 1984, and focused on supporting community-based NGOs working to achieve the ideals of the Universal Declaration of Human Rights (DoS, 1986: 47). The programme was a part of other US assistance activities in South Africa in support of civil liberties, including providing educational scholarships, assistance to black labour unions and improving community well-being through health and education programmes (DoS, 1986: 47). The development programme in southern Africa was designed to help mitigate 'war, economic disruption, racism and foreign intervention' to help the region to achieve these goals and develop without Soviet bloc interference (Crocker, 1986: 35; see also Crocker, 1987: 42). The assistance programme in South Africa, spearheaded by USAID, was also used as an important tool to promote human rights, both in upholding American principals, as well as an example of concrete action against the apartheid regime and in support of the administration's statements against racial discrimination (for example, see Freeman, 1987: 44;[83] McPherson, 1987: 55).

In June 1986, South Africa escalated the level of violence against the ANC through a comprehensive military operation that included cross-border raids into Botswana, Zambia, Zimbabwe, Swaziland and Angola. These actions led to a total loss of confidence in the Botha regime and its intentions to achieve reform, and intensified the criticism of Congress against Reagan's stance in opposition to sanctions (Schraeder, 1994: 229–230). The final termination of Reagan's constructive engagement occurred when Congress overturned Reagan's veto of HR-4868. In September 1986, the House (followed by the Senate in October) forced the President to abandon his foreign policy strategy for South Africa and accept the version offered by Congress (Schraeder, 1994: 230; see also Crocker, 1992: 304–330), and in essence, forced Reagan to match his rhetoric against the apartheid regime with action (Schraeder, 1994: 232). Despite Congress, Reagan continued to stall the implementation of harsher measures called for in the Act,[84] as well as veto a Security Council resolution in 1987 to block economic sanctions against South Africa

(Schraeder, 1994: 233). In an address before the OAU, Secretary Shultz explained that the administration believed 'a more fruitful approach is to help the victims of apartheid build their bargaining power through assistance for education, economic opportunities, and community development for black South Africans.' (Shultz, 1988: 21), and the proposed sanctions would lead to a significant economic loss to American investors in South Africa (Shultz, 1988: 21).

By this time, South Africa and Angola were concluding negotiations on an agreement mediated by the US under the terms of which South Africa would comply with UN resolution 435 and withdraw its hold on Namibia, while the governments of Angola and Cuba agreed to terminate the Cuban mission in Angola and withdraw all Cuban troops. The agreement was finalised in December 1988 and allowed the Reagan administration to claim success of the South African policy, and by extension, of constructive engagement (Crocker, 1992).

Crocker explained to the Senate Foreign Relations Committee (Crocker, 1985: 23–26) that the economic crisis in Africa was anchored in severe mismanagement and flawed economic policies of African nations, as well as in a donor failure to recognise the problems and work to mitigate them. According to the administration, the four main causes of the crisis were: the long-term decline in agricultural productivity, explosive population growth, Africa's debt problem, and inefficient use of resources (Crocker, 1985: 24; Whitehead, 1986: 33). Intensive state regulation and the government ownership of means and resources led to inefficient production systems, overinflated bureaucracies, subsidies, corruption and a small and unprotected private sector. To help African nations overcome their deficits and dependence on imports, multilateral and bilateral strategies were employed. The World Bank Structural Adjustment was the main multilateral initiative which also influenced many of the bilateral programmes (Crocker, 1986: 32). Two main initiatives were devised by the Reagan administration to help Africa recover from the economic crisis, and to reduce political instability, external interference, poverty, malnutrition, and disease (these being humanitarian issues as well as the causes and results of instability). The first was the African Economic Policy Reform Programme which provided assistance to countries that were in the process of reforming their economic policies or were planning to establish 'growth-oriented policy frameworks' and to improve the co-ordination among bilateral and multilateral donors. The second initiative was the Food for Progress programme, which provided food aid as an incentive to those countries that agreed to reform their agricultural sectors 'stressing market approaches in agricultural pricing, marketing, and input supply and distribution' (Crocker, 1985: 25). Crocker linked poverty, environmental challenges, state fragility, and state vulnerability, to the Libyan and other Soviet-backed subversions in Africa, which were interpreted as attempts to weaken the US and its allies (Crocker, 1985: 26).

When Reagan assumed office in 1981 and approached the world through his ideological lenses, the world was still dominated by the bipolar struggle between the Soviet Union and the US. But when Reagan left office in 1989, the world had changed. The Soviet Union was an empire in decline, plagued with a collapsing economy, fragmented by the rise of nationalism and calls for reform in many of its satellite territories. The collapse of the Soviet Union was also one of the main reasons for the Cuban and Soviet withdrawal from Africa. The Soviet Union as an empire was fading, and would dissolve entirely under the Bush administration. This would mean that the contest between the Soviet Union and the US to win hearts and minds in the Third World would disappear, and new justifications for foreign policy and development assistance would emerge.

## Concluding remarks

In this chapter, we have traced the importance of US development assistance policies toward Africa to fight the Cold War from the Truman through to the Reagan administrations. While there were several serious efforts to understand and respond to African development issues, they were mostly secondary to the Cold War. Following WWII, Africa was peripheral to the major US global interests and the US did not foresee the strength of African independence movements and the weaknesses of the colonial powers. The Eisenhower administration, dominated by Secretary of State Dulles, found the Soviet threat almost everywhere. African nationalism was viewed through the prism of the communist threat rather than the legitimate and necessary creation of new independent nations in Africa, and the focus of the policy was to ensure that African nations would align themselves with the US, or at least not align themselves with the Soviet Union. The purpose was to enhance America's position as a superpower as well as domestic prosperity. Richard Nixon who did travel to Africa on behalf of the Eisenhower administration also viewed the world through a fiercely anti-communist lens. It took John F. Kennedy to shift US emphases and assume a new approach in Africa. Kennedy's efforts were centred on investing in the creation of institutions that replicated the American regime of truth. Development assistance was established and focused on creating political, social and economic institutions in Africa consistent with American ideology. The Nixon era began with his lack of concern over Africa only for the coups in Portugal, Sudan and Ethiopia (among others) to force Secretary of State Kissinger to view Africa with increased importance especially after the withdrawal of the US from Indochina. Being a 'realist', Kissinger focused not on African realities but on the potentialities of Soviet and Cuban influence and expansion. Once again, the policy focus was enhancing the position of the US, so it can maintain its position of leadership as the most powerful nation. For this purpose the Nixon-Kissinger-Ford administrations were willing to grant assistance to problematic regimes and for various purposes to win allegiance against the Soviet Union and its allies. Carter sought to refocus on African issues and to lead by example. By treating nations based on the same principles the American government treated its own citizens, Carter wished to flag America's greatness and through this enhance its legitimacy and power. Faced however, with multiple crises and the presence of Cuban troops in Angola and Ethiopia, Carter shifted towards acting based on Cold War priorities rather than African or human rights preferences. Ronald Reagan, who succeeded Carter, viewed his own mission as rolling back communism and blocking the actions of state actors and supporting non-state actors who were attempting to defeat left governments in Africa. This meant a focus on the Cuban presence in Angola, the civil wars (externally fuelled) in Angola and Mozambique, and worries about Qadafi's actions in sub-Saharan Africa. During the Cold War, the complex interests and needs of African nations were not seen to be the most important for the US government. Rather, development assistance was viewed and used primarily as a tool to enhance US strategic interests – political, economic and military – in sub-Saharan Africa.

Throughout the Cold War, the US engagement consisted of two main strategies. The first was to win over the allegiance of African countries by contrasting an American ideology with the Soviet ideology. This strategy was based on a deep belief that the American way of life leads to freedom and prosperity, while the Soviet way constrained various freedoms and led to authoritarianism. Policies associated with this strategy focused on highlighting the benefits of alignment with the US to African countries, the dangers of alignment with the Soviet Union, and by providing benefits to countries, demonstrating that America was prosperous, righteous and powerful and that it paid off to support America and align with its ideology. The second strategy relied upon investing in the creation or supporting of African institutions that would replicate the various ideals and principles of US ideology. Through this America would help install new (and in its eyes) better ideologies that will serve both Africans as well as US power. Development Assistance featured in both strategies as a tool of power. This was done through coercion and/or co-option or a mixture depending upon the circumstances. Both strategies were anchored in the conviction that the US is an exceptional nation, and that it has a duty to lead the world, and re-create it in its own image. To accomplish this, America needed to remain powerful and to be mindful and responsive to all Soviet and Cuban threats. This narrative was repeated by all the administrations from Truman to Reagan in the context of fending off communism.

## Notes

1 See, for example, the Foreign Relations of the United States, 1952–1954, Volume XI, Part 1, Africa and South Asia: documents: 93–103.
2 The Bureau was established in 1958 and headed by Assistant Secretary for African Affairs Joseph Satterthwaite.
  His suggestions were a part of a discussion on a formulation of a US policy statement on Africa, and formed the basis for NSC 5719/1, the main document setting the African policy throughout the Eisenhower administration.
4 G. Mennen Williams was the second Assistant Secretary of State for African Affairs.
5 Nevertheless Nikita Khrushchev declared in January 1961 that the African struggle for independence was an opportunity to spread communism to the continent (Walton, 2007: 31).
6 Portugal and Belgium resisted African nationalism longer than the other colonial powers. In the case of Portugal, Kennedy exercised direct pressure by cancelling commercial arms deals and US aid programmes to Portugal (Muehlenbeck, 2012: 46).
7 It is important to note that the Peace Corps training included an important focus on how to argue against communism and the USSR. The physician for the American Embassy in Guinea, for example, provided information to the CIA and sought information from Peace Corps volunteers to pass on to the agency. Carrying out anthropological field research in Guinea from 1965–1967. Bill Derman was working in Guinea during the time and was friends with several peace corps volunteers and the American doctor who was tasked with caring for them.
8 Rivkin (1965: 118).
9 In reality, the Chinese in Guinea, for example, built a dam, stadium and had other projects between 1965–1970. They also built the TANZAM railroad in early 1970s.
10 In Algeria, Congo, Dahomey, Central African Republic, Upper Volta, Nigeria and Ghana.
11 This memorandum was cleared by Rostow and sent to Secretary of State Rusk from the Bureau of African Affairs.
12 The Strategic Arms Limitation Talks, also known as SALT and later SALT II.
13 Referring to a speech delivered by Secretary of State, William P. Rogers, in 1971 calling for an end to the Cold War in Africa.
14 John Daniel Ehrlichman was the White House Counsel and Assistant to the President for Domestic Affairs.
15 Harry Robbins Haldeman was the White House Chief of Staff.
16 This memorandum was sent by Kissinger to Nixon as part of a series of exchanges between White House staff in preparation for a stag dinner for the African ambassadors planned for early 1970 where the President would make his first statement on African policy. This statement was to precede a longer speech on US African policy planned to be delivered by Secretary of State Rogers in a visit to several African countries in February 1970. The dinner eventually took place on 23 March 1970, after Secretary Rogers returned from Africa.
17 Attached to Haig's memorandum to Kissinger is the DoS draft of US policy towards Africa with comments provided by Kissinger's staff.
18 There was basically only one such facility located in South Africa, and another potential facility located in Mozambique. These were the only shipyards around the continent, excluding the Mediterranean, that could accommodate US Navy needs.

19 Expressed, for example, through the Lusaka Manifesto on southern Africa from April 1969, where Portugal is condemned by African countries along with South Africa and Rhodesia.
20 Also known as National Security Study Memoranda 39.
21 In the US, for example, students demonstrated against the apartheid regime. The first demonstration against US involvement in South Africa was attended by Bill Derman. It was organised by Todd Gitlin and the Students for a Democratic Society at Chrysler World Headquarters to call for Chrysler to leave South Africa.
22 Resolutions 216 and 217 of the Security Council, November 1965. All members voted in favour with the exception of France which abstained.
23 This review was a part of a series of studies commissioned by Kissinger and known as the National Security Study Memoranda (NSSM). NSSM 39 (see NSC, 1969) was a comprehensive review on southern Africa and sought to answer a series of questions formulated by Kissinger and his staff.
24 Dubbed as such later by its opponents (see Lake, 1976: 129; Schraeder, 1994: 206).
25 While South Africa was legally a sovereign nation, Rhodesia was considered an illegal entity.
26 Alexander Haig was the White House Deputy National Security Advisor at that time.
27 Security Council Draft Resolution 9696 (1970) was formulated by a number of African countries and included: provisions for total isolation of Rhodesia, calling for general sanctions on Portugal and South Africa, and the condemnation of the UK for her refusal to use force in Rhodesia. US Ambassador to the UN, Charles Yost, explained that the main reason for casting the veto was that the resolution would have led to the isolation of American citizens in Rhodesia.
28 Introduced by Senator Harry Byrd Jr (Virginia).
29 The other major supplier of chrome was the Soviet Union which charged a very high price from the US (DoS, 1973). Some reports claimed that the Soviet Union was buying chrome from Rhodesia and reselling it to the US (see McManus, 1977).
30 Security Council Resolution 232 (1966) and 253 (1968).
31 The base in the Azores became of material importance during the 1973 October War in the Middle East, and served the US in their effort to support Israel. The October war had a Cold War dimension: the Arab forces relied on Soviet political support and military supplies, and Israel relied on the US for the same purpose.
32 Rondon's recommendations were not acted upon.
33 America provided both military and political support to Israel during the crisis. Military support was flown through the Azores base (Portugal) and political support included backing in the Security Council (see, for example, Kissinger, 2003).
34 It is important to note that due to its significant oil resources, Nigeria was one of the most important countries in Africa and of significant importance to the US. Nevertheless, its relatively stable status and firm policy of non-alignment kept Nigeria off the immediate crisis management approach of US foreign policy in Africa.
35 The involvement of Zaire in supporting the FNLA also helped the US to channel aid to the organisation.
36 Private American organisations granted some support to RENAMO (Crocker, 1992: 250; Nesbitt, 1988: 119–120; Shultz, 1993: 1113, 1116), but the role of the US government, if it played any, remains obscure.

37 Listed in the document: Kenya, Tanzania, Mauritius, Mozambique and the Malagasy Republic.
38 Listed in the document: Ghana, Gabon, Liberia, Guinea and Ivory Coast.
39 There was a limited military presence of the Soviet Union in Somalia; Moscow also backed the liberation movements against Portugal since the early seventies (DoS, 1970); in addition, the Russians had been providing military aid to several African countries for some years.
40 The military and financial support to the MPLA by the Soviet Union was stopped during the first months of 1974 since the organisation was deemed to be militarily ineffective (Bender, 1978: 69).
41 The CIA was already involved in a relatively limited covert operation to support the FNLA since late January 1975. The unified government in Angola (established after the Alvor accords signed on 15 January) began to deteriorate late in February. For a more detailed description of the events in Angola, see Bender (1978) and Stockwell (1978).
42 This concern was also related to the fact that the CIA undervalued the amount of resources needed for the intervention in Angola and was now requesting more funds (Bender, 1978: 102–103).
43 The Senate decided to cut military spending in Angola on December 1975 and the House of Representatives joined the decision on 27 January 1976.
44 Easum made a conscious effort to set the relations between the US and independent Mozambique on track, and was the first foreign diplomat to visit the transitional government in Maputo.
45 This was the military wing of the Zimbabwe African National Union headed ultimately by the current President of Zimbabwe, Robert G. Mugabe.
46 Kissinger's first statement on his Africa trip delivered in Lusaka on 27 April 1976.
47 It is important to note that during his challenge of Ford's nomination as the Republican Party candidate for the Presidential bid, Reagan's main criticism of the Ford–Kissinger administration was related to losing power to the Soviet Union. More specifically, Reagan declared that: 'Under Kissinger and Ford, this nation has become Number Two in a world where it is dangerous – if not fatal – to be second best' (Reagan quoted in Rodman, 2009: 111). This kind of pressure in an election year was one of the reasons why Kissinger had to actively demonstrate that the Ford administration was not ignoring the Soviets in Africa (see also relevant comment by President Ford in NSC, 1976).
48 The initiative covers Mauritania, Mali, Upper Volta, Niger, Senegal, Chad and The Gambia (DoS, 1976b).
49 Parker refers to a message by President Senghor of Senegal communicated to Kissinger, calling for the support of African development to present hope and prevent radicalisation of the youth.
50 The same rhetoric was employed when the African visit was presented to the American people, for example, the comments made by Press Secretary Nessen on 3 August 1976 (Nessen, 1976).
51 Which was mainly dealt with until then through covert assistance now halted by Congress through the Clark Amendment.
52 When it came to action, the policy was focused on addressing the regime in Rhodesia and the independence of Namibia rather than addressing South Africa, where American interests were still significant and the legal status of the country more complicated. Nevertheless, assuming a firmer stand on racial equality was also taking a position of rhetoric against South Africa's policy of separate development.
53 While America was being publicly (mildly) critical of the white minority regimes, it had granted support to Portugal despite their colonial presence;

166   *US policy in Africa and the Cold War*

bought chrome from Rhodesia; opposed OAU statements calling for more severe actions against the Smith regime and the isolation of South Africa's apartheid regime; avoided severe criticism of the white regimes (NSSM, 39); and granted support against the MPLA and other liberation movements when the OAU has recognised their legitimacy.

54  Nigerian support was imperative to the Americans. Nigeria recognised the legitimacy of the MPLA in Angola. Kissinger reported to the NSC that this recognition was influenced by a Soviet bribe of US$25 million (NSC, 1976). The US was conscious of the need to win over Nigerian support as part of the new strategy to prevent African radicalisation.
55  A comment written by Carter's National Security Advisor Zbigniew Brzezinski (1983: 189) in his memoirs about the role of the crisis on the Horn of Africa and collapse of détente with the Soviet Union.
56  The quote is a paraphrase of Carter's points of view summarised for the presidential debate briefing book prepared for President Ford. This particular quote is based on an interview published in the *Washington Post* on 30 July 1976. It is located in the *Developing Nations* folder in the debate briefing book on page 6.
57  See, for example, Carter's statements at Notre Dame University (Carter, 1977).
58  The approach which treated the entire globe as the arena where the Cold War is fought through proxy wars between the Soviet Union and the US.
59  Referring to Section 502B introduced as an amendment to the Foreign Assistance Act in 1974.
60  Nancy Mitchell provides an excellent account of the complicated international response to the Zairean rebels entering Zaire from Angola where there were major Soviet and Cuban interests (2016: 166–174).
61  Conduct of Foreign Policy Folder, page 4.
62  US ambassador to the UN during the Carter administration.
63  The group fighting against the white minority in Rhodesia to create the independent state of Zimbabwe.
64  Vice President Walter Mondale met with Vorster in Austria on behalf of President Carter in May 1977.
65  The killing of the anti-apartheid activist Steven Biko in September 1977 is an example of the hardening line assumed by Vorster.
66  Recalling the American ambassador from Pretoria in protest against the repression of black Africans (Danaher, 1984: 128).
67  Often referred to as the Shaba I conflict.
68  Often referred to as the Shaba II conflict.
69  Odom was Brzezinski military assistant under the Carter administration and director of the NSA under the Reagan administration.
70  Eritrea was part of the Federation of Ethiopia during that time.
71  It is important to note that Ethiopia accepted Soviet aid since 1959 but kept its close ties and traditional alliance with the West under the rule of Emperor Selassie (Jackson, 2007: 37).
72  At the very least, this had rhetorical importance if not matched by policy.
73  But more critical than Africa were the Middle East, South-west Asia, Europe and the Americas.
74  See also Armacost (1987) for a lucid description of the underlying tenets of US policy towards the Third World.
75  Another situation indirectly aggravated by the US policy towards South Africa was the civil war in Mozambique. South Africa was supporting RENAMO in Mozambique, mainly to fight the African National Congress (ANC) and punish the ruling party in Mozambique (FRELIMO) for granting support and refuge to the ANC. For a comprehensive account of the American policy dilemmas

towards Mozambique see Crocker (1992: 232–250), Shultz (1993: 1110–1117) and Cohen (2000: 181–196).

76 The Third World organised through the Non-Aligned Movement in the UN was continuously criticising US policies around the globe, especially the American position on southern Africa (Armacost, 1987: 58–59).
77 Sudan was the only Arab government to endorse the Camp David accords between Egypt and Israel. Consequently, Gaddafi began to undermine Nimeiry's regime.
78 For example, the Libyan attempts to destabilise the governments of Senegal, Mauritania and Ghana from 1980 to 1981, and the Libyan call for the unification of Arabs in Libya, Mali and Niger to wage a war on the West (Crocker, 1982a: 62; Graham, 1985: 54; Hollick, 1982: 300).
79 Deputy Secretary of State, Kenneth Dam.
80 Reagan and his administration stated publicly on numerous occasions that America found the apartheid regime abhorrent (for example, see Armacost, 1986: 56; Crocker, 1986b: 27; Reagan, 1985: 1–2; Shultz, 1986: 30–32; Walters, 1985: 54).
81 Executive Order 12532 issued September 9, 1985.
82 Reagan opposed harsher sanctions and rejected congressional pressure to take firmer action against apartheid. In September 1986 Reagan vetoed the Comprehensive Anti-Apartheid Act suggested by Congress (H.R.4868) because he believed that economic sanctions will be destructive to the people of South Africa rather than punish the government (Reagan, 1986: 35–36).
83 Deputy Assistant Secretary for African Affairs, Charles Freeman.
84 Such as section 401(b) which required that the US would participate in negotiations to co-ordinate multilateral action to bring about the end of the apartheid regime (Schraeder, 1994: 233).

## References

Ambrose, S. E. and Brinkley, D. (1997) *Rise to globalism: American foreign policy since 1938*. Penguin Books, New York.
Apodaca, C. (2006) *Understanding U.S. human rights policy: a paradoxical legacy*. Routledge, New York; London.
Armacost, M. H. (1986) Promoting Positive Change in southern Africa – Address before a Convention at Carleton College in Northfield, 24 January 1986. *Department of State bulletin* 86 (2109): 53–59.
Armacost, M. H. (1987) U.S. Policy Towards the Third World – Address before the National Third World Studies Conference, 17 October 1986, *Department of State bulletin* 87: 56–60.
Attwood, W. (1967) *The reds and blacks; a personal adventure*. Hutchinson, London.
Bender, G. J. (1978) Kissinger in Angola: anatomy of failure, in Lemarchand, R. and Bender, G. J. (eds) *American policy in Southern Africa: the stakes and the stance*. University Press of America, Washington, DC, pp. 65–143.
Bienen, H. (1978) U.S. Foreign Policy in a Changing Africa, *Political Science Quarterly* 93: 443–464.
Brzezinski, Z. (1983) *Power and principle: memoirs of the national security adviser, 1977–1981*. Farrar, Straus and Giroux, New York.
Bush, G. H. W. (1986) Vice President's Visit to Africa – Arrival Statement, Khartoum, 4 March 1985, *Department of State bulletin* 86: 13–18.

Cable (1974) SA press reports Easum to be replaced. US Embassy Cape Town. Retrieved April 25, 2017, from US Ambassy Cape Town www.wikileaks.org/plusd/cables/1974CAPET00893_b.html.

Cable (1975) South African newspapers report Ambassador Hurd to be replaced. US Embassy Cape Town. Retrieved April 25, 2017, from US Embassy Cape Town www.wikileaks.org/plusd/cables/1975CAPET00023_b.html.

Callaway, R. L. and Matthews, E. G. (2008) *Strategic US foreign assistance: the battle between human rights and national security.* Ashgate, Aldershot.

Carter, J. (1977) University of Notre Dame – Address at Commencement Exercises at the University – 22 May 1977.

Carter, J. (1980) The State of the Union Address delivered before a Joint Session of the Congress – 23 January 1980.

Carter, J. (1982) *Keeping faith: memoirs of a president.* Bantam Books, Toronto; New York.

Clough, M. (1992) *Free at last?: U.S. policy toward Africa and the end of the Cold War.* Council on Foreign Relations Press, New York.

Cohen, H. J. (2000) *Intervening in Africa: superpower peacemaking in a troubled continent.* St. Martin's Press, New York.

Cohen, H. J. (2003) *The United States and Africa: non-vital interests also require attention,* www.unc.edu/depts/diplomat/archives_roll/2003_07-09/cohen_africa/cohen_africa.html (accessed November 21, 2013).

Cohen, H. J. (2010) A Perspective on Fifty Years of U.S. Africa Policy: The Nixon Legacy, *American Foreign Policy Interests* 32: 209–218.

Cohen, S. B. (1982) Conditioning United States Security Assistance on Human Rights Practices, *American Journal of International Law* 76: 246–279.

Cowell, A. (1981) In these parts, friendship is a three way street, *New York Times*, 8 November.

Crocker, C. A. (1981) U.S. Interests in Africa – Address before the Council of Foreign Relations in New York City, 5 October 1981, *Department of State bulletin* 82: 23–26.

Crocker, C. A. (1981a) Regional Strategy for Southern Africa – Address before the American Legion in Honolulu – 29 August 1981, *Department of State bulletin* 81: 24–27.

Crocker, C. A. (1982) U.S. Responses to the Challenge of Regional Security in Africa – Address before the Baltimore Council of Foreign Relations, 28 October 1982, *Department of State bulletin* 82: 22–25.

Crocker, C. A. (1982a) FY 1983 Assistance Requests – Statement before the Subcommittee on Foreign Operations of the House Appropriations Committee – 25 March 1982, *Department of State bulletin* 82: 61–63.

Crocker, C. A. (1985) An update of Constructive Engagement in South Africa – Statement before the Subcommittee on African Affairs of the Senate Foreign Relations Committee, 26 September 1984, *Department of State bulletin* 85: 5–7.

Crocker, C. A. (1986) FY 1987 Assistance Requests for sub-Sahara Africa – Statement before the Subcommittee on International Operations of the House Foreign Affairs Committee, 18 March 1986, *Department of State bulletin* 86: 30–6.

Crocker, C. A. (1986a) U.S. and Soviet Interests in the Horn of Africa – Address before the World Affairs Council, 13 November 1985, *Department of State bulletin* 86: 29–32.

Crocker, C. A. (1986b) South Africa: Report on the President's Executive Order – Statement before the Subcommittee on Africa and on International Economic Policy and Trade of the House Foreign Affairs Committee, 9 April 1986, *Department of State bulletin* 86: 27–30.

Crocker, C. A. (1987) Southern Africa: Toward Peace and Stability – Address before the Economic Club in Detroit, 11 December 1986, *Department of State bulletin* 87: 40–42.

Crocker, C. A. (1992) *High noon in southern Africa: making peace in a rough neighborhood*. W.W. Norton, New York.

Dam, K. W. (1985) South Africa: The Case Against Sanctions – Statement before the Senate Committee on Banking, Housing and Urban Affairs, 6 April 1985, *Department of State bulletin* 85: 36–38.

Danaher, K. (1984) *In whose interest?: a guide to U.S.–South Africa relations*. Institute for Policy Studies, Washington, DC.

Davis, N. (1978) The Angola Decision of 1975: A Personal Memoir, *Foreign Affairs*, 1 (vii), 109–124.

Debate Briefing (1976) Carter on foreign policy: debate briefing book (1). Gerald R. Ford Presidential Library.

Derman, B. (1978) Pastoralism, the Sahelian Drought and Famine: Anthropology and Response to a Crisis, *Reviews in Anthropology* 5: 89–99.

Derman, B. (1984) USAID in the Sahel: Development and Poverty, in Barker, J. (ed.) *The Politics of agriculture in tropical Africa*. Sage Publications, Beverly Hills, pp. 77–98.

DoS (1952) Memorandum of Conversation, by the Officer in Charge of West, Central, and East Africa Affairs (Feld): Document 1. Foreign Relations of the United States, 1952–1954, Volume XI, Part 1, Africa and South Asia.

DoS (1952a) The Consul General at Salisbury (Sims) to the Officer in Charge of West, Central, and East Africa Affairs (Feld): Document 5. Foreign Relations of the United States, 1952–1954, Volume XI, Part 1, Africa and South Asia.

DoS (1953) Memorandum prepared by the Officer in Charge of West, Central, and East Africa Affairs (Feld): Document 18. Foreign Relations of the United States, 1952–1954, Volume XI, Part 1, Africa and South Asia.

DoS (1953a) The Consul at Dakar (Corrigan) to the Department of State: Document 96. Foreign Relations of the United States, 1952–1954, Volume XI, Part 1, Africa and South Asia.

DoS (1955) Memorandum from Assistant Secretary of State for International Organization Affairs (Key) to the Deputy Under Secretary of State (Murphy): Document 3, Foreign Relations of the United States, 1955–1957, Volume XVIII, Africa.

DoS (1955a) Letter from the Consul at Nairobi (Barrow) to the Representative at the Trusteeship Council (Sears): Document 6, Foreign Relations of the United States, 1955–1957, Volume XVIII, Africa.

DoS (1955b) Memorandum from the Assistant Secretary of State for Near Eastern, South Asian, and African Affairs (Allen) to the Secretary of State: Document 7. Foreign Relations of the United States, 1955–1957, Volume XVIII, Africa.

DoS (1955c) Memorandum by the Consul General at Leopoldville (McGregor): Document 9, Foreign Relations of the United States, 1955–1957, Volume XVIII, Africa.

DoS (1957a) Report by the Vice President: Document 19, Foreign Relations of the United States, 1955–1957, Volume XVIII, Africa.

DoS (1957b) Memorandum from the Assistant Secretary of State for Near Eastern, South Asian, and African Affairs (Rountree) to the Secretary of State: Document 22, Foreign Relations of the United States, 1955–1957, Volume XVIII, Africa.

DoS (1958) Memorandum from the Secretary of State's Special Assistant (Holmes) to Secretary of State Dulles: Document 1. Foreign Relations of the United States, 1958–1960, Volume XIV, Africa, pp. 1–11.

DoS (1958a) Editorial Note: Document 13. Available at: http://history.state.gov/historicaldocuments/frus1958-60v14/ch1 (accessed: 21 October 2013).

DoS (1959) Memorandum from the Representative at the Trusteeship Council (Sears) to the Representative at the United Nations (Lodge): Document 11. Foreign Relations of the United States, 1958–1960, Volume XIV, Africa.

DoS (1959a) Memorandum of Conversation: Document 14, Foreign Relations of the United States, 1958–1960, Volume XIV, Africa.

DoS (1960) Memorandum of Discussion at the 432nd Meeting of the National Security Council: Document 21. Foreign Relations of the United States, 1958–1960, Volume XIV, Africa.

DoS (1960a) Memorandum of Discussion at the 438th Meeting of the National Security Council: Document 23. Foreign Relations of the United States, 1958–1960, Volume XIV, Africa.

DoS (1960b) Memorandum from the Assistant Secretary of State for African Affairs (Satterthwaite) to the Under Secretary of State (Dillon): Document 24, Foreign Relations of the United States, 1958–1960, Volume XIV, Africa.

DoS (1961) Memorandum from the Assistant Secretary of State for African Affairs (Williams) to the Under Secretary of State (Bowles): Document 201, Foreign Relations of the United States, 1961–1963, Volume XXI, Africa.

DoS (1965) Memorandum from Ulric Haynes of the National Security Council Staff to Robert W. Komer of the National Security Council Staff: Document 196, Foreign Relations of the United States, 1964–1968, Volume XXIV, Africa.

DoS (1965a) Memorandum from Ulric Haynes of the National Security Council Staff to the President's Special Assistant for National Security Affairs (Bundy): Document 197, Foreign Relations of the United States, 1964–1968, Volume XXIV, Africa.

DoS (1965b) Memorandum from Robert W. Komer of the National Security Council Staff to President Johnson: Document 199, Foreign Relations of the United States, 1964–1968, Volume XXIV, Africa.

DoS (1965c) Action Memorandum from the Assistant Secretary of State for African Affairs (Williams) to Secretary of State Rusk: Document 200, Foreign Relations of the United States, 1964–1968, Volume XXIV, Africa.

DoS (1965d) Memorandum from Secretary of State Rusk to President Johnson: Document 201, Foreign Relations of the United States, 1964–1968, Volume XXIV, Africa.

DoS (1965e) Memorandum from the President's Deputy Special Assistant for National Security Affairs (Komer) to President Johnson: Document 202, Foreign Relations of the United States, 1964–1968, Volume XXIV, Africa.

DoS (1965f) Memorandum from President Johnson to Secretary of State Rusk: Document 203, Foreign Relations of the United States, 1964–1968, Volume XXIV, Africa.

DoS (1966) Memorandum from the President's Special Assistant (Moyers) to President Johnson. Document 211, Foreign Relations of the United States, 1964–1968, Volume XXIV, Africa.

US policy in Africa and the Cold War 171

DoS (1966a) Memorandum from the Deputy Assistant Secretary of State for African Affairs (Fredericks) to Secretary of State Rusk: Document 207, Foreign Relations of the United States, 1964–1968, Volume XXIV, Africa.

DoS (1966b) Memorandum from the President's Special Assistant (Rostow) to President Johnson: Document 209, Foreign Relations of the United States, 1964–1968, Volume XXIV, Africa.

DoS (1966c) Report of the Task Force on the Review of African Development Policies and Programs: Document 215, Foreign Relations of the United States, 1964–1968, Volume XXIV, Africa.

DoS (1966d) Memorandum from the Under Secretary of State (Ball) to President Johnson: Document 216, Foreign Relations of the United States, 1964–1968, Volume XXIV, Africa.

DoS (1966e) Memorandum from the President's Special Assistant (Rostow) to President Johnson: Document 217, Foreign Relations of the United States, 1964–1968, Volume XXIV, Africa.

DoS (1966f) National Security Action Memorandum No. 356: Document 221, Foreign Relations of the United States, 1964–1968, Volume XXIV, Africa.

DoS (1967) Memorandum from the Under Secretary of State (Katzenbach) to President Johnson: Document 224, Foreign Relations of the United States, 1964–1968, Volume XXIV, Africa.

DoS (1967a) Paper prepared in the Department of State: Document 226, Foreign Relations of the United States, 1964–1968, Volume XXIV, Africa.

DoS (1968) Paper prepared in the Department of State: Document 232, Foreign Relations of the United States, 1964–1968, Volume XXIV, Africa.

DoS (1970) Intelligence note prepared in the Bureau of Intelligence and Research: Document 92, Foreign Relations of the United States, 1969–1976, Volume XXVIII, Southern Africa.

DoS (1973) Memorandum from Fernando Rondon of the National Security Council Staff to the President's Assistant for National Security Affairs (Kissinger), Washington, 2 January 1973: Document 1, Foreign Relations of the United States, 1969–1976, Volume E–6, Documents on Africa, 1973–1976.

DoS (1973a) Briefing Memorandum from the Assistant Secretary of State for African Affairs (Newsom) to Secretary of State Kissinger, Washington, 5 October 1973: Document 11, Foreign Relations of the United States, 1969–1976, Volume E–6, Documents on Africa, 1973–1976.

DoS (1974) Telegram 175398 from the Department of State to All African Diplomatic Posts, 11 August 1974, 1512Z: Document 18, Foreign Relations of the United States, 1969–1976, Volume E–6, Documents on Africa, 1973–1976.

DoS (1974a) Memorandum of Conversation, Washington, 21 August 1974: Document 19, Foreign Relations of the United States, 1969–1976, Volume E–6, Documents on Africa, 1973–1976.

DoS (1974b) Minutes of the Secretary of State's Staff Meeting, Washington, 23 December 1974: Document 22, Foreign Relations of the United States, 1969–1976, Volume E–6, Documents on Africa, 1973–1976.

DoS (1975) Telegram 84081 from the Department of State to All African Diplomatic Posts, 12 April 1975, 0205Z: Document 28, Foreign Relations of the United States, 1969–1976, Volume E–6, Documents on Africa, 1973–1976.

DoS (1975a) Action Memorandum from Deputy Assistant Secretary of State for African Affairs (Mulcahy) and Director of Policy Planning (Lord) to Secretary of

State Kissinger, Washington, 27 June 1975: Document 29, Foreign Relations of the United States, 1969–1976, Volume E–6, Documents on Africa, 1973–1976.

DoS (1975b) Telegram 566 from the Embassy in Zaire to the Department of State, 21 January 1975, 1415Z: Document 23, Foreign Relations of the United States, 1969–1976, Volume E–6, Documents on Africa, 1973–1976.

DoS (1975c) Telegram 300 from the Embassy in Somalia to the Department of State, 27 February 1975, 1035Z: Document 26, Foreign Relations of the United States, 1969–1976, Volume E–6, Documents on Africa, 1973–1976.

DoS (1975d) Memorandum of Conversation, Washington, August 19, 1975: Document 30, Foreign Relations of the United States, 1969–1976, Volume E–6, Documents on Africa, 1973–1976.

DoS (1976) Intelligence Appraisal DIAIAPPR 4–76 prepared by the Defense Intelligence Agency, Washington, 9 January 1976: Document 33, Foreign Relations of the United States, 1969–1976, Volume E–6, Documents on Africa, 1973–1976.

DoS (1976a) Memorandum of Conversation, Washington, 9 May 1976, 2:45–4:03 p.m.: Document 42, Foreign Relations of the United States, 1969–1976, Volume E–6, Documents on Africa, 1973–1976.

DoS (1976b) Memorandum from the Administrator of the Agency for International Development (Parker) to Secretary of State Kissinger, Washington, March 13, 1976: Document 36, Foreign Relations of the United States, 1969–1976, Volume E–6, Documents on Africa, 1973–1976.

DoS (1976c) Memorandum from the Assistant Secretary of Defense for International Security Affairs (Amos) to Secretary of Defense Rumsfeld, Washington, undated: Document 51, Foreign Relations of the United States, 1969–1976, Volume E–6, Documents on Africa, 1973–1976.

DoS (1976d) Memorandum of Conversation, Washington, 9 May 1976, 2.45–4.03 p.m, *Foreign Relations of the United States, 1969–1976, Volume E–6, Documents on Africa, 1973–1976.*

DoS (1976e) Telegram 188577 from the Department of State to All African Diplomatic Posts, 30 July 1976, 0048: Document 52, Foreign Relations of the United States, 1969–1976, Volume E–6, Documents on Africa, 1973–1976.

DoS (1976f) Telegram 212737 from the Department of State to the Embassy in Tanzania, 26 August 1976, 2336Z: Document 54, Foreign Relations of the United States, 1969–1976, Volume E–6, Documents on Africa, 1973–1976.

DoS (1976g) Memorandum of Conversation, Washington, April 21, 1976: Document 39, Foreign Relations of the United States, 1969–1976, Volume E–6, Documents on Africa, 1973–1976.

DoS (1978) Memorandum of Conversation, Washington, 27 May 1978: Document 115, Foreign Relations of the United States, 1977–1980, Volume VI, Soviet Union.

DoS (1981) Proposed Chad-Libya Merger – Department of State, 9 January 1981, *Department of State bulletin* 81: 31.

DoS (1986) U.S.-Supported Human Rights Program in South Africa, *Department of State bulletin* 86: 47–48.

Easum, D. (2010) Hard Times for the African Bureau 1974–1976 – A Diplomatic Adventure Story. American Diplomacy: Foreign Policy Despatches and Periodic Reports on US Foreign Policy.

Eberstadt, N. (1988) *Foreign aid and American purpose.* American Enterprise Institute for Public Policy Research; Distributed by arrangement with National Book Network, Washington, DC; Lanham, MD.

Ford, G. R. (1979) *A time to heal: the autobiography of Gerald R. Ford.* Harper & Row, New York.
Franke, R. W. and Chasin, B. H. (1980) *Seeds of famine: ecological destruction and the development dilemma in the West African Sahel.* Allanheld, Osmun, Montclair, N.J.
Freeman, C. W. (1987) The Human Rights Dimension in Africa – Address before the World Affairs Council in Philadelphia, 6 November 1986, *Department of State bulletin* 87: 42–45.
Gleijeses, P. (2002) *Conflicting missions: Havana, Washington, and Africa, 1959–1976.* University of North Carolina Press, Chapel Hill.
Gleijeses, P. (2010) A Test of Wills: Jimmy Carter, South Africa, and the Independence of Namibia, *Diplomatic History* 34: 853–891.
Graham, Y. (1985) The politics of crisis in Ghana: class struggle and organisation, 1981–84, *Review of African Political Economy* 12: 54–68.
Haig, A. (1970) Memorandum for Henry A. Kissinger: March 23, 1970 – Subject: State Department's Policy Statement on Africa. Richard M. Nixon National Security Files, 1969–1974 [electronic resource]: Africa. Bethesda, Md.: University Publications of America, 2011.
Haig, A. (1981) A New Direction in U.S. Foreign Policy – Address before the American Society of Newspaper Editors (ANE), 24 April 1981, *Department of State bulletin* 81: 5–7.
Haig, A. (1981a) Peaceful Progress in Developing Nations – Commencement address at Fairfield University, Connecticut, 24 May 1981, *Department of State bulletin* 81: 8–9.
Haig, A. (1981b) Security and Development Assistance – Address before the Senate Foreign Relation Committee, 19 March 1981, *Department of State bulletin* 81: A–C.
Haig, A. (1982) Overview of Recent Foreign Policy – Secretary Haig's Statement before the House Foreign Affairs Committee on 12 November 1981, *Department of State bulletin* 82: 16–18.
Haig, A. (1982a) Proposed FY 1983 Foreign Assistance Program, *Department of State bulletin* 82: 36–37.
Henze, P. B. (1986) *Rebels and separatists in Ethiopia: regional resistance to a Marxist regime.* Rand, Santa Monica, CA.
Hollick, J. C. (1982) Civil-War in Chad, 1978–82, *World Today* 38 (7): 297–304.
Hubbard, J. P. (2011) *The United States and the end of British colonial rule in Africa, 1941–1968.* McFarland & Company, Jefferson, North Carolina.
Isaacman, A. and Davis, J. (1978) US Policy Towards Mozambique, 1946–1976: 'The defense of colonialism and regional stability', in Lemarchand, R. and Bender, G. J. (eds) *American policy in Southern Africa: the stakes and the stance.* University Press of America, Washington, DC, pp. 65–143.
Jackson, D. R. (2007) *Jimmy Carter and the horn of Africa: Cold War policy in Ethiopia and Somalia.* McFarland & Company, Jefferson, North Carolina.
Johnson, D. H. (2011) *The root causes of Sudan's civil wars: peace or truce.* James Currey, Woodbridge.
Johnson, L. B. (1966) Remarks at a Reception Marking the Third Anniversary of the Organization of African Unity, 26 May 1966. www.presidency.ucsb.edu/ws/?pid=27619 (accessed 15 March 2017).
Kennedy, J. F. (1961) Address by President John F. Kennedy to the UN General Assembly: 25 September 1961. Department of State.

Kissinger, H. (1969) Memorandum for the President, December 1969 – Subject: Presidential Speech on Africa. Richard M. Nixon National Security Files, 1969–1974 [electronic resource]: Africa. Bethesda, Md.: University Publications of America, 2011.

Kissinger, H. (1970) United States Policy toward South Africa – National Security Decision Memorandum 38. Nixon Presidential Library & Museum.

Kissinger, H. (1973) Memorandum From the President's Assistant for National Security Affairs (Kissinger) to President Nixon, Washington, June 18, 1973: Document 6. Foreign Relations of the United States, 1969–1976, Volume E–6, Documents on Africa, 1973–1976.

Kissinger, H. (1976) Statement by Secretary of State Kissinger – Implications of Angola for Future U.S. Foreign Policy. Washington, 29 January 1976: Document 67. Foreign Relations of the United States, 1969–1976, Volume XXXVIII, Part 1, Foundations of Foreign Policy, 1973–1976.

Kissinger, H. (1976a) United States Policy on Southern Africa, *The Department of State Bulletin*, pp. 672–679.

Kissinger, H. (1979) *White House years*. Little, Brown, Boston.

Kissinger, H. (2003) *Crisis: the anatomy of two major foreign policy crises.* Simon & Schuster, New York.

Lake, A. (1976) *The 'tar baby' option: American policy toward Southern Rhodesia.* Columbia University Press, New York.

Lebovic, J. H. (1988) National Interests and United States Foreign Aid: The Carter and Reagan Years, *Journal of Peace Research* 25: 115–135.

Lefebvre, J. A. (1998) The United States, Ethiopia and the 1963 Somali–Soviet arms deal: containment and the balance of power dilemma in the Horn of Africa, *Journal of Modern African Studies* 36: 611–643.

Lemarchand, R. (1976) CIA in Africa: How Central? How Intelligent?, *Journal of Modern African Studies* 14: 401–426.

Liebenow, J. G. (1983) American Policy in Africa: The Reagan Years, *Current History* 82: 97ff.

Litwak, R. (1984) *Détente and the Nixon doctrine: American foreign policy and the pursuit of stability, 1969–1976.* Cambridge University Press, Cambridge; New York.

Lyman, P. (1982) Libyan Involvement in Sudan and Chad: Statement before the Subcommittee on Africa of the House Foreign Affairs Committee, 4 November 1981, *Department of State bulletin* 82: 27–29.

Lyons, T. (1994) Keeping Africa off the agenda, in Cohen, W. I. and Tucker, N. B. (eds.) *Lyndon Johnson confronts the world: American foreign policy, 1963–1968.* Cambridge University Press, Cambridge; New York, pp. 245–278.

Mahoney, R. D. (1983) *JFK: ordeal in Africa.* Oxford University Press, New York.

McManus, J. F. (1977) Rhodesia and the Byrd Amendment, *The Sundance Times*, March 10.

McPherson, P. (1987) U.S. Initiative for Southern Africa: Address before the Annual Consultative of the South Africa Development Coordination Conference, 5 February 1987, *Department of State bulletin* 87: 54–5.

Mead, W. R. (2001) *Special providence: American foreign policy and how it changed the world.* Knopf, New York.

Millikan, M. F. and Rostow, W. W. (1957) *A proposal: key to an effective foreign policy.* Harper & Bros, New York.

Mitchell, N. (2007) Tropes of the Cold War: Jimmy Carter and Rhodesia, *Cold War History* 7: 263–83.

Mitchell, N. (2016) *Jimmy Carter in Africa: race and the Cold War*. Woodrow Wilson Center Press, Washington, DC; Stanford University Press, Stanford, California.

Muehlenbeck, P. E. (2012) *Betting on the Africans: John F. Kennedy's courting of African nationalist leaders*. Oxford University Press, Oxford; New York.

Nesbitt, P. (1988) Terminators, Crusaders and Gladiators: Western (Private & Public) support for Renamo & Unita, *Review of African Political Economy* 15: 111–124.

Nessen, R. (1976) Various comments on Kissinger's Africa trip. Gerald Ford Public Library.

Newsom, D. D. (1970) Text of the speech to be given by the Honorable David D. Newsom, Assistant Secretary of State for African Affairs, before the Chicago Committee, 17 September 1970. Richard M. Nixon National Security Files, 1969–1974 [electronic resource]: Africa. Bethesda, Md.: University Publications of America, 2011.

NIE (1953) National Intelligence Estimate: Document 27. Foreign Relations of the United States, 1952–1954, Volume XI, Part 1, Africa and South Asia.

NIE (1956) National Intelligence Estimate: Document 14. Foreign Relations of the United States, 1955–1957, Volume XVIII, Africa.

Nixon, R. M. (1970) U. S. Foreign Policy for the 1970s: A New Strategy for Peace: A Report to the Congress by Richard Nixon, President of the United States: Document 7, Foreign Relations of the United States, 1969–1976, Volume E–5, Part 1, Documents on Sub-Saharan Africa, 1969–1972.

Nixon, R. M. (1970a) Memorandum from President Nixon to the President's Assistants (Haldeman), (Ehrlichman) and (Kissinger): Document 10, Foreign Relations of the United States, 1969–1976, Volume E–5, Part 1, Documents on Sub-Saharan Africa, 1969–1972.

Nixon, R. M. (1971) U.S. Foreign Policy for the 1970s: Building for Peace: A Report to the Congress by Richard Nixon, President of the United States: Document 14, Foreign Relations of the United States, 1969–1976, Volume E–5, Part 1, Documents on Sub-Saharan Africa, 1969–1972.

Nixon, R. M. (1972) U.S. Foreign Policy for the 1970s, The Emerging Structure of Peace: A Report to the Congress by Richard Nixon, President of the United States: Document 18, Foreign Relations of the United States, 1969–1976, Volume E–5, Part 1, Documents on Sub-Saharan Africa, 1969–1972.

Noer, T. J. (2005) *Soapy: a biography of G. Mennen Williams*. University of Michigan Press, Ann Arbor.

NSC (1957) National Security Council Report – NSC 5719/1: Document 24, Foreign Relations of the United States, 1955–1957, Africa, Volume XVIII.

NSC (1958) National Security Council Report: Document 8, Foreign Relations of the United States, 1958–1960, Volume XIV, Africa.

NSC (1969) Paper prepared by the National Security Council Interdepartmental Group for Africa: Document 17, Foreign Relations of the United States, 1969–1976, Volume XXVIII, Southern Africa.

NSC (1976) Minutes of a National Security Council Meeting, Washington, 11 May 1976, 6:15 p.m.–7:15 p.m.: Document 44, Foreign Relations of the United States, 1969–1976, Volume E–6, Documents on Africa, 1973–1976.

Odom, W. E. (1992) *On internal war: American and Soviet approaches to Third World clients and insurgents*. Duke University Press, Durham, N.C.

Packenham, R. A. (1973) *Liberal America and the Third World; political development ideas in foreign aid and social science.* Princeton University Press, Princeton, N.J.

Paterson, T. G., Clifford, J. G. and Hagan, K. J. (1991) *American foreign policy: a history.* D.C. Heath, Lexington, Mass.

Pollack, K. M. (2002) *Arabs at war: military effectiveness, 1948–1991.* University of Nebraska Press, Lincoln, NE.

Reagan, R. (1981). Cooperative Strategy for Global Growth: Address before the World Affair Council in Philadelphia, 15 October 1981. *Department of State bulletin,* 81 (2057), 14–17.

Reagan, R. (1984) American Foreign Policy Challenges in the 1980s: Address before the Center for Strategic and International Studies, 6 April 1984, *Department of State bulletin* 84: 1–17.

Reagan, R. (1985) South Africa: Presidential Actions: Remarks made in the White House upon signing the Executive Order Prohibiting Trade and other Transactions involving South Africa, *Department of State bulletin* 85: 1–3.

Reagan, R. (1986) Economic sanctions against South Africa: Messages to the House and Congress, *Department of State bulletin* 86: 35–37.

Rivkin, A. (1965) Lost Goals in Africa, *Foreign Affairs* 44: 111–126.

Rodman, P. W. (2009) *Presidential command: power, leadership, and the making of foreign policy from Richard Nixon to George W. Bush.* Alfred A. Knopf, New York.

Rostow, W. W. (1960) *The United States in the world arena; an essay in recent history.* Harper, New York.

Ruttan, V. W. (1996) United States development assistance policy: the domestic politics of foreign economic aid. Johns Hopkins University Press, Baltimore.

Schlesinger, A. (1983) Foreign Policy and the American Character, *Foreign Affairs* 62: 1–16.

Schmidt, E. (2013) *Foreign intervention in Africa: from the Cold War to the War on Terror.* Cambridge University Press, Cambridge.

Schraeder, P. J. (1994) *United States foreign policy toward Africa: incrementalism, crisis, and change.* Cambridge University Press, Cambridge; New York.

Shultz, G. (1983) Foreign Aid and U.S. National Interests – Address before the Southern Center for International Studies, Atlanta, Georgia, 24 February 1983, *Department of State bulletin* 83: 25–28.

Shultz, G. (1984) The U.S. and Africa in the 1980s: Address before the Boston World Affairs Council, 15 February 1984, *Department of State bulletin* 84: 9–12.

Shultz, G. (1985) South Africa towards an American consensus: Secretary Shult's address before the National Press Club, 16 April 1985, *Department of State bulletin* 85: 22–26.

Shultz, G. (1986) The Church as a Force for Peaceful Change in South Africa – Address before the Conference on South Africa for American Religious Leaders, 2 June 1986. *Department of State bulletin* 86 (2113): 30–32.

Shultz, G. (1988) Efforts for peace in Africa: Remarks at a Reception in honor of the Organization of African Unity (OAU) in New York City – 4 October 1988, *Department of State bulletin* 88: 20–22.

Shultz, G. P. (1993) *Turmoil and triumph: my years as secretary of state.* Scribner's; Maxwell Macmillan, Toronto, Canada; Maxwell Macmillan International, New York.

Smith, G. (1986) *Morality, reason, and power: American diplomacy in the Carter years.* Hill and Wang, New York.

Stockwell, J. (1978) *In search of enemies: a CIA story.* Deutsch, London.
Stohl, M., Carleton, D. and Johnson, S. E. (1984) Human Rights and U.S. Foreign Assistance from Nixon to Carter, *Journal of Peace Research* 21: 215–226.
Tillery, A. B. (2007) G. Mennen 'Soapy' Williams and the American Negro Leadership Conferance on Africa: Rethinking the origins of multiculturalism in U.S. Foreign Policy, in Walton, H., Stevenson, R. L. and Rosser, J. B. (eds) *The African foreign policy of Secretary of State Henry Kissinger: a documentary analysis.* Lexington Books, Lanham, pp. 45–65.
Ungar, S. J. and Vale, P. (1985) South Africa: Why Constructive Engagement Failed, *Foreign Affairs* 64: 234–258.
USIS (1972) Portugal – United States. Renewal of Agreement on Azores Bases. *Keesing's Contemporary Archives*, 6–13 May 1972, p. 25239.
Vance, C. R. (1983) *Hard choices: critical years in America's foreign policy.* Simon & Schuster, New York.
Walters, V. A. (1985) Statement at the UN Security Council Meeting on the Situation in South Africa – 25 July 1985, *Department of State bulletin* 85: 1–3.
Walton, H. (2007) African foreign policy before the Kissinger Years: The G. Mennen 'Soapy' Williams era 1961–1966, in Walton, H., Stevenson, R. L. and Rosser, J. B. (eds.) *The African foreign policy of Secretary of State Henry Kissinger: a documentary analysis.* Lexington Books, Lanham, pp. 23–43.
Weiner, T. (2007) *Legacy of ashes: the history of the CIA.* Doubleday, New York.
Whitehead, J. C. (1986) The African Economic Crisis – Oral Statement before the Subcommittee on African Affairs of the Senate Foreign Relations Committee – 24 October 1985, *Department of State bulletin* 86: 33–35.
Williams, G. M. (1969) *Africa for the Africans.* Eerdmans, Grand Rapids.
Wright, J. L. (1989) *Libya, Chad and the Central Sahara.* Hurst, London.

# 5 US policy in Africa and the 'new world order'

Superpower peace-making in a troubled world

**Superpower peace-making in a troubled world**

The election of George H. W. Bush was a testimony to the immense popularity of Ronald Reagan despite the numerous controversies that surrounded his presidency. The nickname given to Reagan by Congresswoman Patricia Schroeder, the 'Teflon President', was indeed well earned. Both during his campaign and shortly after he was elected President, Bush signalled that he had no intention of introducing significant policy changes that departed from Reagan's general approach (Ambrose and Brinkley, 1997: 352).

Despite his intentions, however, the events that occurred around the globe in 1989 had a significant impact on US foreign policy and subsequently on the justification for US foreign assistance. Most importantly, the Cold War was fading, and with it, the rationale to conduct foreign policy based on the premise that the Soviet Union and its allies needed to be contained to ensure the continuation of a free, democratic and secure world.

Assistant Secretary of State for African Affairs during the Bush administration, Herman Cohen, expressed a fresh hope for the Africa policy. Now that the Cold War was over, there was no more reason to help 'sleazy African dictators principally because they were deemed "pro-West"' (Cohen, 2000: 1). Instead there was 'a great opportunity to formulate new policies unencumbered by the "communist menace"' (Cohen, 2000: 1).

Secretary Baker had a similar understanding of the main role of the African policy during the Cold War and of the fresh opportunities to engage with the continent in contemporary ways without the need to formulate policy based on the US–Soviet relationship (Baker and DeFrank, 1995: 218).

Nevertheless, with the exception of the policy regarding South Africa, African affairs continued to rank as low priority in relation to almost every other region in the world (Clough, 1992: 54; Cohen, 2000: 54). Ambrose and Brinkley (1997: 352–353) note that 1989 was not only a remarkable year in terms of the 'unprecedented, unpredictable, and unimaginable' geopolitical earthquakes, but also in the sense that America, for the most part, had nothing to do with these events (see also Paterson *et al.*, 1991:

688). With Chinese students protesting for democracy in Tiananmen Square, and Gorbachev's revocation of the Brezhnev doctrine in conjunction with increasingly popular voices across the Soviet satellite nations in Europe demanding to abolish the one-party rule, it seemed evident that the Bush-declared 'new world order' was in the offing. Amid tensions with China following the massacre in Tiananmen Square, the Soviet move towards glasnost and perestroika, the fall of the Iron Curtain, the American involvement in South America (including the invasion of Panama), the stagnated peace process in the Middle East, the Iraqi invasion of Kuwait, Operation Desert Shield, and the financial crisis in the US, Bush had very little time for African affairs.[1]

The changing geopolitics, and particularly the dissolution of the Soviet Union, left America with a sense of victory, and a willingness to assume global responsibility and leadership. But in tension with this self-perception, during the eight years of the Reagan administration America was transformed from the leading creditor nation to a major debtor, rendering the state of the economy as the major concern in the new world order context (Ambrose and Brinkley, 1997: 379–380). Nonetheless, as the leader of the sole remaining superpower, Bush sought to cash in on the peace dividend, and promote the social, political and economic principles of American ideology (Conti, 2002: 3).

As long as the Soviet threat persisted, the unifying rationale for foreign assistance was containment of the Soviet Union. With the Cold War drawing to a close and both the Soviet Union and the US under financial stress, it became difficult to justify maintaining the levels of financial support granted to win the friendship of developing countries (Ambrose and Brinkley, 1997: 370). The Bureau of African Affairs was hopeful that the end of the Cold War would lead to a new policy framework for Africa that could revert to its 'development roots', and eventually to a new kind of partnership with African nations that would help spur their much-needed economic growth (Cohen, 2000: 1–2). This intention was consistent with Secretary Baker's persistent promotion of economic reform policies in the Third World.[2] Cohen (2000: 2) believed that the Bureau could contribute towards achieving this end by concentrating on solving the four ongoing civil wars in Africa (Angola, Mozambique, Ethiopia and Sudan). He believed that these wars were the underlying cause for regional economic stagnation and humanitarian distress in Africa. He also highlighted political corruption and repressive regimes as causes of underdevelopment and explained that conflict resolution and democratisation will become 'centrepieces' of the African policy (Cohen, 2000: 2–3).

This was a new rationale for an American involvement in Africa, born out of the necessity to introduce a framework that could support continued engagement on the continent in the absence of the Cold War (Clough, 1992: 55). Cohen and Secretary Baker favoured an approach that linked (selected) instabilities in Africa to global security, economic development and the promotion of democracy, justifying America's interventionism by the leadership role it assumed in a post-Soviet world. President Bush explained that in the new geopolitical reality, American interests in Africa are 'the promotion of peaceful change and conflict resolution, democracy and improved governance, free market economic policies, sustainable development and effective African action on transnational issues such as AIDS, the environment, population growth and terrorism.' (Bush, 1992: 14). The approach to Africa was justified by emphasising that '[p]rogress toward democracy and respect for human rights are explicit criteria in AID's allocation process and an integral part of U.S. diplomatic agenda in Africa' (Bush, 1992: 15).

Since Moscow was searching for exit strategies from its various costly entanglements around the globe, Bush instructed his administration to work closely with the Russians to help smooth the transition from the Cold War (Cohen, 2000: 4; Paterson *et al.*, 1991: 689). Nevertheless, Bush and his senior advisors who had built their entire careers as 'cold warriors' could not easily shake off their suspicions of the Soviet Union. Coupled with Bush's conservatism and cautiousness, the administration was often hesitant and careful before committing to a course of action (Apodaca, 2006: 117; Paterson *et al.*, 1991: 691). The most important US policy objectives for Africa under the Bush administration were formulated towards the end of his presidency, and were outlined in a response to National Security Review (NSR 30) commissioned by the President, and dubbed American Policy toward Africa in the 1990s. An assessment conducted based on the questions posed in the commissioned review, identified five issue areas in Africa:

- Access to selected African air naval facilities, air space and sea lanes;
- Downsizing African Militaries;
- African military support for democracy, human rights and civilian control;
- Conflict resolution and African regional peacekeeping operations;
- Retaining sufficient US military presence in Africa (Aning, 2001: 45).

*The Apartheid regime*

While the new post-Cold War justification for the African policy was being reshaped, the most difficult policy issue, the apartheid regime, was surprisingly beginning to show signs of significant change. As with the other major events taking place in 1989, the shift in South Africa occurred from within. Following secret meetings between the African National Congress and business and political leaders, President F. W. de Klerk addressed the South African Parliament on 2 February 1990. His address paved the way for the legalisation of the ANC and several other political parties; the abolishment of racial segregation; the ending of the state of emergency, the suspension of capital punishment; and the release of all political prisoners and the safe return of political exiles, including the unconditional release of Nelson Mandela. This was a public and open commitment to begin to dismantle the apartheid regime. Shortly after this announcement, Mandela was released after spending 28 years behind bars. In his speech before Parliament, President de Klerk created a link between the changes he proposed and the events which had mesmerised the world in 1989. This linkage, probably a mixture of political opportunism and real concerns,[3] was created by de Klerk to emphasise that the events in Eastern Europe indicated the failure of the communist economic and political systems. In the eyes of many South Africans and the American government, the failure of the communist system in Europe diminished the perceived threat from communist-backed political organisations such as the ANC[4] (de Klerk, 1998: 105–107, 114). As Bush explained:

> The United States' overriding policy objectives in South Africa is the peaceful transition from apartheid to a nonracial, multi-party democracy based on a free market economy.
> (Bush, 1992: 16)

Schraeder (1994: 236) noted that when Bush took office, he was determined to avoid the 'bruising battles with Congress over South Africa so frequent during the Reagan years'. During the first few months of the administration, Secretary Baker and Assistant Secretary Cohen continued the efforts to express the administration's revulsion of apartheid, and to emphasise the steps taken to convince South Africa to move towards democratisation (Schraeder, 1994: 236). Nevertheless, they also continued to express the administration's opposition to the imposition of further sanctions against South Africa (Baker and DeFrank, 1995: 219; Schraeder, 1994: 236). Baker and DeFrank (1995: 226) recount that during the ceremonies for Namibian independence in March 1990, Bush met with Mandela and several other ANC members. Still wearing his cold warrior lenses, Baker remarked:

> I was disappointed to learn that he was still clinging to long-discredited socialist economic theories. When I asked about the importance of free markets, he'd counter with the need for nationalization of industry. 'It's important to redistribute wealth to give people whom apartheid has denied a chance,' he argued.
> (Baker and DeFrank, 1995: 226)

On this occasion, Mandela asked Baker to intensify American sanctions against South Africa since the 'pillars of apartheid' were still in existence. The US lifted its sanctions against South Africa in July 1991[5] before the ANC, the Black Congressional Caucus and other organisations in the US sought their termination (Schraeder, 1994: 241). In conjunction with lifting sanctions, President Bush also announced that the administration would double its assistance to black South Africans for housing, economic development and education programmes, which was interpreted by some as an effort to neutralise some of the criticism against his decision to revoke the sanctions provided in the Anti-Apartheid Act (Friedman, 1991).

*Ethiopia*

In Ethiopia, the Marxist–Leninist government of Mengistu was entangled in a bloody civil war against a number of ethnic groups. In the north, the Eritreans fought for separation and to regain the autonomy that existed before Emperor Selassie reduced Eritrea to an Ethiopian province. In the Tigray province, immediately south of Eritrea, the Tigrean people were fighting an ideological war against Mengistu's government. And in southern Ethiopia, the Oromo people were fighting for self-determination and freedom to practise their religion and culture. Mengistu's war effort was largely sustained through Soviet military assistance that provided weapons as well as military advisors. Financially burdened and otherwise occupied with internal reforms, the Soviet Union was looking for a responsible way out of Ethiopia. Against this background, the US agreed to collaborate with the Soviet Union to provide assistance to Mengistu's government to enter into a negotiation process to end hostilities in the country (Cohen, 2000: 19–20).

In addition to the standing instructions by President Bush to co-operate with the Soviet Union on the transition out of the Cold War, there were several issues that influenced American policy towards Ethiopia. Domestically, pressure groups lobbied Congress to address the humanitarian crisis in Ethiopia. Their main concerns were the famine in the region, and the diversions of food aid sent as relief for local populations. In addition, there was a strong lobby concerned with the wishes of the Ethiopian Jewish community (the Falashas) to leave and immigrate to Israel. Re-igniting the US–Ethiopian relationship was also an opportunity to help resolve regional tensions and encourage a Marxist–Leninist government to move towards democracy and modify its economic policy.

In a meeting with Mengistu held during the month of August 1989, Cohen listed human rights, economic policy, peaceful resolution to the civil war, and Ethiopia's restrictive emigration policy (in implicit reference to the Falashas), as the basis for improving the US–Ethiopian relations (Cohen, 2000: 24).

Almost immediately, the Bureau doubted Mengistu's sincerity on advancing peace in Ethiopia through negotiations. It seemed as though his main goal was to normalise relations with the US in order to replace Soviet military aid with American arms and achieve an advantage over his enemies (Cohen, 2000: 27). His intentions became transparent when he linked the issue of the Falashas' immigration to Israel and Israeli military aid (Cohen, 2000: 34–36). The Americans allowed some leeway on this issue but made it clear that they would not accept the formula of 'Jews for weapons' (Cohen, 2000: 32).

In 1990 the US reached a conclusion that Mengistu's days were numbered and his downfall imminent.[6] The administration's decision was to continue to advance the humanitarian goals (food assistance and Jewish immigration) and the peace process while waiting for the regime's downfall. Cohen hoped that America's efforts to achieve peace between the fighting factions would lead to a meaningful relationship with a future government in Ethiopia. The strategy was to conduct 'constructive engagement' (Cohen, 2000: 30) with the different factions fighting in Ethiopia and link any future relationship with Ethiopia to the emergence of democratic values and practices:

> This reflected the growing importance of 'democratization' in our overall policy towards Africa. The 'liberalization of politics' was becoming a new conditionality for U.S. development assistance.
> (Cohen, 2000: 29 n15)

In April 1991, the Tigrean guerrilla forces were closing in on Addis Ababa. Under pressure due to rebel military victories, Mengistu asked the Americans to help re-ignite the peace negotiations with all parties. In parallel, the Ethiopian government was pressuring Israel to deliver weapons while stalling the already slow and tedious process of allowing Falashas, a handful at a time, to immigrate to Israel (Cohen, 2000: 43). Since there was a concrete possibility that the 18,000 Falashas waiting in Addis Ababa for a departure approval would be caught in a future battle for the control of Ethiopia, Israel and the US devised a solution based on paying (financially) for the release of the Falashas. To blur the moral *problématique* of what looked like a ransom payment, Cohen pushed and passed an amendment to the Defense Department Appropriation Bill, allocating money to the Office of Humanitarian Assistance for 'immediate emergency airlift assistance' (Cohen, 2000: 45). This money was intended to reimburse the government-owned company Ethiopian Airlines, for 'revenue lost' due to the Israeli airlift of the Falashas (Cohen, 2000: 45). Cohen explains that Mengistu 'insisted that the United States "supply the financial assets to cover costs". We all know what that meant', remarks Cohen (2000: 45), implying that America understood that the money would end up lining Mengistu's pockets.

A round of peace negotiations took place in London in May 1991 while Ethiopian forces continued to suffer defeats inside the country. The basis for these talks was a declaration by the Ethiopian Parliament in April that it accepted a ceasefire with the Tigrean rebels.[7] A few days before the London Conference, Mengistu fled Ethiopia for Zimbabwe. Fearing chaos in Addis Ababa, Cohen asked the leader of the Tigrean rebels to enter the capital and assume responsibility to ensure order. This was seen as a controversial request that was interpreted as an American inclination towards the rebels and potentially undermining the ongoing peace negotiations with the government. Many Ethiopians, especially the Ethiopian–American community in the US, accused the administration of handing over Addis Ababa to the dictatorial rule of the Tigrean rebels (Cohen, 2000: 55). Cohen recounts that this issue became a point of controversy that was used repeatedly to question the American commitment to the link between aid and democratisation. His response to this accusation during a press conference in London was 'no democracy, no development assistance' (Cohen, 2000: 56).

## *Sudan*

Sudan, like Ethiopia was suffering from an ongoing civil war that inflicted a severe humanitarian toll. Here, as in the case of Ethiopia, Congress and other organisations had specific concerns that the administration intended to address (Cohen, 2000: 61). The civil war in Sudan was a mixture of subnational, ethnic, religious, and historical grievances between the north and south (Mamdani, 2013). The first civil war that began in 1955 when colonial rule was fading, subsided as 1972 approached, when President Nimeiry negotiated a peace agreement with the South Sudan Liberation Movement. The agreement created tensions between Nimeiry and the more conservative Muslim parties in Sudan who favoured an Islamic state (Johnson, 2011: 55). Gaddafi, who resented what he viewed as Nimeiry's pro-Western orientation, began granting support to Nimeiry's rivals and sought to undermine his rule.[8] Concerned with Gaddafi's attempts to penetrate sub-Saharan Africa and undermine interests, the US decided to assist Sudan. In the early 1980s, Nimeiry went through a personal process that led him to firmer religious convictions, and eventually to a reconciliation with his Muslim rivals and the imposition of Sharia laws on Sudan in 1983 (Johnson, 2011: 51). This resulted in an uprising in the south led by Colonel John Garang[9] who defected from the Sudanese army and created the Sudan People's Liberation Army (SPLA). The SPLA wanted to re-create Sudan as a multi-ethnic and secular state and end Arab cultural and religious imposition on the non-Muslim population (Natsios, 2012: 67).[10] This was the beginning of the second civil war during which the government of Sudan, still closely allied with the US, used weapons supplied by America to help fend off Libyan and Soviet aggression, to subdue the revolts in the south (Johnson, 2011: 58). The US accused Libya and Ethiopia for backing the SPLA uprising (Johnson, 2011: 67), thus linking the civil war to Cold War issues. This linkage allowed Nimeiry to use American-supplied weapons to fight the rebels in the south without serious American opposition (Johnson, 2011: 67; Natsios, 2012: 69).

In 1985, while on an official visit to the US to secure further American aid, a popular uprising against Nimeiry resulted in his removal by Sudan's defence minister, who eventually ceded power to a civilian government elected democratically in 1986.[11] The new Sudanese Prime Minister, Sadiq al-Mahdi, was an Islamist and the leader of the Umma party, which had attempted a Libyan-backed coup against Nimeiry in 1976. Until the deposition of Nimeiry, Gaddafi assisted the SPLA against the government of Sudan. Once al-Mahdi assumed power and pursued his commitment to an Islamic state, Gaddafi shifted his support and helped the government against the SPLA rebels (Johnson, 2011: 81). The situation in Sudan was rapidly deteriorating. Despite hopes for change, al-Mahdi did not revoke the Sharia laws installed by Nimeiry that brought about the SPLA rebellion. Benefiting from both Libyan and American assistance, al-Mahdi had little incentive to pursue serious peace negotiations with the SPLA (Johnson, 2011: 81). The civil war was causing a humanitarian crisis characterised by massive internal displacement and a severe food shortage. Food aid to the south provided by the international community was often diverted or refused by the government of Sudan as a means to inflict pressure on the SPLA, leading eventually to famine and hunger-related deaths (Natsios, 2012: 75). Sudan's economy was in disarray, suffering from bad management, corruption and the costs of the conflict (Natsios, 2012: 70) and Sudan was delaying its loan payments to the US and the IMF (Cohen, 2000: 62).

Between 1986 and 1989, the conflict between the government forces and the SPLA intensified. The SPLA was winning important military victories while exerting a severe humanitarian toll on the population. The democratically elected government of Sudan was adhering to Sharia laws, had close ties with Libya (Cohen, 2000: 63) and was engaged in human rights violations. On the other hand, America was sympathetic with the aspirations of the SPLA. But the SPLA was also guilty of gross violations of human rights (Cohen, 2000: 63). Early in 1989, the Sudanese military high command was dissatisfied with al-Mahdi military strategy and issued an ultimatum that required him to pursue peace with the SPLA (Cohen, 2000: 62; Johnson, 2011: 84). At the same time, the international community led by the UN were devising a new humanitarian aid programme for Sudan called Operation Lifeline Sudan, which consisted of securing the co-operation of both fighting factions for allowing the delivery of food assistance to save the lives of the starving population (Cohen, 2000: 61; Natsios, 2012: 76).

The reality faced by the Bush administration in Sudan was that of a civil war deeply rooted in ethnic and religious rivalries exacerbated by borders set by colonial powers, and facilitated by the foreign assistance granted under the canopy of Cold War strategies. Cohen recounted that when he assumed his position as Assistant Secretary for African Affairs, he received instructions from Deputy Assistant Secretary Laurence Eagleburger to give

Sudan 'a high policy profile' due to intense congressional pressure on the administration to address the humanitarian crisis (Cohen, 2000: 61). Cohen's policy approach to Sudan was to focus on the elimination of hunger, which could be possible if the 'bureaucratic obstacles' along the 'humanitarian corridors' could be circumvented (Cohen, 2000: 62). For this purpose, the US needed the co-operation of the Sudanese government. Between the need to satisfy the domestic and international pressures to provide urgent humanitarian assistance to southern Sudan, and the need to maintain 'friendly contact with the Sudanese military' because of Sudan's strategic location, America opted to continue to supply the Sudanese military with non-lethal assistance, while US aid personnel would seek permission from the government of Sudan before providing assistance to specific locations in the country (Cohen, 2000: 65).

In June 1989, a military coup lead by Brigadier General Hassan el-Bashir deposed Sadiq al-Mahdi. The coup was staged by al-Bashir and the Islamist leader, Hasan al-Turabi, who played a prominent role in subsequent years as a political advisor to al-Bashir. The deposers opposed a process of peace with the south and the weak coalition led by al-Mahdi (Natsios, 2012: 80). Turabi is considered to be the architect behind the idea of creating an Islamic state in Sudan, as well as the creator of the Popular Defence Force who violently oppressed the people of south Sudan (de Waal, 2004: 719; Natsios, 2012: 85–86). Cohen remarked that the 'Africanist community in the US government' welcomed the deposition of al-Mahdi's 'hopelessly inept regime' (Cohen, 2000: 65). Nevertheless, a military coup meant the termination of aid to Sudan according to Article 508 of the Foreign Assistance Act (Cohen, 2000: 66). The al-Bashir regime proved to be fundamentalist and problematic. The SPLA, who continued to inflict serious losses on the Sudanese military, also proved to be uncompromising. As long as he had the upper hand in the battlefield, Garang refused to meet al-Bashir and discuss peace. He adhered to his demands to form a secular Sudanese state and did not trust al-Bashir and his intentions. This was a serious impasse that both the US and other members of the international community did not manage to overcome. So long as the SPLA was victorious on the battlefield, al-Bashir wanted to achieve a cease-fire to hold off the SPLA momentum and negotiate a settlement. As long as he was winning, Garang refused to meet al-Bashir. In the meantime, the civilian population in Sudan suffered from war and hunger while the international community was unable to deliver humanitarian assistance and food aid. Domestically, Congress was increasingly pressuring the administration to assume a firmer stance against the military regime in Sudan. Cohen explained to Congress that without the ability to grant assistance to Sudan,[12] the administration had very little leverage in that country (Cohen, 2000: 74).

When Iraq invaded Kuwait in 1990, the al-Bashir regime turned against the US in support of Iraq and gave refuge to various anti-American

Islamist groups; this led to the closure of the American embassy and the removal of US personnel from Sudan. Sudan's stance against the international community during the Gulf War resulted in its further isolation. Immediately after the Gulf War, Sudan turned once again to the US in an attempt to de-isolate itself from the international community. Bashir asked America to help to re-ignite the reconciliation process in Sudan (Cohen, 2000: 79). But in May 1991, approximately a month after Sudan approached the US, Mengistu's regime in Ethiopia came to an end. Mengistu's government supplied Garang with arms and 'safe-heaven' camps inside Ethiopia (Cohen, 2000: 80). The regime in Sudan, on the other hand, was assisting the rebels in Ethiopia against Mengistu. Now that Mengistu was gone and the rebels assumed power in Ethiopia, assistance to the SPLA was halted (Johnson, 2011: 88). In July 1991, Cohen received a message from Sudan that US mediation in the conflict was no longer required; the SPLA was weak and al-Bashir felt confident in his ability to crush the rebellion. Cohen stressed that the administration was never 'sanguine about the ability to help Sudan' and that US priorities in Africa had lain elsewhere (Angola and Ethiopia). These priorities were attached to US–Soviet relations while the policy in Sudan was a response to domestic pressure which required, in essence, only a superficial engagement on the part of the US.

## Angola

Turning to Angola, the American involvement in the civil war in Angola resumed under the Reagan administration in 1986[13] with US covert aid to UNITA (Cohen, 2000: 87; Wright, 1997: 126–127). Crocker stated in this context that:

> Now we could play the assistance card so as to guarantee that UNITA could never become the victim of a Cuban withdrawal settlement; it could give us leverage as the question of Angolan reconciliation ripened.
> (Crocker quoted in Wright, 1997: 126)

Under the Bush administration in contrast, the DoS viewed Angola as a good place to strengthen US–Soviet relations through a joint collaboration to achieve reconciliation between UNITA and the MPLA. Once the tripartite agreement between Namibia, Angola and South Africa was achieved in 1988 and Namibia had become independent, South Africa ceased its military support to UNITA. But the US did not agree to recognise the legitimacy of the Marxist MPLA government in Angola without a process of reconciliation with UNITA, and continued its military aid to Savimbi, the leader and founder of UNITA. Wright (1997: 154) notes that the 'Angolan drought crisis became interwoven with US policy towards that country'. Following Savimbi's request in 1989, Cohen declared south-eastern Angola a disaster area and instructed USAID to provide food and medical assistance (Wright, 1997: 155). This collaboration with Savimbi circumvented the MPLA government and allowed the US, and subsequently other international organisations, to deliver food and medicine directly to UNITA-controlled areas (Wright, 1997: 155). The MPLA government was not pleased by the direct aid offered by the US to UNITA. From their vantage point, this was an attempt to sustain UNITA rather than support a peace process in Angola. The US replied to these accusations by blaming the MPLA for withholding assistance during a humanitarian disaster to achieve the objective of weakening UNITA and the areas under its control (Wright, 1997: 155).

There was a considerable ideological gap between the MPLA and UNITA, and bringing them to the negotiation table proved to be a challenging task. While the MPLA was willing to negotiate an agreement where UNITA would be integrated politically and militarily into Angolan institutions, UNITA wanted a process that would lead to free and open elections. In essence, UNITA's position appealed to America as it focused on abolishing the one-party Marxist system in Angola. As in other cases in the region, the side that had a temporary advantage on the battlefield refused to accept a ceasefire during negotiations to leverage the process. Both the US and the Soviet Union wanted a dignified exit from Angola, and worked in tandem to bring both parties to the table. At the same time, both superpowers continued to provide military aid – the Soviets to the MPLA, and the US to UNITA.

Involving Angola's neighbours in the peace process, especially President Mobutu of Zaire, a close US ally who had helped America supply UNITA over the years, proved to be problematic. Mobutu lent himself to the process, but being a dictator, he did not subscribe to Savimbi's position to hold free and open elections. He feared that if this condition was accepted, it might lead to a precedence that would risk his own rule (Cohen, 2000: 92). The process under the auspice of Mobutu ended in a logjam and Savimbi, who felt trapped and betrayed, went back to fighting the MPLA. Since Mobutu was angered by Savimbi's refusal of his peace initiative, he decided to discontinue weapon deliveries to UNITA through Zaire. This was a concern for the US who vowed to support Savimbi. On Cohen's recommendation, President Bush invited Mobutu to a meeting. Then, '[h]aving been properly stroked and reassured of his importance to our African policy, Mobutu agreed to reconcile with Savimbi.' (Cohen, 2000: 97).

After efforts to find negotiated solutions had failed, in December 1990 the Soviet Union and the US agreed to take decisive steps to break the deadlock in Angola. A framework agreement was drafted by the superpowers and included a ceasefire, the establishment of a multiparty process in Angola and the legalisation of UNITA, the integration of UNITA fighters in the military, elections and the end to arms deliveries by the superpowers (Cohen, 2000: 106). Both the MPLA and UNITA agreed in essence with the content of the concept and the process of arranging the first free elections in Angola to end the civil war began. The US remained engaged with Angola until the elections took place in September 1992. Cohen indicated that:

> Whenever I visited Luanda, I met with both sides on an equal basis, but the conversations were on different levels. With dos Santos and the MPLA, conversations focused on implementation. With Savimbi, we talked strategy and tactics aimed at coping with problems and winning the elections.
>
> (Cohen, 2000: 112)

But UNITA's approach and attitude was becoming problematic. Their campaign employed ethnic and racist rhetoric against Angolans of mixed ancestry, which characterised many of the MPLA leadership. In parallel, Savimbi was strengthening his position inside UNITA by assassinating his rivals (Cohen, 2000: 13). Savimbi also indicated directly to Cohen that under the negotiated agreement, his fighters were now free to be present everywhere in the country and that he had the ability to assume power in Angola without elections if he so wished. Cohen (2000: 116) remarks that he 'left the meeting hoping more than ever for a UNITA victory'.

Preliminary counting of the votes on election day indicated that the MPLA was leading. Displeased with the projected outcomes, Savimbi denounced the elections as fraudulent despite the opposite assessment of international observers. He refused appeals by the US to accept the outcome of the elections and to collaborate with dos Santos for the future of Angola. UNITA reverted to an armed struggle, and fighting broke out in Luanda and spread throughout Angola. During the last months of the Bush administration, the situation in Angola disintegrated back into a full-scale civil war, and the administration's goal to end another superpower-assisted and fuelled civil war in Africa had failed.

*Mozambique*

As in Angola, the civil war in Mozambique was also induced by a post-colonial struggle for power aggravated by the interests of the regional white minority regimes and Cold War rivalries. Unlike Angola and Ethiopia, Soviet personnel and Cuban troops were not present in Mozambique (Cohen, 2000: 181). Nevertheless, the Marxist nature of the FRELIMO government and Russian arms during the war against the Portuguese led to the imposition of Cold War paradigms on the analysis of the situation in Mozambique.

FRELIMO assumed power in Mozambique after a long liberation struggle against Portugal. The organisation became a political party once independence was achieved. Almost immediately, Rhodesia and later South Africa, helped create the anti-communist liberation organisation in Mozambique, RENAMO, mainly to remove FRELIMO support for the Zimbabwean ZANU and the South African ANC.

There was an internal discussion in the US on the nature and legitimacy of RENAMO, as well as on the extent of America's involvement in Mozambique. The DoD, CIA and many conservative politicians and organisations were of the opinion that RENAMO was a legitimate movement with a solid basis of support among the rural population as it struggled for liberalism against a Marxist government (Cohen, 2000: 182). The DoS on the other hand, argued that the FRELIMO-led government in Mozambique had been recognised internationally, including by the US, who had an embassy and a USAID mission in the country. RENAMO was seen by the DoS as a problematic organisation which had been supported in the past by the controversial Rhodesian white minority regime whose interests were to undermine FRELIMO to preserve their own rule (Cohen, 2000: 182).

America did not assume a leadership role in the mediation of peace in Mozambique (Cohen, 2000: 189). There were no clear strategic US interests in Mozambique and the foreign policy interests were related to a number of different opinions and strategies. Those in the executive and legislative branches that lobbied for US support for RENAMO were analysing the civil struggle in Mozambique through Cold War lenses. These voices were prominent during the late Reagan administration but continued into the Bush administration despite the lack of direct Soviet or Cuban involvement (Cohen, 2000: 182–183, 186–187). Cohen (2000: 195) recalls a briefing with Under Secretary Arnold Kantor[14] where he outlined US policy towards Mozambique. Kantor wanted to know if there was any reason 'other than doing good' for the US to be involved in Mozambique. Cohen explained to Kantor that the US spends a significant amount of money on humanitarian relief in Mozambique, and that if the war ended, this money could be used for development purposes instead. Kantor was not convinced, however, and later stated in a memorandum to Deputy Secretary Eagleburger that with the absence of 'vital U.S. interests in Mozambique', America should 'drop out of the game' (Cohen, 2000: 195).

*Additional conflicts in Africa*

In addition to the four ongoing civil wars initially prioritised by the Bureau of African Affairs during the Bush administration, a number of other conflicts emerged in Africa, including in Liberia, Somalia and Rwanda. For the most part, the US remained uninvolved in those conflicts, and avoided declaring a concrete position or assuming leadership in conflict resolution.

## Rwanda

The civil war in Rwanda that turned into genocide in 1994 began during the Bush administration. The rivalries between the Tutsi and Hutu at the heart of the civil war were historical and were embedded in cultural practices altered and intensified by colonial practices (see, for example, Mamdani 2001; Wheeler, 2000: 209–211). In October 1990, the Rwandan People's Front (RPF)[15] launched an invasion against the Hutu government of President Habyarimana in Rwanda. The RPF was composed of Tutsi refugees in Uganda, many of whom had served as soldiers and officers in the Ugandan military and were backed by President Yoweri Museveni. Unlike southern Africa and the Horn of Africa, Rwanda was not of any strategic or political importance to the US. This had a direct bearing on the level of involvement of the US in the conflict and its resolution. From the beginning of the conflict in Rwanda, the Bush administration was reluctant to take any active role. This was partly the result of few concrete interests in Rwanda (Cohen, 2000: 165), and partly because of President Museveni's involvement in the instigation of the conflict, as noted by Cohen:

> At the time, the international donor community favored Uganda under Museveni's leadership because of its successful economic reforms, its substantial economic growth, and its revival of Ugandan society after the disastrous years of Idi Amin and Milton Obote. We had no desire to challenge Museveni over Rwanda and thus quietly looked for other avenues for conflict management.
> (Cohen, 2000: 178)

The story of Rwanda is picked up again in Bill Clinton's presidency.

## Liberia

In Liberia, the US had historical ties, a strong pro-Liberian lobby and several strategic facilities belonging to the CIA, US Coast Guard and the United States Information Agency (USIA). When Bush came into office, the relations between the US and the President Samuel Doe of Liberia were strained. Doe came to power in 1980 through a military coup that included the assassination of President William Tolbert, consequently ending the rule of the Americo-Liberian minority which had governed that country for decades. Doe's regime assumed a pro-American posture and accommodated US Cold War efforts in Africa. Liberia was rewarded for its support with increased US foreign assistance that peaked during the Carter administration and continued under President Reagan who invited Doe to an official visit of the US (Cohen, 2000: 129). Approaching the mid-1980s, accusations against Doe's human rights abuses and his financial mismanagement of Liberia began to mount. Doe's domestic unpopularity was reflected in the elections of 1985, when he won by a small margin to the protest of international observers who claimed the elections to be fraudulent (Cohen, 2000: 129). With mounting pressure from the Americo-Liberian lobby, and with growing accusations of human rights abuses, financial mismanagement and corruption, Congress threatened to suspend all aid to Liberia (Wills, 1987). The DoS and USAID objected to this initiative, arguing that they were in the process of working with the Liberian government on instituting financial reforms (Cohen, 2000: 128; Wills, 1987). Doe was displeased; he believed that he had been loyal to the US by supporting its foreign policy objectives in Africa, and was now rewarded with declining foreign aid (Cohen, 2000: 128).

In December 1989, the Libyan-backed and financed National Patriotic Liberation Front of Liberia (NPFL) led by Charles Taylor began an insurgency against Does' regime (Adebajo, 2002: 49). With a strong anti-Doe lobby in America and the mounting evidence of human rights abuses conducted by his regime against tribal minorities related to the NPFL,[16] the US refrained from assuming a definite position against the rebels or in favour of Doe. Instead, the administration adopted a 'pro-Liberian people' posture focusing on the provision of humanitarian assistance (Cohen, 2000: 135). Behind the scenes, the Bureau of African Affairs tried to convince Doe to remove himself into exile in order to stop the bloodshed, protect American facilities and citizens, and help to bring about free elections in Liberia. On a higher level of policy in the NSC, the prevailing opinion was to keep the US out of the Liberian problem. In June 1990, Cohen was informed that President Bush had decided the US would not take charge of the diplomatic efforts to solve the Liberian problem and would restrict its efforts to the protection of American citizens when needed (Cohen, 2000: 144). During the same time, the NPFL was fighting in and around Monrovia against the Armed Forces of Liberia. Internal disagreements between Charles Taylor and some of his commanders led to a split in the NPFL and the formation of the Independent National Front of Liberia (INPFL) led by Prince Johnson. The split aggravated the civil war which turned into a three-way fight. The INPFL was backed by the Economic Community of West African States Monitoring Group (ECOMOG),[17] involved in the conflict because Charles Taylor held a number of hostages from Nigeria and other West African states since he believed they were backing Doe. ECOMOG forces intervened in the fights in Liberia to liberate the hostages and remove the siege from Monrovia which had caused a humanitarian disaster. In September 1990, Johnson backed by ECOMOG, managed to capture and kill Samuel Doe (Adebajo, 2002: 52). This did not end the civil war, but only turned it into a struggle between NPFL (armed with Libyan supplies) and the INPFL, effectively turning Taylor into a warlord. Throughout the rest of the Bush administration, the US remained relatively uninvolved in Liberia (Cohen, 2000: 153–160).

## Somalia

Unlike Rwanda, Somalia was strategically important to the US:

> Because of Somalia's strategic position, US diplomacy felt obliged to cultivate close and cordial relations with one of the world's most vicious despots, Mohammed Siad Barre, President of the Somali Democratic Republic.
>
> (Cohen, 2000: 197)

America had a good and stable relationship with Barre who was benefiting from US assistance since Ethiopia became a Soviet client and Cuban troops helped push back the Somali troops during the Ogaden war. In return, America had access to strategic facilities that helped project 'over the horizon' power towards the oil-rich Middle East.

Cohen notes that Somali irredentism was a central narrative used by Barre to acquire power (Cohen, 2000: 200). Once the prospects of winning back the Ogaden vanished, the internal tribal conflicts in Somalia resurfaced with grievances against Barre and his selective power structure that alienated many clans while favouring others (Cohen, 2000: 200). This was the core reason for the civil war waged by the Somali National Front (SNM) and a number of other groups and organisations against Barre's regime.

Until the onset of the Gulf War, US strategic facilities in Somalia remained important, and the strategy towards the internal conflict in Somalia was based upon building a good relationship with the various fighting factions and encourage negotiations to safeguard continued access to vital installations (Cohen, 2000: 202). When the US was granted direct access to bases in the Middle East as a part of operation Desert Storm, the strategic importance of Somalia as a location for proximate presence of US forces to the Middle East was reduced (Cohen, 2000: 203). Similarly, Siad Barre's hold on Somalia deteriorated and his influence on the various regions of the country diminished. His fading hold on Somalia led the US to reconsider the levels of economic assistance to his regime (Cohen, 2000: 203).

In January 1991 Barre fled Somalia, leaving the country in disorder and at the mercy of warlords fighting to gain power and possession of the few resources left. Somalia descended quickly into chaos while international citizens fled the country with the help of US troops. A major consequence of the conflict was a severe food shortage exacerbated by the inability of the international community to bring emergency food assistance due to diversion of aid by the various fighting factions. With the international community involved in the Gulf War, there was a reluctance to define the Somali situation as a security crisis. 'Conflict fatigue', as Cohen indicates, led to an inclination to view Somalia as a humanitarian issue, thus avoiding the need to intervene militarily on behalf of the people of Somalia

(Cohen, 2000: 206–208). When, the international community was finally ready to mount a peacekeeping operation in November 1992, the Bush administration was in its final months. Nonetheless, Bush committed the US to a six-month mission[18] in Somalia. As Cohen indicates, the main concern of the US under the Bush administration was to ensure continued access to the strategic facilities in Somalia as long as needed. As long as the projections and evaluations indicated that the access would not be interrupted by the deteriorating situation, America refrained from taking decisive action to stop the unfolding humanitarian disaster (Cohen, 2000: 217). Bush's commitment to a peacekeeping mission in Somalia was handed over to the Clinton administration which was tasked with continuing to shape a new foreign policy for a post-Cold War reality.

## Navigating the new world (dis)order

While the collapse of the Soviet Union removed the presiding dominance of the Cold War over foreign policy matters, the exit of a superpower from the international arena left a vacuum that the US hoped to fill. However, there were reasons for optimism with the ending of apartheid, the ending of the civil war in Mozambique, and the growing movements for democracy in Africa. As the sole superpower with hopes for reaping the 'peace dividend', America under Clinton sought to redefine its role in the world as new challenges emerged.

Domestically, the absence of a communist enemy opened up foreign policy to the influence of new actors (Mertus, 2008: 39). Clinton's presidential campaign was able to focus, at least rhetorically, on human rights and the expansion of democracy as the cornerstones of US foreign policy (Hesse, 2001: 106; Mertus, 2008: 40). International trade and globalisation were flagged as the key post-Cold War strategy for prosperity (Hyland, 1999: 18). This focus created a space for a growing number of interest groups and organisations to participate in influencing US foreign policy through direct pressure on the executive branch and through Congress (Mertus, 2008: 39; Scott, 1998: 401–402).

Supporting the transition to democracy in Africa was a common foreign policy objective incorporated into the public narratives of American presidents since WWII. With Clinton, the enlargement of democracy assumed, by default, a new orientation. During the Cold War, supporting democracies or granting assistance to a transition to democracy, meant encouraging an anti-communist stance, even if corruption and human rights violations were common practice in many 'US-friendly' regimes. Without the need to contain communism, human rights gained more prominence as a vital characteristic of democracy and as a stricter conditionality for American assistance (Smyth, 1998: 82). The link between American assistance and human rights criteria had been introduced into law by Congress during the Nixon administration. But as long as the Cold War persisted, national security considerations often overruled human rights considerations (for example, see Apodaca, 2006: 142; Mertus, 2008: 26). In the absence of a Soviet threat, Clinton's human rights rhetoric represented a real hope for change. The strategy of what came to be known as Clinton's 'democratic enlargement' linked free markets and political freedom with the rule of law as necessary conditions for prosperity and as a reflection of American values (Mandelbaum, 1996: 17). Secretary of State, Warren Christopher, defined the threefold goals of the African agenda of the Clinton administration as:

> [B]olster the movement toward democracy and free markets; to address the health, environmental, and population issues that threaten lives and imperil sustained development; and to help Africans build their capacity for preventive diplomacy and conflict resolution.
> (Christopher, 1998: 467)

These goals bound American values and interests together with America's role as a sole superpower in an increasingly globalised world. In such a world, democracy was viewed as the key ingredient for peaceful interaction between nations, and for the expansion of personal freedom as the underlying condition to spur free market competition and mitigate transnational challenges such as crime, disease, environmental degradation and human suffering (Alden, 2000: 357; McCrisken, 2003: 160; Morrison and Cooke, 2001: 4). During the first few years of the Clinton administration, the US shifted its policy to include a focus on poor peripheral countries where local populations were suffering from various kinds of distress. Mandelbaum (1996) defines this approach as 'foreign policy as social work', where the objective became the promotion of American values as the means to create conditions for a peaceful, democratic world with a prosperous global economy based on a free market system. During the Clinton administration, American values and democracy were consciously used to promote American power and its influence on the international economic system to enhance its own interests and security (Cox, 2000: 221).

Brian Atwood, the administrator of USAID during the Clinton years, describes how the world has changed since the end of the Cold War and with it the core principles of foreign assistance:

> [During the Cold War] the success or failure of less-developed nations was measured only partly by whether the lives of citizens improved; how individual governments aligned themselves with the superpowers also figured prominently in judgments of 'success' and 'failure'.
> (Atwood, 1994: 11)

When the Cold War ended, there was no longer a need to secure political alignment against the Soviet Union and its allies:

> Governments can no longer use strategic competition between the West and the Communist bloc to extract assistance. Moreover, the spread of the democratic model, free market economics, and open communications, is forcing nations throughout the world into a more competitive environment, both at home and abroad. Both external and internal factors are forcing governments to open up their economic and political systems or face economic stagnation and social unrest.
>
> (Atwood, 1994: 11)

Atwood emphasised that development, a healthy environment and political freedoms were fundamental conditions for a prosperous economy (Atwood, 1994: 12). According to Atwood (1994: 13), in an interconnected international system, a 'spillover effect' from poverty, conflict and pollution can affect American economic well-being and national security and development assistance is therefore consistent with fundamental American values such as freedom and democracy, as well as national security. These statements were coherent with Clinton's intention to 'make trade a priority element of American security' (Clinton quoted in Cox, 2000: 229; see also Christopher, 1998: 467). The thread Clinton pursued was intended to promote American power by enhancing America's ability to compete in the global market by encouraging countries to adhere to American values (Cox, 2000: 232). The argument linked securing American interests to ensuring its position of leadership in an increasingly globalised world through economic leadership.

These ideas helped define the priorities of USAID under the Clinton administration. The agency's Strategy for Sustainable Development published in 1993, recognised the need to integrate the enhancement of economic growth and political freedoms into the process of poverty alleviation (USAID, 2000: 3). Atwood understood sustainable development as a process focused on maintaining the cohesion of society (Atwood, 1994: 15). He explained that achieving sustainable development depended on the ability of nations to anticipate problems and create the institutions to deal with them and stressed that this form of development was at the heart of USAID's work:

> Under the Clinton administration, USAID is pursuing a policy of sustainable development that fulfils four imperatives: to help nations generate broad-based economic growth; to help nations deal with unsustainable rates of population growth; to help nations protect the environment; and to help nations build democratic systems and societies where law and human rights are respected.
>
> (Atwood, 1994: 15–16)

The links between democracy, economic growth, and development assistance were also underlined by Secretary of State Christopher during an address given in South Africa in October 1996, where he sought to clarify and gain both domestic and African support for US foreign policy (Christopher, 1998: 474). Christopher emphasised that for Africa to realise its economic potential, there was a need to focus on education, gender equality, the fight against corruption, population growth, and management of natural resources, as well as help African nations join the WTO and relieve their debts (Christopher, 1998: 482–483).

But spreading American values as a strategy meant involving the US in world affairs where the linkages to American interests were not immediately apparent. This created domestic scepticism and resistance as America immersed itself in the unfolding events of the post-Soviet world. It led Congress to cut the foreign assistance budgets, and as a result, USAID was closing down missions around the world, many of these in sub-Saharan Africa (Hesse, 2001: 67; Lyman, 2002: 226). Despite Clinton's two visits to the African continent and his rhetorical emphasis on Africa's importance, aid to Africa dropped by 52 per cent from US$1.93 billion in 1992, to US$933 million during his administration (Rothchild, 2001: 201; Schraeder, 2001: 393).

In his forward to a volume summarising Clinton's African policy, Chester Crocker notes once again that American interests in Africa, relative to other parts of the world, were not significant. During the Clinton administration, this was translated into 'retrenchment and timidity'[19] towards the continent (Alden, 2000: 356–357; Rosenblum, 2002: 195; van de Walle, 2009: 2):

> Another thing one hopes for in a book about U.S. African policies is balance and a sense of historical perspective. Africa has never figured near the top of the list of U.S. foreign policy priorities. It does not today – and probably never will. The contributors of this volume take due note of the considerable efforts made during the 1990s to draw greater attention to Africa, raise its rhetorical profile in U.S. policy pronouncements, and orchestrate senior-level travel and frequent, visible consultations with African counterparts. Yet, they underscore the reality that the 1990s have been 'catastrophic' for Africa, that U.S. actions and responses have been empty or ineffectual …
> (Crocker, 2001: viii)

*Somalia*

The catastrophes in Africa during the Clinton administration, which Crocker refers to, began with Somalia. Before Bush left office, he committed America to the leadership of a UN multinational humanitarian mission in Somalia, focusing on restoring supply lines and bringing relief to the starving, war-torn populations. 'Operation Restore Hope' (officially designated UNITAF[20]) began in December 1992, and saw the deployment of over 20,000 American troops. The US-led mission succeeded in quickly bringing desperately needed food and commodities to the starving population of Somalia (Cohen, 2000: 215). President Bush had refused to commit American troops to a mission that included a political goal, such as the disarmament of Somali warlords as suggested by UN Secretary General Boutros-Ghali (Albright and Woodward, 2003: 142; Cohen, 2000: 214). However, President Clinton supported UN resolution 814, approving a second phase of the operation in Somalia (dubbed UNOSOM II[21]) which included a mission goal to create a secure environment for, and assist in, the process of nation-building.[22] This was the first instance where Clinton applied his democratic enlargement agenda.[23] In Somalia, Clinton engaged America in an assertive mission of nation-building, moving beyond the strictly humanitarian objective to which Bush had committed (Apodaca, 2006: 151). The intervention in Somalia, beginning with Bush and continuing with Clinton, signalled a new American post-Cold War doctrine. Under this 'assertive multilateralism' approach, the US would be willing, at least rhetorically, to commit its military power to support humanitarian causes and assist in nation-building from a position of leadership in multinational efforts, and in places where US interests were not necessarily significant (Apodaca, 2006: 149–150; Hyland, 1999: 54; McCrisken, 2003: 160).

It was in the context of Somalia that the term 'mission creep' was coined to describe how initial success leads to the expansion of a mission beyond its original intended goal (Christopher, 1998: 467; Hyland, 1999: 56). Mission creep in Somalia referred to the transformation of the original humanitarian mission under UNITAF into a political mission under the mandate of UNOSOM II (Hyland, 1999: 55–56; Schraeder, 1998: 342). With nation-building as an objective, American troops found themselves engaged in two kinds of operations: development assistance and combat. In terms of the latter, US troops were involved in clan-fighting, including the pursuit and attempted disarmament of various warlords (Schraeder, 1998: 342). As an extension of combat missions, US troops were involved with local communities in efforts to assist in the restoration of civilian local governments and the creation of institutions. These efforts were guided by conditions on the ground, and mainly as needed to facilitate combat operations (Marine Colonel Werner Helmmer quoted in Schraeder, 1998: 343).

On 3 October 1993, a force of US Rangers carried out a mission in Mogadishu against a Somali military faction led by Mohammed Farah Aidid. The Somali forces succeeded in bringing down two Black Hawk helicopters, killing 18 American soldiers, wounding 77 more and capturing one American pilot alive. The American forces killed more than 300 Somalis and wounded more than 700, including many women and children (McCrisken, 2003: 166–167). Pictures of Somali militants dragging the defiled body of an American soldier through the streets of Mogadishu were broadcast by TV networks around the world, and caused shock and anger in the US. This debacle, also known as the Battle of Mogadishu, brought about the end of the American involvement in Somalia, and led to the reformulation of America's role as an assertive power engaged in multinational peacekeeping and humanitarian efforts (Hyland, 1999: 58). The decision Clinton took in assuming a more cautious approach as a result of the events in Somalia, was to be significant for his subsequent African policy, and would lead to hesitant and weak responses to future challenges (Apodaca, 2006: 150; Khadiagala, 2001: 26; Mandelbaum, 1996: 16; McCrisken, 2003: 167).

The events in Somalia had unearthed major limitations to the 'assertive multilateralism' policy. First, it demonstrated the limited willingness of the American people to engage with challenges where the interests of the US were not clear and tangible. Many scholars highlight the link between nation-building, enlargement of democracy and the 'Vietnam syndrome' (for example, see McCrisken, 2003: 168; von Hippel, 2000: 1; Wheeler, 2000: 172). With the scar of Vietnam on American consciousness, the Somali incident triggered fears that America was stepping into another conflict without a clear-cut policy and exit strategy, possibly leading to an extended engagement with many more American and Somali casualties. Second, and in relation to the above, despite being the sole superpower and leader of the free world, building other nations proved to be 'a dangerous hubris', especially when there were no American interests involved and no associated exit strategy (Lake, 1996; see also von Hippel, 2000).

A few days after the Battle of Mogadishu, President Clinton broadcast a televised address where he announced the end of American involvement in Somalia, stating: 'It is not our job to rebuild Somalia's society or even to create a political process that can allow Somalia's clans to live and work in peace. The Somalis must do that for themselves.' (Clinton, 1993). Not wanting to create an immediate vacuum in the face of an ongoing UN mission, Clinton announced that the American mission in Somalia would end by 31 March, 1994.

*Rwanda*

The effects of the Somali debacle on Clinton's assertive multilateralism in Africa were most pronounced in relation to the escalation of violence in Rwanda. America's reaction to the civil war in Rwanda that broke-out during the Bush administration was already hesitant as described above. Following the economic crisis of the 1980s and the civil war of 1990, President Juvénal Habyarimana was under international pressure to conduct political reforms in Rwanda (Des Forges, 2004: 30; Melson, 2003: 332–333; Olson, 1995: 219; Wheeler, 2000: 211). These reforms weakened Habyarimana and his party,[24] which was no longer the sole party allowed to participate in politics. Habyarimana's rule was challenged, sometimes violently, by the formation of opposition parties throughout the country (Olson, 1995: 219). The civil war with the RPF was a further challenge to

Habyarimana's strong grip on the country. In order to maintain his power and preserve legitimacy, Habyarimana eventually agreed to a ceasefire accord with the RPF (the Arusha accords of 1993), a UN peacekeeping mission (UNAMIR),[25] and to a detailed power-sharing agreement where he would maintain his presidency. However, he continued to use violence and propaganda to instigate hate against the Tutsi-led opposition and the RPF (Albright and Woodward, 2003: 148; Olson, 1995: 220).

Rwanda was never considered a high priority country for the US. During the Cold War, Rwanda's co-operation with the US against communism was reciprocated by a modest investment in Rwanda's economic development (Apodaca, 2006: 152; Des Forges, 2004: 29). As in other places in Africa, the US did not assume a strong position against the one-party rule led by Habyarimana, nor did it take a strong position against his human rights violations (Des Forges, 2004: 30). Even after the end of the Cold War and with the rising importance of democracy and human rights criteria in American foreign policy, the US continued to ignore Habyarimana's practice of discrimination against the Tutsi minority in the country (Des Forges, 2004: 30–31; see also Albright and Woodward, 2003: 148–149; Uvin, 1998). It was only in 1993, following reports of war-related massacres conducted by the Habyarimana government, that America decided to cut its aid package to Rwanda from US$19.6 million to US$6 million. As noted by Des Forges (2004: 32), the reduction of aid was explained through mixed messages sent to Habyarimana's government, quoting poor economic performance and human rights abuses as reasons for the cut.

On 6 April 1994, Habyarimana's airplane was shot down while returning from peace talks in Arusha. His death drove 'Hutu Power', an organisation composed of Hutu elites closely tied to Habyarimana,[26] to launch a genocidal campaign against the Tutsi (Melson, 2003: 333). The genocide began on 7 April and lasted for two months during which more than one million people were slaughtered and more than two million displaced (Des Forges, 2014).

During these two critical months, the US, along with other members of the international community, failed to take decisive action to stop the genocide. Instead, the international community engaged in long bureaucratic procedures debating the nature of the violence in Rwanda, subsequently disagreeing on how to respond to the events in that country (Barnett, 1997; Klinghoffer, 1998). Instead of addressing the genocide directly and decisively focusing on the people of Rwanda and the unfolding human catastrophe, the debates focused on the role and future of UNAMIR under the new circumstances. The main debates revolved around the withdrawal of UNAMIR, and began shortly after Habyarimana's plane was shot down.[27] The US argued for a full withdrawal of all UNAMIR troops from Rwanda, flagging responsibility to ensure the safety of UN peacekeepers and the viability of future peacekeeping missions. The American stance was that the unfolding circumstances in Rwanda rendered the goals of UNAMIR untenable (Albright and Woodward, 2003: 150; Barnett, 1997: 571). In addition, America argued that its position on the UNAMIR mission was also meant to warn other countries that deliberate action against UN peacekeepers would carry consequences (Albright and Woodward, 2003: 150; Barnett, 1997: 572). As explained by Madeline Albright[28] in her memoir, the political and public outcry following the American debacle in Somalia heavily influenced the Clinton administration's position on Rwanda, and prevented the US from assuming and pursuing a firm policy against the genocide (Albright and Woodward, 2003: 153; see also Apodaca, 2006: 153; Barnett,[29] 1997: 561–562; Cohen, 2007: 3). In order to circumvent public pressure, the official policy at the White House was to avoid the use of the word 'genocide' when referring to the situation in Rwanda (Apodaca, 2006: 153; Des Forges, 2004: 38). This was in spite of clear information from various American sources and human rights organisations indicating that a genocide was in progress (Cohen, 2007: 129–143; Ferroggiaro, 2001; Lewis, 2001; Power, 2002: 354).

The Clinton administration failed in its first real challenge as the leader of the free world where the values of democracy, freedom and humanitarianism were flagged as the pillars of foreign policy. The lack of concrete national security interests in Rwanda and mounting domestic political and public pressure to keep US forces away from conflicts on distant continents, meant that the sole superpower had been unable to lead a resolute intervention to halt an ongoing genocide. Instead, America led the efforts to discourage an international response to the genocide in Rwanda (Cohen, 2007: 5; Hesse, 2005: 328–329; Power, 2002: 373).

*South Africa*

While genocide was unfolding in Rwanda, the world witnessed the first free elections taking place in South Africa. Nelson Mandela was elected President on 27 April 1994. The South African political transformation served as a new opportunity for the Clinton administration to try to modify the prevailing perceptions of Africa as a continent plagued by violence and corruption held by the American public and US lawmakers. The South African transformation served as an entry point to launch a campaign that explained to the American public the recent policy failures in Africa and convey a way forward for a future African policy built upon past lessons. The first 'White House Conference on Africa' held in June 1994, was convened with the objective of harnessing new domestic support for an African policy (Clinton, 1994: 36; Hesse, 2001: 69). Vice President Al Gore explained during his conference address that America:

> want[s] to promote trade and investment. We want to leverage capital for basic development and infrastructure. We want to support effective government and democracy.

> There are those who argue that democracy and free market economies or, for that matter, attention to the environment are luxuries Africa cannot afford. What patronizing nonsense. Democracy is not a cure-all. But if ever there was a doubt that Africa is ready for democracy, it was surely dispelled when we saw ordinary men and women waiting in line at the polling places for hours and hours in small townships, rural reserves, and great cities along the length and breadth of South Africa. As for those who argue that free trade will only trample Africa's small companies and smother entrepreneurs, well, history shows that when countries choose economic isolation over international economic engagement, their standard of living falls. Democracy, free markets, attention to the environment: all three conditions, like a kind of economic petri dish, can create conditions allowing environmentally sustainable economic development.
>
> (Gore, 1994: 35)

President Clinton emphasised the need to redefine the African continent in a post-apartheid context together with the post-Cold War perspective:

> In the post-Cold War and post-apartheid world, our guideposts have disappeared.... We have a new freedom and a new responsibility to see Africa, to see it whole, to see it in specific nations and specific problems and specific promise.... We'd like to see more prosperity and more well-functioning economies and more democracy and more genuine security for people in their own borders. We'd like to see sustainable development that promotes the long-term interest of our common environment on this increasingly shrinking globe. Africa illustrates also a central security challenge of the post-Cold War era, not so much conflicts across national borders, but conflicts within them which can spill over.
>
> (Clinton, 1994: 37)

Hesse (2001: 99) highlights the links between the administration's interest in Africa and Clinton's doctrine of enlargement, underlining the vast potential of African markets in contributing to the prosperity of the American economy in the global age. Promotion of democracy and economic liberalism was at the heart of this strategy; South Africa was identified as the only 'big emerging market'[30] on the African continent (Hesse, 2001: 107). As such, post-apartheid South Africa presented the perfect arena to exhibit the link between American values, idealism, and the national interest, prompting the Clinton administration to focus on engaging South Africa 'as a partner in enlargement' (Hesse, 2001: 107).

In his speech during the White House Africa Conference, Clinton announced that America would provide US$600 million for trade investments and development programmes with South Africa. The aid package to South Africa included a significant budget increase for USAID programming as well as several trade components aimed at strengthening commerce between the US and South Africa, amidst cuts which affected the agency's work in other sub-Saharan countries (Lyman, 2002: 227).

Mandela was unimpressed with the American gesture. Given the hyped reaction of America (and the world) to the newly formed democracy in South Africa and to Mandela's leadership, he expected a significant strategic US investment on levels similar the investment in the Middle East (Lyman, 2002: 231). Mandela indicated directly to President Clinton, Vice President Gore and later publicly, his opinion of the level of US aid, labelling it 'miserable' and 'peanuts' in comparison to aid granted to South Africa by other countries (Lyman, 2002: 230–231). Secretary of State Christopher rejected Mandela's comparison of South Africa with the Middle East, explaining that in the Middle East the US had 'strategic interests' (Christopher quoted in Lyman, 2002: 231). In the following years, the US and South Africa would clash on a number of foreign policy issues, including Mandela's relations with 'rogue countries' such as Libya, Cuba and Iran; South Africa's weapon sales to Syria; and lingering issues relating to intellectual property rights infringements reminiscent of the apartheid years when major brands boycotted South Africa.

Despite Mandela's dissatisfaction with the administration's aid package to South Africa, the two countries established a Binational Commission (BNC). This was one of two BNCs (the other was with Russia) established during the Clinton administration. The two BNCs are significant attempts to form new relationships with the post-Soviet and post-apartheid regimes. They had the potential to provide entry points to two big emerging markets (Hesse, 2001: 99). The BNC was headed by Vice President Al Gore and Deputy President Thabo Mbeki of South Africa and co-ordinated most of the bilateral foreign policy interactions between the two countries. Some suggest that the main purpose of the BNC was to serve American political goals to protect US investment interests in South Africa (see, for example, Coleman-Adebayo, 2011). Viewed through this prism, supporting the political rejuvenation in South Africa was a crucial element in a foreign policy aimed at creating an environment favouring and facilitating American investment vital for national interests (Hesse, 2001: 99).

### *African Crisis Response Initiative (ACRI)*

Many important foreign policy initiatives for Africa emerged during the Clinton administration. One such initiative was ACRI.[31] ACRI was an attempt to find a way to help manage and resolve conflicts in Africa, which, together with democratic enlargement, economic development, and sustainable development, formed the four-pronged policy approach to Africa during the first Clinton administration (Christopher, 1998: 476–484).

ACRI emerged as an effort to bridge the need to manage conflicts in Africa without engaging American troops in peacekeeping and peace-enforcing missions. ACRI aimed at creating an all-African mechanism that could be activated if peacekeeping, peace-enforcing or humanitarian relief mission where needed on the continent. This could be used to mitigate conflicts undermining American interests and policy objectives without the need to risk American lives (Frazer and Herbst, 2001: 57; Hesse, 2001: 118; Khadiagala, 2001: 264; Levitt, 1998: 102; Omach, 2000).

African troops of select African nations received training packages and equipment to prepare them for proficient responses to deployment needs in peacekeeping and peace-enforcing operations[32] (Aning, 2001; Levitt, 1998).

Congress, in limiting who could participate in ACRI, stated that to qualify for American training and equipment, a participating country must be governed by a democratically elected civilian authority which was not guilty of committing gross human rights violations, and that a participating military force must accept the supremacy of the civilian government (Levitt, 1998: 102). The criteria antagonised many African countries who would be disqualified from participation in ACRI. Some in Africa viewed these conditions as an imposition of 'Western notions of state governance' that could be interpreted as a sort of imperialism (Aning, 2001: 54; Hesse, 2001: 120; Levitt, 1998: 102). This also meant that the DoS would need to satisfy Congress with its ACRI-related policy as well as deal with the dissatisfaction and scepticism of some African states regarding the new assertive US involvement in Africa. Despite these criteria, some ACRI participants such as Uganda and Ethiopia, were in fact governed by a former military government turned civilian (Omach, 2000: 89).

Other issues with ACRI troubled the US and African states. The first was the possibility that military units trained through ACRI would turn on their own governments and depose democratic regimes. Second, ACRI would produce relatively highly-trained military units intended for peacekeeping and peace-enforcing missions, which would then be handed to governments who could potentially use them for their own offensive purposes (Levitt, 1998: 102–104). In other words, ACRI could contribute to shaping a new balance of power in Africa or in some countries. A third issue was who could order the deployment of ACRI forces, and to whom would they answer in case of deployment. Trained for peacekeeping and peace-enforcing missions, ACRI forces would naturally respond to the UN Security Council (Levitt, 1998: 104–105). But additional deployment scenarios related to the nature of the African governance structure were possible, including deployment under orders of the OAU or another sub-regional organisation involved in peacekeeping such as the Economic Community of West African States (ECOWAS) or SADC (Aning, 2001: 52). Moreover, ACRI-trained forces could be ordered to deploy by their home governments in any unilateral scenario unrelated to an international authority (Levitt, 1998: 105–106).

Several African countries, especially South Africa, were concerned with the fact that ACRI was an American initiative (Hesse, 2001: 120). They feared that the US would use ACRI as a tool to advance its own interests through power to influence who participates, the kind of training packages given to recipients, and other related political manipulations (Hesse, 2001: 120; Omach, 2000: 90).

### *Africa Growth and Opportunity Act (AGOA)*

While ACRI was an attempt to help bring stability to the continent through military training linked to democratic processes, the AGOA initiative was focused on bolstering economic growth, trade, and accelerating the integration of Africa into the global economy. Originally, AGOA was initiated by the Africa Trade Caucus in Congress hoping to create a trade policy towards the Africa, the only continent with which America did not have a trade policy (Hesse, 2005: 331). This initiative was appropriated[33] by President Clinton in 1997 and announced as the Partnership for Economic Growth and Opportunity, which passed as law during the 106th Congress in 2000 as AGOA. Assistant Secretary for African Affairs, Susan Rice, referred to AGOA as the 'single most important piece of legislation ... considered on Africa in more than a decade' (Rice, 1999). AGOA was pitched as a beneficial initiative for both America and Africa and indeed enjoyed solid bipartisan support in Congress. Rice emphasised the triangular relationship between stability, development and the economy in Africa, underscoring economic growth as the main long-term US interest in Africa as markets opened up for American products and investment. In testimony before the House International Relations Subcommittee on Africa, Rice explained the importance of AGOA to further advance America's growing economic interests, particularly oil imports and the sale of American commodities to the growing African market (Rice, 1999). She suggested that a 'strong, stable and prosperous' Africa would not only translate into economic dividends for the US, but would also contribute to global stability as African nations would be better placed to assist against transnational threats such as terrorism, crime and environmental degradation (Rice, 1999).

It is important to emphasise that AGOA was structured around unilateral conditionalities determined by the US. Rice explained to Congress that:

> [T]he genius of the bill is its linkage of market access provisions with eligibility criteria that encourage the proper conditions for U.S. trade and investment abroad. Contrary to some critics' charges of 'neocolonialism', these criteria are strictly voluntary and do not penalize countries that choose not to participate in the bill's benefits. To the extent that countries participate, the bill will stimulate and encourage African-led market oriented reforms that enable the United States to

develop stronger mutual beneficial business partnerships with Africa's opening economies.

(Rice, 1999)

As indicated by Rice, no country was forced to accept the predetermined criteria and the conditions associated with benefiting from AGOA; countries could simply choose 'not to participate in the bill'. The AGOA legislation states that in order for a country to benefit from AGOA, the President must conclude that a country:

1. has installed, or is in the process of progressing towards a market-based economy, a lawful governance system, the elimination of trade barriers, corruption and poverty, the protection of workers' rights and the protection of intellectual property rights;
2. 'does not engage in activities that undermine US national security and foreign interests; and,
3. does not engage in gross violations of human rights or provide support for international terrorism' (Fuhr and Klughaup, 2014: 137; Jones and Williams, 2012: 15; Schneidman, 2012: 3).

AGOA contains several provisions focused on protecting the US market, for example, the need to use American raw materials in apparels produced in Africa for export to the US as a condition to enjoy full duty-free benefits.[34] In addition, the President can decide to suspend AGOA-related benefits if the competition damages or threatens the prosperity of the domestic industry in the US (Fuhr and Klughaupt, 2014: 139–140). With these and other provisions in place, the purpose of AGOA seemed to be mostly the promotion of political and economic reforms in Africa that protect American intellectual property rights and encourage the creation of a stable environment to facilitate American investment (Fuhr and Klughaupt, 2014: 140–141; see also Mattoo et al., 2003: 836–837; Lyman, 2002: 248).

Enacting AGOA to accelerate Africa's integration into the global economy produced new interagency processes in the US involving bodies such as the Treasury Department, the Export-Import Bank, the Trade Development Agency and the Overseas Private Investment Corporation. These joined USAID, in an effort to create a broad support for the overall trade policy through development assistance, debt relief and trade-related technical assistance (DoS, 2001: 2).

Some in Africa were critical of the AGOA initiative from the start. Mandela expressed his reservations concerning AGOA and called the terms 'unacceptable'. Deputy President Mbeki openly criticised AGOA for what he characterised as an attempt by the US to substitute aid with trade (Hesse, 2001: 166; Lyman, 2002: 249). South Africa regarded the conditionalities attached to AGOA as neo-colonial and emphasised that Africa needed both trade and aid to overcome poverty. More specifically, the criticism, emanating from South Africa pointed out that AGOA was designed principally to benefit the American market and corporations through the imposition of provisions related to trade and intellectual property rights (Mushita, 2001: 17–19).

With the inception of AGOA in 1997, America indicated the intention to elevate the importance of the African policy during the second Clinton administration (DoS, 2001: 2). Indeed, the appointment of Madeleine Albright as Secretary of State and Susan Rice as Assistant Secretary of State for African Affairs in 1997 and a well-planned presidential trip to Africa in 1998, were all part of an overall plan to foster renewed domestic interest in Africa as a continent of hope rather than a continent plagued by conflict and poverty (Albright and Woodward, 2003: 453; Rosenblum, 2002: 195, 197).

*Promotion of new leadership*

In practice, the second Clinton administration sought to get close to, and empower, a new set of African leaders. Previous alliances were now highly problematic including Somalia, the Democratic Republic of Congo, Sudan and Nigeria. The US–Nigerian relationship was complex; the country was the prime exporter of African oil, accounting for 8 per cent of American oil imports, while four American oil companies were drilling in Nigeria. As the most populous country, Nigeria was considered one of the two[35] most powerful countries in Africa in terms of regional influence, military power and market power (Mikell and Lyman, 2001: 73–74). As such, Nigeria's situation presented a significant challenge to US policy as economic interests and regional security concerns collided with human rights and the democratic enlargement policies (Minter, 2000: 205). Attempting to balance between those, Clinton sent the former US ambassador to the UN, Donald McHenry, to Nigeria in an attempt to convince President Abacha to show moderation (Mikell and Lyman, 2001: 81). But when Abacha executed nine social leaders and human rights activists in 1995,[36] America shifted its policy of moderation and instituted limited sanctions and public condemnation of Abacha's regime and his human rights infractions (Khadiagala, 2001: 262). The sudden and unexpected death of Sani Abacha in June 1998 allowed Clinton to normalise relations with Nigeria and re-awaken a focus on democracy. The US supported the Nigerian transition to democracy by increasing assistance from US$7 million in 1998 to US$170 million in 2000 (Mikell and Lyman, 2001: 81; DoS, 2001). This investment came despite reports of fraud and violence during the election process (Mikell and Lyman, 2001: 82) as well as corrupted exploitation of oil resources by the elected Obasanjo regime in Nigeria (Minter, 2000: 206).

The search for new African leadership during the second Clinton administration occurred against this background and translated into a number of high-level official visits, peaking with a presidential visit in 1998 (Connell and Smyth, 1998: 94). The four leaders the US was attempting to promote as symbols of a new reinvigorated Africa were Yoweri Museveni of Uganda, Paul Kagame[37] of Rwanda, Isaias Afwerki of Eritrea and Meles Zenawi of Ethiopia (Connell and Smyth, 1998: 81–86; Rosenblum, 2002: 195; Schraeder, 2001: 396). These 'new African leaders' (Rosenblum, 2002: 196) were deemed 'agents of change in Africa' (Connell and Smyth, 1998: 82). Despite various differences and disagreements among them, the four had many commonalities. Rosenblum (2002: 195) notes that they all witnessed the rise of corruption in post-colonial Africa and were victimised by post-colonial regimes; they were all ready to accept economic reforms and spoke of self-reliance. In addition, they were not shy to use military force to achieve foreign policy goals (see also Connell and Smyth, 1998: 87ff.; Hesse, 2005: 332). These common perspectives were affirmed in the Entebbe Principles, published as a joint declaration by President Clinton and participating African leaders in March 1998 during Clinton's visit to Africa (Clinton, 1998). However, the promise of new African leadership quickly disintegrated, when in May 1998 an emerging border dispute between Ethiopia and Eritrea led to war. In the Democratic Republic of Congo, Kabila sought to free himself from the Rwandan patronage which had brought him to power, and dismissed his Rwandan Chief of Staff. In response, Kagame allowed an opposition group fighting against Kabila to regroup in Rwandan territory, and with Ugandan support, the second Congolese War was underway. In Tanzania and Kenya, Osama bin Laden's Al-Qaida destroyed the American embassies in a coordinated attack on 7 August 1998, which led to a retaliatory American attack on a pharmaceutical factory in Sudan[38] (Hesse, 2005: 338–339; Rosenblum, 2002: 200–202). The prospects for a peaceful Africa in transition to democracy and economic reforms seemed very remote as critics of Clinton's African policy questioned America's efforts to invest resources in a plagued continent (DoS, 2001: 3; Khadiagala, 2001: 261–262).

Despite the criticism, however, Clinton continued the attempt to form a coherent African policy for democratic enlargement and to strengthen America's economic ties with Africa. In these efforts, Clinton was disinclined to support multilateral efforts, and mostly focused on direct relations between the US and African countries (Khadiagala, 2001: 263–264). During March 1999, a US–Africa ministerial conference was held in Washington DC, aiming to forge a partnership for the twenty-first century. The meeting included representatives from 46 sub-Saharan nations, as well as many North African states and the representatives of the eight African regional organisations. The aim was to forge a partnership through governmental actions, as well as increase private sector and civil society involvement on a wide range of issues: trade, investment, finance, debt, infrastructure, agribusiness, energy, environment, regional integration, development assistance, human capital, HIV/AIDS, transnational threats, democracy, governance, human rights and conflict resolution (DoS, 1999). The promotion of AGOA was high on the agenda and was presented as the 'way forward' framework of the blueprint for the partnership (DoS, 1999).

*Fighting HIV/AIDS*

One important legacy of the Clinton administration, which was carried forward with great fervour by his successor, George W. Bush, was the fight against HIV/AIDS in Africa. Seen as much more than a humanitarian issue, HIV/AIDS was described as a threat to social stability with a possible wide range of security implications, as well as a threat to economic growth and development (Albright and Woodward, 2003: 452; Morrison, 2001: 13–14). Addressing HIV/AIDS issues in Africa caught traction during the last two years of the Clinton administration (Morrison, 2001: 19). In 1999, the President and Vice President launched the Leadership and Investment in Fighting an Epidemic (LIFE) initiative aimed at expanding the global US expenditure to combat HIV/AIDS. In January 2000, Vice President Al Gore chaired a special UN Security Council session aimed at raising the awareness of the threat posed by HIV/AIDS to global security and economic development (Morrison, 2001: 19). Later that year, President Clinton signed the Global AIDS and Tuberculosis Relief Act of 2000, passed by Congress as H.R.3519. The Act authorised funds to expand US efforts to combat HIV/AIDS, including funding to USAID programming and the creation of a World Bank AIDS fund (Clinton, 2000). The fight against AIDS encompassed both a humanitarian objective to alleviate the suffering of millions, as well as national security objectives through threats to the stability of nations (Morrison, 2001: 22). The focus on combating the HIV/AIDS threat was carried over to the Bush administration, where PEPFAR became the centrepiece of the administration's Africa Policy.

## Concluding remarks

As a testimony to the importance of development assistance as a tool of power, the main struggle during the Bush and Clinton administrations when it came to aid was to re-define and justify development assistance in the absence of a Soviet enemy. During the Cold War, the various administrations used development assistance to influence African preferences to be more aligned with the US. With the break-up of the Soviet Union and the weakening of Soviet domination over Eastern Europe, the Bush administration claimed that the end of the Cold War was a victory of American principles and ideals; American exceptionalism was thus vindicated in the discourses of both the Bush and Clinton administrations. As the sole superpower and the exceptional nation that can and should lead the world, development assistance was re-defined to both enhance American power, as well as help re-create a world in its image. With some African nations re-establishing democratic processes, good governance became an important part of US development assistance to Africa.

The Bush administration focused on granting assistance to African nations to solve a series of issues which were partly due to the Cold War and partly over national struggles for power. The Clinton administration focused on assisting the creation of various institutions that would lead to the enlargement of democracy and the adoption of free market principles. Both administrations used development assistance to enhance American leadership and to develop African institutions toward adopting principles consistent with American ideology. Once again, the objective of the assistance policy was first and foremost to help enhance American power, legitimising US leadership, and creating institutions in developing countries that would enhance the power of the American economy and trade, decrease poverty and create better livelihoods in developing countries, and lead to a peaceful and democratic world. Despite their focus on the importance of development assistance both administrations struggled to convince Congress that development assistance was as important as during the Cold War.

## Notes

1 In a biography co-authored by Bush and his National Security Advisor, Brent Scowcroft, focusing on the geopolitical transformations during the Presidency, very few pages are devoted to events in Africa (see Bush and Scowcroft, 1998).
2 A policy which he advocated extensively as the Secretary of Treasury during the Reagan administration.
3 The expressed concern was that if power was to be turned over to the black majority for rule, especially if given to the Soviet-backed ANC, South Africa would turn towards socialism.
4 See de Klerk's speech before the Parliament on 2 February 1990. In this address he also underlines that the global changes were brought forth by an intrinsic process that is 'without the involvement of the Big Powers and the United Nations', to emphasise the responsibility of the government of South Africa to assume responsibility and bring about real reform.
5 A few months after they were lifted by the European Community.
6 There was also information that Mengistu was preparing a personal contingency plan should his regime collapse, including sending his family (1991) to live on a farm he had purchased in Zimbabwe a year earlier (Cohen, 2000: 47).
7 The only precondition issued by the Parliament was that the 'unity of Ethiopia should not be compromised' (Cohen, 2000: 44).
8 Gaddafi backed the leader of the Umma party, Sadiq al-Mahdi, who attempted to depose Nimeiry in an unsuccessful coup in 1976 (see Johnson, 2011: 55–56).
9 Garang was a military officer who was educated in the US and held a PhD in economics (see Cohen, 2000: 60; Natsios, 2012: 61–65).
10 Andrew Natsios was the director of USAID's Office for Foreign Disaster Assistance during the Bush administration and was involved in US policymaking on Sudan (see Cohen, 2000: 64). He later became the Administrator of USAID (2001–2005).

11 The South was excluded from the vote under the pretext of SPLA insurgency (Natsios, 2012: 71).
12 Under article 508 of the Foreign Assistance Act prohibiting the US government to grant assistance to a country where democracy was overturned by a military *coup d'état*.
13 The Clark Amendment had prohibited US assistance to UNITA since 1976. It was repealed by Congress in 1985 during the Reagan administration.
14 Kantor replaced Robert Kimmit in 1991 (Cohen, 2000: 195).
15 A group of young Tutsi exiles, many of whom had served in the Ugandan military.
16 Namely the Gio and the Mano ethnic groups.
17 An armed force formed under the mandate of ECOWAS.
18 Known as 'Operation Restore Hope'.
19 See also Minter (2000: 200) and Hesse (2005: 331, 333) as examples of elevating the importance of Africa in foreign policy during the Clinton administration on the rhetorical level, while in practice, Africa remained a low priority when it came to American engagement and investment of resources.
20 Unified Task Force.
21 United Nations Operations in Somalia.
22 Under UNOSOM II, the number of American troops in Somalia would be significantly reduced and the overall command of the operation would transfer to a UN commander (Hyland, 1999: 55).
23 The official document issued in 1993 by Clinton which links humanitarian issues to international peace and security and US interests is known as Presidential Review Directive 13 (PRD-13). This document was the basis for US involvement in peacekeeping missions until it was modified by Presidential Directive Decision 25 (PDD-25) issued in 1994 following the debacle in Somalia. PDD-25 introduced limitations to US involvement in peacekeeping missions, established conditionalities and more clearly linked US involvement to tangibility of interests and mission outcomes (Alden, 2000: 363; Cohen, 2007: 49–53).
24 The Hutu-dominated National Republican Movement for Democracy and Development in power since 1975.
25 United Nations Assistance Mission to Rwanda composed mainly of Belgian troops and commanded by a Canadian General. Its main mandate was to monitor the ceasefire and help prepare democratic elections.
26 The ideology of Hutu Power held that the Tutsi were an alien race in Rwanda and a remnant of colonial occupation (for example, see Mamdani, 2001: 189–196).
27 In addition, the Prime Minister Agathe Uwilingiyimana along with 10 Belgian UNAMIR peacekeepers assigned to protect her were assassinated. Agathe Uwilingiyimana was an ethnic Hutu from the Democratic Republican Movement (MDR), one of the opposition parties established after the one-party rule was abolished in Rwanda. After the death of Habyarimana, she became the head of the government and served in this position for half a day until murdered by Rwandan troops loyal to the late President's party.
28 Then the US Ambassador to the United Nations.
29 Michael Barnett was a Somalia and Rwanda 'expert' at the US Mission to the UN during the unfolding of these events (see Barnett, 1997: 554–558).
30 The Clinton administration identified many 'big, emerging markets' important for American interests (see Garten, 1997).
31 Initially dubbed the African Crisis Response Force (ACRF). The allusion to a 'force' was understood by many as reference to a standing army and led to initial scepticism among African countries (Aning, 2001: 49; Omach, 2000: 87).

ACRF was also hard to sell to Congress, who failed to see how the initiative would benefit the US (Hesse, 2001: 123).
32 Providing troops for deployment under Chapter VI and Chapter VII operations under the UN Charter.
33 Some say hijacked (Hesse, 205: 331).
34 Known as the Rules of Origin Requirement.
35 The other country being South Africa.
36 Known as the Ogoni nine.
37 Who served as Vice President of Rwanda until he assumed Presidency in 2000.
38 The factory, which was suspected to be manufacturing chemical weapons, was in fact just a vaccine and medicine producer; the American attack, dubbed operation Infinite Reach, led to the destruction of production lines for important medicine, as well as a large number of civilian casualties, attracted worldwide criticism against the US.

## References

Adebajo, A. (2002) *Building peace in West Africa: Liberia, Sierra Leone, and Guinea-Bissau.* Lynne Rienner Publishers, Boulder, Col.

Albright, M. K. and Woodward, W. (2003) *Madam Secretary.* Miramax Books, New York.

Alden, C. (2000) From Neglect to 'Virtual Engagement': The United States and its New Paradigm for Africa, *African Affairs* 99: 355–371.

Ambrose, S. E. and Brinkley, D. (1997) *Rise to globalism: American foreign policy since 1938.* Penguin Books, New York.

Aning, E. K. (2001) African Crisis Response Initiative and the New African Security (Dis)order, *African Journal of Political Science* 6: 43–67.

Apodaca, C. (2006) *Understanding U.S. human rights policy: a paradoxical legacy.* Routledge, New York; London.

Atwood, B. J. (1994) Nation Building and the Crisis Prevention in the post-Cold War World, *Brown Journal of World Affairs* 2 (1): 11–17.

Baker, J. A. and DeFrank, T. M. (1995) *The politics of diplomacy: revolution, war, and peace, 1989–1992.* Putnam, New York.

Barnett, M. N. (1997) The UN Security Council, Indifference, and Genocide in Rwanda, *Cultural Anthropology* 12: 551–578.

Bush, G. H. W. (1992) The U.S. and Africa: The Republican Record. *Africa Report*, 37 (5): 13–17.

Bush, G. H. W. and Scowcroft, B. (1998) *A world transformed.* Knopf, Distributed by Random House, New York.

Christopher, W. (1998) *In the stream of history: shaping foreign policy for a new era.* Stanford University Press, Stanford, Calif.

Clinton, B. (1993) Transcript of a televised address on Somalia. 7 October 1993.

Clinton, B. (1994) White House Conference on Africa, 26–27 June *Foreign Policy Bulletin* 5: 36–38.

Clinton, B. (1998) Communique: Entebbe Summit for Peace and Prosperity. The American Presidency Project.

Clinton, B. (2000) Statement on Signing the Global AIDS and Tuberculosis Relief Act of 2000. The American Presidency Project.

Clough, M. (1992) *Free at last?: U.S. policy toward Africa and the end of the Cold War.* Council on Foreign Relations Press, New York.

Cohen, H. J. (2000) *Intervening in Africa: superpower peacemaking in a troubled continent*. St. Martin's Press, New York.
Cohen, H. J. (2007) *One-hundred days of silence: America and the Rwanda genocide*. Rowman & Littlefield Publishers, Lanham.
Coleman-Adebayo, M. (2011) *No fear: a whistleblower's triumph over corruption and retaliation at the EPA*. Lawrence Hill Books, Chicago, Ill.
Connell, D. and Smyth, F. (1998) Africa's New Bloc, *Foreign Affairs* 77: 80–94.
Conti, D. B. (2002) President Bush's trade rhetoric: retaining the free trade paradigm in an era of managed trade, in Bose, M. and Perotti, R. (eds) *From Cold War to New World Order: the foreign policy of George Bush*. Greenwood Press, Westport, Conn., pp. 3–17.
Cox, M. (2000) Wilsonianism resurgent? the Clinton administration and the promotion of democracy, in Cox, M., Ikenberry, G. J. and Inoguchi, T. (eds) *American democracy promotion: impulses, strategies, and impacts*. Oxford University Press, Oxford; New York, pp. 218–239.
Crocker, C. A. (2001) Forward, in Morrison, J. S. and Cooke, J. G. (eds) *Africa policy in the Clinton years: critical choices for the Bush administration*. CSIS Press, Washington, DC, pp. vii–xiv.
De Klerk, F. W. (1998) *The last trek – a new beginning: the autobiography*. Macmillan, London.
de Waal, A. (2004) Counter-Insurgency on the Cheap, *Review of African Political Economy* 31: 716–725.
Des Forges, A. (2004) Learning from disaster – U.S. human rights policy in Rwanda, in Liang-Fenton, D. (ed.) *Implementing U.S. human rights policy: agendas, policies, and practices*. United States Institute of Peace Press, Washington, DC, pp. 29–50.
Des Forges, A. L. (2014) *Leave none to tell the story: genocide in Rwanda*. Red Sea Press, Trenton, NJ.
DoS (1999) *U.S.–Africa ministerial: blueprint for a U.S.–Africa partnership for the 21st century* http://1997-2001.state.gov/www/regions/africa/blueprint.html (accessed 11 September 2014.
DoS (2001) *History of the Department of State during the Clinton Presidency (1993–2001): Africa*, http://2001-2009.state.gov/r/pa/ho/pubs/8531.html (accessed 7 September 2014.
Ferroggiaro, W. (2001) The US and the genocide in Rwanda 1994: evidence of inaction. The National Security Archive. George Washington University, Washington, DC.
Frazer, J. E. and Herbst, J. I. (2001) U.S. investment in security operations in Africa, in Morrison, J. S. and Cooke, J. G. (eds) *Africa policy in the Clinton years: critical choices for the Bush administration*. CSIS Press, Washington, DC, pp. 55–72.
Friedman, T. L. (1991) Bush lifts a ban on economic ties to South Africa, *New York Times*, 11 July 1991.
Fuhr, D. and Klughaup, Z. (2014) The IMF and AGOA: A Comparative Analysis of Conditionality, *Duke Journal of Comparative & International Law*, 14 (1): 125–148.
Garten, J. E. (1997) The Big Ten: The Big Emerging Markets and How They Will Change Our Lives, *Foreign Affairs*.
Gore, A. (1994) White House Conference on Africa. 26–27 June, *Foreign Policy Bulletin* 5: 34–36.
Hesse, B. J. (2001) *The United States, South Africa and Africa: of grand foreign policy aims and modest means*. Ashgate, Aldershot; Burlington.

Hesse, B. J. (2005) Celebrate or hold suspect? Bill Clinton and George W. Bush in Africa, *Journal of Contemporary African Studies* 23: 327–344.

Hyland, W. G. (1999) *Clinton's world: remaking American foreign policy*. Praeger, Westport, Conn.

Johnson, D. H. (2011) *The root causes of Sudan's civil wars: peace or truce*. James Currey, Woodbridge.

Jones, V. C. and Williams, B. R. (2012) U.S. trade and investment relations with sub-Saharan Africa and the African Growth and Opportunity Act, *Congressional Research Service*, Washington, DC.

Khadiagala, G. M. (2001) The United States and Africa: Beyond the Clinton Administration, *SAIS Review* 21: 259–273.

Klinghoffer, A. J. (1998) *The international dimension of genocide in Rwanda*. New York University Press, New York.

Lake, A. (1996) Defining missions, setting deadlines: prepared remarks Anthony Lake, Assistant to the President for National Security Affairs, George Washington University, Washington, Wednesday, 6 March 1996, *Defense Issues*.

Levitt, J. (1998) The African crisis response initiative: a general survey, *Africa Insight* 28: 100–108.

Lewis, N. A. (2001) Papers show U.S. knew of genocide in Rwanda, *New York Times*, 21 August 2001.

Lyman, P. N. (2002) *Partner to history: the U.S. role in South Africa's transition to democracy*. United States Institute of Peace Press, Washington, DC.

Mamdani, M. (2001) *When victims become killers: colonialism, nativism, and the genocide in Rwanda*. Fountain Publications, Kampala.

Mamdani, M. (2013) *Saviors and survivors: Darfur, politics and the war on terror*. Makerere Institute of Social Research, Kampala, Uganda.

Mandelbaum, M. (1996) Foreign Policy as Social Work, *Foreign Affairs* 75: 16–32.

Mattoo, A., Roy, D. and Subramanian, A. (2003) The Africa Growth and Opportunity Act and its Rules of Origin: Generosity Undermined?, *World Economy* 26: 829–851.

McCrisken, T. B. (2003) *American exceptionalism and the legacy of Vietnam: US foreign policy since 1974*. Palgrave Macmillan, Basingstoke, Hampshire; New York.

Melson, R. (2003) Modern genocide in Rwanda: ideology, revolution, war and mass murder in an African state, in Gellately, R. and Kiernan, B. (eds) *The specter of genocide: mass murder in historical perspective*. Cambridge University Press, New York, pp. 325–338.

Mertus, J. (2008) *Bait and switch: human rights and U.S. foreign policy*. Routledge, New York.

Mikell, G. and Lyman, P. N. (2001) Critical U.S. bilateral relations in Africa: Nigeria and South Africa, in Morrison, J. S. and Cooke, J. G. (eds) *Africa policy in the Clinton years: critical choices for the Bush administration*. CSIS Press, Washington, DC, pp. 73–95.

Minter, W. (2000) America and Africa: Beyond the Double Standard, *Current History* 99: 200–210.

Morrison, J. S. (2001) U.S. policy toward HIV/AIDS in Africa: momentum, opportunities, and urgent choices, in Morrison, J. S. and Cooke, J. G. (eds) *Africa policy in the Clinton years: critical choices for the Bush administration*. CSIS Press, Washington, DC, pp. 13–32.

Morrison, J. S. and Cooke, J. G. (2001) *Africa policy in the Clinton years: critical choices for the Bush administration*. CSIS Press, Washington, DC.

Mushita, T. A. (2001) An African Response to AGOA, *Southern African Economist*, pp. 17–19.
Natsios, A. S. (2012) *Sudan, South Sudan, and Darfur: what everyone needs to know.* Oxford University Press, Oxford; New York.
Olson, J. (1995) Behind the Recent Tragedy in Rwanda, *An International Journal on Human Geography and Environmental Sciences* 35: 217–222.
Omach, P. (2000) The African Crisis Response Initiative: Domestic Politics and Convergence of National Interests, *African Affairs* 99: 73–95.
Paterson, T. G., Clifford, J. G. and Hagan, K. J. (1991) *American foreign policy: a history.* D.C. Heath, Lexington, Mass.
Power, S. (2002) *'A problem from hell': America and the age of genocide.* HarperCollins, London.
Rice, S. (1999) The African Growth and Opportunity Act Introduction: AGOA at a Pivotal Point in Relations: Susan E. Rice, Assistant Secretary for Africa Testimony, House International Relations Committee, Subcommittee on Africa Washington, DC, 11 February 1999. US Department of State Archive.
Rosenblum, P. (2002) Irrational Exuberance: The Clinton Administration in Africa, *Current History* 101: 195–202.
Rothchild, D. S. (2001) A New Foreign Policy for Africa?, *SAIS Review* 21: 179–211.
Schneidman, W. (2012) The African Growth and Opportunity Act: Looking Back, Looking Forwards, *Africa Growth Initiative at Brookings*. Brookings Institution, Washington, DC.
Schraeder, P. J. (1994) *United States foreign policy toward Africa: incrementalism, crisis, and change.* Cambridge University Press, Cambridge; New York.
Schraeder, P. J. (1998) From ally to orphan: understanding U.S. policy toward Somalia after the Cold War, in Scott, J. M. (ed.) *After the end: making U.S. foreign policy in the post-Cold War world.* Duke University Press, Durham, pp. 330–357.
Schraeder, P. J. (2001) 'Forget the Rhetoric and Boost the Geopolitics': Emerging Trends in the Bush Administration's Policy towards Africa, 2001, *African Affairs* 100: 387–404.
Scott, J. M. (1998) Interbranch policy making after the end, in Scott, J. M. (ed.) *After the end: making U.S. foreign policy in the post-Cold War world.* Duke University Press, Durham, pp. 389–407.
Smyth, F. (1998) A New Game: The Clinton Administration on Africa, *World Policy Journal* 15: 82–92.
USAID (2000) *Clinton-Gore adminstration history project: USAID's role 1993–2001.* USAID, Washington, DC.
Uvin, P. (1998) *Aiding violence: the development enterprise in Rwanda.* Kumarian Press, West Hartford, CT.
van de Walle, N. (2009) US Policy towards Africa: The Bush Legacy and the Obama Administration, *African Affairs* 109 (434): 1–21.
von Hippel, K. (2000) *Democracy by force: U.S. military intervention in the post-Cold War world.* Cambridge University Press, New York.
Wheeler, N. J. (2000) *Saving strangers: humanitarian intervention in international society.* Oxford University Press, Oxford; New York.
Wills, K. J. (1987) Liberia Reported to Divert Millions in U.S. Aid, *New York Times*, 22 February 1987.
Wright, G. (1997) *The destruction of a nation: United States' policy towards Angola since 1945.* Pluto Press, London; Chicago, Ill.

# 6 The arc of instability
## US policy in Africa after 9/11

### Africa: 'a nation that suffers from incredible disease'[1]

George W. Bush's lack of experience in foreign policy was mitigated by a team of individuals who built their careers working in foreign policy and national security. One such individual was Secretary of State Colin Powell, a former Chairman of the Joint Chiefs of Staff and a former National Security Advisor. As a veteran of the armed forces, Powell had experienced first-hand the quagmire of Vietnam. He viewed foreign policy through 'realist' lenses, and was wary of unilateral military action, especially openended missions without a clear exit strategy (LaFeber, 2002: 550). Powell was the first African-American to serve as Secretary of State, and his first stop during his tour of the DoS was the Bureau of African Affairs (Perlez, 2001). During the presidential campaign, Bush stated that 'while Africa may be important, it doesn't fit into the national strategic interests, as far as I can see them' (Bush quoted in Behrman, 2004: 246, and Fisher, 2001; see also Copson, 2007: 7). This statement raised initial concerns that the continent would be placed on the backburner of foreign policy. Powell's ancestry and symbolic choice to honour the Bureau of African Affairs raised hopes among Africanists and African leaders that despite Bush's initial statement, the administration would maintain an interest in Africa.

The Bush team had criticised the Clinton administration's African policy for being overly activist and unrealistic in its (mainly rhetorical) promotion of a grand vision of transformation for the African continent (Perlez, 2001; Schraeder, 2001: 387–388). Powell stated that his approach to Africa would be anchored in geopolitics rather than activist rhetoric (Perlez, 2001; Schraeder, 2001: 388). He rejected Clinton's over-reliance on a set of new African leaders through personal diplomacy, which he believed, gave them a certain amount of power over American foreign policy objectives for the continent (Schraeder, 2001: 396). Instead, Powell suggested focusing on regional powers such as South Africa, one of the most important economies and the most significant military power on the continent, and Nigeria, the most populated African nation and one of the most important oil suppliers to the US (Schraeder, 2001: 395). The emerging strategy for the African policy under the Bush administration used a three-pronged approach: boosting the co-operation with regional powers; promoting US trade investment in Africa through strengthening Clinton's AGOA initiative; and working towards minimising the need for foreign interventions to solve African challenges, both through capacity-building initiatives (such as ACRI), and by encouraging Africans to channel profits from natural resources towards infrastructure and improvement of social services (Schraeder, 2001: 396–397).

Powell's intention to promote the African policy was demonstrated by a formal tour of Africa undertaken only a few months into the Bush administration (Powell, 2001a). His visit took place in May 2001, and included stops in Kenya, Mali, South Africa and Uganda. The stated objectives of the Africa tour were: to demonstrate that the administration and the Secretary have an interest in the African policy; to assess positive transitions towards democracy, peaceful elections and regional co-operation; to examine and evaluate the HIV/AIDS threat and the American response to the spread of the disease; to evaluate the implementation of AGOA; and to strengthen the American engagement in conflict resolution on the continent (DoS, 2001).

The choice of destinations for the tour combined objectives concerning political, strategic, economic, and health issues: Mali was one of the only countries where a transition to democracy had occurred through an internal process disconnected from economic development; South Africa was the most important economy and most powerful country in Africa; Kenya was an import regional ally in an election year; and Uganda was of interest both because of the role it played (together with Rwanda) in the Congo conflict, and for its programmes to fight HIV/AIDS through education and prevention (Powell, 2001).

In reply to specific questions on the upcoming African policy, Powell indicated that the Bush administration intended to continue training African troops for assuming a greater role in peacekeeping missions on the continent. The rationale was to eliminate a future need for American combat troops to be sent in response to crisis in Africa (Powell, 2001). The Secretary also indicated that the administration intended to continue providing humanitarian aid to Sudan and engage in an attempt to foster a solution for the political and economic problems plaguing that country (Powell, 2001). Powell emphasised America's commitment to the sustainable economic development of Africa and indicated the intention of the US to relieve the debt burden of developing countries to help promote economic development (Powell, 2001b).

## *Africa and Oil*

One of the most important issues on the African policy agenda was the increased reliance of the US on African oil. Powell was a member of the

National Energy Policy Development Group (NEPDG), a task force led by Vice President Cheney, created by Bush shortly after his election to develop an energy policy. The NEPDG was established to address one of America's main concerns: the declining production of oil around the world and the subsequent impact on the US economy (Chouala, 2009: 145). The issue was framed by Secretary of Energy, Spencer Abraham, as a threat to US national security by undermining the American way of life (Abraham quoted in Chouala, 2009: 145). The final report of the NEPDG, also known as the Cheney Report, identified the importance of African oil for US strategic interests. Despite the fact that the events of 9/11 overshadowed the Cheney Report, it is crucial to acknowledge its importance and influence on the post-9/11 African policy.

The NEPDG (2001: Chapter 8, pp. 11–12) determined that African oil is a highly desirable product due to its low sulphur content. The report identified Nigeria and Angola as the most important African oil suppliers, but also noted the oil production potential of other countries such as Gabon, Congo and Chad. It also mentioned the importance of USAID's role in providing technical assistance to West Africa to construct and improve its oil and natural gas infrastructure, allowing for the enhancement of oil production to supply US energy needs, as well as providing business opportunities for American oil companies.

While not stated explicitly as 'corruption', the Cheney Report recommended that the President takes steps to increase 'transparency, sanctity of contracts, and security', both to achieve a more reliable energy procurement environment for the US, and to ensure a safe investment for American companies in Africa (Klare and Volman, 2006: 613). Energy security in Africa thus converged with national security, economic prosperity and development assistance. After 9/11, security was mostly linked to the GWOT. The juncture between security, domestic prosperity and development assistance required the involvement of the DoD, DoS and USAID, along with other departments (such as Energy and Treasury) and the private sector (namely oil companies) in a closer relationship with each other.

### Combating HIV/AIDS

During the Africa tour, Powell emphasised the commitment of President Bush to support the fight against HIV/AIDS in Africa. Combating HIV/AIDS became one of the pillars of the African policy during the Bush administration. In the pre-9/11 context of the African tour, the main commitment to HIV/AIDS was embodied in a US$200 million contribution to the newly established Global Fund to fight HIV/AIDS, tuberculosis and malaria. This commitment as well as the subsequent efforts of the Bush administration to elevate the importance of the fight against HIV/AIDS was applauded both in Washington and around the world. Bush's interest in fighting HIV/AIDS was contradictory to his earlier record. As Governor and a conservative new-born Christian, Bush was uncomfortable dealing with AIDS issues which were associated with sex and the LGBT community (Behrman, 2004: 245). Shortly after his election, the position of senior advisor for international health at the NSC was cancelled by Condoleezza Rice. This step was viewed as an indication of how the administration perceived the link between health and security created during the Clinton administration (Behrman, 2004: 247). However, consistent domestic pressure as well as a global effort by the international community to address global health issues kept the administration involved in the fight against HIV/AIDS (Behrman, 2004: 264–265). Pressure exercised by UN Secretary General Annan and Secretary of State Powell, led Bush to commit the US to become the first contributing nation to the newly established Global Fund (Behrman, 2004: 263; Bush, 2010: 336; Rice, 2011: 225). The American commitment to fight HIV/AIDS in Africa would become one of the most lauded legacies of the Bush administration, especially through the post-9/11 PEPFAR programme.

Despite Powell's intention to elevate the importance of the African policy, it is essential to note that in general, until the events of 9/11, President Bush was reluctant to commit the US to assuming a new leadership role on African issues. He preferred instead to continue the general policy of bolstering democracy, increasing trade and fighting HIV/AIDS. Africa remained a relatively low priority foreign policy concern (Rothchild and Emmanuel, 2005: 78, 84).

## Africa and the Global War on Terror

Powell's initial approach to Africa had no time to fully mature. The events of 9/11 brought about a significant change of focus to America's foreign policy, and had important implications for the African policy (van de Walle, 2009: 3). The underlying approach after the events of 9/11, otherwise known as the Bush doctrine, was stated by the President in a sentence uttered shortly after the terrorist attacks (Cheney and Cheney, 2011: 9; Rice, 2011: 77; Rumsfeld, 2011: 423; Tenet and Harlow, 2007: 170): 'We will make no distinction between the terrorists who committed these acts and those who harbor them.' (Bush, 2001). This statement was an indication of the fierce unilateralism that would characterise the attitude towards international affairs during the Bush administration (LaFeber, 2002: 549; see also Gurtov, 2006: 36–48). While elements of unilateral foreign policy under the Bush administration were present even before the events of 9/11,[2] the attacks prompted Bush to declare publicly that America's engagement in world affairs would be characterised by pre-emptive unilateralism. The nations of the world would be given the opportunity to pledge their allegiance to combat terrorism, or otherwise, stand against America (Bush, 2001a). The Bush doctrine evolved into a four-pronged approach known as the 'Freedom Agenda':

> First, make no distinction between the terrorists and the nations that harbor them – and hold both to account. Second, take the fight to the enemy overseas before they can attack us again here at home. Third, confront threats before they fully materialize. And fourth, advance liberty and hope as an alternative to the enemy's ideology of repression and fear.
>
> (Bush, 2010: 396–397)

In his autobiography, Bush professes that he viewed his doctrine as both idealistic and realistic (Bush, 2010: 397). His idealism was deeply anchored in his religious beliefs and American exceptionalism (LaFeber, 2002: 552). But what he regarded as realism was blended with his brand of idealism – expressed as: 'freedom is the most practical way to protect our interest' and 'America's vital interests and our deepest beliefs are ... one' (Bush, 2010: 397) – which was more an expression of his neo-conservative inclination than of realism à la Morgenthau. The rising importance of Africa in the aftermath of 9/11 was illustrated in remarks made by National Security Advisor Rice at the AGOA forum at the DoS on 7 November 2001. Addressing more than 100 African representatives, Rice stated that Africa 'has an historic role to play in the global battle against terrorism' (Rice, 2001). The administration recognised the strategic importance of Africa as a bridge between geographical regions (physical), religions (cultural) and multilateral forums (political). Africa was not only an important partner in the battle against terrorism, but also a potential breeding ground and a hideout for terrorists (Schraeder and Crouzel, 2005: 43–44). The reach of Al-Qaida in Africa had already been demonstrated by the bombings of the American embassies in Nairobi and Dar-es-Salaam in 1998. Given the vastness of the continent and the nature of the borders between African states, it was important for the US to co-opt African nations to collaborate in the global fight against terrorism.

As a function of the Bush doctrine, the US began to classify the vulnerability of nations to threats from non-state actors such as Al-Qaida. In this context, the vulnerability of some states in Africa could potentially affect American regional political, security and economic interests on the continent, as well as influence the progression of the GWOT (Natsios, 2006; NSS, 2002). State vulnerability and African oil production became two important cornerstones of the post-9/11 approach to the GWOT on the African continent (Rothchild and Emmanuel, 2005: 78–79). Both AGOA and the fight against HIV/AIDS were important elements of the African policy during the Bush administration. They were expressions of American compassion rooted in the neo-conservative understanding of idealism and exceptionalism, in addition to being important parts of the strategy to contribute to the stability of vulnerable nations (Rothchild and Emmanuel, 2005: 78–79). The various categories of vulnerable states in Africa linked underdevelopment (poverty, corruption, diseases, lack of education, poor governance and lack of democracy) to security (breeding grounds for terrorism and criminal networks). This became the central component of the post-9/11 policy of the US in Africa, combining the efforts of the DoS and the DoD to help Africa develop on the parallel tracks of security and development to achieve the overarching objective: combat terrorist networks. In many ways, the post-9/11 African policy was a reminder of the Cold War where foreign policy was determined according to an enemy's current or potential endeavours. Only this time, the enemy was not another superpower or state, but a group of elusive individuals exercising various forms of shifting influence in countless contexts ranging from high governments to very local settings, mainly in underdeveloped countries.

As noted by Taylor (2010: 25), the African policy priorities of the Bush administration were, in essence, almost identical to the Clinton administration: promoting US economic interests (primarily oil), conflict resolution, democracy and human rights, development assistance and reducing the impact of HIV/AIDS. The most significant difference is the security prism through which these elements were regarded and formulated in the Bush policy, or in other words, the securitisation[3] of foreign policy in light of the 9/11 attacks (Taylor, 2010: 27).

The post-9/11 securitisation of foreign policy launched a process to improve the coherence among the different departments and agencies to more effectively fight the war on terror, and to increase the efficiency and effectiveness of the different policy tools available to the US government.[4] With reference to Africa, the most important policy bridges were built among the DoD (in charge of fighting the GWOT), the DoS (in charge of diplomacy), and USAID (in charge of designing and applying assistance programmes on the continent).[5]

The US regarded Africa as a continent particularly vulnerable to terrorism (Lyman and Morrison, 2004). A number of geopolitical realities support this view of Africa. The continent is in proximity to both Europe and the Middle East, and eastern Africa to Asia. It is therefore close to substantial US interests in the oil-rich Middle East and to southern Europe. In the context of the wars in Afghanistan and Iraq, this linkage was viewed as providing a natural geographical escape corridor for terrorists (Keenan, 2009: 158–175;[6] Lyman and Morrison, 2004). Northern Africa's Arab orientation and Islamic regimes were hosts to various radical groups with problematic ideologies. The Saharan and Sahelian regions were regarded as under-governed regions containing possible hideouts for many radical groups and criminal networks. African governments were plagued by poverty, corruption, poor governance, disease, food insecurity and general lack of economic development. These facts linked US economic interests to various forms of security issues. During the post-9/11 Bush administration, Africa gradually became a 'second front' of the GWOT (Schraeder, 2007: 171).

An effective strategy in Africa, therefore, needed to create a bridge connecting military, development, and economic assistance in order to address both contextual and regional challenges on the African continent.

In terms of military assistance, the Bush administration undertook a number of steps to develop the capacity of African nations to combat terrorism and enforce peace on the continent. These efforts evolved throughout the eight years of the Bush administration with the objective of creating a coherent process to pull together the various USG resources to effectively combat terrorism.

In 2002, the US replaced ACRI with the African Contingency Operations Training and Assistance Program (ACOTA). ACOTA was a revamped version of ACRI and intended to address a number deficiencies in its programming, including the lack of training for peace enforcement, the absence of tailored training packages and the lack of capacity of African troops to sustain readiness by training independently (Handy, 2003: 59). An HIV/AIDS module was also introduced as a part of the training, mainly to address the loss of trained personnel to the disease, leading to the loss of military knowledge and expertise (Handy, 2003: 60; Shanahan and Francis, 2005: 3). While ACOTA is supported by the DoD by providing instructors, trainers and advisors, the programme is under the management of the DoS. Similar to ACRI, ACOTA contains built-in conditionalities for recipient countries to be eligible for training and equipment, including an elected civilian government, capacity to deploy peacekeepers when needed, and a track record which does not include the abuse of human rights.

In June 2004, the Global Peace Operations Initiative (GPOI) was announced by President Bush during a G8 summit as a part of the effort to meet the forum's Africa Action Plan (Shanahan and Francis, 2005: 4). Copson (2007: 106), quoting the Deputy Secretary of Defence Wolfowitz, emphasised that the main purpose of the GPOI was to ensure that US forces would not become entangled in African conflicts by building capacity of African forces to independently enforce peace on the continent.

### *Regional security initiatives and AFRICOM*

In addition to peacekeeping training, the US launched a number of regional security initiatives in Africa to more effectively fight the war on terror. These programmes included a development assistance component to help remove the underlying causes of poor governance and radicalisation. This component was initially devised and carried out by the military rather than the DoS and USAID.[7]

Before proceeding with an overview of these initiatives, it is important to note that until 2008, the African continent fell under the responsibility of three US-unified combatant commands: the European Command (EUCOM), assigned with responsibility for most of the African continent excluding Egypt, Sudan, Kenya, Ethiopia, Somalia, Djibouti and Madagascar; the Central Command (CENTCOM), assigned with responsibility for the countries mentioned above excluding Madagascar; and the Pacific Command (PACOM) which was responsible for the island of Madagascar. With the increased importance of the war on terror in Africa, the plurality of initiatives and missions imposed on the combatant commands, and the need to form coherent and centralised processes to fight the war on terrorism, the USG authorised the creation of the African Command (AFRICOM) in 2006, and established it as an operational command on 1 October 2008. AFRICOM assumed responsibility for the entire African continent with the exclusion of Egypt, which remained under the responsibility of CENTCOM. The various regional initiatives in Africa described below began under the responsibility of different commands and were eventually gathered under the AFRICOM after it became operational. Under AFRICOM, various mission parameters were modified and extended because of the geographical flexibility that came along with the creation of a unified command for the continent.

### The Combined Joint Task Force – Horn of Africa (CJTF-HOA)

The CJTF-HOA was established in 2002 under CENTCOM as the military component of Operation Enduring Freedom – Horn of Africa, the designation for the GWOT on the continent. The initial mission specifications of CJTF-HOA's regional security programme included 'supporting international agencies working to enhance long-term stability to the region' (DoD, 2003). In addition to active combat operations to seek and destroy terrorists and their support networks (on land and sea), the Task Force worked to enhance the capability of host nations to fight the GWOT within their borders (DoD, 2003). The CJTF-HOA operates from Camp Lemonnier in Djibouti, and its direct area of activity includes Eritrea, Ethiopia, Kenya, Seychelles, Somalia and Sudan. Additional areas of interest relating to the Task Force's mission include Burundi, Chad, Comoros, the Democratic Republic of Congo (DRC), Madagascar, Mauritius, Mozambique, Rwanda, Tanzania, Uganda and Yemen (Ploch, 2010: 27). The CJTF-HOA activities to modify the underlying social realities that allowed terrorists and their doctrines to encroach, included development assistance projects traditionally carried out by USAID, such as building schools, hospitals, provision of veterinary and medical services and digging wells (Copson, 2007: 114).

### The Pan Sahel Initiative (PSI)

In the western part of the African continent, a second regional security initiative emerged, initially under the command of EUCOM. The Pan Sahel Initiative (PSI) was announced in November 2002 as a programme designed to help Chad, Mauritania, Mali and Niger to 'protect borders, track movement of people, combat terrorism and enhance regional cooperation and stability' (DoS, 2002). The goals of the PSI were to 'support two US national security interests in Africa: waging the war on terrorism and enhancing regional peace and security' (DoS, 2002). One of the main concerns of the US was that terrorists fleeing from US forces in Afghanistan and Iraq would seek refuge in the vast 'ungoverned' spaces of the Sahara and Sahel regions (Schraeder, 2007: 177). The PSI was a mission of relatively limited scale focused on the training of about 150 special troops from each of the participating countries by US Special Forces and providing basic military equipment (AFRICOM, 2010; Copson, 2007: 111).

Initially, the main terrorist threat in the Sahara and Sahel regions was the presence of an Algerian Islamic group identified by its French Acronym GSPC.[8] This group was a splinter organisation from the Armed Islamic Group (GIA),[9] and was involved since the late 1990s in insurgency against the Algerian government. The insurgency included attacks against oil resources and eventually the kidnapping of Western civilians for ransom, which placed the GSPC on the radar of Europe and the US (see, for example, Keenan, 2009: 23–26). While originally from Algeria, the GSPC used the vast spaces of the Sahara and Sahel, preferring the areas of northern Mali, but also Niger, Mauritania and Chad, to hide hostages and evade pursuing forces. Because the PSI was perceived as a success after having inflicting casualties upon the GSPC and eventually leading to the capture of the leader of the GSPC in Chad in 2004, it was expanded in 2005 to become the Trans-Sahara Counter Terrorism Initiative[10] (TSCTI). The programme was initiated in a meeting between various US ambassadors to the region in an attempt to bolster a regional approach to reduce the vulnerability to terrorist attacks (Warner, 2014: 23). The TSCTI expanded on the PSI to include Senegal and Algeria as participating countries, with the addition of Nigeria, Morocco and Tunisia as observer countries (Schraeder, 2007: 178). The overall approach of TSCTI was to:

> build indigenous capacity and facilitate co-operation among governments in the region that are willing partners (Algeria, Chad, Mali, Mauritania, Morocco, Niger, Senegal, Nigeria and Tunisia, with Libya possibly to follow later) in the struggle with Islamic extremism in the Sahel region. TSCTI helps strengthen regional counterterrorism capabilities, enhance and institutionalize co-operation among the region's security forces, promote democratic governance, foster development and education and ultimately benefit our bilateral relationships with each of these states.
>
> (Jones, 2005: 17)

In essence, the TSCTI was a much more ambitious version of the PSI geographically and in terms of scale and scope. The inclusion of development and education in the goals, as well as a focus on building bilateral relationships, meant expanding the war on terror in the region to include securitised and militarised development and diplomatic objectives. The TSCTI military component accounted for 20 to 30 per cent of the total budget, with the rest devoted to other government agencies, including USAID, to foster economic development and engage in various efforts of development assistance to provide essential social services, water, health, education, nutrition, infrastructure and governance training, as a part of the effort to fend off terrorism in the region (Copson, 2007: 112). The DoD supports the programme through AFRICOM[11] under the umbrella of Operation Enduring Freedom-Trans Sahara (OEF-TS). The DoS planning of support for TSCTI (and later TSCTP) is conducted through various Bureaus in Washington, including the Bureau of African Affairs, Near Eastern Affairs, Political-Military Affairs and Counterterrorism. On the individual country levels, decisions are made by the Country Team which includes the Ambassador, the USAID Mission Director and the Defence Attaché (Warner, 2014: 27–33).

*East Africa Counter-Terrorism Initiative (EACTI)*

Another regional programme launched in 2003 under the DoS is the East Africa Counter-Terrorism Initiative. EACTI includes Djibouti, Ethiopia, Kenya, Tanzania and Uganda focusing on legal and policy training, border control and aviation security to improve the capabilities of participating countries to counter terrorism (Ploch, 2010: 23; Schraeder, 2007: 178–179). The programme funding accounts included Development Assistance (DA), Peace Keeping Operations (PKO), the Economic Support Fund (ESF), Foreign Military Financing (FMF), International Narcotic and Law Enforcement (INLE), and Nonproliferation, Antiterrorism, and Demining and Related programmes (NADR). As in the case of the sister programmes, EACTI demonstrates the administration's policy of preferring regional activity and movement to improve coherence and co-operation between the various government instruments to fight the war on terror. In 2009 EACTI was transformed into the East Africa Regional Strategic Initiative (EARSI) to resemble the TSCTI/TSCTP and the practices of co-ordination among the various arms of the USG (Ploch, 2010: 24).

Schraeder (2007: 179–181) remarked that US regional interests in Africa are arranged in a four-tier hierarchy:

1 fighting the GWOT in regions in proximity to the Middle East;
2 stabilisation of regional powers such as Algeria, Ethiopia, Kenya and Senegal, as precursors for regional stability and 'anchor' states for the GWOT;
3 protecting important US economic interests, namely oil, especially in countries located in regional proximity to the Gulf of Guinea;

4   addressing issues in the rest of sub-Saharan Africa (the tier which receives the least policy attention and resources).

The policy emphasis follows a globalist logic (Schraeder, 2007: 180), where instead of focusing on individual regimes and the set of social and political challenges within each country, the US assumes a strategic approach to contain terrorism and tailor diplomacy, development and defence interventions to achieve the end goal. Schraeder (2007: 180) also notes that the driving force behind the abovementioned policy was the Pentagon, and as a result, the policy assumed a militarised character and subsequently led to tension between the DoD and the DoS on the focus and execution of the African policy.[12]

## AFRICOM

Secretary of Defence Donald Rumsfeld created an interagency planning team in 2006 to establish an independent military command for Africa. The team included representatives of DoS, USAID, and other federal agencies working in Africa. In 2007, the new Secretary of Defence, Robert Gates, announced the creation of AFRICOM stating that:

> The President has decided to stand up a new unified, combatant command, Africa Command, to oversee security cooperation, building partnership capability, defense support to non-military missions, and, if directed, military operations on the African Continent. This command will enable us to have a more effective and integrated approach than the current arrangement of dividing Africa between Central Command and European Command, an outdated arrangement left over from the Cold War.
> (quoted in AFRICOM, 2011: 9; and in Garamone, 2007)

Reflecting the development assistance dimension attached to the military missions in Africa, the relationship between security and development was emphasised by President Bush in a statement released in 2007 on the establishment of AFRICOM:

> This new command will strengthen our security cooperation with Africa and create new opportunities to bolster the capabilities of our partners in Africa. Africa Command will enhance our efforts to bring peace and security to the people of Africa and promote our common goals of development, health, education, democracy, and economic growth in Africa.
> (Bush quoted in AFRICOM, 2011: 9; and in Feleke, Picard and Buss, 2011: 35)

AFRICOM included the integration of personnel from other government agencies for better co-ordinating and supporting of civilian components of security stabilisation in the particular African environment, as well as using the expertise and capabilities of other government agencies to increase the efficiency and effectiveness of missions (Ploch, 2011: 4–6). This process became increasingly coherent with the whole-of-government approach during the Obama administration.

### Transformational diplomacy

Aside from the military initiatives incorporating diplomacy and development resources to increase the effectiveness of the GWOT, the DoS and USAID formulated a strategic plan for transformational diplomacy during the second Bush administration (DoS, 2007). The overarching purpose of the plan was to outline how defence and diplomacy would actively seek to support the policy of the President as described in the NSS (DoS, 2007: Preface). The various objectives of the strategic plan tie together three basic convictions outlined in the document:

> [O]ur freedom is best protected by ensuring that others are free; our security relies on a global effort to secure the rights of all; and our prosperity depends on the prosperity of others.
> (DoS, 2007: 10)

These convictions bring together American exceptionalism, idealism and the preservation of the American way of life. Based on these truisms, the document outlines seven joint strategic goals for the DoS and USAID, including (DoS, 2007: 10):

- Achieving peace and security (counter-terrorism; weapons of mass destruction and destabilising conventional weapons; conflict prevention and mitigation and response; transnational crime; homeland security).
- Governing justly and democratically (rule of law and human rights; good governance; political competition and consensus building; civil society).
- Investing in people (health; education; social services and protection for especially vulnerable populations).
- Promoting economic growth and prosperity (private markets; trade and investment; energy security; environment; agriculture).
- Providing humanitarian assistance (protection, assistance and solutions; disaster prevention and mitigation; orderly and humane means for migration management).
- Promoting international understanding (offer a positive vision; marginalise extremism; nurture common interests and values).

The DoS/USAID strategic plan begins by quoting Secretary of State Rice, '[o]ur policy toward Africa is rooted in partnership not paternalism, in doing *with* the peoples of Africa not *for* the peoples of Africa' (Rice quoted in DoS, 2007: 44 – emphasis in original). The African policy was based on a view of the continent as a region of opportunity and challenges. On a positive note, the strategy lists an increasing number of democracies in Africa, a decreasing number of conflicts, the fight against corrupt leaders and war criminals, and an increasing number of countries eligible for an MCA compact (see below). On a negative note, the document lists the fragility of some African states and the proximity of fragile states to newly-emerged democracies, extreme poverty, vulnerability of the health system and the burden of diseases, together with the lack of economic freedom affecting investment and growth. Based on this outlook:

> U.S. policy is committed to peace and security, democracy, free markets and economic integration, a healthy environment, and humanitarian assistance. These principles support vital U.S. interests in Africa, one of the last large emerging markets that will soon supply 25 percent of U.S. oil imports. The U.S. priorities in Africa derive from the President's charge to make the world safer and better, and the Secretary's vision of transformational diplomacy to use America's power to help foreign citizens improve their own lives.
>
> (DoS, 2007: 44)

The fundamental message of the African policy is that clear and tangible economic and security interests are driving the American commitment to Africa. Regional priorities of this policy include: strengthening the capacity of African countries to fight terrorism through regional programmes, and the fight against criminal networks and corruption, especially in the trans-Saharan countries of West Africa and across the Sahel towards the Horn of Africa. On other fronts, the document lists four additional overarching priorities: bolstering democracy and human rights with special focus on women and youth; building the capacity of regional organisations to manage threats on the continent; encouraging economic growth in Africa by creating an atmosphere for private investment; and improving education and infrastructure. AGOA is mentioned as an important instrument for economic growth, as is the pledge to reduce the debts of African countries. The strategy document also mentions the commitment of the US to the MDGs and to the reduction of hunger in Africa.

### *Sudan*

The joint DoS-USAID Strategic Plan (DoS, 2007) specifically indicates a number of priority countries for US policy, stating that resolving the conflict in Sudan–Darfur is on the top of the agenda. In the literature, the interest of President Bush and his administration in the Sudan is mostly portrayed as a humanitarian-driven concern. While it is certainly accurate to invoke American idealism and the religious convictions of the President, there were also underlying national security concerns occasionally mentioned, which tie the war on terror to regional stability and access to oil.

It is important to provide a background to explain the situation in Sudan when America under Bush assumed an important role as mediator. Sudan had been added to the list of countries sponsoring terrorism on 12 August 1993, mainly because it provided sanctuary and training facilities to various terrorist organisations (Carney, 2005: 125). Hosting organisations with Islamist ideologies was a part of al-Turabi's plan to encourage the formation of a global Islamist state (Natsios, 2012: 93–94). Between 1991 and 1996, Sudan hosted Osama bin Laden after Hassan al-Turabi granted him sanctuary in exchange for a substantial investment in Sudan. Towards the end of the 1990s, President al-Bashir began to view al-Turabi's radical ideas as a liability. In addition to Sudan's listing as a sponsor of terror, many African governments began to grow wary of the situation in Sudan, especially after the attempted assassination of President Mubarak of Egypt, which was linked to Bashir's government. In 1999, al-Turabi attempted to limit Bashir's power through the National Assembly. Bashir reacted by sending his troops, dissolving the Assembly, and declaring new elections in Sudan. This marked the end of the alliance between al-Bashir and al-Turabi. A new political constellation emerged in Sudan, forcing Bashir to consider a path of reconciliation with the south to assure the survival of his regime (Natsios, 2012: 101–107). With al-Turabi out of the way, there was neither the room nor the need for Bashir to adhere to the Salafist ideas that guided al-Turabi's agenda (Natsios, 2012: 112). The ongoing conflict with the SPLA was not going well for Bashir. Despite the atrocities committed by Bashir's troops, government-sponsored raids on civilians, bombing of civilian targets by the Sudanese air force, and systematic ethnic cleansing campaigns against tribes associated with the SPLA, Bashir failed to curb a southern rebellion.

Against this background, Sudan was enjoying an oil boom during the second half of the 1990s. The majority of oil resources were located in the south, while the main outlet for oil export was Port Sudan located in the north. The oil in Sudan was both a cause of friction between the government and southern separatists, and a motivation for Bashir to seek a solution for the conflict, as oil was a major source of economic revitalisation for the country and served al-Bashir's basis of power in the north (Natsios, 2012: 109–110).

Several experts and politicians note the distinct change of US policy towards Sudan from a non-interventionist policy during the Clinton administration to a policy of 'constructive engagement' during the Bush administration (see, for example, Iversen, 2007: 33 and references). Sudan became an important policy issue for President Bush before the events of

9/11, for many reasons. In his monograph on Sudan, Andrew Natsios[13] (2012: 166–169) notes the influence of both Colin Powell and Condoleezza Rice in persuading the President to assume a proactive role in resolving many ongoing conflicts in Africa and prioritising Sudan in this respect. In addition, Natsios points to the influence of the evangelical minster Franklin Graham (a close personal friend of George W. Bush) in convincing the President to initiate a peace process in Sudan (Natsios, 2012: 166–169). In this context, it is important to note the historical involvement of American religious conservative groups in humanitarian relief efforts in southern Sudan (Iversen, 2007: 24–32). One of these relief organisations was Graham's Samaritan's Purse (Iversen, 2007: 28; Natsios, 2012: 166). In his biography, President Bush emphasises the deep impact Graham had on his life, especially in relation to his rebirth as a Christian and his decision to run for Presidency (Bush, 2010: 31–33). It is therefore not surprising that the sudden interest of the US in Sudan is often linked to the religious convictions of the President and Graham's interests in Sudan. Iversen (2007: 32–34) notes the marked difference in rhetoric on Sudan, not only between the Clinton and Bush administrations, but also by Bush himself before and after his election. Where Sudan was clearly a marginal issue during the Clinton administration, and marginal for President Bush before his election, Sudan and US involvement in the resolution of the conflict began to accumulate traction almost immediately after Graham's visit to the Oval Office after Bush moved into the White House (Natsios, 2012: 166). US involvement materialised into action on 6 September 2001 with the appointment of Senator (and Episcopalian minister) John Danforth as Special Envoy for Peace in the Sudan.

While the administration's interest in Sudan seems to have been motivated by the President's sense of idealism, Assistant Secretary for African Affairs, Walter Kansteiner, outlined several other justifications in his testimony before the House Committee on International Relations on 5 June 2002:

> We will seek to deny Sudan as a base of operations for international terrorism even as we work to bring about a just and lasting peace, push for unhindered humanitarian access, and improved human rights and religious freedom. These goals represent a complex balancing act which I will try to make a bit clearer through my remarks. What I hope is immediately clear is the need for your continued support as we aggressively pursue an end to the suffering which has tragically marked the lives of too many Sudanese people.
>
> (Kansteiner, 2002)

In addition to Evangelical idealism and the war on terror, some scholars tie the new American interest in Sudan to its booming oil production since 1999 (see, for example, Huliaras, 2006: 721–723 and references).

The efforts invested by the administration to resolve the conflict in Sudan, most importantly naming a special envoy and a team of experts to support him, were not repeated in attempts to resolve other civil strife in Africa (Copson, 2007: 90). The intersection of the war on terrorism, access to oil and evangelical activism brought about the US involvement in bringing about the Comprehensive Peace Agreement (CPA) of 2005.[14]

### The Millennium Challenge Corporation

Another important American initiative in relation to the general concept of granting development assistance was the creation of the MCC. As a new and independent US foreign aid agency for the fight against global poverty, the MCC created the MCA, a bilateral development fund which still serves as an important source of development assistance for certain African countries. While the MCC is not generally referred to directly as a part of the GWOT, some scholars indicate that it is one of the tools in the holistic approach that recognises the links between poverty and terrorism and which targets the reduction of security risks by helping eligible developing countries to address governance, human rights and economic growth issues (See, for example, ICG, 2005: 29; Owusu, 2007). This is in addition to the initial linkage between poverty and terrorism made by the President when he announced the establishment of the new agency. In this respect, Acting Assistant Secretary of State for African Affairs, Charles Snyder,[15] stated during a conference on US National Security Interests in Africa that:

> The foundation of an effective long-term strategy is not security assistance by itself, but rather programs that promote justice and the rule of law, encourage agricultural production, and foster lasting economic development. With that in mind, the Millennium Challenge Account, which the President announced two years ago, represents a creative new approach to foreign assistance. It will form a critical part of our long-range counter-terrorism strategy.
>
> (Snyder quoted in Ellis, 2004)

The main rationale behind the MCC is similar to the one often invoked during the Clinton administration. While Clinton focused on encouraging democratic and free market principles through development assistance, Bush used the MCC to measure eligibility for US development assistance[16] according to the presence of democracy and free market principles.[17] Generally, through the MCC, the US grants support to countries which can demonstrate an investment in their people, rule justly and advance economic freedom (Copson, 2007: 28; MCC, 2014; Nowels, 2003: 2; Tarnoff, 2010: 2).

Conceptually, the MCC was intended to be different from other US foreign assistance mechanisms on several levels (Tarnoff, 2010: 1–2):

- In the MCC process, countries' performances are measured by 17 indicators that determine eligibility for US assistance using a competitive process.
- While aid funds are usually influenced by US foreign policy interest, the MCC funds were intended to be independent and based on strict criteria and indicators.
- Programme proposals for the MCC are to be developed by the requesting countries with strong involvement of civil society.
- Countries applying for an MCC compact are responsible for the implementation of their MCC-funded programmes.

Eligibility for an MCC compact does not guarantee assistance. Once a country qualifies for assistance, it must submit a plan for review by the MCC board. The plan must be designed and implemented with civil society in order to work toward the support of economic growth and poverty reduction. The idea of the MCC was intended to induce a 'transformational development' process (Copson, 2007: 29), by encouraging countries to reform their policies to be able to apply for and receive substantial aid grants from the US.[18] By the end of the Bush administration, the MCC had signed compacts with nine African countries (Benin, Burkina Faso, Ghana, Lesotho, Madagascar,[19] Mali, Mozambique, Senegal and Tanzania) and five Threshold programmes (Kenya, Liberia, Niger, Sao Tome–Principe and Uganda).

According to the Bush administration the underlying causes and effects of underdevelopment provided fertile ground for terrorist ideologies as well as a relatively safe operational environment for terrorist activities. The African context allowed terrorists to target important Western interests and take control of vast regions, resources and populations. While initially the American approach rested heavily on military-led assistance, over the years the administration moved towards better co-ordination between the various government agencies to produce a more effective African policy.

### 'Africa's future is up to Africans'

When Obama was elected President of the US, the main author was conducting research in Uganda. In daily contact with many Ugandans ranging from poor villagers, through middle-class workers, to highly educated well-off city dwellers he was struck by their excitement over the election of an African-American as President of the US. The discourse in the media portrayed Barack Obama as not just the President of the US, but as an African. The conversations about Obama revolved around hopes for an elevated importance of Africa on the international agenda now that an

'African' dwelled in the White House. Ugandans viewed him as the son of a fellow African from neighbouring Kenya with immediate family still living on the continent.

Obama was certainly proud, both of his African heritage and of his personal story realising the 'American dream' (see, for example, Obama, 2008; Obama, 2008a: 283). He emphasised his heritage as a candidate for the Senate in 2004[20] and as a presidential candidate in 2008,[21] referring to his father's modest beginnings in Kenya, his education in the US, and the fact that he himself rose to the leadership of the most powerful country on earth.

With this background in mind, the entrance of Obama into the White House raised hopes in Africa and among Africanists in the US that America's policy towards the continent would gain more prominence (Schraeder, 2011: 305; Wiley, 2010: 16). These expectations were enhanced after Obama appointed known Africanists to many key positions. Susan Rice, the former Assistant Secretary of State for African Affairs under the Clinton administration, was appointed as the US Ambassador to the United Nations. Gayle Smith, a former journalist who was based in Africa for over 20 years, had been Clinton's senior director for African affairs at the NSC, and had occupied senior positions at USAID, was now re-appointed to the NSC by Obama. Johnnie Carson, a former ambassador to several African countries was appointed to the position of Assistant Secretary of State for African Affairs, and Samantha Power, a scholar with expertise in human rights who wrote a critical account of the US inaction during the Rwandan genocide and the slaughter in Darfur, was appointed Senior Director for Multinational Affairs at the NSC.[22]

In July 2009 Obama travelled to Africa where he delivered the 'Accra Speech' entitled 'A New Moment of Promise'. This was the first of three trips conducted during his tenure, more than any other American President. His speech in Accra outlined his vision for Africa's future based on the promotion of democracy, human rights and good governance. Invoking his African heritage, Obama stressed that the continent was not only close to his heart, but also important to America's prosperity and security. The speech underlined a basic premise of the Obama policy towards Africa: 'Africa's future is up to Africans' (Obama, 2009a). But despite a rhetoric emphasising that he did not wish to 'impose any system of government on any other nation', Obama did outline a main ingredient that must be in place for a better future – good governance: 'Africa doesn't need strongmen, it needs strong institutions.' (Obama, 2009a). He then proceeded to discuss the various areas in need of better governance, and by extension, how the US would invest its assistance dollars in the years to come: fighting corruption, advancing human rights, mitigating climate change and its effects on underdevelopment, fight emerging diseases, investing in development of the energy sector, and help building capacity in Africa to combat transnational threats and mitigate internal conflicts.

Over the next years these promises translated into a strengthening of initiatives installed by his predecessors such as PEPFAR and the extension of AGOA, as well as creating new initiatives such as Feed the Future, Trade Africa, the Young African Leaders Initiative (YALI), and Power Africa.

But what Obama outlined as his vision during the Accra Speech was not actually different from Bush's African policy (van de Walle, 2009: 17). As pointed out in an editorial published in *The Economist* shortly after Obama's address,[23] what stood out in his Accra speech was the omission of explicit rhetoric linking Africa to the war on terror and to the growing American dependency on African oil.[24] This omission was consistent with Obama's overall strategy of shifting towards a 'smart power' approach to foreign policy in an attempt to mitigate the drain of American power caused by Bush's unilateral application of his doctrine.

A month after Obama's speech in Accra, Secretary of State Hillary Clinton embarked on a seven-nation tour of the continent to 'highlight the Obama administration's commitment to making Africa a priority in US foreign policy'.[25] The tour began in Kenya where Clinton attended the eighth AGOA forum, and continued to South Africa, Angola, the DRC, Nigeria, Liberia and Cape Verde.

Throughout her trip, Clinton emphasised the need for good governance and strong democratic institutions in Africa, paying particular attention to fighting corruption. An article in the Washington Post published on 15 August 2009 concluded that despite Secretary Clinton's Africa tour, the relative importance of Africa in relation to other areas of the world remained unclear. Nevertheless, the article stated, the Africa agenda was influenced by the administration's understanding of the importance of Africa as an oil supplier, and a potential harbour for terrorism and transnational crimes, a reality linked to weak governance and fragile states (Sheridan, 2009). The main purposes of the trip was to ease tensions with South Africa, the strongest economy on the continent, and with Angola, 'a rising oil power whose leaders fought US-backed rebels during the Cold War' (Sheridan, 2009). One of the central messages the Secretary repeated during her tour was that the administration would continue to support the PEPFAR initiative and the MCC mandate, as well as expand US outreach with new initiatives. As such, the Obama administration signalled that there would be a strong measure of continuity extending from the African policy of the Bush administration. On several occasions during her tour, Secretary Clinton was met with cynicism anchored in the past involvement of the US in Africa (Sheridan, 2009).

Five elements became the core of the Obama administration's Africa Policy.[26] The first and most important element was to help Africa strengthen its democratic institutions and improve governance. Democracy was seen as a crucial element for long-term stability and the development of the continent. During a speech before the African Union in Addis Ababa on 13 June 2011, Clinton openly condemned African leaders (without naming them) for their preoccupation with securing the longevity of their rule, associating this practice with self-interest rather than engaging with the needs of people (Clinton, 2011). She underlined the statement made by Obama emphasising the need to promote strong institutions rather than strong men. '[T]he old ways of governing are no longer acceptable', said Clinton. 'It is time for leaders to lead with accountability, treat their people with dignity, respect their rights, and deliver economic opportunity.' (Clinton, 2011).

Helping Africa to improve its economic performance and undertake reforms to ensure the growth of economies was the second element. The development of the vast natural resources on the continent, especially oil, gas and minerals was seen as fundamental for the growth of African economies. The role of development programmes in this respect was to create strong institutions and 'spark economic activity', encourage investment by the private sector, and facilitate the creation of jobs (Clinton, 2011). But as Clinton emphasised, in order to maximise these efforts, there is a need to battle the corruption and lack of transparency which plagues the political, enforcement and private sectors in Africa (Clinton, 2011).

The third element was to work with Africa to mitigate, prevent and resolve crises. In 2011, countries including Sudan, Somalia, and Eastern Congo were viewed as significant sources of political, economic and social instability on the continent.[27] The absence of stability was considered one of the main causes behind the lack of ability to spur economic growth and promote strong democratic institutions in many African nations. A fourth element was to continue supporting the improvement of public health on the continent. The PEPFAR initiative of the Bush administration was supplemented through the GHI and it expanded US support to combat malaria, tuberculosis, cholera and other diseases. A prominent objective of this element in the African policy was to strengthen Africa's public health institutions.

The fifth and final core element was to strengthen the collaboration to help African countries to deal with a variety of transnational challenges. This element covered a wide array of issues from climate change to proliferation, including narcotics-trafficking, maritime security, trafficking of people and terrorist threats. The emphasis of this element was based on multilateral cooperation because these issues transcended national borders. The emphasis of the administration on democratic institutions and the fight against corruption was, and still is, heavily related to this element of policy towards Africa.

These five core elements matured into four foundations of US policy towards sub-Saharan Africa. These formed the basis of a strategy document published by the US government in June 2012, shortly before the elections leading to Obama's second term. This was the first published US strategy regarding sub-Saharan Africa, and signalled the administration's commitment to elevate the status of the African policy. The document listed four pillars and a commitment to improve US efforts to promote the first two (Obama, 2012: preamble):

1   Strengthen democratic institutions.
2   Spur economic growth, trade and investment.
3   Advance peace and security.
4   Promote opportunity and development.

Strengthening of democratic institutions was a foundational strategy linked to the NSS published in 2010 by the administration, and was described as 'critical to US interests, and ... a fundamental component of American leadership abroad' (Obama, 2012: 2). As outlined by Obama in the preamble to the African strategy:

> Strong, accountable, and democratic institutions, sustained by a deep commitment to the rule of law, generate greater prosperity and stability, and meet with greater success in mitigating conflict and ensuring security. Sustainable, inclusive economic growth is a key ingredient to security, political stability, and development, and it underpins efforts to alleviate poverty, creating the resources that will bolster opportunity and allow individuals to reach their full potential.
> (Obama, 2012: preamble)

Obama's message was that the US would stand fast by its commitment to bolster democratic governance in Africa, and not allow subversive elements, be they internal or external, to undermine democratic institutions in Africa. The strategy suggested that the administration should address Africa's problems in a holistic fashion, understanding the circular links between lack of democracy, lack of development, lack of economic progress, weak institutions, corruption and the ability to address security threats. To encourage American investment for economic growth in Africa, to secure steady and reliable access to the natural resources on the continent, and to bolster investment in development, there was a need for some sort of stability and long-term predictability on political, economic, and security issues.

Despite the intention to elevate the status of the African policy in relation to other issues, the inherited reality from the Bush administration imposed constraints during the first years of Obama's presidency. Other pressing issues such as the domestic economic crisis and ongoing engagements in Iraq and Afghanistan occupied a position of prominence on the President's agenda (Wiley, 2010: 20). Schraeder (2011: 307–311) mentions several additional constraints to Obama's intention to elevate the status of the African policy, including the 'historical White House neglect of the African continent' due to a continuous need to attend to matters in other regions of the world. This entrenched an institutional bias that continuously prioritised other issues over Africa, leaving precious little time for the President to deal with African issues (Schraeder, 2011: 308). This was supplemented by 'historical congressional neglect of the African continent' (Schraeder, 2011: 309), meaning that the government's legislative branch often attached more importance to other regions of the world and to domestic issues than to the African continent. Most of the African policy was therefore left in the hands of the bureaucracies (Schraeder, 2011: 311), with minimal involvement of the White House and Congress. In most cases, presidential or congressional attention would be given to Africa only when issues required special attention, such as a humanitarian crisis or an impending national security issue relating to the US or its allies.[28] In the opinion of various DoS officials,[29] Obama's African strategy stemmed from a genuine and continuous intention to change that reality. The Bush administration began to recognise the importance of Africa through the lenses of the GWOT. Its engagement with the continent was based on the unilateral characteristics of the Bush doctrine. Obama wanted to continue the trend of recognising the importance of Africa and US policy towards the continent. He acknowledged that some of the policies installed during the Bush administration were effective in terms of raising the importance of the continent, and he built upon them to continue elevating the importance of Africa. Nevertheless, Obama wanted to entrench a partnership approach 'grounded in mutual responsibility and mutual respect' (Obama, 2009) to tackle the challenges of the continent rather than a unilateral, paternalistic approach driven by the need to fight the GWOT that seemed to characterise the Bush policy.

Trying to change that pattern was described by a Bush official who observed that the US consciously granted assistance to African countries putting on a show of democracy to secure US assistance rather than having real and transparent institutions.[30] Assistant Secretary Johnnie Carson indicated that this was exactly what Obama wanted to change:

> We have stood up for democracy and human rights publicly and behind the scenes – often when taking such positions was unpopular. Our message to those who attempted to derail the democratic process has been clear: Africa does not need strongmen, it needs strong institutions, and the United States will not stand on the sidelines when legitimately elected governments are threatened or democratic processes are manipulated.
>
> (Carson, 2013: 318)

This objective proved hard to attain despite a genuine will in the executive branch to elevate the status of the continent. Low priority coupled with constant reductions in expenditures on diplomatic resources, contributed to understaffed embassies in Africa filled with junior staff (van de Walle,

2015: 55–56). Such conditions create a discrepancy between intentions and the ability to implement change.

Like previous administrations, President Obama introduced a number of initiatives designed to create a partnership with Africa to help countries meet challenges and achieve the American vision for the development of the continent. Since the Obama administration had to deal with a severe recession, especially through the first four years of his Presidency, there were subsequent cuts in fund allocations to the MCC and PEPFAR (van de Walle, 2015: 54). To overcome this, the initiatives introduced by the Obama administration were based on encouraging and facilitating private sector investments. The most notable programmes, such as Power Africa, Feed the Future, Trade Africa, YALI, the extension of AGOA, and the African Leaders Summit hosted by the White House in 2014 revolved around encouraging and creating the conditions for current and future private sector investments in Africa which would help the economy and at the same time overcome budgetary cuts.

Towards the end of the first Obama term, Assistant Secretary Carson (2013) flagged many important policy issues which the administration addressed in an attempt to bolster democracy, economic development and stability on the continent. Among the most important security issues that made it to the President's desk were the violence in Sudan, the Islamists in Somalia, the pursuit of Joseph Kony and his Lord's Resistance Army (LRA), the efforts to stabilise the DRC and resolving the crisis in Mali and the Sahel.

*Mali and the Sahel*

The crisis in the Sahel serves as a good example of a failure of American policy based on the Bush doctrine to achieve its objective through the assistance efforts, namely to support and strengthen democracy and to fight terrorism. The events that took place in Mali after 2011 indicate the challenges of promoting American values through assistance, in relation to self-interests and national security objectives in complex geopolitical contexts. While occurring during the Obama administration, these events were rooted in the history of the region, and to some extent, were influenced by the policies of the US during the Bush administration. These dynamics and relationships contributed to the collapse of the Malian regime in 2012. We do not intend to imply here that US policies led to the dynamics in Sahel and subsequently caused the collapse of Mali. The purpose is to indicate how these policies, anchored in the distinct American interpretation of the purpose of foreign assistance, affected an already complex situation.

To understand the unfolding events and the geopolitical context in the Sahel during the Obama administration we need to place the complex dynamics leading to the collapse of the Malian regime in 2012 in historical context.

The Republic of Mali emerged in 1960 after achieving independence from France.[31] After independence, Mali was ruled by Modibo Keïta who led the anti-colonial party US/RDA.[32] From the beginning of its history as an independent state, tensions ran high between the sub-Saharan population of Mali and the Tuareg tribes inhabiting the Sahel and Sahara desert in the north.[33] The many complex reasons for these tensions have historical, societal, racial, ethnic, cultural, and political dimensions, and they are well documented in literature (see, for example, Lecocq, 2010). A key aspiration of several Tuareg clans was the creation of an independent state in northern Mali. This aspiration led to three rebellions[34] against the state of Mali between 1960 and 2011. The brutal crackdown of the Malian government against the Tuareg dissidents crushed the first rebellion, and led to many years of grievance and harsh treatment of the population in the north. The severe droughts during the 1970s and 1980s and the lack of investment by the Malian government in the northern regions enhanced these grievances. As a result, many Tuareg sought refuge and better opportunities in other countries in the Maghreb, West Africa and Europe. In parallel to the tensions between Tuareg rebels in the north and the regime in Bamako, the Malian state suffered from a number of *coups-d'état*. In 1968 the Keïta government was overthrown in a military coup installing Moussa Traoré as the leader of a military committee, and later (in 1974) as the leader of a one-party state. In 1991 the Traoré regime was overthrown in another coup by Amadou Toumani Touré (ATT), the head of Traoré's personal guard, and in connection with a popular demand manifested through protests in Bamako to install a multiparty democracy in the Republic of Mali. When ATT assumed power by force, he promised to move Mali toward democracy. Indeed, a year later, ATT yielded power to a democratically elected civilian government led by President Alpha Oumar Konaré. At that time, ATT was lauded both internationally and domestically for transforming Mali into a truly democratic country, the only one in the region (see, for example, Wing, 2008).

In the meantime, many Tuareg who had left Mali during the drought years were slowly returning from Algeria and Libya to resettle in northern Mali. These returnees did not abandon their aspirations for an independent state, and contributed to increased tensions between Bamako and the north. Eventually a second Tuareg rebellion took place between 1992 and 1996. This rebellion ended in an accord dubbed 'the Peace of Timbuktu' based on an understanding that the government of Mali would loosen its grip on the north, and allow civil society to step in and help create conditions for peace, development, security and better integration of the displaced population in Mali (Poulton and Youssouf, 1998: 85–123). The process included the integration of Tuareg leaders and fighters into the Malian government and army, as well as the disarmament of armed rebel groups (Poulton and Youssouf, 1998: 85–123).

In 2002, ATT who gave Mali its democracy through his coup in 1991, was democratically elected as president of the republic. During that time, the US was engaged in the post-9/11 war against terrorism around the globe. A number of events involving the Sahara desert and Mali brought the fight against terror and Al-Qaida to the western regions of Africa.

The association of this region with the GWOT began in 2003 when the Algerian Islamic Salafist Group for Preaching and Combat (GSPC) began abducting Western tourists venturing in the Sahara region of Algeria. The GSPC was an Islamist organisation whose members were involved in fighting against the Algerian regime since 1991[35] with the purpose of replacing the government in Algeria with an Islamic state. The tourists abducted by the GSPC in 2003 were held captive for ransom in the vast spaces of the Sahara desert between Algeria, Mali, and Niger. Against this background, the American Pan-Sahel Initiative and subsequently its successor, the TSCTP, were established by the US to help train local troops to combat terrorism and the GSPC threat. The schemes included the provision of funds for local governments for development programmes designed to help counter extremism. While these initiatives helped local governments to fight the GSPC and eventually capture its leader, they did not manage to stop the abduction of Western tourists and the subsequent payment of large sums of ransom money by various European governments to secure their release.

As the West assisted the governments of West Africa to combat terror, bin Laden's deputy at that time,[36] Ayman al-Zawahiri, announced in 2006 that the GSPC had become part of bin Laden's organisation. In 2007 the GSPC was rebranded as Al-Qaida in the Maghreb (AQIM), thus aligning itself with Osama bin Laden and his war against the West. As such, combating AQIM in West Africa became a central strategic objective for the newly-formed AFRICOM, and the Sahara–Sahel stretch became another front of the American war on terror (see references in Keenan, 2009: 214 note 1).

In addition to the terrorist threat, a substantial increase in transnational crime occurred in the region, especially the trafficking of cannabis and cocaine. The Sahara was increasingly being used by criminal organisations as transition corridors for illicit goods and human trafficking towards the Middle East and Europe. According to a number of sources,[37] members of the Tuareg tribes, AQIM (and affiliated organisations), local politicians, and members of the Malian government were in collusion with these criminal organisations, and profited from the illicit traffic of drugs, arms, and humans in the Sahara. The ties between Malian politicians and the criminal activity in the Sahara included profits generated from various forms of mediation leading to the payment of large ransom by European countries to free their hijacked nationals (see, for example, Lacher, 2013: 69–75).

A third Tuareg rebellion emerged between 2007 and 2009. This rebellion began as the Tuareg population expressed their dissatisfaction with the implementation of the Peace of Timbuktu, specifically with the government in Bamako who failed to invest resources in the north. Among their claims was that some Tuareg leaders, now in charge of the governance of the northern areas on behalf of the government of Mali, were involved in all sorts of corruption. These accusations were directed at Tuareg elites residing and working in Bamako and charged them with being in collusion with criminal organisations, as well as diverting aid money to line their own pockets. The rebellion led to several clashes between the Malian army and Tuareg rebel groups. The hostilities ended when the Malian government reached an agreement with a large faction of rebels via Algerian mediation. A smaller faction of rebels led by the Tuareg leader Ibrahim ag Bahanga, opposed this agreement and fled to exile in Libya. Ibrahim ag Bahanga would be one of the leaders of a fourth rebellion which began in 2011 and eventually led to the collapse of Mali in 2012.

Against this setting, the Obama administration entered into the geopolitical reality of the Sahara. In 2010, the popular uprisings known as the 'Arab Spring' took place in various locations in north Africa. In Libya, protests against the rule of Qaddafi led to the collapse of his regime, and his death in October 2011. As a result, several hundred Tuareg who had served in Qaddafi's army began their journey to return to Mali. Among them was Ibrahim ag Bahanga, who allied himself with the Malian diaspora in Libya and helped rally their leadership around the idea of creating a free independent state in northern Mali. Well trained and organised as organic military units with relatively sophisticated weapons, these Tuareg moved back into Mali and formed the National Movement for the Liberation of Azawad (MNLA), resurrecting the struggle for an independent state in the north. Between October 2011 and January 2012, the MNLA formed an alliance with AQIM and the Movement for Oneness and Jihad in West Africa (MUJAO),[38] and began a fourth rebellion against the Malian government by attacking and brutally executing Malian soldiers stationed in the northern city of Gao.[39] On 21 March 2012, the Tuareg Islamist organisation Ansar Dine was formed by Iyad ag Ghaly, a Tuareg elder who was one of the leaders of the uprising against the Malian government in the 1990s. Ansar Dine proceeded by seising control of key towns on the Mali–Algeria border, taking many Malian soldiers as prisoners and capturing their bases and weapons.

Displeased with the management of the conflict by the Malian president, family members of captured and slain Malian soldiers marched in protest in the streets of Bamako. A group of soldiers led by a young army officer named Amadou Sanogo led a *coup d'état* on 22 March 2012, ousting President ATT and installing a military junta,[40] ending two decades of democratic governance. Capitalising on the confusion and chaos in Bamako, the MNLA (backed by the Islamist organisations AQIM, MUJAO and Ansar Dine) quickly consolidated their control of the regions of

Timbuktu, Kidal and Gao declaring an independent state called Azawad on 5 April 2012.

One of the destabilising factors that led to the collapse of Mali, related to the formation of the MNLA by Tuareg veterans serving in Qaddafi's army returning to Mali after the collapse of Libya. Leaving aside political and normative questions relating to UN Security Council Resolution 1973 which adopted provisions of Chapter VII to authorise military action in Libya against Qaddafi's forces,[41] the collapse of the Libyan regime led to a change in the balance of power in Mali. While the US did not assume a leadership role in the UN-led operations against Qaddafi, it certainly supported the operation both logistically and militarily. One of the results of this operation was the return of armed Tuareg veterans to Mali and the beginning of the fourth uprising against the Malian regime.

Another important observation relates to the collapse of the Malian army in the north. The Malian army benefitted for many years from US military assistance which included training under the PSI and TSCTP to combat terrorism. US assistance included military and civilian training modules in democracy and the role of the military in upholding the democratic institutions of a country. In terms of combating terrorism, the Malian army failed almost immediately, disintegrating in the face of the MNLA, AQIM, MUJAO and Ansar Dine virtually without a fight. While unable to combat terrorism in the north, the same Malian army when led by an officer trained by the US (Arieff, 2013: 7),[42] turned against the Malian government and toppled a democratically elected regime four months before elections.[43] This series of events raises important questions about the efficiency and effectiveness of the American projection of power in the region since 2003. It is important to note that Mali was an MCC compact country, selected as a beneficiary mainly because it constituted a model for democracy in the region. The fact that various US officials indicated in interviews that it was clear that several members of the Malian government (including President ATT) and military officers were in collusion, to varying degrees, with organised crime in the north,[44] raises further questions concerning the efficiency, effectiveness and moral basis for the assistance policy during the Bush administration. In terms of American foreign policy interests, the situation in Mali presented the Obama administration with four overlapping concerns: a deteriorating humanitarian crisis instigated by the conflict; the loss of a democratic partner in the region (and by extension, the legal necessity to halt all American assistance to that country[45]); renewed tensions between the northern and southern populations of Mali; and the presence of AQIM and other Islamic organisations in the vast desert regions of northern Mali[46] (Carson, 2012). This led to an accelerated militarisation of US policy in the Sahel region (van de Walle, 2015: 56), and the greatest increase of US military footprint on the continent (Moore and Walker, 2016: 701). Events in Mali weakened the entire Sahel, as well as undermining US strategic objectives in the region. True to his conviction of modifying the way America interacted with the world, Obama's militarisation of US foreign policy on the African continent occurred through cooperation with African governments as well as European allies. In other words, the administration aim was to take a back-seat, and assist France's visible leadership of a militarised intervention. Nevertheless, the US continued to project power in Africa while minimising political flak and the need to use American soldiers (van de Walle, 2015: 56).

To help contain the escalating situation in the Sahel, France had launched operation Serval in January 2013. The French effort to fend off Islamic rebels in the Malian desert was backed with an extensive American support operation spearheaded by AFRICOM, providing crucial airlift, tanker support and intelligence to the French military and the African troops fighting alongside (Moore and Walker, 2016: 703). In parallel, the US continued to use the TSCTP to fund activities by the DoD, DoS and USAID in efforts to support livelihood, education, messages of tolerance and support youth employment with the aim of propagating peace through development (GAO, 2014).

## Sudan

On 3 January 2014, Mark Landler from the *New York Times*, wrote:

> South Sudan is in many ways an American creation, carved out of war-torn Sudan in a referendum largely orchestrated by the United States, its fragile institutions nurtured with billions of dollars in American aid.
> (Landler, 2014)

The Republic of South Sudan became an independent state on 9 July 2011, following a referendum scheduled by the CPA, and an agreement negotiated through American, British and Norwegian mediation during the years of the Bush administration. During the second Obama administration, a civil war erupted within the Republic of South Sudan, linked to ethnic tensions between the Nuer and Dinka tribes. Princeton Lyman, who served as Obama's second special envoy to Sudan said during an interview with TV channel *France 24* on 14 January 2014 that:

> The reason we felt the referendum had to go forward was that if it didn't go forward on time, civil war would likely have resumed. And the overwhelming attention then was to end the civil war between the North and South. Now there were people then saying this SPLM were not up to leading this country. Well a lot of assistance was being given to them to build that capacity, not only from the U.S. and Europe, but also Ugandans, Kenyans, Ethiopians were there training. Where we did not exert direct influence, and it would have been hard to do so,

was within the ruling party, where these divisions and eruptions took place. And we couldn't really get a handle during this period on the fact that the national army was really a coalition of militias, not really an integrated army.

(Lyman, 2014)[47]

Sudan had been a high priority on Obama's African agenda since the beginning of the administration. The American involvement in Sudan during the Bush administration was of material importance for achieving the CPA. Despite the CPA, the Bashir government continued to employ violence against the civilian population in Darfur. This led the US Senate to adopt in 2006 a resolution[48] co-sponsored by Obama, Clinton and Biden (who were senators at the time) to call upon the Bush administration to assume concrete steps to end the violence of Khartoum against the civilian population in Darfur (Blanchard, 2012: 27). As a senator, Obama had stated that it was a 'moral imperative' of the US to ensure that crimes against humanity in Darfur were stopped (Blanchard, 2012: 27). As a president, Obama assumed a hard stance against President Bashir's policy in Darfur (see, for example, DoS, 2009).

According to the terms of the CPA, the southern region of Sudan, which fought a civil war led by the SPLA against the government in Khartoum, would vote in a referendum scheduled for 2011 on the separation of the south from the north and the creation of the independent state of South Sudan.

Two months into his Presidency, Obama appointed Scott Gration, a retired air force major general, as a special envoy to Sudan. In October 2009, after a comprehensive review process initiated by Gration, the DoS announced its new policy towards Sudan (Blanchard, 2012: 27). The announcement explained why Sudan was an important policy issue for the US:

> Sudan's implosion could lead to widespread regional instability or new safe-havens for international terrorists, significantly threatening U.S. interests. The United States has a clear obligation to the Sudanese people – both in our role as witness to the Comprehensive Peace Agreement, and as the first country that unequivocally identified events in Darfur as genocide – to help lead an international effort.
>
> (DoS, 2009)

The main justifications for the Sudan policy were highlighted in the statement: national security and moral imperatives. As noted by Dagne (2011: 8–9) and Smith (2013: 342), the relations between the US and Sudan had been strained since the early seventies. The renewed attention beginning with the Bush administration and continuing with the Obama administration was largely driven by the GWOT and a sense of moral responsibility as a reaction to the genocide in Darfur and the pressure exercised on President Bush by evangelical organisations (Huliaras, 2008: 170–171). The US added Sudan to the list of states sponsoring terrorism during the Clinton administration in 1993.[49] Since then, Sudan has been involved in granting asylum and training to members of several terror organisations, actively participating and sponsoring terror plots, and harbouring arch terrorists like Osama bin Laden.[50] In the context of the GWOT and the history of Sudan in relation to terrorism, an American policy towards that country needed to convince Sudan to move away from its role as a state sponsor of terror (Smith, 2013: 343). Since Sudan is located in a sensitive geographical location, American policymakers feared that further fragmentation of that country, should it collapse, would have devastating effects on the GWOT and regional efforts to contain insurgency and terrorism in countries across the Sahel from Somalia to Mali (Smith, 2013: 343). A peaceful political settlement to the conflict in Sudan was therefore seen as a sound policy choice to help create stability and resolve a long political and ethnic conflict.

The new policy towards Sudan announced by the Obama administration in 2009 had three strategic objectives (DoS, 2009):

1  Protecting civilians and the end of the conflict in Darfur.
2  Promoting the CPA, resolving open issues in the CPA, and helping to create a democratic South Sudan living peacefully with its neighbour in the north.
3  Preventing Sudan from descending into chaos and becoming a hub for warlords and terrorists.

To achieve these objectives, the policy stated that the US was prepared to provide both bilateral and multilateral assistance, including military, economic and development assistance (DoS, 2009). In terms of the promotion of governance and transparency in South Sudan, the policy stated that:

> The United States will work to improve security for the southern Sudanese people by supporting DDR[51] and conflict prevention initiatives and strengthening the capacity of the security sector and criminal justice system. The United States will also work to improve economic conditions and outcomes. The United States will provide technical advisors to vital ministries and will work to strengthen entities such as the U.N. Development Program's Local Government Reform Program (LGRP). The United States will work with international partners to implement the World Bank Multi-Donor Trust Fund South Strategy in a timely manner and to improve access to capital, particularly microfinancing, for agricultural enterprises and local private sector ventures. The United States will support efforts and initiatives that assist in

increasing trade between Sudan and its neighbors. Transparency in fiscal expenditures will be critical to attracting investment, and the United States will support World Bank anticorruption efforts in Southern Sudan.

(DoS, 2009)

Special envoy Gration worked consistently with Bashir's National Congress Party (NCP) ruling in the north and with the Sudan People's Liberation Movement (SPLM)[52] in the south to keep the CPA on track and advance US policy objectives. In September 2010, the Obama administration introduced a new policy initiative on Sudan which included a number of incentives to Bashir's government to continue moving towards fully implementing the CPA and securing a peaceful resolution for the Darfur conflict. These incentives included the proposition to ease sanctions and restrictions against the Sudan government, steps towards removing Sudan from the State Sponsors of Terrorism list, and increase US diplomatic presence in Sudan (Dagne, 2011: 11–12).

In January 2011 after a successful referendum, the government of Sudan agreed to respect the outcome and the wishes of the people of South Sudan, thus paving the way for establishing the Republic of South Sudan as an independent state. The separation of the Sudan into two states was scheduled for July 2011. In March 2011, Scott Gration[53] was replaced with Princeton Lyman as special envoy to the Sudan. Despite the referendum, a number of crucial issues remained on the table. Among these were the unresolved conflict in Darfur; the future status of the disputed border areas of Abyei, Blue Nile and the Nuba Mountain region; debt sharing; and oil-related issues. The status of Abyei was more complicated due to historical ethnic rivalries in this border region between the north and the south, and the fact that it was an oil-rich area and an important source of income for both the north, and the future South Sudan (Natsios, 2012: 172).

Many conflicts erupted between Sudan and South Sudan during 2011 to 2013 in relation to these unresolved issues. In addition to these, in December 2013, an internal power struggle inside the government of South Sudan led to violent confrontations and fragmentation within the country (see Blanchard, 2014). While the struggle between President Salva Kiir (a Dinka) and his Vice President, Riek Machar (a Nuer) reflected the internal ethnic rivalries, the roots of the conflict are deep and complicated, and include internal rivalries and power struggles within the SPLA since the 1990s, and Machar's subsequent alliance with Bashir during those years (Blanchard, 2014: 6). At the end of 2016, the situation in South Sudan remains tense, and the possibility of South Sudan becoming a failed state looms large. In an article published in 2013, Princeton Lyman wrote that Sudanese officials had warned him in 2011 that the internal rivalries in South Sudan would lead to an implosion of that country:

You Westerners will be sorry. You are so supportive of South Sudan's right to self-determination. But you will see that South Sudan will not be governable. It will be torn apart by ethnic divisions and the SPLM will prove incapable of governing. What you will get is a failed state.

(Quoted in Lyman, 2013: 335)

Before the secession of South Sudan from the Sudan, the country was one of the top global recipients of US foreign aid in terms of bilateral, emergency and humanitarian assistance, as well as hosting ongoing UN peacekeeping operations (Blanchard, 2012: 30). During the Obama administration, South Sudan has been one of the largest beneficiaries of US aid in Africa (Blanchard, 2014: 15). Assistance is being given to South Sudan to achieve the objectives of the policy, including 'to reduce ethnic tensions in the south, speed up development programmes, and improve government performance' (Carson, 2013: 320). US bilateral assistance to South Sudan is channelled through different mechanisms, with most funds being allocated through the Economic Support Fund to promote economic and political stability, through USAID's Global Health Program, and through peacekeeping operations (Blanchard, 2014: 17). With the onset of internal rivalries, the future of US assistance is subject to restrictions and remains unclear. From a current perspective, US assistance to South Sudan since its independence has not achieved its objectives of reducing ethnic tensions, spurring economic growth, or helping to create a viable and transparent government in the south.

## *Somalia*

Another US foreign policy priority during the Obama administration was Somalia. Somalia was plunged into anarchy with the collapse of the Barre regime in 1992. Fighting between various warlords brought about American-led UN operations to ensure the deliverance of humanitarian aid to the Somali people (UNITAF under the George H. W. Bush administration), and the failed mission to reconstruct Somalia and fend off warlords (UNSOM II under the Clinton administration). After the US pulled its troops out of Somalia in March 1994, the country suffered from fragmentation, chaos and clan-based violence. Many attempts to reconcile the fighting factions in Somalia and restore a central government have been initiated by various African countries since 1996. In 2004 after several attempts to form a central authority and continuous clashes, the Transnational Federal Government (TFG) was formed but did not manage to inspire unity and defeat the warlords until the end of 2006 during a joint Ethiopian and TFG military campaign.

During the Bush administration, the Somalia policy was focused on combating terror. Within these efforts the administration (through the CIA) supplied payments to warlords to turn over terror suspects, encouraging Ethiopia to intervene militarily in that country, and conducting US air strikes against the Islamic Court Union (ICU), who enforced Sharia law on parts of Somalia and fought against the TFG (Copson, 2007: 89).

True to its purpose of changing the unilateral fashion in which America addressed global challenges, the Obama administration opted for a constructive way forward in Somalia. Until October 2010, Obama had supported the so-called Djibouti Peace Process, which focused on stabilising Somalia through the TFG. But minimal progress made by the TFG over the years, as well as accusations of corruption from within the TFG, led the US to adopt a 'dual track' approach to Somalia.[54]

As explained by Assistant Secretary Carson in a presentation of the dual track policy on 20 October 2010,[55] the ongoing chaos in Somalia during the past two decades has escalated from a local problem, to a regional challenge, to a global concern which represents a grave political and security problem. The instability in Somalia has created a humanitarian crisis that spills into neighbouring countries, affecting their politics, economy and security. For example, in 2010, Kenya hosted more than 300,000 Somali refugees who strained the country's infrastructure and resources. Somali piracy, rooted in the problems on land, has had a global impact which burdens the international community. By 2010 over 450 ships were taken by pirates and many hostages were held for ransom. Ships and prisoners were released against large sums of money, which was used to further finance warlords and criminal activity. To protect commerce, the international community dispatched a significant number of navy ships at great cost to protect civilian shipping lanes in the Red Sea and off the coast of Somalia.

In addition, Somalia had become a safe haven for criminals and terror organisations. The Somali Islamist organisation Al-Shabab, a splinter of the ICU, took control over large areas of Somalia, enforced Sharia law, and conducted terror operations inside Somalia and in neighbouring countries, thus creating both local and regional destabilisation. A number of Al-Qaida operatives also took refuge in Somalia, including some of the organisers of the 1998 American embassy bombings in Nairobi and Dar es Salaam (Dagne, 2011a: 1).

Assistant Secretary Carson explained that to counter these threats, a global co-ordinated effort was needed. He emphasised that there could not be a solution for Somalia based on the interests and efforts of a single country. He underlined that the US would continue to work and co-ordinate its efforts with the international community to help Somalia find long-term solutions and promote policies to enhance stability, security, economic recovery, development and address the humanitarian crisis in Somalia.

As outlined by Carson, the dual track approach consisted first of continued support to the TFG and government institutions, including support to the African Union Mission to Somalia (AMISOM) and the UN. This first track was in essence a continuation of the humanitarian, development, economic, military and educational support the US had provided since 2009. The main purpose of this track was to back the institutional development of the TFG and help make it more effective, inclusive and financially transparent. Nevertheless, Carson indicated that some leaders of the TFG were corrupt and concerned with safeguarding their power and profit rather than governing the country. For this reason, and since the US recognised the complex nature of the Somali society and politics, a second policy track would be developed in parallel to the first.

The essence of the second track was to extend US support and assistance to the autonomous regional governments of Somaliland and Puntland, as well as to other smaller units opposing the Al-Shabab organisation. Carson indicated that the US would seek and support those governments and units, and would allow more diplomats and USAID experts to travel to areas controlled by those governments to engage directly with local officials and initiate small-scale development projects. The relative stability of these areas was viewed by the US as a contribution to regional stability. Carson praised the free democratic election that took place in Somaliland in 2010 and the peaceful transition to a new government.

As a coastal region located on the horn and with a coastline situated on the Gulf of Aden and the Indian Ocean, Puntland was an essential partner in the fight against piracy. Carson indicated that the US wanted to forge a relationship with the leaders of Puntland, in order to assist the government and NGOs working there to address the root causes of instability and piracy. With regard to other local governments, Carson explained that the US would extend its support to those who opposed and fought Al-Shabab in order to reduce the instability of Somalia, with emphasis on development assistance to combat the root causes of instability.

One of the elements of the policy was the fact that America understood it could not achieve success in Somalia by acting alone. This was a consistent feature of American foreign policy rhetoric under Obama, focusing on multilateralism and the doctrine of leading from behind[56] (see, for example, Holmes and Carafano, 2010).

By the end of 2012, it appeared that America's Somalian policy had paid off. Carson (2013: 321) points out that Al-Shabab had been degraded, Al-Qaida members killed, the TFG dissolved, a new president elected, and a new constitution adopted. In June 2012, Carson was the first American diplomat to visit Somalia since the battle of Mogadishu in 1993. Somalia's situation improved 'largely because of American diplomacy and diplomatic partnership with key African states in the region' (Carson, 2013: 321).

### Uganda

Together with Sudan and Somalia, Joseph Kony's LRA received most of the attention of American policymakers during the Obama administration (Carson, 2013: 322). The LRA became a policy priority for many complex reasons, including intense lobbying of advocacy groups, think tanks and the Ugandan government (Carson, 2013: 321; Fisher, 2014). There was also a link between the two other main policy priorities (Sudan and Somalia) and the LRA (White House, 2010: 8).

Since 1987, the LRA insurgency in northern Uganda against President Museveni had caused a massive humanitarian crisis and had led to the displacements of millions. The LRA employed violent tactics such as the massacre of civilians, abduction of children and their employment as soldiers, porters, sex slaves and cooks. They also inflicted severe punishment on civilian populations including mutilations (Arieff and Ploch, 2012: 5; Carson, 2013: 321; Fisher, 2014: 689). Since the 1990s, the LRA received support from the government of Sudan to undermine the Museveni regime in Uganda. In retaliation, Uganda supported Garang and the SPLA in their insurgency against the Bashir government in Sudan. This proxy war between Sudan and Uganda involved many other guerrilla organisations and was largely fought inside the DRC (see Prunier, 2004: 367ff.). The reasons for the conflict between Sudan and Uganda and their support to the LRA and SPLA included ethnic and cultural rivalries linked to the Arab–Muslim dominance of the Sudanese government as opposed to the sub-Saharan African–Christian emphasis of the Ugandan government (Prunier, 2004: 381–382). After signing an agreement in 1999 for the cessation of hostilities and support for rebel groups, Sudan withdrew its support for the LRA (Arieff and Ploch, 2012: 5–6). Ugandan troops were granted permission by Sudan to conduct operations against the LRA on Sudanese territory in 2002 (Arieff and Ploch, 2012: 5–6). The LRA continued to operate in the region, moving its forces between southern Sudan (including Darfur), the DRC, and the Central African Republic (CAR), affecting civilian populations in those countries and contributing to humanitarian disasters and regional instability (White House, 2010: 6).

The US has maintained a close relationship with Museveni's government in Uganda since he rose to power in 1986. Uganda was considered a relatively stable democratic country and a strategic partner of the US, particularly since its major contribution to the AMISOM in 2007 (DoS, 2013). Uganda was viewed by the US as a major contributor to regional stability. During the Clinton and Bush administrations, Museveni worked with the US on terror-related threats in connection with Bashir's government in Sudan, and he alleged a connection between Al-Qaida and the LRA after 9/11 (Arieff and Ploch, 2012: 17; Fisher, 2014: 698). In terms of foreign assistance, Uganda has been receiving important amounts of military and development assistance since the Bush administration, especially through presidential initiatives and USAID (ICG, 2010: 2, footnote 10) despite the government's growing authoritarianism.

The LRA was viewed by many US-based think-tanks, advocacy groups, the Ugandan government, Congress and members of the executive branch as a threat to the regional stability of central Africa (White House, 2010: 8). The objective of the American strategy was to eliminate the LRA threat and to 'positively impact other priorities in the region' (White House, 2010: 8).

In terms of concrete steps to eliminate the LRA threat, the US deployed 100 military personnel to serve as advisors to local forces in their efforts to pursue Kony (Arieff and Ploch, 2012: 10). While these advisors participated in field missions and were combat-equipped, their purpose was to offer information, advice and assistance to the Ugandan, CAR, South Sudanese and DRC forces and would only engage in combat in the capacity of self-defence (Arieff and Ploch, 2012: 10).

In addition to military advisors, the efforts to combat Kony were supplemented by humanitarian relief efforts, building early warning mechanisms and encouraging desertions from the LRA. These relief and capacity-building mechanisms were channelled through USAID bilateral missions and the DoS. They included: rehabilitation of infrastructure, distribution of humanitarian supplies, increase of communication capacities through the provision of radios transmitters and the formation of community communication networks, and funds aimed at supporting 'disarmament, demobilization and reintegration of former LRA combatants, especially child soldiers' (Arieff and Ploch, 2012: 13; Carson, 2013: 322; White House, 2010: 23–24).

Despite the fact that Kony has not been apprehended to date, Carson (2013: 322) views the American support for defeat of the LRA as a successful example of regional collaboration. During the Obama administration, as had been the case with Somalia, Sudan, Libya and Mali, the US focused on collaboration with partners and multilateral solutions to regional challenges. Unlike the policy during the years of the Bush administration, the Obama administration's rhetorical emphasis underlined support and collaboration rather than unilateral action. In terms of foreign assistance, the military components focused on logistical support, combat support, intelligence and training rather than direct (open) engagement in combat. When it came to development and economic assistance, the American focus was on strengthening democratic institutions to 'foster peace and stability', and the promotion of economic growth, trade and investment (Carson, 2013: 323).

Despite the initial optimism and the intentions to elevate the status of Africa to the levels of Asia, Europe and the Middle East,[57] Africa remained a low foreign policy priority on the President's agenda throughout the Obama administration (Schraeder, 2011: 301; van de Walle, 2015: 54–55). Van de Walle (2015: 60) holds that Obama was the first 'post-foreign-aid president' in the sense that his initiatives sought to replace the asymmetric relationship created through foreign aid, with a genuine attempt to create a real and equal partnership with African nations. Nevertheless, foreign aid during the Obama administration was explicitly an element of a triad together with diplomacy and defence. In this sense, a partnership to spur African development is still a part of an American projection of power. While the Obama administration signalled that the US would transform its relations with Africa to establish a real partnership, the message also indicated that foreign aid was still seen as an instrument to achieve predefined American objectives, despite the partnership discourse. In other words, the approach of the Obama administration was consistent with his 'smart power' discourse where the purpose remains the same: to encourage African development that first and foremost serve American visions and interests.

## Concluding remarks

The post-9/11 African assistance policy expresses the tension between securing national interests and the moral discourse of development assistance. The new threat to US security and ideology has created a clear policy priority for the US. Similarly to the Cold War years, fighting an enemy became the main purpose of US foreign policy in the post-9/11 era. This led once again to the securitisation of development assistance.

One distinct element of the post-9/11 years was that in addition to securitising assistance, we witnessed a militarisation of assistance, whereby various arms of the DoD assumed responsibility for delivering development assistance, both directly and as support to USAID, DoS, and other agencies, based on needs and mission parameters.

Between the Bush and the Obama administration, we can observe a process that was meant to create more cohesion and coherence between the various tools of power available for US government. The militarisation of development assistance began during the Bush years, and continued during the Obama administration. Obama focused on elevating the roles of the DoS and USAID as instruments of power to win back the confidence of the world, and signal to the world that America leads through cooperation and not through coercion. As demonstrated by the outcomes of the Bush doctrine, the over reliance on hard power to achieve policy objectives, undermines American power.

Since the onset of the Cold War, through the post-Cold War years to the post-9/11 years, the development assistance policy of the US served both in rhetoric and in practice as a tool of power designed to achieve the national security and foreign policy interests of the US. While this statement seems to be fairly trivial, the emphasis here is placed on two issues. The first is that using development assistance as such not only contradicts the moral purpose of assistance, but it also leads to perpetuating a range of problematic political, social and economic practices in African states. Ultimately, the outcomes undermine not only the concept of development assistance, not only the livelihood of people defined by the policies as underdeveloped, but also the long term strategic objectives of using assistance as a projection of power to achieve specific national security and foreign policy objectives. We turn now to how difficult it has been for the US through the use of its power to achieve its strategic goals, constantly undermined by unintended consequences of power projection.

## Notes

1. Adapted from a quote on Africa by President George W. Bush during a press conference after meeting EU leaders in Gothenburg, Sweden on 14 June 2001. The full quote is: 'We spent a lot of time talking about Africa, as we should. Africa is a nation that suffers from incredible disease'.
2. Exemplified by the withdrawal from the Kyoto Protocol in March 2001.
3. As explained by Buzan *et al.* (1998), securitising various issues through discursive practices justifies action that would otherwise be politically difficult to defend.
4. The creation of the Office of the Director of Foreign Assistance at the Department of State as mentioned above was a part of this attempt to form better coherence between the various foreign policy instruments under the Department of State.
5. This linkage came to be known as the 'three Ds' during the Obama administration, referring to Defence, Diplomacy and Development.
6. See also references in Keenan.
7. The tendency to conduct military-led development assistance missions, to increase the capacity of the civilian population to improve their resilience to terrorists independently of the DoS and USAID, changed under the Obama administration with the introduction of the 'whole-of-government' approach in the NSS issued in 2010 (see, for example, CJTF-HOA, 2012: 1–2).
8. *Groupe Salafiste pour la Prédication et le Combat*, translated into Salafist Group for Preaching and Combat. In later years the GSPC became a part of Al-Qaida, and was designated Al-Qaida in the Maghreb (AQIM).
9. Groupe Islamiste Armée.
10. See, for example, the statement of General James Jones before the Senate Foreign Relations Committee (Jones, 2005: 16–18). The TSCTI was later replaced by the Trans Sahara Counter Terrorism Partnership (TSCTP).
11. Since 2008.
12. The co-ordination between the various departments improved towards the end of the Bush administration. The focus on diplomacy together with DoS bureaucracy as the leader of foreign policy characterises the Obama administration which inherited and continued various initiatives begun in the Bush administration.
13. Who served as the Administrator of USAID under the Bush administration between 2001 and 2006, and then as US Special Envoy to Sudan through 2007.
14. Also known as the Naivasha Agreement.
15. Before joining the Department of State, Charles Snyder served as an intelligence officer for Africa in the CIA. He was also a retired colonel of the US army where he served in a post related to operations and training in sub-Saharan Africa.
16. Nowels (2003: 2) remarks that the innovation here is not the eligibility of aid based on performance but rather that an extensive aid package would be entirely based on performance and results as criteria.

17 This was a condition for eligibility to apply for an MCC compact. In the MCC process, countries can also be eligible for threshold programmes. These grants are designed for countries close to passing the MCC criteria and show commitment to improve their democracy and free market policies.
18 For example, Table 3 in Tarnoff (2010: 29) lists over 20 compacts ranging from roughly US$60 million to US$700 million, which is substantially higher than any programmes carried by USAID in each of the countries.
19 The compact with Madagascar was terminated in 2009 after an undemocratic change of government (Tranoff, 2010: 16).
20 See, for example, Obama's keynote address at the Democratic National Convention in Boston on 27 July 2004.
21 See, for example, Obama (2008a: 271).
22 During the second Obama administration, Samantha Power replaced Susan Rice as the US Ambassador to the UN.
23 *The Economist*, 16 July 2009: 'Barack Obama and Africa: How Different is his Policy?'
24 One of Obama's stated objectives for his presidency was to reduce America's dependency on foreign oil.
25 As indicated by the Department of State Spokesman Ian Kelly in a press conference on 27 July 2009.
26 The five core elements were described by Assistant Secretary of State for African Affairs, Johnnie Carson in a personal communication during a visit to the Department of State on 22 June 2011.
27 Johnnie Carson, personal communication (22 June 2011).
28 This is also true when a pressure group that is important to Congress or the President manages to mobilise enough pressure to elevate an issue to the President's desk.
29 Information gathered through interviews.
30 Private communication during an interview with a senior US diplomat conducted in 2013.
31 First as the Federation of Mali with Senegal achieving independence in June 1960, and later (September) as the independent Republic of Mali after Senegal withdrew from the Federation.
32 Union Soudanaise-Rassemblement Démocratique Africain.
33 While the focus here is on the Tuaregs of northern Mali, these tribes belong to a larger group scattered around a vast region stretching from western Sahara to Sudan, including areas of Maghreb states such as Morocco, Algeria and Libya.
34 The first between 1963 and 1964; the second between 1990 and 1996; and the third between 2006 and 2009.
35 The GSPC was founded in 1998 by dissenting members of the GIA, who had conducted fights against the Algerian regime since 1991.
36 Presently serving as the current leader of Al-Qaida.
37 Including DoS, Pentagon and Malian sources interviewed for the purpose of this research, as well as academic sources such as Lacher (2013) and references.
38 An Islamic group that broke off from AQIM in December 2011.
39 Also known as the Battle of Aguelhok.
40 Named the National Committee for the Restoration of Democracy and State (CNRDR).
41 These questions are simply irrelevant to the current research.
42 See also the article in the *Washington Post* by Craig Whitlock entitled 'Leader of Malian military coup trained by the US' published on 24 March 2012.
43 Parliamentary elections in Mali were planned to take place in July 2012.
44 Interviews conducted for the purpose of this research with Pentagon and DoS officials.

45 Not including humanitarian assistance.
46 These organisations, especially Ansar Dine led by Iyad ag Ghaly, managed to capitalise on the MNLA success and assume leadership for the 'state' of Azawad, which resulted in the creation of an Islamic state governed by Sharia laws.
47 The quote is taken from a televised interview with Ambassador Lyman.
48 S.Res. 559 passed on 13 September 2006.
49 Thus joining Iran, Iraq, Libya, Syria, North Korea, and Cuba already on that list.
50 The Policy of President Bush on the Sudan is described above and as specified, largely related to the involvement of evangelical NGOs in the south and to Bush's own religious convictions.
51 Disarmament, Demobilisation and Reintegration.
52 The SPLM was the political wing of the SPLA which turned into a political party in the process towards referendum for the secession of South Sudan from the Sudan.
53 Scott Gration was appointed US Ambassador to Kenya.
54 Somalia: US Dual Track Policy (French Ministry of Defense, undated document accessed 12 April 2015).
55 Johnnie Carson, 'A Dual Track Approach to Somalia'; Speech at the Center for International and Strategic Studies, Washington, DC, 20 October 2010.
56 This is not to conclude that the actions under the foreign policy of the Obama administration do not include unilateral actions or actions designed to protect US interests in a unilateral fashion.
57 Johnnie Carson, personal communication.

## References

AFRICOM (2010) Trans Sahara Counter Terrorism Partnership. U.S. Africa Command, Public Affairs Office.
AFRICOM (2011) United States African Command: the first three years. U.S. Africa Command Public Affairs Staff, Stuttgart.
Arieff, A. (2013) Crisis in Mali. *Congressional Research Service*, Washington, DC.
Arieff, A. and Ploch, L. (2012) The Lord's Resistance Army: The U.S. Response. *Congressional Research Service*, Washington, DC.
Behrman, G. (2004) *The invisible people: how the U.S. has slept through the global AIDS pandemic, the greatest humanitarian catastrophe of our time*. Free Press, New York.
Blanchard, L. P. (2012) Sudan and South Sudan: Current issues for Congress and U.S. Policy. *Congressional Research Service*, Washington, DC.
Blanchard, L. P. (2014) The Crisis in South Sudan. *Congressional Research Service*, Washington, DC.
Bush, G. W. (2001) Address to the Nation on the Terrorist Attacks. The American Presidency Project.
Bush, G. W. (2001a) Address Before a Joint Session of the Congress on the United States Response to the Terrorist Attacks of September 11 – 20 September 2001. The American Presidency Project.
Bush, G. W. (2010) *Decision points*. Crown Publishers, New York.
Buzan, B., Wæver, O. and Wilde J. de (1998) *Security: A New Framework for Analysis*. Lynne Rienner Publishers, Boulder, Col.
Carney, T. (2005) The Sudan: Political Islam and Terrorism, in Rotberg, R. I. (ed.) *Battling terrorism in the Horn of Africa*. World Peace Foundation, Cambridge, Mass., pp. 119–140.

Carson, J. (2012) Addressing Development in Mali: Restoring Democracy and reclaiming the North: Testimony before the Senate Committee on Foreign Relations Subcommittee on African Affairs, Washington, DC.

Carson, J. (2013) The Obama Administration's Africa Policy: The First Four Years, 2009–2013, *American Foreign Policy Interests* 35: 317–324.

Cheney, R. B. and Cheney, L. (2011) *In my time: a personal and political memoir*. Threshold Editions, New York.

Chouala, Y. A. (2009) Securing access to African oil post-9/11: The Gulf of Guinea, in Smith, M. (ed.) *Securing Africa: post-9/11 discourses on terrorism*. Ashgate, Farnham; Burlington, VT, pp. 143–159.

CJTF-HOA. (2012) Combined Joint Task Force – Horn of Africa: Partner in a New Paradigm. US African Command, Camp Lemonnier, Djibouti.

Clinton, H. R. (2011) Remarks at African Union – 13 June 2011, U.S. Department of State.

Copson, R. W. (2007) *The United States in Africa: Bush policy and beyond*. Zed Books; David Philip; Distributed in the USA exlusively by Palgrave Macmillan, London; New York; Cape Town.

Dagne, T. (2011) Sudan: The Crisis in Darfur and Status of the North-South Peace Agreement. *Congressional Research Service*, Washington, DC.

Dagne, T. (2011a) Somalia: Current Conditions and Prospects for a Lasting Peace. *Congressional Research Service*, Washington, DC.

DoD (2003) Joint Task Force Horn of Africa Briefing by Major General John F. Sattler, USMC, Combined Joint Task Force Horn of Africa. News Transcript: Department of Defense.

DoS (2001) Briefing to the Press on the Secretary's Upcoming Trip to Africa – Nancy Powell, Acting Assistant Secretary for African Affairs, Briefing to the Press, Washington, DC: 17 May 2001, US Department of State Archive.

DoS (2002) Pan Sahel Intimate: Office of Counterterrorism, Washington, DC, 7 November 2002.

DoS (2007) Strategic Plan – Fiscal Years 2007–2012: Transformational Diplomacy. Department of Stated; U.S. Agency for International Development, Washington, DC.

DoS (2009) Sudan: A Critical Moment, A Comprehensive Approach – Media Note. Department of State – Office of the Spokesman.

DoS (2013) U.S. Relations with Uganda – Fact Sheet, 8 October 2013. U.S. Department of State, Bureau of African Affairs.

Ellis, S. (2004) U.S. National Security Interests in Africa Outlined: State Dept. official lists key programs that tie Africa to America, *IIP Digital – U.S. Department of State*. Department of State.

Feleke, E., Picard, L. A. and Buss, T. F. (2011) African security challenges and AFRICOM, in Buss, T. F., Adjaye, J., Goldstein, D. and Picard, L. A. (eds) *African security and the African command: Viewpoints on the US role in Africa*. Kumarian Press; Matthew B. Ridgway Center for International Security Studies, Sterling, VA; Pittsburgh, pp. 9–39.

Fisher, I. (2001) Africans ask if Washington's sun will shine on them. *New York Times*, 8 February 2001.

Fisher, J. (2014) Framing Kony: Uganda's war, Obama's advisers and the nature of 'influence' in Western foreign policy making, *Third World Quarterly* 35: 686–704.

GAO (2014) Combating Terrorism: US efforts in Northwest Africa would be strengthened by Enhanced Program Management, *Report to the Committee on Foreign Relations, US Senate.*
Garamone, J. (2007) DoD Establishing U.S. Africa Command, *American Forces Press Service*, 6 February 2007.
Gurtov, M. (2006) *Superpower on crusade: the Bush doctrine in US foreign policy.* Lynne Rienner Publishers, Boulder, Col.
Handy, R. J. (2003) Africa Contingency Operations Training Assistance: Developing Training Partnership for the Future of Africa, *Air & Space Journal* Fall 2003: 57–64.
Holmes, K. R. and Carafano, J. J. (2010) Defining the Obama Doctrine, Its Pitfalls, and How to Avoid Them, *Backgrounder*. The Heritage Foundation.
Huliaras, A. (2006) Evangelists, oil companies, and terrorists: the Bush administration's policy towards Sudan, *Orbis* 50 (4): 709–724.
Huliaras, A. (2008) The Evangelical Roots of US Africa Policy, *Survival* 50: 161–182.
ICG (2005) Islamist Terrorism in the Sahel: Fact or Fiction? International Crisis Group, Africa Report 92. p. 42.
ICG (2010) LRA: A Regional Strategy beyond Killing Kony. International Crisis Group, Africa Report 157.
Iversen, I. A. (2007) Foreign policy in God's name: evangelical influence on US policy towards Sudan. Norwegian Institute for Defense Studies, Defence and Security Studies.
Jones, J. L. (2005) Statement of General James L. Jones, USMC, Commander, United States European Command before the Senate Foreign Relations Committee on 28 September 2005. Senate Foreign Relations Committee, Washington, DC. http://web.archive.org/web/20070110031318/www.senate.gov/~foreign/testimony/2005/JonesTestimony050928.pdf (accessed 15 March 2017).
Kansteiner, W. H. (2002) U.S. Policy Towards Sudan, US Department of State.
Keenan, J. (2009) *The dark Sahara: America's war on terror in Africa.* Pluto Press, London.
Klare, M. and Volman, D. (2006) The African 'Oil Rush' and US National Security, *Third World Quarterly* 27: 609–628.
Lacher, W. (2013) Organized crime and conflict in the Sahel-Sahara region, in Wehrey, F. M. and Boukhars, A. (eds) *Perilous desert: insecurity in the Sahara.* Carnegie Endowment for International Peace, Washington, DC, pp. 61–86.
LaFeber, W. (2002) The Bush Doctrine, *Diplomatic History* 26: 543–558.
Landler, M. (2014) U.S. is facing hard choices in South Sudan. *New York Times*, 3 January 2014.
Lecocq, B. (2010) *Disputed desert: decolonisation, competing nationalisms and Tuareg rebellions in northern Mali.* Brill, Leiden.
Lyman, P. N. (2013) Sudan–South Sudan: The Unfinished Tasks, *American Foreign Policy Interests* 35: 333–338.
Lyman, P. N. (2014) Princeton Lyman, former US Special Envoy for Sudan and South Sudan – interview with Philip Crowther. *France 24*, 14 January 2014.
Lyman, P. N. and Morrison, J. S. (2004) The Terrorist Threat in Africa, *Foreign Affairs*. The Council on Foreign Relations, New York.
MCC (2014) *About MCC.* Millennium Challenge Corporation, www.mcc.gov/pages/about (accessed November 25, 2014).

Moore, A. and Walker, J. (2016) Tracing the US Military's Presence in Africa, *Geopolitics* 21: 686–716.
Natsios, A. (2006) USAID in the Post-9/11 World, *Foreign Service Journal* June 2006: 19–24.
Natsios, A. S. (2012) *Sudan, South Sudan, and Darfur: what everyone needs to know.* Oxford University Press, Oxford; New York.
NEPDG (2001) National Energy Policy: Report of the National Energy Policy Development Group. The Office of the President of the United States.
Nowels, L. (2003) The Millennium Challenge Account: Congressional Consideration of a New Foreign Aid Initiative. *CRS Report*, Washington, DC.
NSS (1987–2012) National Security Strategy of the United States.
Obama, B. (2008) *Dreams from my father: a story of race and inheritance.* Canongate, Edinburgh; New York.
Obama, B. (2008a) *Change we can believe in: Barack Obama's plan to renew America's promise.* Canongate, Edinburgh; New York.
Obama, B. (2009) Inaugural Address – 20 January 2009.
Obama, B. (2009a) Remarks by the President to Ghanaian Parliament – 11 July 2009. The White House.
Obama, B. (2012) US Strategy towards Sub-Saharan Africa. The White House.
Owusu, F. Y. (2007) Post-9/11 US Foreign Aid, the Millennium Challenge Account and Africa: How Many Birds Can One Stone Kill?, *Africa Today* 54: 3–26.
Perlez, J. (2001) Powell gives Africa a hard new look. *New York Times*, 14 January 2001, New York.
Ploch, L. (2010) Countering Terrorism in East Africa: The US Response. *CRS Report*, Washington, DC.
Ploch, L. (2011) Africa Command: US Strategic Interests and the Role of US Military in Africa. *CRS Report*, Washington, DC.
Poulton, R. and Youssouf, I. a. (1998) *A peace of Timbuktu: democratic governance, development and African peacemaking.* United Nations, New York.
Powell, C. L. (2001) Remarks to the press aboard aircraft en route to Bamako, Mali – Secretary Colin L. Powell, Remarks to the press, Bamako, Mali: 22 May 2001, US Department of State Archive.
Powell, C. L. (2001a) Press availability with Malian Foreign Minister Madibo Sidibe following meeting with President Konare – Secretary Colin L. Powell, Press remarks with Foreign Minister Sidibe, Bamako, Mali: 23 May 2001, US Department of State Archive.
Powell, C. L. (2001b) Remarks at the University of Witwatersrand – Secretary Colin L. Powell, Remarks to University of Witwatersrand, Johannesburg, South Africa: 25 May 2001, US Department of State Archive.
Prunier, G. (2004) Rebel movements and proxy warfare: Uganda, Sudan and the Congo (1986–99), *African Affairs* 103: 359–383.
Rice, C. (2001) *Remarks by National Security Advisor Condoleezza Rice To African Growth And Opportunity Act Forum*, www.somaliawatch.org/archivesep01/011107301.htm (accessed October 9, 2014).
Rice, C. (2011) *No higher honor: A memoir of my years in Washington.* Crown Publishers, New York.
Rothchild, D. S. and Emmanuel, N. (2005) United States: the process of decision-making on Africa, in Engel, U. and Olsen, G. R. (eds.) *Africa and the north: between globalization and marginalization.* Routledge, London; New York, pp. 74–91.

Rumsfeld, D. (2011) *Known and unknown: a memoir.* Sentinel, New York.

Schraeder, P. J. (2001) 'Forget the Rhetoric and Boost the Geopolitics': Emerging Trends in the Bush Administration's Policy towards Africa, 2001, *African Affairs* 100: 387–404.

Schraeder, P. J. (2007) The African Dimension of U.S. Foreign Policy in the Post-9/11 Era, in Franco, M. (ed.) *Estrategia e Seguranca na Africa Austral.* Luso – American Foundation and Portuguese Institute of International Relations, Lisbon, Portugal, pp. 171–196.

Schraeder, P. J. (2011) The Obama's Administration Engagements in Africa within Historical Context: Great Expectations versus Daunting Challenges, in Havnevik, K. J., Dietz, A. J., Kaag, M. and Østigård, T. (eds) *African engagements: Africa negotiating an emerging multipolar world.* Brill Academic Publishers, Leiden; Boston, pp. 300–324.

Schraeder, P. J. and Crouzel, I. (2005) La Guerre contre le Terrorisme et la Politique Américaine en Afrique, *Politique africaine* 2: 42–62.

Shanahan, M. and Francis, D. (2005) U.S. Support to the African Capacity for Peace Operations: The ACOTA program, *Peace Operations Factsheet Series.* The Stimson Center, Washington, DC, pp. 1–6.

Sheridan, M. B. (2009) Clinton's Africa trip ends with a promise, *Washington Post.* 16 August 2009.

Smith, D. F. (2013) Sudan: Survival Depends on Getting to Inclusive Government, *American Foreign Policy Interests* 35: 339–345.

Tarnoff, C. (2010) Millennium Challenge Corporation, *CRS Report for Congress.* Congressional Research Service, Washington, DC.

Taylor, I. (2010) *The international relations of sub-Saharan Africa.* Continuum, New York.

Tenet, G. and Harlow, B. (2007) *At the center of the storm: my years at the CIA.* Harper-Collins, New York.

van de Walle, N. (2009) US Policy towards Africa: The Bush Legacy and the Obama Administration, *African Affairs* 109 (434): 1–21.

van de Walle, N. (2015) Obama and Africa: Lots of Hope, Not Much Change, *Foreign Affairs* 94 (5): 54–61.

Warner, L. A. (2014) The Trans Sahara Counter Terrorism Partnership: Building Partner Capacity to Counter Terrorism and Violent Extremism. Center for Stability and Development, CNA Corporation.

White House (2010) Strategy to support the disarmament of the Lord's Resistance Army. The White House.

Wiley, D. (2010) Superb Intentions and US Policy Constraints, *African Studies Review* 53: 16–21.

Wing, S. D. (2008) *Constructing democracy in transitioning societies of Africa: constitutionalism and deliberation in Mali.* Palgrave Macmillan, New York.

# 7 Explaining assistance as power projection

In Chapter 1, we described a conceptual map combining a number of perspectives on power. This map allowed us to navigate and observe critically the space where culture, history, geopolitics, development assistance and policy co-exist and interact. In this context, power is the thread that governs relationships between developed and undeveloped countries. We use notions of power to demonstrate how an American identity has been and is performed through the assistance policy. In turn, projecting identity through power has undermined the meaning and purpose of development assistance. We also use theories of power to explain the constitution of the identities contained within hierarchies (developed, underdeveloped), the clash of identities (ethnic, religious, national, class due to or supported by development assistance policies, and the unintended empowerment effects occurring through projections of power. This narrative serves to form a critique of the concept of development assistance when it is used as a soft power tool or linked to hard power tools to achieve national security and foreign policy objectives. The contradictions we highlight here are between the moral and value-based purpose of development assistance, and the use of it to achieve US national security goals rather than those of development. We continue to find that US national security objectives override development objectives. Power is a key ingredient that governs this contradiction, and as we discuss, has led to problematic and often undesired and unintended outcomes. This chapter also demonstrates how difficult it can be to get African leaders to fully adopt a US determined agenda. In the cases described below alternative African national objectives alter or block US policies. For example, US policies and resources can be turned to support Somali, Ethiopian and Sudanese own-defined agendas.

This chapter will be divided into two main sections. The first will thread power through the assistance discourse in post WWII American history, its objectives, and its application in the African policy. It will illuminate how an American identity is performed through the justification for using assistance to achieve national security interests. The assistance policy aims at creating social institutions that reproduce what Foucault would call an

American 'regime of truth'. What differs mostly between various administrations is the tactic employed to construct social institutions that achieve this end.

In the second section of this chapter, we will sketch the long-term effects of using assistance as a tool of power. We focus on outcomes that have undermined the moral and value-based purpose of assistance. Quite possibly there was no policy that the US could have followed that would have realised its objective due to a range of factors including the unintended empowerment of groups within African nations opposed to elements of US policy. In the examples described in this chapter we point to groups and interests that thwart US policies and objectives.

Regimes of truth, despite their historical depth, can become unstable. While George W. Bush created AFRICOM, Obama expanded it and enlarged its military operations and training exercises. He also permitted the military's increased role in 'doing development' thus weakening the long-standing development aims of the US. African nations worry if the security interests of the US dovetails with those on the continent as well as their economic interests. AFRICOM has created substantial concern on the continent (Buss, 2011), and domestic US worries about the militarisation of US foreign policy (Adams and Murray, 2014). It is possible that the militarisation of US development assistance may undermine, over time, the regime of truth because of the overwhelming emphasis upon terrorism rather than development. The US currently assumes that the existence of 'terrorists' in particular countries should be their most important priority in the same way that the US had sought African countries to regard Cubans and Russians as their most important enemies during the Cold War.

Before threading power through the specific case analysis in this book linking American exceptionalism, history, the American development discourse and the American foreign policy in Africa, we would like to explain the circular track on which power moves – from Foucault's regime of truth, through Lukes' dimensions of power, and back to Foucault's regime of truth. It is the complex nature of this mechanism, as we will argue below, which creates the unintended consequences associated with the assistance policy, including its failure to spur development for those viewed as in need of assistance.

## Projection of power through the assistance policy

In discussing Foucault and the formation of a regime of truth, we observe that this concept refers to a stratified social construction that is self-generating and self-reinforcing. The regime of truth in our case refers to two interconnected mechanisms: the mechanism that forges 'American' (that is, the discourse of Americanism as discussed below), and the mechanism that combines Americanism with historical contexts to produce the assistance discourse. The unique American regime of truth is based on three principles. First, it is founded on the basic undeniable (God-given) rights of the *individual*; these rights being life, liberty and the pursuit of happiness (and the subsequent sense that no *collective* should have the ability to infringe on these God-given rights). The second principle is that the system of government which is derived from the consent of the governed, is installed to protect these individual rights from the possible dictatorship of a collective. The third principle is that the US is an exceptional nation and has a distinct role to play in the history of the world.[1] Projected onto historical contexts, these elements produce a regime of truth that manifests in the assistance discourses. That is not to say, as indicated throughout the book, that there are no distinctions among foreign policies of different administrations and the subsequent paths chosen in international relations, but to emphasise that there is a common denominator to the different foreign policy approaches. This common denominator is a regime of truth that grants basic justification to any foreign policy path chosen by its originators/inceptors. The arguments within America on foreign policy courses are, in essence, debates on how to reflect and protect the fundamental American regime of truth, not to question its core tenets.

The regime of truth does more than grant justification to that policy. It also grants justification for the ways in which policy is operationalised.[2] American policymakers often disagree on policy matters, policy courses and policy preferences. In a theoretical sense, these disagreements revolve around how America should express its exceptional role in the world, how American values should be reflected in that expression, and how to secure American interests, or in other words, how to secure the continuation of the regime of truth. The disagreements do not concern the fundamental basis of Americanism, but instead on how it should be expressed in the operationalisation of policy. In this space we move from the Foucauldian concept of power to the Lukesian concept of power.

Lukes' conception of the third dimension of power offers a conceptual framework explaining the ways in which regimes of truth are projected through the formulation and operationalisation (in our case) of the assistance policy. The assistance policy, labelled as 'soft power' in Nye (2004, 2011), is used intentionally to create social institutions through which agents are moulded to believe in and accept the basic tenets of the American regime of truth. Through Lukes' third dimension of power, where A uses social forces in addition to institutional capacities and individual decisions to shape the basic belief, preferences and perceptions of B; certain assistance interventions can be understood as an attempt by America to encourage and influence the creation of social institutions with recipients, which either replicate or enhance the American regime (or both). The purpose of assistance as such, is to develop mechanisms or enhance the institutions that serve America, and by extension, safeguard the regime of truth at home.

In relation to foreign assistance strategies two concepts have been used:[3] a 'missionary' policy that can be defined as a conscious attempt to create institutions through granting assistance that expand and replicate the American regime of truth. When it comes to aid, missionary development discourses focus on helping underdeveloped nations to create institutions to form and enhance democracy, individual freedoms and free market strategies. This type of projection of power is consistent with Lukes' third dimension of power. 'Exemplary' policies are when the assistance discourse focuses on demonstrating to recipients of foreign aid that America is a model worth emulating, rather than actively engaging in the creation of institutions with recipients of assistance. To be worthy of imitation means that America must possess some desired qualities worthy of reproduction. There are different interpretations of how America can be, become, and/or can remain a model for other nations. In many instances during the Cold War, for example, American policy was focused on convincing and demonstrating that it was worthy of echoing and trying to deter other nations from emulating the Soviet Union.

We locate two principal ways through which an exemplary approach to the assistance policy is displayed in the discourse of presidential administrations:

First is to demonstrate the ability to command various kinds of power. These include military, political and economic power. As such, America being the most powerful state enacts its success. However, for the US to be worthy of the title required consistency and clear values and goals. A paradox is embedded in this path, since accumulating power in cases of competition often leads to practices which do not fall into the exemplary category. We have detailed in earlier chapters examples of amoral policies of support to human rights abusers or to problematic regimes to win their allegiance to enhance the position of the US as a superpower. Winning allegiance in such cases may have temporarily increased US power but at a cost to being viewed as a model state. Second, is to consistently deal with the world according to a set of values and principles that the nation upholds at home and which are worthy of emulation. This requires attaching conditions to assistance by granting it only to those who uphold or take steps to achieve democracy, human rights, and individual freedoms. This approach is not a missionary approach (as defined above) since it does not seek to intervene actively by granting assistance for the creation of specific institutions. Rather it supports those who 'adopt' an American path. It does this by creating incentives for those who do not uphold these principles to move towards what are labelled American values.

Based on the terms *missionary* and *exemplary* as descriptions of foreign assistance strategies and tools of power, we can observe in the American assistance discourse the following:[4]

1   Missionary approach – helps create American-like regimes of truth by actively assisting the creation of specific institutions that spur democracy, free market economy, respect for human rights and individual freedoms.
2   Exemplary approach (1) – ensures that America can remain the example of the best system through the enhancement and preservation of domestic principles at home. In order to be that example, America needs to preserve and enhance its power (political, military and economic) as the basis for domestic prosperity. The assistance policy is used to ensure that these objectives are achieved by granting various streams of benefits in different contexts to recipients of assistance, even in cases where granting such assistance negates the very basic principles America upholds at home.
3   Exemplary approach (2) – ensures that America demonstrates that it is worthy of emulation by upholding the American way of life at home, and by interacting with the world through foreign policies that adhere to the same principles, values and morals without double standards. Assistance, in theory, is granted based on morals and principles. Its aims are not only to promote good in the world, but also to indicate to the recipients and the world at large that America is an exceptional nation that adheres to higher principles and is worthy of emulation.
4   Flexible approach – differentiates between contexts and combines the missionary and exemplary stances as needed to achieve specific objectives. The assistance policy is tailored to contexts and used to build institutions, buy allegiance and demonstrate that America acts according to worthy principles, depending on contextual interests and specific objectives in different geopolitical realities.[5]

Over the historical span covered here, it is possible to assign to different administrations a preferred approach based on presidential and executive branch discourses. This does not mean that a preferred approach propagated by a president was the only policy course assumed during an administration through the application of foreign assistance. The reality is such that circumstances, geopolitics, and domestic power relations have led every administration to assume a flexible approach rather than an exclusively missionary or exemplary one.

## The regime of truth and the assistance discourse

A distinctly American regime of truth features in the assistance discourse of every administration from Truman to Obama. It manifests in a variety of ways as the justification for various policies. While the analysis below locates clear distinctions between the assistance discourses of various administrations, it is important to emphasise that the political realities yield policies which are not always fully consistent with the discourse.[6]

## The Cold War years

After the end of WWII, the justification to create an assistance policy and engage in developing military and civilian institutions, the economy, and infrastructure of underdeveloped countries revolved around two interconnected narratives. The first was centred on the Soviet Union as the antithesis of Americanism. Soviet ideology focused on the duty of individuals towards the collective and loyalty to a system of governance based on a single party, dedicated to the promotion of collective consciousness at the expense of individual rights. A second concern of the US was that if Soviet ideology gained traction through Soviet imperialism, it would threaten American interests, the American way of life and weaken American power. Communist parties which were an important part of the political scene in western Europe, the United States, Asia and Central and South America were seen as agents of the USSR. The assistance discourse was justified by promoting freedom, individualism and democratic governance to counter Soviet activities as an assertion of the American regime of truth. The preservation of the American way of life meant the preservation of American military, political and economic power and basic freedoms including religion. To have a healthy and prosperous America that thrived domestically and served as the leader of the free world, there was a constant need to secure US global interests. The importance of the American people being chosen by divine providence provided the ideological foundation for US leadership. As Restad observed: the US at the end of WWII 'created an order that would allow for the kind of influence and freedom of action it needed' (2015: 11). The US saw itself as having the responsibility to assume a leadership role to preserve and to disseminate[7] the rights bestowed upon humans by the creator. By extension, those who try to deny humans these rights are in direct conflict with the creator,[8] and, were, although not always, regarded as evil and should be stopped. These two narratives appear consistently in the assistance discourse of the US as outlined in previous chapters.

Truman's doctrine was very clear concerning the Soviet threat to the freedom of nations and their economic prosperity. NSC-68, the most significant policy statement of the US issued during the Truman administration, is based entirely on these narratives. It speaks of the fundamental purpose of assuring the integrity and validity of American society, referring directly to the individual freedoms and the democratic system mentioned in the declaration of independence and the constitution. It draws on divine providence and American exceptionalism to justify assisting the free world to build up its military, economic and political institutions to counter the Soviet Union and its agenda of expansionism. The Foreign Assistance Act of 1950 was explained publicly by Truman as a direct attempt to contribute to world peace through the promotion of health, education, literacy and economic prosperity in the underdeveloped areas of the world with the objective of strengthening freedom and combating Soviet imperialism.

In the 1950s when African nationalism was on the rise, the interests of America's European allies in Africa were undermined. The Soviet Union was playing an active role in supporting various anti-colonial forces on the continent. Subsequently, the DoS expressed concern that the Soviet Union was exploiting African nationalism to advance Soviet ideology. A main concern was that the free world, and therefore US strategic and economic interests, would be jeopardised, consequently weakening American power. At that time the legitimacy and autonomy of African independence movements were downplayed or misunderstood.

During the Eisenhower years, the assistance discourse was increasingly used to explain the dangers of Soviet ideology and to negate it. While the discourse during the Truman years was arguing that America should help to create institutions that strengthen freedom, democracy, rights and promote free economy in the underdeveloped areas of the world, Eisenhower's discourse was more focused on strengthening the capacity of nations to uphold peace and justice. Eisenhower stated that the intention of foreign assistance was not to modify the cultural, political or economic patterns of nations, but to prevent them from becoming Soviet satellite states. The objective was to preserve and strengthen the leadership of the US by granting foreign assistance, first and foremost, to ensure the preservation and protection of the American way of life at home. Assistance, according to this reasoning, would be given to strengthen the orientation of nations towards the US and against the Soviet Union, not to necessarily create institutions that replicate and uphold the American regime of truth.

The US sought to simultaneously balance support of the interests of European allies in Africa with the support of African aspirations for independence. The Soviet Union however assumed a pro-African independence stance that included support to socialist-oriented dissenting forces. Within this context, America was preparing for the 'day after colonialism' on the continent and to thwart Soviet intentions as they were understood in Washington. The US was prepared to support African independence if the new nations would keep their pro-Western stance, consider America as an ally, and help secure current and future American interests. One of the concrete concerns of the US was to ensure that African nations would support American agendas in the UN and other multinational forums. Foreign assistance, including technical and development assistance, was framed in this discourse as a way of allowing moderate leaders in Africa to gain popular support by helping them show tangible results to their constituencies. This policy was justified both as a humanitarian duty, as well as a national security imperative against Soviet subversive actions in Africa. During the Eisenhower years, African policy documents often referred to Africans as unsophisticated and immature. By extension, the purpose of aid was to help Africans move towards the 'right' political positions that would serve American, European and African interests.

With the election of Kennedy, the assistance discourse assumed a missionary stance. The discourse emphasised both a duty to help people in need, as well as create democratic institutions to advance individual freedoms and economic prosperity. The establishment of the Peace Corps and USAID as independent agencies for development assistance is a further testament to the missionary character of the assistance discourse during the Kennedy years. All of these elements were repeatedly tied to fending off communism on the African continent and securing American interests by helping to shape African institutions which respected individual freedoms, choose the path of democracy, and encouraged a free market system. While Kennedy did occasionally mention that the US had no intention to dictate to Africans which system of governance they should assume, he emphasised that a system of governance should be based on the consent of the governed.

Being occupied with the Vietnam War, President Johnson was not concerned with African issues. While he shared Kennedy's approach to the assistance policy, most of the resources were channelled towards dealing with the crisis in Indochina. The President's involvement in the African policy was mostly limited to public statements that attempted to indicate that America was a friend to Africa. The policy was mostly devised by the bureaucracy and was based on a combination of helping Africans create institutions conducive to economic development, and counter communist ideology. Some resources were also devoted to granting assistance to friendly leaders regardless of the political regimes they commanded, as long as their allegiance supported American interests and rejected Soviet ideology. This was, in effect, a combination of missionary and exemplary strategies. The need to have a form of exemplary stance in Africa was linked to increasing criticism against the US stemming from their involvement in the Vietnam War and the association of such involvement with colonialism. Therefore, the policy attempted to demonstrate that the US was not trying to impose its ideology on Africans.

Nixon and Ford often invoked American exceptionalism in their assistance discourse. The moral qualities of America were flagged as the underlying reason to engage in aid, at least rhetorically. Nixon stated that the assistance programme helped to build respect for the US, and increased the security of the American people at the same time as it elevated the dignity of people around the globe. But his suggestion of reducing government involvement in economic aid while increasing its focus on military assistance was more consistent with the realpolitik approach than a mission to disseminate American values. The new directions in foreign assistance suggested by USAID during the Nixon administration also emphasised an exemplary stance by assuming the role of negotiator of peaceful solutions, deliverer of assistance to combat poverty and alleviate suffering, and intervene with assistance during man-made and natural disasters in order to indicate the generosity of the American people. While the main discourse emphasised humanitarianism through assistance, an element of reforming institutions was also present.

The African policy during those years was consistent with the realpolitik approach. In this case, the exemplary policy sought to enhance American power through the assistance policy. Nixon and Ford's African policy was based on the idea that American power would be enhanced by winning over nations using various tools, including foreign assistance. This rationale stipulated that when nations align themselves with America, the Soviet Union loses ground. It is significant that the context of the Cold War and the Nixon–Ford–Kissinger realpolitik yielded policies that were not based on the principles America upheld at home and so eagerly tried to protect with that same foreign policy. In Africa, this translated into granting support for the problematic apartheid regime, conducting economic transactions with the illegal Smith regime in Rhodesia, and providing assistance and support to the last colonial power on the continent – Portugal.

The realpolitik approach to Africa persisted during the Ford years. Africa still scored low on the foreign policy priorities of the President. Kissinger listed four main reasons to engage with the continent: strategic, economic, political and, satisfying the domestic lobby for Africa. Politically, the US wanted to continue securing access to natural resources and to ensure that African nations would support the US in multinational forums. Assistance was once again framed as a tool that should be tailored to advance interests and channelled to countries where US interests were most significant. The most important role of aid was to induce political impacts – in other words, to strengthen alliances between the US and strategic African nations to gain political, economic and strategic dividends.

Carter wanted to bring back morality to foreign policy. His approach was also anchored in the exemplary stance towards foreign policy. He believed that America, by divine providence, had the responsibility to assume the role of 'the city upon the hill' to be emulated. But the exemplary stance he propagated was very different from the one employed by the Nixon–Ford–Kissinger administrations. For Nixon, Ford and Kissinger, to be the example America needed to be strong to preserve the American way of life. This translated into an amoral foreign policy, addressing the world in ways which would be deemed illegal and unconstitutional in the US. This approach created a dichotomy between upholding the regime of truth at home, and ignoring its principles when dealing with the world at large. The protection and preservation of American power was Kissinger's philosophy. In a similar manner to the Nixon and Ford administrations, Carter emphasised that America could not be strong internationally unless it was strong at home. But he also stressed that since America was an exceptional and moral nation, it had a duty to act abroad in ways that were consistent with its basic ideals and how it acted at home. His intention was to bring back morality to foreign policy so that America could serve as the example worthy of emulation.

Carter tried to apply his approach in Africa but faced with efforts to support Somalia's break from Russia, keeping Ethiopia supplied with arms and delaying measures against South Africa meant that he could not adhere to his principles. Trying to block further Cuban interventions (unsuccessfully) and Soviet designs meant in practice that Carter was also a 'cold warrior'. He proclaimed the Carter Doctrine which committed the US government to repel any Russian intervention in the Persian Gulf including the use of military force. As noted earlier, Carter sought to have Rhodesia end its white racial domination based upon his experiences in Georgia. While he remained true to his intention to further racial justice his other objective was to use the search for justice as a means to keep the Cubans from intervening further in southern Africa (Mitchell, 2016). Toward Uganda, Carter initiated an embargo on products until it became democratic again. Carter could not avoid Cold War politics in supporting highly repressive governments in Ethiopia, Somalia, Zaire and continuing to back FNLA and UNITA in Angola. By the end of 1977 Carter had institutionalised a human rights focus by establishing the Bureau of Human Rights and Humanitarian Affairs within the DoS.

Reagan believed that Carter's approach weakened the US. Like Carter, Reagan trusted that America was guided by divine providence, having been chosen to be a beacon for other nations. He also believed that the Soviet Union was an evil empire which stood against everything that America represented. He was weary of the perceived weakening of American power, which he linked to the Vietnam debacle exacerbated by Carter's approach to foreign policy. To be able to fight the Soviet evil, America needed to command power. For Reagan, this meant both economic and political power. A strong US with a flourishing economy would be the basis of American strength. A powerful America would be able to influence nations and reject the tyranny and oppression offered by the Soviets. America would demonstrate by example to the nations of the world that democracy and freedom lead to economic growth, prosperity and happiness. Reagan's discourse assumed a very clear position on the fact that America was exceptional, the example for all other nations. But he also believed in the qualities of democracy in opposition to Soviet ideology. His predisposition to support democratic movements around the world produced a mixed assistance policy, assuming both exemplary and missionary stances. On the one hand he wanted America to be the supreme example of a prosperous nation. But on the other hand, for being the example of success American interests needed to be safeguarded, even at the expense of ideals and principles. For him, foreign assistance would be given to strategic nations that helped to achieve these objectives, even if this meant supporting human rights abusers and dictators. But to support democracy, Reagan was also prepared to assume a missionary stance and grant assistance to help create institutions which promised to emulate the American regime of truth.

For these purposes, America granted support to those various groups willing to overthrow communist or socialist regimes in the name of democracy and free market principles against Soviet ideology. Reagan preferred granting assistance bilaterally rather than multilaterally to better serve the security and economic interests of the US.[9] The purpose of assistance was essentially to serve the interests of the US while ensuring the prosperity of the American economy (the basis for American power), and repelling Soviet ideology. The idea was that well-conceived assistance programmes would lead to partnership with recipient nations and enhance their confidence in America as an ally. In addition to granting assistance in return for support, the Reagan administration also recognised that spurring economic growth in the Third World and resolving the debt problem meant helping to create proper institutions. Hence, another objective of American assistance during the Reagan administration was to help re-create the basic elements of the American regime of truth through structuring institutions that advanced democratic governance, and protected individual rights and freedom. This type of approach allowed the Reagan administration to follow two parallel tracks, the first of which was to grant assistance to gain support for America, which led to certain policy choices being deprived of a normative yardstick. The purpose of such policies was to maintain America's position as the leader of the free world as an example of a strong, prosperous nation which thrives based on the basic idea of its regime of truth. The second track was to assist nations in building institutions to advance democracy, individual freedoms and a free market system, which would not only enhance American power, but would also move the world towards being like America and unlike the Soviet Union.

The constructive engagement policy with South Africa, for example, embodied elements of the approach above. On one hand, it allowed the US to access strategic minerals, continue trade with South Africa, and support South Africa in its struggle against what it claimed was a total communist onslaught against it (Marks and Trapido, 1987). On the other hand, USAID was engaged in programmes in South Africa to help victims of apartheid, promote civil liberties, provide scholarships for students and black leaders for education in the US, and in general enhance the orientation of the population towards the US. This policy was aimed at helping to shape a post-apartheid South Africa that would choose freedom over communism.

To summarise the assistance policy and the formation of the African policy of the US during the Cold War years, we can observe the following:

First, bearing in mind Foucault's concept of regime of truth, we can clearly locate in all presidential discourses a validation for the assistance policy that links American exceptionalism, democratic governance, freedom and market economy as the anchors of an anti-Soviet foreign policy.

Second, the concept of American exceptionalism yields two distinct approaches to foreign policy that are carried to the assistance policy: the exemplary and the missionary. Each approach exhibits different nuances in varying contexts and through different administrations. Both approaches are interventionist in their nature, that is, isolationism is not a foreign policy strategy of any administration.[10] Through the assistance policy, the missionary approach emphasises the need to create institutions that seek to advance democratic regimes which adopt the concepts of life, liberty and the pursuit of happiness. In foreign assistance, these are expressed as respect for human rights, free enterprise and adoption of free market principles. The exemplary stance yields two different kinds of assistance policies. The realpolitik approach of the Nixon–Ford–Kissinger administrations was mostly concerned with safeguarding the American way of life at home by defeating communism abroad. These administrations created a dichotomy between the principles America upholds domestically and the way America projects power through its foreign policy. The second exemplary approach is represented in the intended foreign policy of President Carter. He emphasised the need for America to act in an exemplary way when dealing with the world rather than an active conversion of the world to American principles. Carter stated clearly in his inaugural address that the best way for America to enhance freedom around the globe was to demonstrate that America was worthy of emulation. His emphasis was not placed on re-creating America by assisting the formation of American-like institutions abroad, but on the need to grant assistance and act in foreign policy according to the morals, values and principles that make America an exceptional nation and guide life at home. According to Carter's rationale, the world would follow America because the country was just, in addition to being powerful. Carter's approach could not be sustained in the face of growing Cold War issues in Africa.

An interesting combination of the exemplary and missionary approach to foreign policy can be located in the assistance discourse of the Reagan administration.[11] Reagan's assistance discourse was less directional than that of other presidents in the sense that it emphasised both the need to intervene in foreign countries through the creation of institutions that emulate the American regime of truth where appropriate, and in other cases, granted assistance based on the objective of winning over (politically, economically and militarily) the allegiance of other nations.

Third, during the Cold War, both approaches yielded policies that consciously projected American power through foreign assistance to achieve the end result of blocking the spread of communism. With the exception of some humanitarian aid as a response to a crisis such as drought, foreign assistance was designed to create institutions that conform to the US regime of truth, and/or to move countries towards the American sphere of influence, and by extension, adopt US ideological approaches rather than Soviet ones. The most important aspect of that policy was to preserve

US power so that the American way of life at home and its global influence would persist in the face of the Soviet and Cuban threats.

## The post-Cold War years

The transition from a Cold War world to a unipolar world created difficulties for US assistance policy. The rationale that linked assistance to American power and the need to fend off communism, was gone. For the American policymakers during the George H. W. Bush administration, the post-Cold War 'new world order' meant the triumph of American values that defined the core of the US. 'The age of democratic peace' was at the gate for President Bush. The vision of a new world order was a world led by the US as the promotor and defender of democracy, individual freedoms, human rights and free market economies. President Bush sought to legitimise US leadership by working through the UN. To be the leader of the free world, domestic vitality was an imperative. The objective of foreign policy became to promote a global transition towards a better world as envisaged by the US. Among the challenges Bush hoped to address through foreign policy, was the promotion of free market principles, the creation of a friendly environment for US competitiveness, promotion of peace and resolution of conflicts, and a global commitment for addressing various humanitarian disasters and transnational issues.

With the end of the Cold War, there was no longer a justification for granting assistance to problematic regimes to secure their allegiance as a part of the geopolitical puzzle built to fend off communism. Aid became increasingly contingent upon democratisation and liberalisation. As a result, the US began to distance itself from regimes which had been traditional Cold War allies such as Sudan, Zaire (Democratic Republic of the Congo) and Liberia. In Africa, foreign assistance was channelled towards those countries that were emerging from conflicts exacerbated by the Cold War including South Africa, Mozambique, Angola and Ethiopia. The African policy was focused on granting assistance to resolve conflicts, supporting the creation of democratic institutions, and addressing humanitarian crises.

The American-led peacekeeping operation in Somalia was an example of the new world order approach of the Bush administration. Somalia faced a humanitarian disaster due to a breakdown of government and a severe drought. The decision of President Bush to lead a UN peacekeeping mission by sending American soldiers to a foreign country to achieve a humanitarian objective, was a foreign policy precedent. It symbolised the intention of America to assume responsibility as a leader, to work through multilateral institutions and a broad-based legitimacy, and to uphold as well as disseminate principles based on the American regime of truth.

The new world order experiment of the Bush administration in Somalia did not last long. American involvement in the peacekeeping mission was carried into the Clinton administration and evolved from a humanitarian operation (an exemplary stance) into a nation-building undertaking (a missionary stance). With American casualties in the battle of Mogadishu, President Clinton withdrew the American forces, and Somalia was left in a precarious state and civil war. The Somalian debacle led the Clinton administration to formulate a policy of disengagement from involvement in UN peacekeeping operations unless deemed necessary to advance US national security interests. US leadership in 'nation-building' came to an end only to be resurrected in the Iraq and Afghanistan wars.

Criticised at home for not formulating a clear foreign policy, Clinton was under pressure to devise a strategy that would clarify how America intended to promote its global interests in the post-Cold War world. True to his promise during his presidential bid, Clinton focused on the revitalisation of the American economy. Subsequently, his foreign policy strategy was based on promoting democracy, free market economy and lifting barriers to trade. The American discourse identified a number of features characterising the post-Cold War world. The first was that the US could be regarded as the sole superpower. Second, the dissolution of the Soviet Union together with its grip on various nations, caused a flare of ethnic conflicts in former satellite states but also opened new economic opportunities in the former East Bloc. Third, the US sought to shape the privatisation of state industries, businesses and agriculture in the former USSR and eastern Europe. Lastly, Clinton sought to foster globalisation which he saw as increasing the economy of the US but also as a path to diminish conflicts. Identifying these features,[12] the Clinton administration devised a policy of engagement and enlargement. The explicit objective of this policy was to help mould a world that was willing to adopt democratic institutions and the free market. The underlying assumption was that a democratic world operating through the free market system would be a peaceful and secure world. Such a world would help to entrench American leadership and enhance America's ability to project power to secure its interests.

One pillar of Clinton's engagement policies was the use of foreign assistance as a power projection tool. With foreign assistance, the US would provide aid and create institutions that lead to democratic governance and the adoption of free market principles (Lake, 1993). Assistance would be granted to help enlarge democracy in developing countries. Resources would be allocated for this purpose, preferring locations where American interests would be most significant. In sub-Saharan Africa, for example, Nigeria and South Africa were identified as strategic states whose stability and prosperity would have a positive regional effect and serve US interests. Assistance would be withheld, according to this discourse, from nations who abused human rights and did not support the principles of democracy and a free market economy. Countries choosing these paths would face global isolation instigated by American leadership.

The humanitarian and development agenda of the Clinton administration was justified rhetorically in a many ways. Through development assistance, the US would help to stimulate the creation of institutions that encouraged democracy and free market economy. Increasingly, the US would fund the strengthening of governance institutions. When these institutions had fully developed, American legitimacy as a leader would be strengthened. All nations would look to America as the nation that functions according to these principles and pursues justice and humanitarianism around the globe.

During his second term as president, Clinton focused on a greater integration of Africa into the global economy. African countries ready to adopt free market principles received preferential access to the American market through the AGOA scheme. While AGOA helped to develop a free market system in Africa, criticism emanating from various sources including African countries such as South Africa and Nigeria, highlighted that the scheme was serving the American market and protecting the American economy from competition.

ACRI, (now known as ACOTA) was a US initiative to assist selected African states to build a military force capable of responding to a crisis on the continent and conducting UN-led peacekeeping missions. ACRI was conceived as a way to resolve African conflicts without the need to involve American troops in the process. ACRI was created in response to the incident in Somalia, and to the subsequent American reluctance to intervene in the Rwandan genocide. Optimistically, ACRI would enable future mobilisation of an all-African force to solve crises without the need to use American troops in combat.

Despite the disappearance of the Soviet threat the US assistance policy was justified based on the American regime of truth and to serve as a tool of power to secure US national interests. The purpose became to ensure that the world would adopt principles consistent with the ideological foundation of the US as a basis to enhance global prosperity under US leadership. Both missionary and exemplary strategies were employed, mostly in a mixed approach, during the Bush and Clinton administrations. But while Bush's focus leaned towards the exemplary stance, Clinton assumed a missionary policy. Bush wanted to enhance and secure American leadership by being the example and conducting policy based on American values and principles. Clinton wanted to create institutions that would re-create American principles with recipients, to spur democratic governance and the adoption of free market principles.

*The post-9/11 years*

After America was attacked on 9/11, President George W. Bush announced that the US had a responsibility to lead the world in a mission to eradicate the evil that produced terrorism. He emphasised that the US would lead in a unilateral fashion and that US security, interests and objectives would overrule all other considerations. In his foreign assistance discourse, Bush created a link between his faith, the role America was destined to play in the world, poverty and the war on terror. These elements connected his religious interpretation of American exceptionalism to the need to fight evil, now meaning global terrorism instead of communism. James Traub (2008) wrote that 'realism died on 9/11' when Cold War pragmatists shifted gears away from narrowly defined US interests. What happened inside other states became a matter of national interest with underdevelopment viewed as a path which could lead to evil if left unchecked. The war on terror led to the creation of the Millennium Challenge Corporation (MCC) which was to undo the process whereby failures of development might lead to terrorism. In the eyes of Bush, the only country that could fulfil this global role was the United States.

Designed to safeguard America and its interests against the new enemy, the assistance programme was conceived around two principles. The first was the promotion of values: freedom, justice and human dignity, the intention to combat tyranny, promote democracy and expand prosperity through free market policies and development assistance. The second overriding principle was to ensure that America was leading the world towards that vision.

The Bush assistance policy was based on rewarding those who chose to follow America and accept its values. The MCC would give significant amounts of assistance to countries with systems of democratic governance in place, or to countries clearly moving in that direction. Economic freedom and investment in people were two other main indicators for eligibility for assistance according to the Bush administration. The main emphasis of this type of assistance was that America would not devise a development plan for eligible countries, but rather let a country come up with its own agenda based on the selection criteria and indicators of the MCC. In effect, to be eligible for MCC assistance, a country would commit itself to building institutions that conformed in one way or another, to the American regime of truth.

Another focus of the assistance policy of the Bush administration was on humanitarian interventions, especially targeting the HIV/AIDS pandemic through PEPFAR. This programme had a security component to it, but most importantly it was a humanitarian mission justified by American values and moral principles, to demonstrate to the recipients that the US was a compassionate nation[13] worthy of praise and emulation.

Aside from the humanitarian interventions of the US in Africa (such as PEPFAR), the African policy of the Bush administration focused on regional strategies to increase security, boost stability, secure economic interests and fight terrorism. The creation of AFRICOM was indicative of the securitisation of the African policy, as well as the militarisation of aid. The CTJF-HOA, the TSCTI, the EACTI, and ACOTA were all designed to increase regional co-operation to fight terrorism. They all included development assistance components designed to win hearts and minds and reduce the potential for radicalisation. Underlying these trends was a realisation by the Bush administration that to more effectively fight terrorism, there was a need to engage in parallel nation-building efforts to reduce the fragility of states and their vulnerability to transnational challenges. Development assistance was once again viewed as a tool to help the US achieve its national security objectives in a post-9/11 context. Directive 3000.05 and the mission of AFRICOM are testimonies to this statement and to the increased militarisation of the assistance policy.[14]

The rhetoric of the Obama administration centred around the concept of smart power. He elevated the status of development assistance as a foreign policy tool to be on par (theoretically) with defence and diplomacy, and intended to deploy all three elements through a 'smart power' approach to secure American interests. He sought multilateral cooperation in contrast to the former administration. Development assistance was considered an essential tool for nation building in the belief that failing states suffered from many underlying conditions that could be mitigated through development assistance. Obama believed that the essence of state failure was located in a dysfunctional system of governance that did not draw legitimacy from consent of the governed. He flagged the problem of powerful leaders in African countries who were mostly concerned with the prolongation of their own rule to continue to enjoy the benefits of power while embezzling the resources of their nation for their own profit. He therefore made democratic governance and accountable leadership the centrepiece of his assistance policy.

His African policy centred on the assertion that stability and prosperity of states are based on a system of governance that respects the governed and rules without coercion. In his Ghana speech (Obama, 2009), he observed that a lack of transparency and democracy was at the heart of many failing states in Africa. Such states also abused the human rights of their citizens and provided opportunities for the growth of 'terrorism'. Political stability and democratic governance were, in his view, the missing ingredients for development and prosperity. He vowed that the US would create a partnership with African nations to help promote political stability and good governance on the continent.

Obama chose diplomacy as the main instrument to mitigate, prevent and resolve local conflicts. He dedicated resources to humanitarian missions to improve public health on the continent. However, through AFRICOM he has retained the military component of assistance to Africa, and continued to train African forces to combat terrorism, to support African forces in their fight against terror and crime, and encouraged regional organisations to bear the major burdens of responsibility for solving African conflicts including military intervention when necessary. His smart power approach differed from Bush's GWOT concept, attempting to balance the use of defence, diplomacy and development as tools for achieving strategic objectives and not to overemphasise the use of force and the military.

The post-9/11 foreign policy of the US has been characterised by a drive to address the new enemy. The assistance policy during the Bush years was based on supporting the effort to combat terrorism. Foreign assistance went to strategic countries if their allegiance was needed to combat the terror threat – regardless of their regime or human rights record of accomplishment. The characterisation of nations as 'fragile' and 'failing' was based on their abilities to address transnational threats. The war on terror was linked to the ability to govern and address the underlying causes of terrorism, including poverty, lack of education and lack of economic prosperity. During the Bush administration, the largest part of investment in assistance was carried through the MCC mechanism that focused on helping nations committed to democratic governance and free market principles. In addition, large sums of money were invested in humanitarian assistance, especially the PEPFAR programme. While in practice the Bush administration did engage in building institutions in developing countries that supported democracy and the free market principle, his preferred approach (discursively) was more consistent with the exemplary stance. He was set on carrying the objectives of the GWOT unilaterally, but was willing to assist those who would accept American principles, as well as demonstrate that America was a powerful and compassionate country. His main mission was to secure America and guarantee the continuation of the American regime of truth at home.

The assistance policy of the Obama administration leaned heavily towards the missionary approach. Obama's purpose was to actively engage nations to adopt the principles of democracy, just governance, human rights and free market principles. His tools of choice were development, diplomacy and defence in a balanced smart power approach focusing on creating partnerships for a way forward. He sought to tone down unilateralism, and concentrated on achieving America national security objectives through the creation of an atmosphere of partnership and co-operation rather than coercion. Nevertheless, there have been growing fears in the later years of the Obama administration that regional movements that grew after 9/11 such as AQIM, Boko Haram and al Shabab contribute to the rise and further spread of ISIL. ISIL has also been expanding in Libya with implications for Mali, Niger and Chad. While Obama toned down the crusading spirit of the Bush administration, and replaced hard power with smart power, hard power tactics were still heavily present, but remained in the background in the form of shadow wars to defeat new and old enemies (Kibbe, 2014).

### American assistance discourse and national identity

The most consistent justification for the American assistance discourse is based on the ideas forwarded in the Declaration of Independence that life, liberty and the pursuit of happiness are divine rights protected by a democratic system of governance, combined with the idea that the US is an exceptional, and for many Americans, a God-chosen nation. When combined, these elements can be described as a practised system of ideology – in other words, a regime of truth. This regime of truth is then carried through history and is used to address the world at large in different historical contexts. This combination has produced discourses through which justification for policy and its practice are granted.

The assistance policy, whether justified as a mission of mercy, of duty, or as realpolitik, draws consistently on the regime of truth attached to the larger context of foreign policy. Assistance strategies vary from administration to administration, but what remains constant is that development assistance is used as a tool of power to achieve a set of objectives defined by the US based on the regime of truth. While the discourse varies between exemplary, missionary or a combined approach, they each draw legitimacy from a fundamental identity and act to secure it at home and to varying extents, reproduce it elsewhere. The assistance policy is used to project and reproduce American power. This use of power can be viewed eclectically in terms of Foucault and Lukes. In a Foucauldian sense the use of assistance reinforces American national identity at the same time as it works to keep the US powerful. US assistance policy has in a Lukesian sense, sought to maintain American domination of the governance and economic systems of other nations.[15] When viewed from both a Foucauldian and Lukesian perspectives, it reveals how the projection of power can lead to unintended consequences as discussed below.

### Unintended consequences of power projection through assistance in Africa

In this section we highlight some of the longer-term consequences of utilising development assistance to achieve national security objectives. What we argue in this section is that the unintended consequences of projecting power through assistance for achieving national security objectives have had devastating effects on geopolitics in Africa. Ultimately, the examples below illustrate that using assistance as a tool of power can undermine rather than strengthen US power.

We contend that the way in which the overarching objectives of US assistance policy as a tool of power, has interacted with the complex realities and existing social constructions in Africa to produce unintended consequences often, although not always, results in, or prolongs, conflict and human misery.

The accounts below are not an in-depth overview of historical events. They are constructed based on the information outlined in previous chapters, and focus on the conjuncture over time between US assistance policy in the context of larger strategic objectives, with local realities, social constructions and domestic divisions within African countries. We are emphasising the US but recognise that other foreign actors have also been involved which in turn have altered or determined US policies. It has primarily been the case that the US does not involve itself in African nations unless there are also foreign involvements. The analyses below focuses on a selection of countries which became main policy concerns over the timespan covered here.

## *The Sudan*

Sudan's complex history under Egyptian–Ottoman rule and Anglo-Egyptian colonialism combined with religious differences and a high degree of ethnic diversity, has led to an unstable nation-state. Rather than deeply consider the complexity of Sudanese history and the important divergences among and within its religions and regions (Mamdani, 2013), Sudanese conflicts have all too often been reduced to Arab versus non-Arab and Muslim versus Christian. Analysing the conflicts in this manner in part makes them true since these fault-lines are used to generate external support of the various actors

A long history of the Sudanese state serving the northern part of Sudan rather than the north and south equally led to a call by elements in the south for an independent state. This led to a rebellion by the south seeking its independence shortly after Sudan's own independence in 1956. The war ended with an agreement in 1972[16] that granted greater autonomy to the south. Shortly after this (1978), the American company Chevron discovered large reservoirs of oil in the south. The discovery exacerbated the dispute between the north and the south on border demarcations, adding the aspect of oil ownership to the religious and ethnic disputes (Natsios, 2012: 58). A second civil war erupted in 1983 and lasted until the Comprehensive Peace Agreement between north and south Sudan in 2005. Both conflicts had ethnic and religious foundations which were exacerbated by Cold War geopolitics and the discovery of oil.

Sudan became a site for Cold War competition between the US and the USSR as well as Islamic social and political movements. In 1958, the US provided a small aid package to Sudan as a part of the Eisenhower doctrine to help countries resist Soviet influence. In 1967, Sudan broke diplomatic ties with the US in protest against America's support of Israel during the Six Day War. In 1969, the democratically elected government of Sudan was toppled by a military coup headed by Nimeiry. Nimeiry followed a combined ideology of pan-Arabism and socialism and took power in Sudan with the backing of the Communist Party (Woodward, 2006: 30).

In the beginning of his regime, Nimeiry turned to the Soviets and received military and economic aid (Woodward, 2006: 30). But his Arab nationalistic inclinations led the Communist Party to stage a failed coup against him in 1971. Consequently, Nimeiry turned to the US and reinstated diplomatic relations in 1972. Nimeiry began to receive substantial aid packages from the US including economic and military assistance. The purpose of the American aid to Sudan was to forge a pro-Western alliance to form a counterbalance to Soviet influence in the region, especially after the most powerful American ally in the region, Ethiopia, became a Soviet client in 1974. Under President Carter, the Sudan was the largest beneficiary of US foreign assistance in sub-Saharan Africa (Clough, 1992: 88; Schmidt, 2013: 205). Because of the US views on Libya, it cultivated Sudan to counter Qaddafi's expansionary dreams. In addition, Nimeiri allowed the US to use Sudan as a base for covert operations against Qadaffi (Schmidt, 2013: 207). In 1983, Nimeiry imposed Sharia on Sudan, thus abrogating the terms of the Addis Ababa agreement, leading to a renewal of the civil war with the south (Natsios, 2012: 60–61). The second civil war was led by the SPLA, formed by John Garang.

US economic and military assistance to Sudan persisted and intensified during the Reagan administration to keep Sudan allied with the US in exchange for the ability to use that country as a platform for regional power projection. In 1985, Nimeiry was overthrown in a bloodless military coup, ironically, while visiting the White House. The coup was followed by democratic elections that placed Sadiq al-Mahdi, the leader of the Islamic Umma Party, in power (Clough, 1992: 89; Woodward, 2006: 32).

Under the rule of Nimeiry, and despite American foreign assistance,[17] the fiscal situation in Sudan was steadily deteriorating (Clough, 1992: 88–89). The economy of Sudan was at its lowest in the early 1980s, to the point that Nimeiry's government was unable to deal with the severe drought-induced famines of 1982 to 1983 (Clough, 1992: 88–89), causing an acute humanitarian crisis leading to the deaths of hundreds of thousands of people from hunger (Natsios, 2012: 70).

Until 1989, Sudan remained the largest recipient of American aid in Africa as a regional ally to balance against the Soviet-backed regime in Ethiopia (Natsios, 2012: 69). From 1983, Ethiopia supported Garang's SPLA who displayed 'early Marxist rhetoric' and was fighting the pan-Arabic government in the north (Natsios, 2012: 69).

The al-Mahdi government in Sudan was toppled by another bloodless military coup in 1989 by Omar al-Bashir. The coup came in the midst of another famine mismanaged by the al-Mahdi government and while Sudanese forces were deliberately exacerbating the famine in the south by withholding food supplies to subdue the SPLA rebels (Natsios, 2012: 74–75). As a result of the coup, the US suspended all bilateral assistance to Sudan.

The Islamic ideology of Sudan together with Bashir's support of Saddam Hussein's invasion of Kuwait against the international community, led to a change of US policy towards that country. Sudan became a major source of concern when it began to host terrorists and actively support training and attacks, including the attempted assassination of the Egyptian President Hosni Mubarak in 1995. As a result, Sudan was entered into the DoS's list of State Sponsors of Terrorism in 1993, and all assistance to that country was halted. In 1997, President Clinton issued an executive order[18] blocking Sudanese government property and prohibiting transactions with Sudan. In a span of seven years, Sudan went from being a major ally and recipient of American aid to an embargoed country that provided direct support to terrorists fighting the US. In parallel, the US and some of its African allies began to provide military and logistical support to the SPLA, once a Soviet client, fighting now against the al-Bashir regime. The north was waging the war against the SPLA using many militias while building on ethnic rivalries in Sudan between Dinka and Nuer to encourage devastation in the south (Natsios, 2012: 79). The LRA in northern Uganda was also supported by al-Bashir during those years and they were used to attack the SPLA in parallel to their war against the Museveni government in Uganda (Natsios, 2012: 79). This also brought Garang and Museveni closer to the point where the President of Uganda was considered as Garang's closest ally in Africa (Natsios, 2012: 173).

After the embassy bombings in Kenya and Tanzania, the US accused Sudan of direct co-operation in an attack against the United States by hosting and supporting Al-Qaida terrorists, and assumed a policy of confrontation towards Sudan (Natsios, 2012: 114; Woodward, 2006: 95). In this period USAID and the DoS initiated the Sudan Transitional Assistance Relief programme, focusing on granting humanitarian assistance and constructing civil society in the south through the SPLA regime (Woodward, 2006: 107).

Increasing pressure from Congress and evangelical organisations involved in humanitarian charity work in the south prompted the pre-9/11 Bush administration to deepen the engagement of the US through diplomacy to help reach a resolution for the civil war in Sudan. The events of 9/11 and the GWOT further elevated the importance of finding a way to remove Sudan as state sponsor of terrorism. In addition, the government of Sudan was accused of genocide in its region of Darfur (Flint and de Waal, 2008; Prunier, 2008). The atrocities committed by the Bashir regime in Darfur in 2003 required an international intervention to stop a genocide,[19] and the prospects of a possible US military intervention in Sudan in a post-9/11 reality served as an incentive for the Bashir regime to negotiate a peaceful conclusion for the ongoing civil war (Natsios, 2012: 167).

The Comprehensive Peace Agreement (CPA) between Sudan and southern Sudan was achieved in 2005, largely due to the involvement of the Bush administration. The independence of South Sudan became a reality after a referendum and despite substantial violations of the agreement between 2005 and 2011. Over the past four decades, the US has been using foreign assistance to the Sudan as a foreign policy tool to achieve its own national security objectives as they changed over time. During the Cold War, assistance was granted to Nimeiry to keep Sudan as a Cold War ally, to counterbalance Soviet power projected through its Ethiopian ally, and for the ability to use Sudan as a platform to project power towards the Gulf and Libya. While the objective of preventing Sudan from becoming a Soviet satellite state was achieved in the short term, the US supported a leader who turned Sudan into an Islamic state. When this happened in 1983, a second civil war of the south against the north occurred. At the beginning of the Civil War, the US supported the government of Sudan against the Marxist-oriented SPLA, who was supported by Soviet-backed Ethiopia. But as the Cold War subsided, and with it Soviet interest in Ethiopia and the subsequent re-engagement of the US with that important regional power (see below), the importance of Sudan lessened. In parallel, the government in Sudan changed, and as it became more radical, it began to sponsor terrorism against the US, its allies and its regional interests. As a result, the US began supporting the SPLA against the government in Sudan and worked for the isolation of Sudan from the international community. After 9/11 – and in relation to the war on terror, oil interest, domestic pressure and an ongoing regional effort to end the civil war in Sudan – the US pushed for the accomplishment of the CPA, strongly supporting the establishment of an independent South Sudan. After its establishment, and despite US assistance to that country from USAID, the DoS and the DoD (and other Western nations), South Sudan remains riven by internal rivalries and conflicts leading, perhaps, to a new civil war this time ethnically based, within the south itself.

The brief overview above indicates that in the case of Sudan, the initial policy of keeping Sudan out of the Soviet orbit more or less succeeded. However, since then the assistance policy of the US failed to remove Sudan's growing support of terrorists, achieving greater regional stability, and ending a civil war that inhibited democracy and economic development. Sudan and South Sudan did not turn into prosperous democracies that respected human rights, placed the interests of their people first, or adopted free market principles. Instead, the recipients used US development assistance as a means to achieve what their national governments defined as their objectives using the additional resources toward other avenues that included old ethnic rivalries, corruption and the spread of particular branches of Islam.

### *Ethiopia and Somalia*

Together with Liberia, Ethiopia was a US foreign policy priority (albeit marginal) in Africa long before there was greater policy emphasis upon the whole continent. Ethiopia was one of the only countries which did not fall under colonial rule. The Italian invasion of an independent Ethiopia sparked major concerns among African-Americans especially those associated with Marcus Garvey. Emperor Haile Selassie was both an expression of, and a symbol of, an independent Africa. The Ethiopian emperor Menelik II had defeated the Italian army coming from its colony of Eritrea in 1896 and in this way kept its autonomy. The second attempt in 1935 saw the Ethiopians defeated by a combination of the Italian army assisted by troops from the Italian colonies of Eritrea, Somalia, and Libya.

After WWII and the restoration of Haile Selasse to his throne, the relatively good relations between Ethiopia and the US led the US to support Ethiopian sovereignty over Eritrea in 1948. The strategic aspect of this support was related to the Cold War, and allowed America to access military facilities in Asmara[20] (Schraeder, 1994: 118). A further agreement with Ethiopia established an extended access to military facilities in Ethiopia in exchange for a limited military assistance programme (Schraeder, 1994: 119). Nevertheless, Ethiopia and the African continent were not considered vital for America as long as colonialism persisted, and European allies managed interests on the continent. The rise of nationalism in Africa towards the mid-1950s, and the subsequent increased influence of the Soviet Union on some nationalistic movements led the US to reconsider its policy towards the continent. Located geographically in a sensitive area in the proximity of the Horn, the Red Sea and Egypt,[21] Ethiopia and its monarchy became a strategic ally in the Cold War.

Aware of these dynamics, Emperor Selassie travelled to the Soviet Union in 1959 to signal to the US that he was prepared to shift allegiance if needed (Schraeder, 1994: 122–123). He pressured the US to support Ethiopian foreign policy and grant him military and economic assistance, which later had an important effect on geopolitics and the formation and makeup of Somalia as an independent nation (Lefebvre, 1991: 51; Schraeder, 1994: 122–123). When Somalia emerged as an independent nation in 1960, a merger of an Italian and British colony, the US and Ethiopia were close allies. This placed the US on the Ethiopian side for any future dispute with Somalia.[22] American military, political and economic support to Ethiopia pushed the newly-formed Somalia towards the Soviet Union, which responded by granting aid packages to strengthen Somalia's military (Schmidt, 2013:148). Ethiopia and Somalia clashed many times during the 1960s over border issues. These clashes were not instigated by the two superpowers, and both America and the Soviet Union were pressuring their clients not to engage in a cross-border war but to respect the territorial integrity of the other country. The US even threatened to withhold its assistance to Ethiopia if it did not comply (Schraeder, 1994: 129).

The military coup instigated by Barre in Somalia in 1969 toppled a democratically elected government, and brought Somalia closer to the Soviet Union as a client. Until the coup, the US was engaged in diplomacy with Somalia. Barre escalated the relationship with the US, and undertook a number of actions that antagonised Washington, including the expulsion of 100 US Peace Corps volunteers, claiming they were CIA agents (Schraeder, 1994: 133–134). But most importantly, by accepting large amounts of Soviet arms and by providing the port of Berbera which the Soviets turned into a naval and air base.

Ethiopia continued to be the most important strategic ally for the US in the region. Both economic and military assistance increased steadily in exchange for unhampered access by the US military to strategic facilities in Ethiopia. But in 1974, the Emperor was ousted by a commission of military officers called the Derg. It is important to note that the Ethiopian army was trained and equipped by the US; thus, troops trained by the US played an important role in ousting the Emperor.[23] The Derg assumed a communist ideology in 1975, and steadily moved towards the Soviet Union. In December 1976, the leader of the Derg, Mengistu Haile Mariam, signed a military aid agreement with Moscow. Up until then, the US had still supplied the Derg with military equipment approved by Kissinger true to his realpolitik stance. Kissinger attempted to keep this important Cold War ally on the US side by continuing to deliver important military and economic assistance to Ethiopia (Schraeder, 1994: 139). As Mengistu eliminated his opponents in Ethiopia, Castro visited Somalia and Ethiopia, and the Russians agreed to supply arms to Ethiopia while Carter ceased most military aid to its government.

Carter instructed his national security bureaucracy to attempt to befriend Somalia and provide limited assistance to Barre, despite the fact that he was seen and understood in Washington as a radical nationalistic leader (Mitchell, 2016: 176–202). As noted by Schraeder (1994: 144), Carter wished to signal that the US would grant support to any country ready to distance itself from Moscow. The attempt to befriend Somalia was in contrast to Carter's human rights rhetoric and influenced by the Cold War reality. It was also influenced by Saudi Arabia and Egypt's ongoing support for the Somali government (Mitchell, 2016: 191–199)

External powers were unable to stop Barre from attempting to incorporate the Somali areas (the Ogaden) into Somalia resulting in the Somalia–Ethiopian war which was launched by Somali troops entering Ogaden in July of 1977 under Carter's watch. The Somali army was initially successful and was only pushed back by Ethiopia with the strong support of the USSR and Cuba. This involved Soviet transport for 12,000 Cuban soldiers and 6,000 Cuban advisors thus enabling what the US had been trying to avoid – Cuban troops again on the battlefields of Africa (Mitchell, 2016: 369; Schmidt, 2013: 152).

Carter however, did not support the Somali offensive and attempted a diplomatic solution, pressuring Barre to retreat from the Ogaden in return for a promise that the US would supply him with defensive weapons. This was unsuccessful as the Somali army was pushed out of

Ogaden. Nonetheless, in the following years, Somalia replaced Ethiopia as the regional strategic ally, and granted US troops access to strategic military facilities, allowing America to project power towards the Gulf and balance Soviet influence in the region.

The dispute between Somalia and Ethiopia ended in 1988 through a peace agreement signed between Mengitsu and Barre (Lefebvre, 1991: 245–247). Both countries suffered from internal insurgencies, and the Cold War was fading into the background as the Soviet Union faced economic difficulties at home. Both regimes where overthrown in the beginning of 1991. At the same time, the US was realising that a new world order was in the offing. The Soviet Union was slowly disengaging from the Horn of Africa, and the US agreed to help Russia transit out of the region (Cohen, 2000).

Mengitsu approached the US for help as the Soviets were pulling out and civil war was threatening his regime. The US under the Bush administration agreed to negotiate with Mengitsu and facilitated talks between the rebels and the government (Schmidt, 2013). In 1991, responding to a US request to prevent further bloodshed, the Tigrean rebels assumed power in Addis Ababa, and eventually formed a coalition that shifted the country into democracy (temporarily) in 1995.

In Somalia, Barre faced a number of rebel groups, some of whom had been supported since the 1980s by the Soviet-backed Derg regime in Ethiopia. In 1991, after fighting to retain control of Mogadishu against rebels, Barre was overwhelmed by the forces of Mohamed Farrah Hassan Aidid and was forced to flee the country. With the national government gone, competing clan leaders used violence to expand their control and the county fell into anarchy.

The United Nations sought to ameliorate Somali civilian suffering caused by the internal wars. Civilian interventions were blocked by warlords and the UN expanded its mission in 1993 to neutralise local militias in order to deliver humanitarian relief (Schmidt, 2013: 204). The US took the lead but in a highly controversial action attacked a meeting held to consider a UN peace initiative. Intent on defeating Aidid US forces lost two helicopters to militia guns. In an incident made even more famous by the movie Black Hawk Down, 18 US troops and approximately 500 civilians were killed in the fighting. This led to the US withdrawal from the UN mission and Somalia for the time being. The Clinton administration decided to disengage from Somalia and move the US away from assuming leadership for military interventions. Over the years, Somalia fell to the control of Islamists enforcing strict Sharia laws over the civilian population. Terror, transnational crime and piracy became the trademark of Somalia over the next decade.

While the Bush administration opted for the hard power approach towards Somalia, the Obama administration slowly moved towards diplomacy and development, and helped African efforts to move Somalia out of chaos by providing both diplomatic and development assistance to the TFG and the functioning autonomous governments in the regions of Somaliland and Puntland. Obama also provided military assistance to defeat terror threats, namely against the radical al-Shabab organisation. As we write, al-Shabab still operates in Somalia and carries out terror attacks against civilians in neighbouring countries which it claims are responses to the use of Kenyan and other troops in its borders, contributing to regional destabilisation in East Africa.

When making a critical historical overview of the unintended consequences of power projection through assistance, we can conclude that US policy contributed to regional chaos. During the Cold War, assistance was given to Ethiopia to ensure that the US military had access to strategic facilities. This assistance allowed Ethiopia to build up its own power, which it projected against the newly independent state of Somalia and block the independence of Eritrea. In addition, to prevent Ethiopia from aligning with the Soviet Union (which it threatened to do several times over the years), the US assumed certain positions that were interpreted as anti-Somalian. Somalia aligned itself with the Soviet Union in return for assistance, while Ethiopia received military and economic assistance from the US. When Emperor Selassie was replaced by the Derg in a coup, US assistance to Ethiopia did not halt, and was granted to keep that country aligned with the US against the Soviet Union. This did not prevent the Marxist-oriented Derg regime from turning towards Moscow. Invoking human rights and American principles, Carter ended US assistance to Ethiopia, which allowed that country to fully ally itself with the Soviet Union, granting permission to Cuban troops to enter the region. In an attempt to keep a strategic foothold in the Horn of Africa, Carter began supporting Barre's regime in Somalia. While Ethiopia resumed a limited democratic system and slowly regained its position as a regional ally, Somalia fell into chaos. A US-led United Nations attempt to bring down the warlords ended in failure as the military option generated increased resistance to the UN (Schmidt, 2013). Somalia became a centre for regional political Islam, piracy and a global destabiliser. American foreign assistance in the past decade has been given to various countries in the region in order to help contain spill-overs from the Somali chaos across the Horn and eastern Africa.

The American strategic policy of assuming that military and development assistance would bring about long lasting loyalty to US objectives have failed in Somalia. Ethiopia is a more complicated case as the US remains active in the development arena. The assistance provided to Ethiopia and Somalia during the Cold War years did not bring about democracy, respect for human rights or the adoption of free market principles. Instead, it bought temporary strategic benefits through alliances and gave the US certain advantages (though limited in time and impact) over the Soviet Union. However, both Ethiopia and Somalia used US assistance to project their own regional power, mainly on each other, leading to conflict, heavy civilian casualties and human rights violations.

*Southern Africa*

In this section we show that while the US benefited strategically and economically from its ties with Portugal, Rhodesia and South Africa, it breached its fundamental principles, as well as contributed to war and human misery across the region. Since the end of WWII, the geopolitics of southern Africa has been through substantial transformations. It has posed a series of challenges to US policy due to the continued existence of Portuguese colonialism in Angola and Mozambique and the systems of racial domination in Namibia, South Africa and Zimbabwe. While much of Africa was becoming independent Portugal insisted that its colonies were overseas parts of the greater Portuguese nation. It refused to set up a process to guarantee national independence.

The US kept close ties with the apartheid regime in South Africa which raised both domestic and international criticism of US policies. These voices intensified in the 1950s along with the African struggle for independence from colonialism. The issue of US relations with the apartheid regime in South Africa continued to be a major source of friction not only between the US and the rest of Africa, but also within the US government until the free elections of 1994 when apartheid was abolished. The US South African policy was the result of a geopolitical strategy that placed South Africa as a fundamental ally in the region. In addition, South Africa was a major trade partner on the continent, and supplied the US with minerals crucial for American industry and power.

Rhetorically and throughout the Kennedy and Johnson administrations, the US attempted to distance itself from South Africa and its apartheid regime, but continued quietly to forge a relationship to secure strategic interests and kept military and intelligence contacts (Schraeder, 1994: 205).

Until the Carnation Revolution of 1974, Portugal under the rule of the Estado Novo regime clung to its African colonies, refusing to allow them to become independent. In opposition to its propagation of self-determination and human rights, the US continued to support Portugal with assistance, including the military assistance diverted from NATO. The assistance to Portugal was given for strategic reasons and in exchange for usage rights of the Azores base and the ongoing practice that the colonial power had the right to shape policies. In return, Portugal received economic and military assistance packages, including political support.[24]

When Nixon came to power in 1969, southern Africa was composed of Portuguese colonies locked in a conflict against nationalists, a white minority regime in Rhodesia, an apartheid regime in South Africa, and the large territory of South-west Africa under a South African mandate.

The situation in southern Africa presented a dilemma for US policymakers. The American discourse emphasised justice, self-determination, human rights, democracy and economic liberalism all of which was absent in southern Africa. The preferred policy option of the Nixon administration, known as the 'tar baby' option, was based on communication and relaxation of tensions with the white minority regimes (Rhodesia,[25] South Africa and Portugal), and a toned-down rhetoric.[26] In parallel, the US continued granting diplomatic and economic aid to other African nations in order to balance criticism against US policy in southern Africa, securing US national security, economic and political interests, and encouraging black African states to reject communist interests in Africa. However, this policy had a short life due to events in Portugal and southern Africa.

After the coup in Portugal, Portuguese African colonies moved quickly towards independence. In Mozambique, the Soviet and Chinese-backed FRELIMO party which had waged a guerrilla war against the Estado Novo regime since 1964, finally came to rule. Fearing a communist-backed state on its borders, together with the prospect of a safe haven for the rebel group ZANU, Ian Smith's regime backed the formation of RENAMO. Beginning in 1976 and lasting until the peace agreement of 1992, RENAMO fought a bitter civil war against FRELIMO in Mozambique sponsored by Rhodesia and later by South Africa.[27] The FRELIMO government initially assumed an anti-American stance, remembering the support US granted to Portugal during colonial times through the tar-baby policy option but became more aligned with the West in the 1980s.

In post-colonial Angola, the destructiveness of Cold War rivalries emerged. The United States, the USSR, China and Cuba became involved, to be followed by South Africa. While the three liberation organisations were to form a united government (the Alvor Accord, 1975) they were unable to agree. The American Secretary of State saw the MPLA (which was now Soviet backed) to be their proxy and had arms and support channelled to the FNLA and UNITA. When South African troops began entering Angola to chase Namibian rebels this changed the nature of the conflict due to the overwhelming hatred on the continent of South Africa and its apartheid regime. This was followed by a South Africa effort to unseat the Angolan government which was blocked by the intervention of Cuban troops. Angola's 'civil war' lasted with a few pauses until 1992.

The US government's 'secret' support especially for UNITA created political difficulties domestically. Congress refused to continue US covert support to the fight against the MPLA by passing the Clark amendment in 1976, a decision that went against the executive branch preference. Kissinger viewed the evolving situation in southern Africa with concern, fearing that without US involvement, Soviet and Cuban presence in Angola would lead to the creation of a pro-Soviet independent state in

Namibia as well as Angola. Kissinger feared the risk that a post-Smith Rhodesian regime, as well as a post-apartheid regime in South Africa would be pro-Soviet because Moscow provided support both to ZAPU and the ANC.

Frustrated by the restrictions imposed by Congress, Kissinger devised a new policy for Africa. His goal was to contain the Soviet Union, find a way to remove the Cubans from Angola, ensure that no more countries would call on Cuban and Soviet support, and secure various American strategic interests. He hoped to achieve support by sponsoring bilateral and multilateral assistance programmes for several key African nations (NSC, 1976).[28] In addition, Kissinger understood that to satisfy other African nations, the US would have to adopt a harsher line against the apartheid regime, and find a solution that would remove the illegal Smith regime in Rhodesia. With the electoral defeat of President Ford, Kissinger's views were no longer dominant.

The Byrd Amendment from 1971 was repealed during the Carter administration, and a stronger line against the white minority regimes in southern Africa was adopted. Nevertheless, the most important objectives of the US in the region were to end white racial domination in Rhodesia forestalling Cuban and Soviet intervention and to remove Cuban troops and Soviet influence from Angola. Carter expended substantial energy and resources to a negotiated settlement between the Smith government and the national liberation groups.[29] Carter also assumed a harsher stance against South Africa, calling for the abolition of apartheid. This led to the deterioration of the relationship between the US and the Vorster government in South Africa.

During the Reagan administration, the main concern remained the Cold War and how to block and roll back the presence of Soviet and Cuban troops in southern Africa. The administration opted for a regional policy of what they labelled 'constructive engagement' towards southern Africa. The policy involved persuading the South Africans to grant Namibia (South-west Africa) independence. In exchange, Washington would work to oblige Cuban troops to leave Angola. In southern Africa more generally, the Reagan administration appeared to accept the idea that South Africa was the anti-communist bulwark in the region and therefore should not be weakened. The constructive engagement policy aimed to locate a diplomatic solution for Namibia and apartheid without isolating South Africa. Resisting domestic and international pressure, Reagan opposed the imposition of comprehensive sanctions against South Africa until he was forced to do so by Congress in 1986. In general, the Reagan administration viewed the African National Congress (and other African liberation movements) as Soviet sponsored terrorist organisations. Cuban troops eventually left Angola after South Africa reached an agreement with Namibia for independence in 1988.

The sanctions against South Africa imposed by Congress were lifted by the Bush administration in 1991 after Mandela was released from prison and before apartheid was abolished and against the position of the ANC. In parallel Bush granted development and economic assistance to South Africa.

In its focus on the USSR and Cuba, US policies paid little attention to the grievances and concerns of Angolans, Mozambicans, Namibians, *et al.* but rather viewed them as pawns of the Russians and/or Cubans. The outcome for the region was long and destructive wars which arguably were aggravated by US policies on the continent. In Angola, America together with Rhodesia and South Africa, provided support to the FNLA and UNITA against the Soviet and Cuban-backed MPLA. This support inflamed a civil war that lasted a decade longer than the Cold War.

In opposition to the international community, the US traded with Rhodesia and provided extensive assistance to South Africa, including economic, military and political assistance in exchange for access to strategic military bases, trade, access to strategic minerals and an alliance against Soviet subversive actions in the region. These policies were undertaken to secure American interests. As a result, many African nations were antagonised. When the US through Kissinger decided to change its policy after Congress hampered the ability of the executive branch to support rebels against Angola, it used development and economic assistance as a way to gain guarantees from a number of African nations that they would oppose Cuban and Soviet involvement in Africa and help locate a solution to the presence of Cuban troops in Angola.

In this example, foreign assistance – which included military, economic, development and political assistance – was granted by the US to support problematic regimes and political movements (UNITA and FNLA) as a part of the Cold War rationale. Assistance was used as a power tool in a box of tools to strengthen America's leadership, secure American interests, and help fight communism. As history unfolded, the antagonised Portuguese colonies turned to the Soviet Union, while America continued to support problematic minority regimes in the region against communism, helping to perpetuate apartheid and the Rhodesian regime, and by extension the violence created by the struggles for independence by national liberation movements.

### *Projecting power through assistance*

US foreign assistance as an extended element of foreign policy is viewed in the examples above as a tool to project power. It has been used to support and strengthen allies and to help repel enemies. It has also been used in exchange for US access to strategic facilities and strategic minerals. It has been used as a political tool to ensure support for US policies, and in return for supporting US national security objectives. The assistance was given knowingly to problematic and corrupt regimes which adhered to principles that were in stark contradiction to US principles and to the American regime of truth. In the examples given above, the actual welfare of the people in developing countries was, at best, a secondary consideration of the US.

Granting economic, military and development assistance in such a fashion had severe side effects with incalculable and unpredictable costs. These exerted a toll in terms of loss of human rights, suffering, conflict and corruption. In the cases of Sudan, Ethiopia and Somalia, for example, the assistance granted to these countries to fend off Soviet ideology did not achieve the desired goal. Instead, governments and militaries took US assistance and transformed it to achieve their own objectives, whether these were linked to ethnic or political rivalries or were for the personal economic gain of the leadership. Attempts by the US to achieve regional stability through assistance to Ethiopia, to Sudan, to Portugal, and to South Africa backfired. Assistance to Portugal resulted in national liberation movements seeking assistance elsewhere including Cuba and the USSR leading, as it turns out, to temporarily socialist governments in Angola, Guinea-Bissau and Mozambique. Labelling national liberation movements as terrorist probably lengthened the time it took to grant independence to Namibia and for white minority rule to end in Zimbabwe and South Africa. In sum, US policies led to the further radicalisation of these movements but in the end with the collapse of the USSR and the turn toward capitalism by China, radicalism has at least for the time being come to an end (Southall, 2013).

## Conclusion

Throughout this book we have examined a particular aspect of foreign assistance. The particular space we highlight is that in which assistance is granted to promote the national security and interests of the donor.

Throughout the book we focused on showing how assistance is justified as a power projection tool and on the overarching rationales attached to these justifications. In the case of the US, justification of the assistance policy is linked to the American regime of truth. Foreign or international assistance is presumably given to enhance life, liberty and the pursuit of happiness for nations that are in need and meet conditions set forward by the US. America engages in assistance because it sees itself as an exceptional nation that has a role to play in the world, as well as having a duty to its people to keep them secure and to share the benefits of the American way of life. Democracy and free enterprise are viewed as the keys through which the basic God-given rights are to be secured. An economic system that allows people to pursue the American dream which is linked to these basic rights, is secured and enhanced through the democratic system. These basic elements that forge a distinct American understanding of itself and its role in the world, interact with historical contexts to produce a distinctly American assistance discourse.

The assistance policy of the US is a power tool through which America projects its exceptionalism and secures its system at home. This is the same as saying that assistance in these instances is just another foreign policy tool. This last statement can be considered as fairly trivial; nevertheless, it is important to understand that when development assistance is subjugated to the foreign policy and national security objective of the donor, it becomes a means to project power through *domination* rather than a tool designed first and foremost to help people who are defined as being in need of development. While at times there may be a genuine attempt to help people achieve development, in the cases described in this book, it is granted primarily to achieve goals which were linked to the Cold War, to American power in a post-Cold War reality, and now to fight terrorism. We would like to emphasise that development assistance has been all too often attached to national security objectives. Efforts to provide assistance 'to people in need' has been rarely sufficient to convince a reluctant congress to fund such programmes. A path toward generating development assistance on the basis of compassion, or from adherence to human rights, seems as distant as ever.

Building on the dominant terminology that links exceptionalism to foreign policy, we categorise the assistance discourse of the US into four dominant approaches located in the discourse. These are: the missionary, the exemplary type 1, the exemplary type 2, and the mixed approaches. We also emphasise that while certain administrations prefer, discursively, one approach to another, most administrations adopt a mixed approach in practice, combining in contexts missionary and both types of exemplary approaches. The underlying thread linking these approaches is the need to preserve the American regime of truth at home and safeguard the exceptional nature of the US through the projection of power. It would seem that to date, no amount of failures of US foreign policy has been sufficient to challenge the regime of truth.

Granting assistance to encourage development, be it military, political, economic or human, has unintended consequences (as well as the intended ones). In terms of those implementing policies they could also be indifferent or powerless toward the outcomes for different categories of people. New actors are empowered or old elites are re-empowered by how assistance is structured and delivered. By supporting UNITA and FNLA in Angola and using the government of Mobutu in Zaire to deliver the arms, the US supported the militarisation of the MPLA and its reliance upon Cuba. Rather than leading to democratisation or free enterprise it has led to an oil oligarchy. In this sense, we speak of unintended empowerment linked to the projection of power through assistance, and the impact of the unintended empowerment and subsequent consequences. This, not only towards the strategic objectives of the policy, but also towards issues such as encouraging democracy, human rights, free market systems and development as it is defined in contexts. We provide examples of impacts such as prolonged civil wars, empowerment of problematic regimes, of coups d'état, of encroachment of terrorism and transnational crime, and of corruption.

When analysed through the theoretical frameworks that bind it, development assistance is viewed as various types of aid which are given to governments or other agencies and organisations, to modify conditions of underdevelopment (as defined by various taxonomies), to conditions of development. When using the power lens, development assistance is a tool used by government to modify the underdeveloped (be it people, governments, or organisations) in ways that will produce an end result consistent with the preferences of the donor. The US government does not engage in an attempt to hide the links between the assistance policy and its national security objectives. It identifies very clearly the links between granting assistance and securing interests, but consistently links those to a concrete set of values and principles which it sees as supreme. The justification helps to create a bridge between a collective identity and the pursuit of unilateral interests. As such, development assistance serves an extra-theoretical purpose of achieving predefined national security interests of a donor. When used for such a purpose, the basic usefulness of the concept of development assistance as a global good is undermined.

However, we are entering a new period of US engagements with Africa. The establishment of AFRICOM, the shift in what had been thought of 'development' funding to the DoD potentially represents major changes in US assistance policy. According to Anderson and Veillette (2014), DoD activities include not just countries in conflict but also at peace. In many of the same ways that all conflicts in Africa were viewed through a Cold War lens from 1945 until 1990, all current conflicts are viewed from an Islamic and 'terrorism' perspective. These new conflicts are also taking place in a multipolar world where other major actors are active. Can and will the American regime of truth hold in the US? What forces and actors might lead to its fragmentation within the US even as much of the world does not view the US in idealistic terms? Will the contested state of American democracy pose a new challenge for American exceptionalism? 'America First' as the new basis for US foreign policy according to President Trump does not signal a withdrawal from the global arena but perhaps making explicit what has always been the underlying practice of development assistance. Whether or not the US regime of truth will hold is uncertain. Given the increased reliance upon the military without a comprehensive analysis of its impacts in Africa since 2001 may undermine the broader moral purposes and goals of development and lead to reframing and reshaping the regime of truth.

## Notes

1 This is very much like Lieven's explanation of the American creed and American civic nationalism: 'The essential elements of the American Creed and American civic nationalism are faith in liberty, constitutionalism, the law, democracy, individualism and cultural and political egalitarianism.' (2004: 49).
2 This does not mean that all Americans accept a specific justification, but only to emphasise that all justifications, from ultra-liberal to ultra-conservative, will be pinned in the regime of truth.
3 We use here the terms 'Missionary' and 'Exemplary'. These two terms are widely used to distinguish between US foreign policies (as discussed in Chapter 3). We build on these terms to characterise sorts of power in US development assistance policy.
4 We would like to emphasise here that these strategies are propagated through discursive practices, not necessarily in the application of policy which is more nuanced than the discourse.
5 This approach appears explicitly in discursive practices. It is also the approach that most administrations adopt in practice, even when the discourse propagates a less nuanced interpretation of the role of foreign assistance.
6 For a discussion on the mutual constitution of foreign policy and identity, the tension arising from it, and the role of foreign policy in creating an image of stability, see Hansen (2006).
7 Actively or by setting the example.
8 This is very often translated in the discourse as 'good versus evil'.
9 Bilateral engagement offers opportunities to incorporate specific agendas and to use various sorts of leverage instruments.
10 This fact was observed by Restad (2015) and is thoroughly discussed in her book.
11 In practice, most administrations assume a similar type of policy in different contexts even if the discourses state a different preference.
12 See, for example, Lake (1993).
13 We write these lines without the intention of sounding cynical or insinuating that America is being deceitful. US policymakers do believe in a mission of mercy to help people in distress overcome hardship. This mission is part of the American ethos, but it is also part of a rationale that views these missions as a way to increase American power and influence. There is no dichotomy by doing both at the same time from a political point of view and this type of approach is based on the exemplary stance in foreign policy.
14 See, for example, Adams and Murray (2014) for a comprehensive analysis of militarisation of the foreign assistance trend in the US since 9/11.
15 Not surprisingly, American policy advice and practices are said to be in the best interests of the nations involved.
16 The Addis Ababa agreement of 1972.
17 And assistance provided by other countries and multilateral organisations.
18 Executive Order 13067 signed on 3 November 1997.
19 There remains much debate as to whether events and violence in Darfur constituted genocide (Mamdani, 2013).
20 Namely Kagnew station.
21 The most powerful Arab nation at that time and a Soviet ally.
22 The Ogaden region of Eastern Ethiopia was inhabited by a majority of ethnic Somalis, and was considered by many Somali nationalists as part of greater Somalia. This issue became the cause of several conflicts between Ethiopia and Somalia.

23  See also Schraeder (1994: 137). It is not insinuated here that the US played any role in the putsch against Selassie.
24  For example, Kennedy's abstention from a UN vote calling for sanctions against Portugal and its colonial policies in Africa in July 1963.
25  Which led to the adoption of the Byrd Amendment in 1971 allowing the US to trade with Rhodesia against sanctions imposed on Smith's regime by the international community.
26  Based on the idea that these regimes were not going to disappear from the arena.
27  When Maputo allowed the ANC to operate from Mozambique.
28  A type of Marshall Plan for Africa (NSC, 1976).
29  The Rhodesian problem was resolved through British and UN mediation in 1979 but strongly supported over the years by President Carter (Mitchell, 2016).

## References

Adams, G. and Murray, S. K. (2014) *Mission creep: the militarization of US foreign policy?* Georgetown University Press, Washington, DC.
Anderson, G. W. and Veillette, C. (2014) Soldiers in sandals, in Adams, G. and Murray, S. K. (eds) *Mission creep: the militarization of US foreign policy?* Georgetown University Press, Washington, DC, pp. 97–119.
Buss, T. F. (2011) *African security and the African command: viewpoints on the US role in Africa.* Kumarian Press, Sterling, VA.
Clough, M. (1992) *Free at last?: U.S. policy toward Africa and the end of the Cold War.* Council on Foreign Relations Press, New York.
Cohen, H. J. (2000) *Intervening in Africa: superpower peacemaking in a troubled continent.* St. Martin's Press, New York.
Flint, J., De Waal, A. and International African Institute. (2008) *Darfur: a new history of a long war.* Zed Books; Distributed in the US exclusively by Palgrave Macmillan, London; New York.
Hansen, Lene. (2006). *Security as Practice: Discourse Analysis and the Bosnian War.* The New International Relations, Routledge, New York.
Kibbe, Jennifer, D. (2014). The Military, the CIA, and America's Shadow Wars, in Adams, G. and Murray, S. K. (eds) *Mission creep: the militarization of US foreign policy?* Georgetown University Press, Washington, DC, pp. 201–231.
Lake, A. (1993) From Containment to enlargement – remarks given at Johns Hopkins University, 21 September 1993.
Lefebvre, J. A. (1991) *Arms for the Horn: U.S. security policy in Ethiopia and Somalia, 1953–1991.* University of Pittsburgh Press, Pittsburgh, Pa.
Lieven, A. (2004) *America right or wrong: an anatomy of American nationalism.* Oxford University Press, New York.
Mamdani, M. (2013) *Saviors and survivors: Darfur, politics and the war on terror.* Makerere Institute of Social Research, Kampala, Uganda.
Marks, S. and Trapido, S. (1987) *The politics of race, class, and nationalism in twentieth-century South Africa.* Longman, London; New York.
Mitchell, N. (2016) *Jimmy Carter in Africa: race and the Cold War.* Woodrow Wilson Center Press, Washington, DC; Stanford University Press, Stanford, Calif.
Natsios, A. S. (2012) *Sudan, South Sudan, and Darfur: what everyone needs to know.* Oxford University Press, Oxford; New York.

NSC (1976) Minutes of a National Security Council Meeting, Washington, 11 May 1976, 6:15 p.m.–7:15 p.m.: Document 44, Foreign Relations of the United States, 1969–1976, Volume E–6, Documents on Africa, 1973–1976.

Nye, J. S. (2004) *Soft power: the means to success in world politics*. Public Affairs, New York.

Nye, J. S. (2011) *The future of power*. Public Affairs, New York.

Obama, B. (2009) Remarks by the President to Ghanaian Parliament – 11 July 2009. The White House.

Prunier, G. r. (2008) *Darfur: a 21st century genocide*. Cornell University Press, Ithaca, New York.

Restad, H. (2015) *American exceptionalism: an idea that made a nation and remade the world*. Routledge, Milton Park, Abingdon, Oxon; New York.

Schmidt, E. (2013) *Foreign intervention in Africa: from the Cold War to the War on Terror*. Cambridge University Press, Cambridge.

Schraeder, P. J. (1994) *United States foreign policy toward Africa: incrementalism, crisis, and change*. Cambridge University Press, Cambridge; New York.

Southall, R. (2013) *Liberation Movements in Power: Party & State in Southern Africa*. James Currey Ltd, Woodbridge.

Traub, J. (2008) *The freedom agenda: why America must spread democracy (just not the way George Bush did)*. Farrar, Straus and Giroux, New York.

Woodward, P. (2006) *US foreign policy and the Horn of Africa*. Ashgate, Aldershot, England; Burlington, VT.

# Index

Page numbers in *italics* denote tables, those in **bold** denote figures.

9/11: and development 21; *see also* post-9/11 assistance discourse

'A New Moment of Promise' speech 233–4
Abacha, S. 207
abolitionist movement 37–8
Abraham, S. 218
Abyei 246
accountability 276
Accra Speech 233–4
Act for International Development, 1950 65
Afghanistan 76, 87, 91, 93, 151, 152
Africa: divisions of 30;; historical context 9; increasing importance to US 112, 122, 127; low priority for US 125–6, 133, 178, 219, 237; perceived vulnerability 115, 160, 220, 228; US post-Cold War interests 179–80, 194, 198, 202, 272–4
Africa as underdeveloped: colonialism 45–9; context and overview 29–31; cultural hierarchies 41–3; developed-undeveloped frames 32–5; political systems 43–5; race and development 35–41; summary and conclusions 52–3; US view of Africa 49–53
Africa for the Africans 117–20
Africa Growth and Opportunity Act (AGOA) 205–7, 209, 217, 220, 228, 234, 274
Africa Trade Caucus 205
African Command (AFRICOM) 223, 226–7, 240, 243, 261, 275, 276
African Contingency Operations Training and Assistance Program (ACOTA) 222, 274, 275–6
African Crisis Response Initiative (ACRI) 203–5, 222, 274
African Development Fund 142–3
African Economic Policy Reform Programme 160
African independence, US disillusionment 126
African National Congress (ANC) 159, 181–2
African Party for the Independence of Guinea and Cape Verde, international support 128
*African Political Systems* (Fortes and Evans-Pritchard) 44–5
African states, vulnerability of 220–1
African Union Mission to Somalia (AMISOM) 249
Afro-Asiatic bloc, as source of concern 115
ag Bahanga, I. 241
ag Ghaly, I. 241
Age of Democratic Peace 81
age of democratic peace 272
agency, and power 12
aid, and policy alignment 18
aid spending, congressional barriers 71, 73–4, 82–3, 86, 99, 124, 126–7, 139–40, 148, 186, 192, 197, 288–9, 292.
Aideed, M.F. 198, 285
al-Bashir, O. 186–7, 229, 244, 280
al-Mahdi, S. 185–6, 280
Al-Qaida 87, 208, 220, 248, 281
Al-Qaida in the Maghreb (AQIM) 240
Al-Shabab 249

298  *Index*

al-Turabi, H. 186, 229
al-Zawahiri, A. 240
Albright, M.K. 83, 201, 207
Alger, H. 59
Algeria 240
Algerian Islamic Salafist Group for Preaching and Combat (GSPC) 240
Alvor Accords 135, 288
Ambrose, S.E. 75, 178
America First 293
American Colonisation Society 49
American dream 59
American ideology 10
American values, under threat 61
American way 75
American way of life, preservation of 265
Americanism 58–9
amorality 263
*An American Dilemma* (Myrdal *et al*) 51
analysis of truth 8
Anderson, G.W. 293
Angola: civil war 135, 138; concerns 144–5; conflict with Zaire 147–8, 151; covert missions 140; foreign involvement 138–9; Kissinger's view 139–40; liberation movements 135; new world order 187–9; Reagan's aims 155; relations with South Africa 146, 160; unintended consequences 288–9; withholding of aid 140
Annan, K. 219
Ansar Dine 241
anti-colonial forces, Soviet support 266
anti-colonial position 109
anti-war movements 73
Aouzou Strip 156
apartheid 145–6, 180–2, 287; *see also* racial segregation
Apodaca, C. 75, 76, 78, 82, 152
Arab Spring 241
arc of crisis 151
archaeology, Foucauldian method 7–8
Armitage, R. 14, 94
Arusha accords 200
assertive multilateralism 198–9
assistance discourse: after collapse of Soviet Union 79–86; Bush, G.H.W. 79–83; Bush, G.W. 87–92; Carter, J. 74–6; Clinton, W.J. 83–6; Cold War 62–79; context and overview 58–62; Eisenhower, D.D. 65–6; Ford, G. 73–4; Johnson, L.B. 69–71; Kennedy, J.F. 67–9; and national identity 278; Nixon, R.M. 71–3; Obama, B. 92–9; post-9/11 87–99; Reagan, R. 77–9; strands of 292; *see also* exemplary strands; missionary strand; mixed approach; summary and conclusions 99; Truman, H. 62–5; unique culture 58–9
Atwood, B.J. 85, 195–6
Azores 130–1

Bacevich, A.J. 60–1
Bachrach, P. 11
Baker, J. 82, 178, 179–80, 181
balancing strategy 266
band-aid diplomacy 83
Baratz, M.S. 11
Barre, S. 149, 150, 193, 283–5
Battle of Mogadishu 198–9
Behrman, G. 219
bilateral programmes 78, 82, 270
bin Laden, O. 229
Binational Commissions (BNCs) 203
Black Africa: reactions to US policy 131; use of term 30–1
Black Caucus 136
Black Congressional Caucus 181–2
Boas, F. 43
book: aims 1–2, 3, 19; application of Foucaldian perspective 9–10; application of Lukes' framework 12–13; chapter outlines 24–5; questions asked 2; scope 2–3, 4; summary and conclusions 291–3
Botswana 141–2
Boutros-Ghali, B. 198
Bowles, C. 119
Brainard, L. 23
Brinkley, D. 75, 178
Brown versus the Board of Education 52
Brzezinski, Z. 77, 144, 145, 147, 148, 150–1
Bureau for Near Eastern, South Asian and African Affairs 108
Bureau of African Affairs 112, 122, 179, 190, 192, 216, 225
Bureau of Human Rights and Humanitarian Affairs 269
Bush doctrine 219–20, 237
Bush, G.H.W. 79–83, 178ff, 209–10, 272, 289
Bush, G.W. 61, 87–92, 209, 216ff, 274–6, 277, 285

Buxton, T. 38
Byrd Amendment 130, 131, 145, 289

Cairo Resolution 149
Callaway, R.L. 87, 88
Carington, P. (Lord Carrington) 151
Carleton, D. 76
Carlucci, F. 78
Carnation Revolution 287
Carson, J. 233, 237, 238, 248–9
Carter doctrine 152, 269
Carter, J. 74–6, 143–52, 192, 250–1, 268–9, 271, 280, 284–5, 289
Castro, F. 149, 284
Central Command (CENTCOM) 223
Central Intelligence Agency (CIA) 134, 138, 147–8, 247–8
Centre for Strategic and International Studies (CSIS) report 14–15
Chad 156
chain of power relations 18
chapter outlines 24–5
Cheney, D. 218
Cheney Report 218
Christopher, W. 195, 196–7, 203
civil rights 73
Civil Rights Act, 1964 70
Civil Rights Movement 51
civil wars 179, 243–4; *see also* new world order
civilisation, sociocultural evolution 34–5
Clinton doctrine 84–5, 202, 273
Clinton, H. 94–5, 234–5
Clinton, W.J. 83–6, 194ff, 209–10, 230, 272–3
co-operation scheme, Europe and US 112
co-operative strategy for global growth 153
Cohen, H. 178, 179–80, 181, 182–3, 185–6, 187–9, 190, 192, 193–4
Cold War 51, 133–42, 179, 265–72, 279
Cold War assistance discourse: Carter, J. 74–6; Eisenhower, D.D. 65–6; Ford, G. 73–4; Johnson, L.B. 69–71; Kennedy, J.F. 67–9; Nixon, R.M. 71–3; Reagan, R. 77–9; Truman, H. 62–5
Cold War neutrality 117–18
collaboration 235, 251
colonial administrations 46–7
colonial powers, relations with US 108–9

colonial wars, southern Africa 133
colonialism 2, 45–9
colonisation, as means of development 38
Combined Joint Task Force – Horn of Africa (CJTF-HOA) 223, 275–6
Commission on Security and Economic Assistance 78
communism 63, 78, 108–9, 115–16, 121, 134, 181
communist expansion doctrine 62–3
comparative method 44–5
Comprehensive Peace Agreement (CPA), 2005 231, 244, 246, 279, 281–2
concepts and terms, of evolution 35
conceptual map 19–24, **22**, 260
conditionality 118
conduct of conduct 12
conflict, and use of power 11
conflict fatigue 193
conflict resolution 235
Congress 124, 127
Congress–executive branch relationship 73–4, 134, 140, 159–60
Congress Foreign Assistance Bill Authorisation S. 2662 74
constructive engagement 157–9, 183, 229, 270
Contact Group 146
containment 63, 69, 71, 75, 80, 83, 117, 118, 119, 125
Copson, R.W. 222, 232
core values 74
corruption 241
Council on Foreign Relations 94
crime 240–1, 248
crisis resolution 235
critique of power 8
Crocker, C.A. 155, 157–9, 160, 187, 197
Cuba 155–6, 160, 269, 284; *see also* Angola
cultural development, as context-determined 43
cultural hierarchies 41–3

Dahl, R.A. 10–11
Dam, K.W. 158
Darfur 244–5, 246, 281; *see also* Republic of South Sudan; Sudan
Davidson, A.I. 4, 6, 7, 8
Davis, N. 135, 138
de Gaulle, C. 115
de Klerk, F.W. 180–1

300   *Index*

Decade of Development 68, 119
Declaration of Independence 130, 278
decolonisation, and development 2
DeFrank, T.M. 181
democracy 79, 86, 194, 234–5, 236, 269–70, 276
democratic enlargement 195, 198
democratic humanism 64
Democratic Republic of Congo (DRC) 208
democratisation 272
Department of Defence, aid delivery 89
Department of State 109ff; transformational diplomacy agenda 227–8
Derg 133, 148, 284, 286
Des Forges, A. 200
détente 132
developed, use of term 9
development: duality of term 47; evolution of idea 34–5; and fight against terrorism 21; and race 35–41
development aid, contingency 272
development assistance: as core pillar 94; dual motivation 61; economic burden 116; guiding principles 70, 78; hierarchy 31–2; historical context 2; increasing impact 121; institutional politics of 23–4; morality of 132, 268–9; policy review Task Force 122–4; as political weapon 120; purpose of 2, 266–7, 270; as redemption 38; as strategic tool 64, 68–9; as technology of power 29–30; value-based rationale 67; *see also* foreign assistance
development categories 2
development challenges, responding to 116
development objectives, transformation of 18
development policy, relation to foreign policy 1
development promises, post-World War II 1
diplomacy 276
direct relations 208–9
Directive 3000.05 92
Director of Foreign Assistance (DFA) 89, 91
discourse analysis, of paradigms 6
Divon, S. 20
Djibouti Peace Process 248
Doe, S. 191–2

domestic concerns 80
domestic criticism 74–5
domestic dissatisfaction 126–7, 137, 197
domination 6–7, 15–18, 19–20
DoS USAID Strategic Plan 228–9
dual motivation 61
dual track approach, Somalia 248–9
Dubois, W.E.B. 50
Dulles, J.F. 66, 109

Eagleburger, L. 185–6
East Africa Counter-Terrorism Initiative (EACTI) 225–6, 275–6
East Africa Regional Strategic Initiative (EARSI) 225–6
East–West conflict 155
Easum, D. 134–5
economic and trade initiatives 83
Economic Community of West African States Monitoring Group (ECOMOG) 192
economic contact 46
economic crisis, Africa 160
economic integration 274
economic interests 136, 155, 205
economic opportunities, post-Cold War 273
economic power, desire for 61
economic prosperity, conditions for 196
economic relations, power asymmetry 46–7
economic well-being, importance of 153
economy, centrality of 61
Eisenhower, D.D. 65–6, 112, 116–18, 266–7
Eisenhower doctrine 279
el-Bashir, H. 186–7
elections: 1956 112; 1976 143; 2016 41; Angola 189; Mali 240; Rhodesia 145; South Africa 201
elements of global development 95
eligibility for aid 90
elitism, European 43
Emerson, R.W. 40, 52
energy crises 76, 132
engagement policies 273–4
Engels, F. 17
Entebbe Principles 208
environmental specialisation 36–7
Eritrea 148, 182, 208
Ethiopia: civil war 133, 134; conflict with Somalia 147; international

relations 148–9; new world order 182–4; and regional balance of power 157; relations with Soviet Union 149; relations with US 149; and Sudan 187; treaty with Libya 156; unintended consequences 280, 282–3, 284, 285, 286–7; war with Eritrea 208
European Command (EUCOM) 222–3
European countries, policies and strategies 115
European elitism 43
Evans-Pritchard, E.E. 44–5
evolution 35, 36–7
exceptionalism 58, 59–61, 88, 153, 271, 278, 292
executive branch: and Congress 73–4, 134, 140, 159–60; power of 73–4
exemplary strands 60, 263–4, 267–9, 271–3, 274, 277, 292

Falashas 182–3
fatal impacts 94
Feed the Future (FTF) 98
Ferguson, J. 18
fight against terrorism 21; *see also* Global War on Terror (GWOT)
flexible approach 264
Flohr, M. 17
food aid programme 69–70
Food for Progress programme 160
Ford, G. 73–4, 134–42, 267, 268, 289
foreign assistance: budget cuts 197; changes to aid programme 89; guiding principles 70, 78; and human rights 194–5; and national security 66, 67–8, 76, 88, 91–2, 154–5; rationale for 80; reduction of 86; and world peace 73; *see also* development assistance
Foreign Assistance Acts: 1950 265–6; 1961 66, 68, 72; 1974 74; 1991 82
Foreign Assistance Bill, 1971 73
foreign policy, influence of exceptionalism 60–1
foreign policy issues, DoS summary 124
Forrestal, J. 64
Fortes, M. 44–5
Foucauldian methods 7–9
Foucault–Habermas debate 8
Foucault, M. 4–10, 11–12, 20, 261–2, 278
four-pronged approach 119–20
France 115–16, 243

Fraser, N. 8
Freedom Agenda 219–20
fresh approach 71–2
friendly autocratic regimes 77
Fulbright, J.W. 64, 93–4
*Future of Power* (Nye) 14

Gaddafi, M. 155, 184–5
Garang, J 184, 281
Garvey, M. 50
Gates, R.M. 95, 226
genealogy, Foucauldian method 8
genocide, Rwanda 200
geopolitics 216–17, 221, 241, 279
Global AIDS and Tuberculosis Relief Act, 2000 209
Global Climate Change Initiative (GCCI) 98
global development, elements of 95
Global Fund to fight HIV/AIDS, tuberculosis and malaria 218
Global Health Initiative (GHI) 98, 235
Global Peace Operations Initiative (GPOI) 222
global position, of US 1, 29, 81
global power, shift to communism 134
Global War on Terror (GWOT) 88, 219–22, 240, 244–5, 274–5, 281
globalisation 86, 273
globalism 152
Goldwater-Nichols Department of Defence Reorganisation Act, 1986 80
good versus evil narrative 87
Gorbachev, M. 179
Gordon, C. 4, 5, 6
Gore, A. 86, 201–2, 209
Goukouni, O. 156
governance 274, 276
government, conduct of conduct 12
governmentality 7
Graham, G. 230
Gramsci, A. 17
Gration, S. 244, 246
Gromyko, A. 151
GSPC 224
guiding principles for strategic foreign assistance 70, 78
Guinea 115–16
Gulf War 187, 193

Habermas, J. 8
Habyarimana, J. 199–200
Haig, A. 129–30, 153–4
hard power 87–8, 93, 285

hegemony 17, 62
Hesse, B.J. 202
hierarchical characterisations 29–31
hierarchies: Africa and the West 30–1; cultural 41–3; development assistance 31–2; manifestations 45; political systems 43–4; power relations 46; racial 35–6, 39–40; structuring of 40; US regional interests 225–6
historical particularism 43
HIV/AIDS 90–1, 209, 218–19, 275
Holmes, J.C., African tour 113–14
Holmes report 114
Horn of Africa 134, 144, 148, 155, 285
hostage crisis 76, 152
House Committee on International Relations, 2002 230
Hoy, D.C. 6
HR-4868 159
H.R.3765 85–6
human rights: abusive regimes 76; Carter's commitment to 145–6, 152; as criteria for aid 74; and foreign assistance 194–5, 273–4; as foreign policy focus 144; increased awareness 73; and national security 195; redefinition of 77–8; US inconsistency 144
humanism 64
humanitarian crises 185, 248, 250
humanitarian missions 276
humans, progression of 34–5
Hunt, M. 39
Hutu Power 200
Hyland, W.G. 85

idealism 61; Bush, G.W. 220; and national interests 86; return to 75–6; and self-interest 33–4
identity, and power 260
ideologies: American 10; of the powerful 17–18; US and Soviet Union 265–6
imperialism 121–2
independence 126, 266–7, 288
Independent National Front of Liberia (INPFL) 192
indirect rule 47–9
instability, Africa 109
institutional bias 237
institutional politics, of development assistance 23–4
intellectual capabilities, and race 38–9

interdependency 73, 81
interest groups 72
international collaboration 79
International Development Coordination Administration (IDCA) 75
International Development Corporation 72
international terrorism, and human rights 77–8
internationalisation 72
internationalism, unilateral 60
interventionism 60
intolerant puritanism 64
Iranian revolution 152
Iraq 91, 93, 186–7, 280–1
Iraq–Iran war 76
Iraq War 88
irredentism, Somalia 193
isolationism 60
Iversen, I.A. 230

Jim Crow laws 50, 51
job creation, aid and trade 68
Johnson Doctrine for Africa 120
Johnson, L.B. 69–71, 120–4, 267, 287
Johnson, P.Y. 192
Jordan, W.D. 40

Kabila, L. 208
Kagame, P. 208
Kansteiner, W. 230
Kantor, A. 190
Katanga 147–8, 151
Keïta, M. 239
Kennedy, J.F. 67–9, 117–20, 267, 287
Kenya 208, 217, 248, 281
Kiir, S. 246
Kilson, M. 52
Kirkpatrick, J.J. 77
Kissinger, H. 126, 133, 134–5, 138–40, 284, 289; Africa visit 140, 141–2; as filter 132; policy review 128–30; promise to Black Caucus 136
knowledge: restriction of 4–5; subjugated 6, 8
Komer, R. 121–2
Kony, J. 250–1
Korean War 65
Korry report 122–4
Kuwait, invasion 186–7, 280–1

Lake, A. 84
Lancaster, C. 89, 91

Landler, M. 243
Lazarus Effect 88
Leadership and Investment in Fighting an Epidemic (LIFE) initiative 209
'Leading Through Civilian Power' 95
Lebovic, J.H. 152
legitimacy, of African claims 9
Lemke, T. 6, 7, 12
Lesotho 18
Levitt, J. 204
liaison posts 108
liberalisation 272
Liberia 191–2
Libya 155–7, 241, 242
linkage, development and fight against terrorism 21
Litwak, R. 132
local character of criticism 4
long-term policy approach 123, 133–4
Lord's Resistance Army 250–1, 281
Lowie, R. 44
Lugard, F.J.D.B. 47–8
Lukes, S. 3–4, 10–13, 15, 16, 17, 19, 262–3, 278
Lusaka Manifesto 129–33
Lydon, G. 30
Lyman, P.N. 207, 243–4, 246–7
lynchings 51

Machar, R. 246
Mair, L. 45–6, 48
Mali 217, 238–43
Malian diaspora 241
Mamdani, M. 48
Mandela, N. 181, 201, 203, 284
Mandelbaum, M. 195
manifest destiny 61
Marshall Plan 63
Marshall-type-plan, for Africa 111
Marx, K. 17
Marxism, southern Africa 134
Matthews, E.G. 87, 88
Mau Mau rebellion 51
Mbeki, T. 206
McHenry, D. 207
Menelik II 283
Mengistu, H.M. 149, 182–3, 187, 284, 285
messianic approach 152–3
Mikell, G. 207
militarisation 242–3, 261
military assistance 222, 242, 250–1, 276–7
military coups 122

military involvements 83–4, 92
military power 61
military significance, Africa for US 111
Millennium Challenge Account (MCA) 89, 228, 231
Millennium Challenge Corporation (MCC) 231–2, 234, 242, 275, 277
Mills, C.W. 10
mission creep 198
missionaries 38, 46, 49
missionary strand 60, 263–4, 267, 271–2, 273, 277, 292
Mitchell, N. 74, 76, 133, 144
mixed approach 292
Mobuto, S.S. 147–8, 151, 188
modernisation 64
moral capabilities, and race 38–9
moral commitment 69, 71, 143, 144
moral duty, and national security paradigm 64–5
moralism, strands of 64
morality, of development assistance 132, 268–9
Morgan, L.H. 42
Mozambican National Resistance (RENAMO) 135, 189–90, 288
Mozambique 135, 138, 141–2, 189–90, 288
Mozambique Liberation Front (FRELIMO) 128, 135, 189–90, 288
Muehlenbeck, P.E. 119
Mugabe, R. 145, 151
multilateralism 72, 78, 82, 249
multinationalism 83
Museveni, Y. 191, 250, 281
Muslim National Liberation Front of Chad (FROLINAT) 156
Mutual Security Program 65
Muzorewa, A. 145
Myrdal, G. 51

Nagl, J.A. 85
Namibia 144, 146, 155, 288–9
nation-building 198, 273, 276
National Congress Party (NCP), Sudan 246
National Energy Policy Development Group (NEPDG) 218
national identity, and assistance discourse 278
National Intelligence Estimate (NIE) 109, 112
National Liberation Front of Angola (FNLA) 135, 288

304  *Index*

National Movement for the Liberation of Azawad (MNLA) 241–2
National Patriotic Liberation Front of Liberia (NPFL) 192
national security: associated factors 218, 220–1; and development 21; and foreign assistance 66, 67–8, 76, 88, 91–2, 154–5; and human rights 195
national security paradigm, and moral duty 64–5
National Security Review (NSR 30), policy response to 180
National Security Strategy (NSS), US 13, 64, 80–1, 85, 88, 91, 95
National Union for the Total Independence of Angola (UNITA) 135, 187–9, 288
nationalism 67, 108–10, 119, 266, 283
Natsios, A. 230
neo-conservatism 220
new African leaders 207–9
New Approach 72
New Directions 72, 127
new era in American policy 141–2
new world order 62, 80, 81, 82, 83, 87, 285; Africa Growth and Opportunity Act (AGOA) 205–7; African Crisis Response Initiative (ACRI) 203–5; 'American Policy toward Africa' 180; Angola 187–9; apartheid 180–2; background and context 178–9; disorder 194–7; economic opportunities 273; Ethiopia 182–4; geopolitical change 179–80; HIV/AIDS 209; Liberia 191–2; Mozambique 189–90; new African leaders 207–9; optimism 194; power projection 272–4; Rwanda 191, 199–201; Somalia 193–4, 197–9, 272–3; South Africa 201–3; spreading American values 196–7; Sudan 184–7; summary and conclusions 209–10; *see also* Bush, G.H.W.
Nichols, R. 7
Niebuhr, R. 60
Niger 156
Nigeria 144, 207, 216–17
Nimeiry, G. 157, 184–5, 279–80
Nixon doctrine 125
Nixon–Ford–Kissinger realpolitik 268
Nixon–Kissinger realpolitik 74, 125, 132
Nixon, R.M. 71–3, 112–13, 125–33, 126, 267–8, 287–8

Nkomo, J. 151
normativity 8–9
North Atlantic Treaty Organization (NATO) 134
NSC-68 64–5, 117–18, 265
NSC 5719/1 113–14
NSSM 39 128, 129, 133
nuclear weapons, fear of 65
Nye, J.S. 3, 13–16, 19, 24, 94

Obama, B. 92–9, 232ff, 276–7; *see also* self-determination
Obama presidency 285; concerns in Mali 242; constraints on 236–7; core policy 234–5; four policy foundations 235; policy militarisation 242–3; policy, Sudan 245–6; priorities 237–8; reactions to 232–3; summary and conclusions 251–2
October War, 1973 132
Odom, W. 148
Office of African Affairs 108
Official Development Assistance (ODA) 21
Ogaden 147, 149–51, 193, 284–5
oil 207, 217–18, 229, 230, 279
oil dependency 76
oil embargo,1973 134
Oil Producing and Exporting Countries (OPEC) 134
one-dimensional view of power 10–11
operation Desert Storm 193
Operation Enduring Freedom – Horn of Africa 223
Operation Enduring Freedom-Trans Sahara (OEF-TS) 225
Operation Lifeline Sudan 185
Operation Restore Hope 197–8
Operation Serval 243
oppressive regimes, aid to 76, 77
optimism, post-World War II 1
Organisation for African Unity (OAU) 122–3, 149, 156, 160
Oromo people 182

Pacific Command (PACOM) 223
Pan African Congress, 1919 50
Pan-Sahel Initiative (PSI) 223–4, 240
paradigm shifts 6
paradigms, discourse analysis of 6
parallel development 47–9
Parker, D. 140–1
Partnership for Economic Growth and Opportunity 205

paternalism 38
peace, shared interests 155
Peace Corps 67
peace dividend 81
Peace of Timbuktu 239, 241
peaceful change, as US aim 81
Peck, J. 64
People's Movement for the Liberation of Angola (MPLA) 128, 135, 187–9, 288
Perham, M. 47, 48
Peterson, R. 72
piracy 248
policy alignment, and aid 18
policy bridges, interdepartmental 221
policy during Cold War: Africa for the Africans 117–20; aid priorities 114; anti-neutrality 117–18; Carter, J. 143–52; categories of interest 136–7; co-ordination of interests 115–16; commitments secured 141–2; courses of action 111–12; creating sense of importance 116; dangers of delay 119; economic burden 116; Eisenhower, D.D. 112, 116, 117, 118; execution strategies 116; five tenets 117–18; Ford, G. 134–42; goals of independent policy 110–12; human rights focus 144; increased importance of Africa 144; increasingly nuanced 116; Johnson, L.B. 120–4; Kennedy, J.F. 117–20; need for independent policy 110; Nixon, R.M. 125–33; Nixon's priorities 125–6, 131; NSC 5719/1 113–14; policy issues 113; policy objectives 116; policy tools 113; post-World War II period 108–9; pre-World War II background 108; priority shift 134–5; Reagan, R. 152–61; reformulation proposals 112; self-determination 118; Soviet strategy 115; strategic interests 134, 144; sub-Saharan Africa 135–8; summary and conclusions 161–2; US interests in Africa 110; World War II background 108
policy review Task Force 122–4
policy shift, Clinton administration 195
political contact 46
political development 44–5
political interests, US in Africa 136–7
political systems, simple and complex 43–5

Popular Defence Force, Sudan 186
Portugal 127–8, 130–1, 133, 134, 287–8
post-9/11 assistance discourse 87–99
post-9/11 conceptualisation of development 21
post-9/11 policy: Africa and oil 217–18; context and overview 216–17; Global War on Terror (GWOT) 219–22; HIV/AIDS 218–19; military assistance 222; Millennium Challenge Corporation (MCC) 231–2; regional security initiatives 222–7; securitisation 220–1; Sudan 228–31; summary and conclusions 252–3; summary and evaluation 277; transformational diplomacy agenda 227–8; *see also* self-determination
post-9/11 power projection 274–7
post-Cold War: economic opportunities 273; power projection 272–4; *see also* new world order
post-Cold War doctrine 198
Poulton, R. 239
poverty 33, 89, 90, 231
Powell, C. 216–17, 218–19, 230
power: concepts of 3–4; defining 3; as distinct from domination 6–7; Foucauldian perspective 4–10, 11–12; instruments of 81; Lukes' perspective 10–13; Nye's perspective 13–16; one-dimensional view 10–11; regaining 95; and resistance 17; Scott's perspective 16–19; third dimension 262–3; three-dimensional view 11–12; two-dimensional view 11
power as domination 15–18, 19–20; conceptual framework *20*
power asymmetry, economic relations 46–7
power games 6–7
power/knowledge mechanism 53
power projection: assistance discourse and national identity 278; Bush, G.H.W. 272, 289–90; Bush, G.W. 274–6; Carter, J. 268–9, 271, 284–5, 289; Clinton, W.J. 272–3; context and overview 260–1; Eisenhower, D.D. 266–7; Ford, G. 267, 268, 289; Johnson, L.B. 267, 287; Kennedy, J.F. 267, 287; new world order 272–3; Nixon, R.M. 267–8, 287–8; Obama, B. 276–7; post-9/11 274–7; post-Cold War 272–4; Reagan, R. 269–70, 271,

306   *Index*

power projection *continued*
  289; regime of truth and assistance discourse *see* separate heading; summary and conclusions 291–3; through assistance policy 261–4, 290–1; Truman, H. 265–6; unintended consequences *see* separate heading;
power relations 12, 18–19, 29, 46–7
Power, S. 233
pragmatism 79
Presidential Policy Directives on Development (PDD) 95–6, 97–9
Presidential Task Force on International Development 72
President's Emergency Plan for AIDS Relief (PEPFAR) 89, 90–1, 231, 235, 275, 277
pride of race 50
private enterprise 72
privatisation, of industry 273
'pro-Liberian people' posture 192
progress, operationalisation 35
protest movements 51–2
Puntland 249, 286
puritanism 64

Qaddafi, M. 241
Quadrennial Diplomacy and Development Review (QDDR) 13, 95–8

race, and development 35–41
race doctrines 36
racial difference 36
racial equality, Carter's commitment to 145–6
racial hierarchies 35–6, 39–40
racial segregation 41, 48, 51, 52, 127–9; *see also* apartheid
racial tension, southern Africa 144
racism, origins 40
Radcliffe-Brown, A.R. 44–5
radicalisation 139, 140, 142
rags-to-riches narrative 59, 61
Reagan, R. 77–9, 152–61, 178, 179, 192, 269–70, 271, 280, 289
realism 61, 220, 275
realpolitik 74, 125, 132, 268, 271
redemption, development assistance as 38, 74
regime of truth 9–10, 53, 59–60, 260–2, 264, 265–72, 278, 293
regional organisations 277

regional security initiatives 222–7
regionalism 150–1
religion 40, 88–9
religious conservative groups 230
religious contact 46
Republic of South Sudan 243–4, 246–7, 281–2; *see also* Darfur; Sudan
resistance, and power 17
resources 29, 73, 110, 118, 136–7, 144, 153, 235
Restad, H. 60, 265
Rhodesia 127, 128–30, 135, 138, 144–6, 152, 190, 269, 289; *see also* Zimbabwe
Rice, C. 87, 220, 228, 230
Rice, S. 205–6, 207, 233
Rogers, W.P. 132
Rondon, F. 131
Rosenblum, P. 208
Roskins, R. 82
Rostow, W. 71, 118, 122, 123–4
Rumsfeld, D. 142, 226
Rusk, D. 121–2
Russell, B. 3
Ruttan, V.W. 61, 69–70, 72, 75, 78–9, 82
Rwanda 191, 199–201, 208
Rwandan People's Front (RPF) 191, 199–200

Sahel 132, 140, 155, 156, 238–43, 245
SALT II agreement 150–1
Sanogo, A. 241
Savimbi, J. 187–8, 189
Schlesinger, A. 152
Schraeder, P.J. 148, 159–60, 181, 225–6, 236–7
Scott, J.C., on power 16–19
Sears, C. 50–1
second Congolese War 208
securitisation 92, 220–1
security, and democracy 236
security challenges, post-9/11 91
segregation 41, 48, 51, 52, 127–9
Selassie, H. 283
self-determination 109; background and context 232–3; as continuation of policy 234; Mali 238–43; partnership 238; as policy aim 118; policy document 235; Sahel 238–43; Somalia 247–9; strengthening and creating initiatives 234; Sudan 243–4; summary and conclusions 251–2; Uganda 250–2; *see also* Obama presidency
self-interest, and idealism 33–4

semi-warriors 64
Senate Foreign Relations Committee 139
Shaba conflicts 148, 151
shadow war 277
Sheridan, M.B. 234
Shultz, G. 78, 154–5, 160
skin colour 35, 40, 42
slavery 37–8, 40–1, 49
smart power 13–15, 94, 234, 276–7
Smith, G. 233
Smith, I. 127, 128, 145, 288
Snider, D.M. 80–1, 85
Snyder, C. 231
social constructions, Foucauldian perspective 5–6
social Darwinism 39–40, 41
sociocultural evolution 34–5
soft power 88–9, 113, 142, 151, 262, 285–6
Somali National Front (SNM) 193
Somalia 147, 149, 193–4, 197–9, 247–9, 272–3, 283–7
Somaliland 249, 286
South Africa 127, 128–30, 144, 145, 217; action against ANC 159; Angola and Mozambique 135; apartheid and new world order 180–2; constructive engagement 270; as emerging market 202; and Mozambique 190; new world order 201–3; relations with Angola 146, 160; sanctions 146–7, 158–9, 181–2; segregation 51; unintended consequences 287, 289; US programmes 159; US relations with 145–6, 155
South African Human Rights Programme 159
South-West African People's Organization (SWAPO) 146
southern Africa: colonial wars 133; concerns 144–5; continued tension 155; increased priority 135; Kissinger's policy review 128–30; liberation movements 134; racial tension 144; strategic interests 134; unintended consequences 287–90; worsening situation 139
southern Yemen 156
Soviet Union: collapse 79; dissolution 179; and Ethiopia 149–50, 283; ideology 265; increased assistance 118; interventions 135; offers of aid 112; Reagan's view of 153, 269; risk of African alignment 112; and Somalia 149–50; in southern Africa 155–6; sub-Saharan Africa 138; support of anti-colonialism 266
Soweto uprising 146
Special Fund for African Development 142
Special Messages to Congress on Foreign Aid 69, 71
spectrum of power behaviours 14
spillover effect 196, 248
stability 235
Stability, Security, Transition and Reconstruction operations (SSTR) 92
Stanley, H.M. 49
state failure 276
states of domination 12
Stevenson, A. 112
Stohl, M. 76
strategic interests, US in Africa 136, 144
Strategy for Sustainable Development 196
stratification, of knowledge 5–6
sub-Saharan Africa 30–1, 135–6, 137–8, 157–8
subjugated knowledge 6, 8
Sudan 156–7, 208; conflicts with South Sudan 246–7; economy 280; new world order 184–7; oil 229, 230; policy objectives 245–6; post-9/11 policy 228–31; self-determination 243–4; and Uganda 250; unintended consequences 279–82; as US priority 244; *see also* Darfur; Republic of South Sudan
Sudan People's Liberation Army (SPLA) 184–5, 229, 281
Sudan People's Liberation Movement (SPLM) 246
Sudan Transitional Assistance Relief 281
superpower 2, 80, 83, 84, 179, 194, 195
superpower politics 29, 130, 132, 155, 188–9, 194, 195–6, 273
sustainable development 86, 196

Tanzania 141–2, 208, 281
tar baby option 288
Tarnoff, C. 232
Task Force, policy review 122–4
Taylor, C. 192
Taylor, I. 220–1
technical assistance programmes 66, 72, 118, 218

technology of power 29–30
terms and concepts, of evolution 35
terrorism 229, 231, 232, 240–2, 245, 248, 275–6, 281
Tet offensive 71
Thatcher, M. 151
*The German Ideology* (Marx and Engels) 17
The Millennium Challenge Corporation (MCC) 89–90
theoretical frameworks 293
theories of evolution 35
theory of evolution, race doctrines 36–7
Third World 67, 153, 154–5
three-dimensional view of power 11–12, 262–3
Tiananmen Square 179
Tigray province 182–4
Tobias, R. 91
Touré, A.T. (ATT) 239, 240
trade investment 118
Trans-Sahara Counter Terrorism Initiative (TSCTI) 224–5, 275–6
Trans-Sahara Counter Terrorism Partnership (TSCTP) 240, 243
transformational development 232
transformational diplomacy agenda 91, 227–8
transnational crime 241
Transnational Federal Government (TFG), Somalia 247–8, 249, 286
Traoré, M. 239
Traub, J. 274–5
tripartite agreement 187
tripartite consultation on African strategy 115–16
Truman doctrine 62, 265–6
Truman, H. 1, 32–4, 35, 62–5
Trump, D. 293
Tuareg 239, 240–1
two-dimensional view of power 11
Tylor, E.B. 41–2

Uganda 191, 217, 250–2, 269, 281
Umma party 185
UN Financing for Development Conference, 2002 89
UN operations, Somalia 247
UN Security Council Resolution 1973 242
UNAMIR 200–1
underdeveloped, use of term 9
underdevelopment 64, 232
unilateral internationalism 60
unilateralism 219
unintended consequences 292–3; Angola 288–9; Ethiopia 282–3, 284, 285, 286–7; Mozambique 288; Somalia 285–7; South Africa 287, 289; southern Africa 287–90; Sudan 279–82; summary and conclusions 290
UNITAF 197–8
United Nations 51, 83, 115, 285
United Negro Improvement Association 50
United States: balancing strategy 266; debt 179; economic revitalisation 273; global position 1, 29, 81, 275; hegemony 62; hierarchy of regional interests 225–6; increasing importance of Africa 112; loss of power 94, 134, 153; military involvements, Clinton administration 83–4; post-Cold War doctrine 198; post-World War II 51; potential for change 9; race 39–41; racial segregation 41; relations with colonial powers 108–9; unique culture 58–9; view of Africa 49–53
United States Agency for International Development (USAID) 68, 70; criticism of 85; elevation of status 95; objectives 73; post-Cold War strategy 82–3; presidential initiatives 97–9; report 1989 82; response to Korry report 124; review of 85–6; Strategy for Sustainable Development 196; White Paper, 2004 91
Universal Races Congress, 1911 50
UNOSOM II 198
US–Africa relations: benefits of development assistance 140–1; and communism 121; context 29; direct relations 208–9; downturn 134; influences on 29; race in US 39–41; shared objectives 155
US African Policy, major review 133–4
US Department of State, Quadrennial Diplomacy and Development Review (QDDR) 13
US foreign policy, and race 39
US leadership, trends impairing 153
US liaison posts 108
US–Nigerian relationship 207
US president, determination of American power 24
US–Russia relations 180

US–South Africa relations 146
US–Soviet relations 78–9, 138–9, 182, 187

value-based rationale for aid 67
Vance, C. 144, 145, 146–7, 148, 150–1
Veillette, C. 293
Vietnam 69–70, 71, 72, 75, 93–4, 124, 126–7, 134, 267, 269
Vorster, B.J. 146
vulnerability, of African states 220–1

Wallace, A.R. 36–7
War on Hunger 70
Washington, B.T. 50
Watergate 73, 134
weapons of the weak 16–19
Weatherley, U.G. 50
West Africa, terrorism 240
White House Conference on Africa, 1994 201–3
white supremacy 41
whole-of-government approach 95

Williams, G.M. 117, 119, 121
Williams, M.J. 132
Woodson, C. 50
Woodward, W. 83
world, stages of development 2
World Bank Structural Adjustment 160
world peace, and foreign assistance 73
Wright, G. 187

Yalta Conference 62
Young, A. 145
Youssouf, I. 239

Zaire 147–8, 151, 188
Zambia 141–2
Zimbabwe *see* Rhodesia
Zimbabwe African National Union (ZANU) 145
Zimbabwe African Peoples' Union (ZAPU) 145
Zimbabwean African National Liberation Army (ZANLA) 138
Zimmerman, R.F. 80, 82

# Taylor & Francis eBooks

## Helping you to choose the right eBooks for your Library

Add Routledge titles to your library's digital collection today. Taylor and Francis ebooks contains over 50,000 titles in the Humanities, Social Sciences, Behavioural Sciences, Built Environment and Law.

Choose from a range of subject packages or create your own!

**Benefits for you**
- Free MARC records
- COUNTER-compliant usage statistics
- Flexible purchase and pricing options
- All titles DRM-free.

**Benefits for your user**
- Off-site, anytime access via Athens or referring URL
- Print or copy pages or chapters
- Full content search
- Bookmark, highlight and annotate text
- Access to thousands of pages of quality research at the click of a button.

REQUEST YOUR FREE INSTITUTIONAL TRIAL TODAY

**Free Trials Available**
We offer free trials to qualifying academic, corporate and government customers.

## eCollections – Choose from over 30 subject eCollections, including:

| | |
|---|---|
| Archaeology | Language Learning |
| Architecture | Law |
| Asian Studies | Literature |
| Business & Management | Media & Communication |
| Classical Studies | Middle East Studies |
| Construction | Music |
| Creative & Media Arts | Philosophy |
| Criminology & Criminal Justice | Planning |
| Economics | Politics |
| Education | Psychology & Mental Health |
| Energy | Religion |
| Engineering | Security |
| English Language & Linguistics | Social Work |
| Environment & Sustainability | Sociology |
| Geography | Sport |
| Health Studies | Theatre & Performance |
| History | Tourism, Hospitality & Events |

For more information, pricing enquiries or to order a free trial, please contact your local sales team:
www.tandfebooks.com/page/sales

 Routledge
Taylor & Francis Group

The home of Routledge books

www.tandfebooks.com